3⁰⁰
8v

ALSO BY CARL SAFINA

Song for the Blue Ocean

Eye of the Albatross

Eye of the
Albatross

> ⥽ ⥽ ⥽ ⥽

VISIONS OF HOPE AND SURVIVAL

⥽ ⥽ ⥽ ⥽

CARL SAFINA

A JOHN MACRAE/OWL BOOK · HENRY HOLT AND COMPANY · NEW YORK

Henry Holt and Company, LLC
Publishers since 1866
115 West 18th Street
New York, New York 10011

Henry Holt ® is a registered trademark of
Henry Holt and Company, LLC.

Library of Congress Cataloging-in-Publication Data
Safina, Carl, 1955–
    Eye of the albatross : visions of hope and survival /
Carl Safina.—1st ed.
        p.   cm.
    "A John Macrae book."
    Includes bibliographical references and index.
    ISBN 0-8050-6229-7 (pbk.)
    1. Albatrosses.   I. Title.
QL696.P63 S24 2002
598.4'2—dc21   2001051644

Henry Holt books are available for special promotions and premiums.
For details contact: Director, Special Markets.

First published in hardcover in 2002 by Henry Holt and Company

First Owl Books Edition 2003

A John Macrae / Owl Book

Designed by Fritz Metsch
Photographs are by the author, except as otherwise indicated.

Printed in the United States of America
1   3   5   7   9   10   8   6   4   2

For Jenna,
who offered her couch

The spirit who bideth by himself
In the land of mist and snow,
He loved the bird that loved the man
Who shot him with his bow.

—SAMUEL TAYLOR COLERIDGE
"The Rime of the Ancient Mariner," 1798

It is impossible to communicate to you a conception of the trembling sensation, half pleasurable and half fearful, with which I am preparing to depart. I am going to unexplored regions, to "the land of mist and snow," but I shall kill no albatross; therefore do not be alarmed for my safety or if I should come back to you as worn and woeful as the "Ancient Mariner." You will smile at my allusion, but I will disclose a secret. . . . There is something at work in my soul which I do not understand . . . a love for the marvelous, a belief in the marvelous . . . which hurries me out of the common pathways . . . to the wild sea and unvisited regions I am about to explore. . . . Shall I meet you again, after having traversed immense seas, and returned? . . . I dare not expect such success. . . . I love you very tenderly. Remember me with affection, should you never hear from me again.

—MARY SHELLEY
Frankenstein, 1818

CONTENTS

PREFACE

*E*ARLIER IN LIFE I spent much of a decade studying seabirds, mainly the fishing habits of two types of terns. I came to love them through the power of beauty and fascination combined, and by them I learned the systematic pursuit of truth that we call the scientific method. The place in my heart reserved for seabirds gets newly refreshed each time I'm at the shore or at sea, because they seem always full of grace. But beyond the visible, the *unseen* aspects of seabirds are astounding, particularly their travels.

Recently, I traveled with albatrosses through much of their range, asking them to reveal their world. The fraction of their lives that I saw—and what it said of the life we share—tells a story of struggle and hope and the power of sheer persistence and of life's resilience. They taught me much.

The most renowned albatross species is the Wandering Albatross, and wandering the oceans was precisely my reason for choosing albatrosses as traveling companions. Albatrosses introduced me to many kinds of ocean wildlife. Along the way, I found albatrosses so continually remarkable in so many ways that I began not just seeing the world albatrosses encounter, but—in a subtle shift of perception—seeing the world as an albatross encounters it. And so, much of this journey is about the travels of one particular Laysan Albatross, named Amelia.

Most people recognize the physical beauty in nature; beyond that we tend only to see (and more often, merely presume) that life for wild animals is difficult and dangerous and short. I let Amelia draw me a map of her world so I could visit her country and its neighboring nations populated by other beings. From what I started seeing, it seemed to me that the basic struggles within the lives of many animals and of people differ mainly in detail. Though human societies have not solved the problems of our own violence and inhumanity, we tend to see—or imagine—the lives of animals as exaggeratedly brutal. Yet in some other species life can be remarkably stable and long, and rich with affection and tenderness. The main reason we usually don't see this is that we have almost never asked another animal to show us what its day is like. I hope that you, as I, may feel awestruck by Amelia and her fellow creatures, see yourself as part of the whole vibrant living family, and feel inspired to help care for the soul of the world.

THIS IS A WORK OF NONFICTION, with one asterisk. The people, places, and events are true as I came to know them during my travels, and correct to the best of my knowledge. Amelia is a real bird. Where she went is what really occurred, and we know this because she wore a transmitter that told us her locations. The maps of her travels are made directly from the transmitter data. However, what she encountered and experienced is conjecture, based on the track of her true travels, on what I've seen albatrosses do, and what albatrosses are known to do. Thus Amelia's travels are where she actually went in particular; her experiences during those travels are what happens to albatrosses in general.

One stylistic note: I have capitalized the species names of all creatures, because the adjectives in unfamiliar names can be confusing. For instance, if you read of a black-footed albatross or a magnificent frigatebird, it isn't exactly clear whether "black-footed" and "magnificent" are visual descriptions of the bird's appearance, the impression the bird made on the writer, or part of its name. So I capitalize Black-footed Albatross and Magnificent Frigatebird to let you know for certain that these are their species names. The general rule I've followed is to capitalize all the names of particular species; group names do not get capitalized.

Amelia's transmitter battery eventually died, so we don't know where Amelia is now. That matters less to her than it does to us. She doesn't need us in order to be an albatross; albatrosses knew what they were doing millions of years before people appeared. But because people were born into a world that included albatrosses, we need them—to prove to ourselves that we can be fully human.

September 2001
Montauk, Long Island

ACKNOWLEDGMENTS

ALBATROSSES ROAM on their own wings, but people like me need help getting around. Dr. David J. Anderson of Wake Forest University and Chuck Monnett of the United States Fish and Wildlife Service made this book possible. Dave very generously provided access to data, and Chuck facilitated my repeated visits to the Northwest Hawaiian Islands. Dr. Beth Flint cheerfully aided in my acquisition of needed details, archives, and reports. I likewise thank Patty Fernandez, David Hyrenbach, Robert Smith, John Twiss, Bud Antonelis, George Balazs, Lee Ann Woodward, Dominique Horvath, and Cindy Rehkemper for helping me see and understand challenges facing Pacific wildlife.

For revealing new worlds to me at French Frigate Shoals, Laysan Island, and Midway Atoll, I warmly thank John Bone, David Itano, Nancy Hoffman, Rob Shallenberger, Mark Thompson, Rick Gaffney, Gary Eldridge, Bill Gilmartin, Cynthia Vanderlip, Gately Ross, Leszek Karczmarski, Binka Bone, Joyce King, Anthony Viggiano, Brian Allen, Chris Lowe, Brad Wetherbee, Greg Marshall, Birget Buhleier, Laura Carsten, Mark Defley, Frans Juola, Shiway Wang, Brendan Courtot, Carrie Holt, Karen Fischer, Julie Rocho, Vanessa Pepi, Aaron Dietrich, Nick Nickerson, Catherine Tredick, Tim Clark, Mitch Craig, Melissa Shaw, Mary Donohue, Jason Baker, Dr. John Lamkin, George Grigorovitch, Petra Bertilsson, Brenda Becker, Walter Machado, Amber Pairis, Rebecca Woodward, Alex Wegmann, Ray Bolland, Jerry Leinecke, John Sikes, Russ Bradley, and Michele Reynolds. For travel in the Gulf of Alaska I am indebted to Mark Lundsten and the crew of the *Masonic*.

I deeply thank Stephanie Glenn, Eric Gilman, Mercédès Lee, Merry Camhi, Mike Testa, Paul Engelmeyer, Candyce Mason, Carrie Brown-stein, Russ Dunn, and Myra Sarli of Audubon's Living Oceans Program for their terrific efforts and support.

The many travels that informed this work and helped me see oceanic wildlife are not readily apparent on the surface of the final narrative. Various people helped me to begin to understand albatrosses and other wildlife in the eastern tropical Pacific, Antarctic Peninsula, and sub-antarctic Southern Ocean. Lisa Ballance, Bob Pitman, Jim Cotton, Mike Force, Laura Morse, and *David Starr Jordan* commander John Herring brought me into the eastern tropical Pacific and Humbolt Current region. My travels along the Antarctic Peninsula, South Georgia Island, and the Falkland Islands were flawlessly facilitated by Wayne Trivelpiece, Susan Trivelpiece, and Laina Shill, who welcomed me into their field study of penguin ice-ecology, and by Polly Penhale and Guy Guthridge of the National Science Foundation's Office of Polar Programs and NSF's Antarctic Artists and Writers Program. Victoria Underwood of Abercrombie and Kent, Kim Crosbie, Victor Emanuel of Victor Emanuel Nature Tours, and the crew of the cruise ship *Explorer* got us to and from the Antarctic in exemplary safety and comfort. Dave Anderson and Tui De Roy facilitated my travels in the Galápagos Islands. Special appreciation to Tui for such breathtaking adventures. I also thank Victor Apanius, Kate Huyvaert, and Henrik Mouritsen. I applaud the courageously dedicated people of the Charles Darwin Research Station and the Galápagos National Park, including Polly Robayo, Rodrigo Bustamante, Felipe Cruz, Mario Piu, Maria Eugenia Proaño, Robert Bensted-Smith, and Howard Snell. Particular additional thanks go to Godfrey Merlen, Dolores Diaz, and Capitan Fulton Divas of the *Guadalupe River*. Capitan José "Pepín" Jaramillo ran a superb diving expedition on the boat *Lammer Law*. The amazing glimpse of Royal Albatross global circumnavigations result from the research of Christopher J. R. Robertson and David G. Nicholls.

I thank Elliot Norse for his special encouragement. Patricia Paladines did everything from travel reservation to language translation to sharing walks to the bay. For important information I thank Suzanne Iudicello, George Burgess, Dave Cline, Bruce Babbitt, Ellen Pikitch, Pete Desimone, Pete Osswald, Stan Senner, Will Novy-Hildesley, Norbert Wu, Vikki Spruill, Daniel Pauly, and Richard Ellis. Additional help came from Diane Glick-Morris, Nancy Anderson, Alexandra Srp, Paul Srp, Bill Sladen, Dave Witting, Alice Tasman, Katy Hope, and Cynthia Robinson. Joanna Burger and Michael Gochfeld first involved me in seabird studies many hazy summer days ago, and though I have wandered far, I continue to make my nest nearby.

Wherever I settled in to write, Jennifer Chidsey arrived with encouragement, insightful comments, binoculars, chopsticks, and an inexplicable desire to read each draft. Faith and very helpful criticism from Jean Naggar, Jack Macrae, Jennifer Weltz, Bonnie Thompson, and Steve Fraser saved the narrative from wandering around like a nonbreeding albatross.

For travel assistance I am deeply grateful to Jocelyn Sladen and Anne Alexander Rowley of the Greenstone Foundation, and Monica Jain and the Avina Foundation. A big literary boost arrived from the Lannan Foundation in the very same month I sat down to begin working on this manuscript, and it very much helped me get focused and going. A most astonishing fellowship from the John D. and Catherine T. MacArthur Foundation altered time and space for thought and work. I thank also Emly McDiarmid and Gus Speth of the Yale School of Forestry and Environmental Studies for extending to me a visiting fellowship and warm welcome.

For generosity and high expectations in our shared efforts to restore ocean wildlife I deeply thank Julie Packard, Jeanne Sedgwick, and Mike Sutton of the David and Lucile Packard Foundation, Wolcott Henry and Angel Braestrup of the Munson Foundation, Leslie Harroun of the Oak Foundation, Richard Reagan of the Norcross Foundation, Josh Reichert of the Pew Charitable Trusts, Andy Sabin and the Evan Frankel Foundation, H. B. and Jocelyn Wallace and Eric Gilchrist of the Wallace Research Foundation, Bob Kearney and Royal Caribbean Cruise Lines, Paul Tudor Jones, George Denny, Eliot Wadsworth, Mark Winkelman, Robert Campbell, Geoffrey T. Freeman and Marjorie M. Findlay, Mike Northrup of the Rockefeller Brothers Fund, the Streisand Foundation, Bacon-Moore Foundation, Lemmon Foundation, Daniel Thorne Foundation, French Foundation, Josie Merck and the Merck Foundation, Nat Reed, Michael Steibner, Richard Worley, Willard Overlock, Christopher Mailman, Fred Garonzik, George Trumbull, Martin Lane, Michael Egan, Vaim Nikitine, Jennifer and Ben Freeman, Frederick Khedouri, Patricia and John Rich, Caroline Mason, Jonathan Ilany, Robert and Birgit Bateman, Pat and Rosemarie Keough, Bret Lyons, Bill Michealcheck, Walter Giles, and Rick Burnes.

I often wrote in the cabin of my twenty-four-foot boat, and I thank the terrific staff of the Westlake Marina in Montauk, Long Island;

Captain Mike Brumm of the Montauk-based charter boat *Daybreaker;* and Jerry and Marie Borriello of the *Marie* for providing the surroundings and camaraderie that made those long hours pleasant and productive. Tim Dykman provided necessary distraction by sharing his boat, his e-mail connection, and his trampoline.

The human heroes of this story are people on the front lines of efforts to preserve and restore albatross populations around the world. Among others, they include Nigel Brothers, John Cooper, Sandy Bartle, John Croxall, Rosemary Gales, Henri Weimerskirch, Hiroshi Hasegawa, Graham Roberston, Jim Ludwig, Julia Parrish, Ed Melvin, Kim Rivera, Beth Clark, Mark Lundsten, Eric Gilman, Charles Wurster, Denise Boyd, Kent Wohl, Patrick Gould, Chris Boggs, Euan Dunn, Janice Molloy, Peter Ryan, Narelle Montgomery, Marilyn England, Dave Chaffey, Ingrid Holliday, Richard Thomas, Esteban Frere, Carles Carboneras, Aldo Berruti, and Deon Nel. Special acknowledgments go to the Western Pacific Fisheries Management Council for their Black-footed Albatross population analysis workshop, New Zealand Department of Conservation, Australian Fisheries Management Authority, Commission for the Conservation of Antarctic Marine Living Resources, BirdLife International, Environment Australia, The Forest and Bird Protection Society, Environmental Defense, Defenders of Wildlife, World Wildlife Fund, Greenpeace, American Bird Conservancy, Audubon's Living Oceans Program, the Antarctica Project, Antarctic and Southern Ocean Coalition, International Southern Oceans Longline Clearinghouse, Pacific Seabird Group, Humane Society International, Oceana, The Ocean Conservancy, and several others, whose omission by name here is a reflection on me, not on them or their hard work and critically important efforts. I celebrate and thank all of you and can only hope my contribution here proves worthy.

Eye of the Albatross

PRELUDE

When the wind drops in late afternoon, Amelia, already hundreds of miles from land, rises on her own power, flapping more than she'd prefer. With her breast muscles pulling on the long bones of her wings, those wings biting like propellers to pull her through the air, she is using up more of the energy she's here to replenish. After rising on a small gust of breeze, Amelia lets gravity take over the work again, gliding downward and forward like a wind-driven snowflake. When her flight line dips, her wing tip traces a thin line on the sea, leaving her spare signature upon the waters. This evanescent track, the only mark of her passage, vanishes in moments, fleeting as her presence here in a body built to move only forward.

When the wind returns, she sets her wings and, without anything perceivable as bodily movement, continues for another hundred miles, flying in long undulations on the propellant energy of the breeze. Hers is the billowy motion of a life under sail. As Archibald MacLeish wrote, "A poem should be wordless as the flight of birds"; and so Amelia is a kind of living poetry upon the ocean.

These immense creatures we call "albatross" are the greatest long-distance wanderers on Earth. Big birds in big oceans, albatrosses lead big, sprawling lives across space and time, traveling to the limits of seemingly limitless seas. They accomplish these distances by wielding the impressive—wondrous, really—body architecture of creatures built to glide indefinitely.

The physics of an albatross's wing differs from that of most other birds, whose bodies are designed for powered flight. That is because albatrosses are constructed more to float in the air than to fly. Compared to many other birds, which power flight with elongated "hand" bones, the proportions of an albatross wing are humanlike—long arm bones, short "hand" bones—almost as though humans were also meant to glide. Or as if, were we suddenly transformed into birds, we would most naturally become albatrosses.

Our physical parallels with albatrosses suggest our metaphorical relatedness. In Coleridge's "Rime of the Ancient Mariner," the sailor who kills an albatross is compelled to wear around his neck the evidence of his crime against nature. Even two centuries ago, the bird symbolized good luck and beneficent companionship, harmed only at our peril—a seabird with power enough to convey a universal cautionary tale. Coleridge, who never saw an albatross, sensed this. We sense it still.

Many of us harbor a different metaphorical albatross within. Beneath the daily overburden, our truer nature is this wandering spirit on expansive wings, hungering for a chance to search new horizons, to hurtle along with the wind, taking chances, taking the world as it comes, making tracks that will endure only in our memory, forming our personal map of life and time.

AN ALBATROSS IS a great symphony of flesh, perception, bone, and feathers, composed of long movements and set to ever-changing rhythms of light, wind, water. The almost overwhelming *musicality* of an albatross in air derives not just from the bird itself but from the contrapuntal suite of action and inaction from which this creature composes flight. It drifts in the atmosphere at high speed, but itself remains immobile—an immense bird holding stock-still yet shooting through the wind. Just as individual notes become music by relationship to other notes, the bird's stillness becomes movement by context. Following your traveling ship with ease, watching you, circling stern to prow and back at will, it flies with scarcely a flinch, skimming wave upon wave, mile after mile. Watching it, you invariably wonder, *How* can it do that?

Exerting no propelling power of its own over long distances, it is driven by the tension between the two greatest forces on our planet: gravity and the solar-powered wind. An albatross's flight relies on exploiting what all other flying creatures struggle to overcome. By working *with* wind and gravity, its flight surpasses all others'. That it holds still while being propelled by invisible forces may be why painters so rarely attempt the albatross, though it is one of the sea's greatest conceptual icons. The author and wildlife painter Richard Ellis explains, "An albatross is motion, and capturing it is too daunting for most artists working in fixed media." Indeed, watch an albatross speeding over the ocean to streak across your wake; it does not so much fly as pilot the great body it inhabits. Exquisitely so.

Albatross flight looks easy. You have no idea. A Wandering Albatross's heart actually beats slower during flight than while sitting on the sea. Black-browed Albatrosses use no more energy while flying than when brooding a chick upon their nest. Scientists who studied metabolic efficiency in Gray-headed Albatrosses at sea discovered "the lowest cost of flight yet measured." Here's one of the birds' secrets: for the long hours and days of flying, albatrosses needn't really hold their wings out; using an extraordinary wing lock at the shoulder and an elbow lock for rigidity, they snap them into the unfolded position like opened switchblades.

The huge birds' placid mastery of gales never fails to impress mariners distressed by heavy weather. Charles Darwin, in a tempest near Cape Horn while aboard the *Beagle* in 1833, wrote, "Whilst we were heavily laboring, it was curious to see how the Albatross . . . glided right up the wind." Not far from there a few years ago, in a storm so great it stopped our 270-foot ship for a day, I too watched albatrosses somehow gliding directly into seventy-knot winds in hurricane conditions, circling our paralyzed ship with surreal serenity, seeming oblivious to the shrieking, spume-filled gusts. When the fascinated nineteenth-century sea captain Jean-Marie LeBris killed an albatross and held its wing in the breeze, the lift it generated so astonished him that he suddenly "comprehended the whole mystery of flight." Later, in Brittany, he built out of wood and cloth a "winged boat" named, of course, *Albatross.* On a Sunday in 1856 his device was mounted on a horse-drawn cart and driven downhill at a gallop. The craft rose a hundred meters into the air—with LeBris at the controls. Modern aviation awaited only invention of an engine capable of powering such an aircraft.

While mariners marveled at the sheer size and stamina of albatrosses for centuries, the birds' oceanic travels were impossible to cipher. Where did they go? Sailors speculated, and some came close. Scientists guessed wrong. No one could have fully imagined, because albatrosses exert almost unimaginable lives.

In the last few years albatrosses have been tracked by Earth-orbiting satellites, and their true travels outdistance all previous conjecture. Before maturing, albatrosses remain at sea for years, never alighting upon a solid surface, perhaps not even glimpsing land all the while. During their whole lifespan they expend 95 percent of their existence at sea—flying most of that time. Theirs is a fluid world of wind and wild waters, everything in perpetual motion. Land is little more than a necessary inconvenience for breeding. When they do breed, albatrosses haunt only the most removed islands, hundreds, sometimes thousands of miles from any continent. And even at the most isolated island groups, albatrosses often choose to nest on the tiniest offshore islets, as though they can't tolerate too much land. When need compels them to return to a remote isle to feed a famished chick, an albatross may make round-trip foraging treks of several thousand miles, sleeping aloft, foraging in darkness and daylight, searching out food enough for a single feeding for their single offspring (a large, ravenous chick may wait two weeks for a meal). And so they span long stretches of space and time, distant from any shore, seldom within sight of a coast, embedded in the breeze. Doing so, they cover distances equivalent to flying around the Earth at the equator three times every year. A fifty-year-old albatross has flown, at minimum, 3.7 million miles.

Albatrosses are creatures of air inside and out; air sacs surround their organs and extend even into their hollow wing bones. An albatross's entire skeleton accounts for only 13 percent of the bird's total weight. You expect massive flight muscles, and again these birds surprise you. In most birds, flight muscle accounts for about 16 percent of body weight, but most albatrosses' flight muscles amount to only 9 percent of body mass; in the great Royal and Wandering Albatrosses, flight muscle is a paltry 6 percent, with very reduced biceps. These creatures are *gliding* machines. More than anything, albatrosses' long, narrow wings make them extreme-range mileage mechanisms. The ratio of wingspan to wing width of a Wandering Albatross is 18 to 1, similar to the best-perfected human-made gliders. Their wings' lift-to-drag ratio—lifting force to air resistance—is a remarkable 40 to 1, more than triple that of many eagles.

Although exquisite at mining energy from the weather, the gigantic Royal and Wandering Albatrosses are gliding-adapted to a fault; they are incapable of sustained flapping flight. Calm weather leaves them stranded on the sea surface. Their existence utterly depends on the prospect that the winds will continue blowing. Fortunately for them, wind remains plentiful, at least for now. Indeed, albatrosses as we know them could only have evolved in the windiest place on Earth—the Southern Ocean, where an abundant supply of moving air breathed creation into Life's most surpassing capacity for flight.

. . .

ALMOST EVERYTHING about albatrosses is superlative and extreme. Extreme in size, in duration, in endurance. Even the smallest species have six-foot wingspreads. Wandering and Royal Albatrosses wield the longest wings in nature—over eleven feet tip to tip. Wandering Albatrosses weigh up to twenty-six pounds—twice the weight of the largest Bald Eagles; that's a very large flying creature. Wanderer chicks grow to as much as thirty-three pounds—larger than adults—before losing weight prior to fledging. After taking years to mature, an albatross embarks upon courtship and "engagement," which can last two full years or longer. Royals and Wanderers first breed as late as age thirteen. Their single egg, which can weigh over a pound, requires more than two months' incubation. Mates take shifts on the nest. Albatrosses whose mates fail to return may sit incubating, waiting, for unimaginably extreme lengths of time. If the mate deserts or dies, a bird may sit on an egg for two months, losing a third of its weight before hunger drives it to sea. One albatross whose mate failed to return faithfully incubated an infertile egg for 108 days. The death of a mate costs the survivor one to four full breeding cycles, because a new courtship takes years. Breeding stretches at least eight months; some albatross species require a full year to raise a chick. During that whole time from egg to fledger, mates may

The longest wings in nature—Wandering Albatross

spend only five to ten days together. Many albatrosses breed only every other year; Light-mantled Sooty Albatrosses raise one chick every three or four years—the lowest reproductive rate of any bird.

For creatures with such extraordinarily slow reproduction—their exceptionally long reproductive lives constitute a life pattern closer to humans' than virtually any other animal—the continuity of their race depends on equally extraordinary adult survival from year to year. Like a human's, an albatross's lifetime may endure for many decades. The oldest albatross found—and probably the oldest known marked wild bird—was a Royal still living at over sixty years of age. Some believe that the maximum albatross life span may approach the century mark. No one yet knows, because they haven't been studied that long.

In addition to sharing similarities with us, albatrosses living so far from humanity increasingly share a human-dominated destiny. Because they range so far and live so long, albatrosses intersect and contend with almost every effect that people exert upon the sea. Forged in the elemental world of wind, water, weather, and other wildlife, the albatross inhabits a realm that has come to encompass everything from fishing boats to human-caused climate changes. Everything people are doing to oceans, albatrosses feel.

"I NOW BELONG to a higher cult of mortals, for I have seen the albatross!" exalted the American ornithologist Robert Cushman Murphy during his first trip to the South Atlantic, in 1912. Being near these birds touches people with something so profound it seems spiritual. Returning from several Wandering Albatross nests on a subantarctic island one morning, one of my companions remarked, "I feel like I've been to church." My first experience among nesting Royal Albatrosses on New Zealand's Campbell Island had caught me off guard, too, seeming less like the expected visit and more like an audience with beings who did not merely occupy but somehow *populated* the place. They seemed to give the island its rationale, embodying the slow sweep of deep time in the splendor of their magisterial seascape. Before I turned my back to walk downhill, the nest inspection had become a pilgrimage. Being in their presence infused a penetrating sensation each of us later described with the same word: *serenity*. The eminent ornithologist Dr. Frank Gill, who has studied birds throughout the world, remembered this from a day observing nesting Wanderers: "There was such wisdom in those beautiful eyes that have seen so many years. In all my lifetime of experiences with birds, no moment was so moving."

During their prodigious travels albatrosses cross paths with a spectacular array of creatures near the ocean surface, including other seabirds, fishes, whales, sharks, sea turtles, seals, and some extraordinary people. Following albatrosses will enlarge your life, and they will be sure to introduce you to the splendid company they keep; all truly awesome envoys of the magnificence of life on this ocean planet.

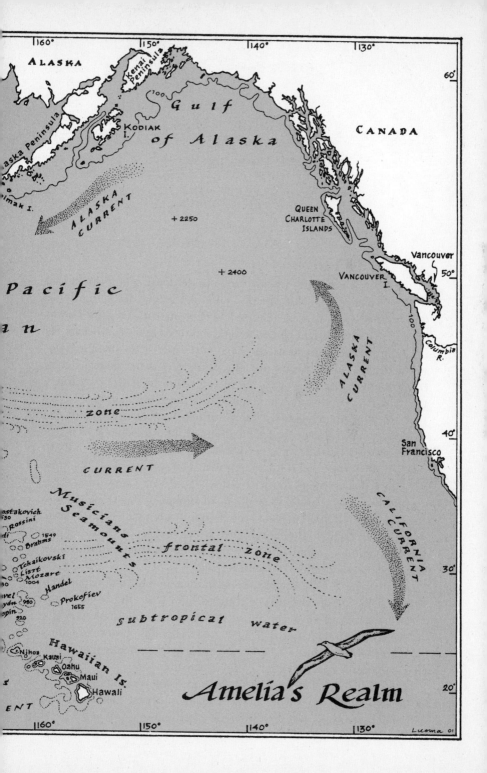

> >

GREETINGS

*T*URN THIS WHOLE VIEW upside down, and it would look the same. There's the blue disk of sky above, the blue disk of sea below, and clouds floating between. Simple and elemental, it's a seabird's world.

Beneath these bright clouds, a dark, limitless expanse of ocean. Flying over and through so much ocean and vapor in so small a plane, we're being reminded that our blue-and-white planet takes its color from clouds and the sea, two forms of water. You can let your eye follow the pale circular horizon, or roam across the skies above or the sea beneath. The realm below is a barely ruffled theater-in-the-round, with us always at center stage under the dome of sky, no matter how fast or far we travel. I'm realizing anew that, when you stop thinking and just *look* at it, the ocean seems numbingly vast. The realization takes a while to build. It delivers a slow shock to your senses, leaving a deep impression.

It's been several hours since the main Hawaiian islands melted into the tropical sea behind us like pats of butter in a hot skillet. Since dawn, with the sun rising higher and higher at our backs, our churning propellers have been pulling our five-seater west from Honolulu across five hundred measured miles of nautical space.

From up here, you can see patterns in the water. Intriguing patterns. Much of the ocean is simply a crinkled light blue. But some of the crenellated surface forms concentric whorls, like enormous fingerprints, or swirls, or fanning patterns being etched by breaths of wind. And lines of lighter blue run through darker expanses in long streaks, like stretch marks upon the curving belly of Mother Earth.

Over there, a line extending out beyond vision separates a vast area of lighter-colored water from a darker realm of ocean. That front, that boundary separating two very different water masses, hints at the great fact that rules the lives and travels of everything that roams and flows below: the ocean is not just a bowl of all-the-same water but a glittering, swirling mosaic of grand proportions.

AFTER SEVERAL ANIMATED HOURS of suspension aloft, a slight aquamarine smudge appears in that blue ocean disk. Slowly it begins attaining focus: shallows surrounding a wide, bright lagoon. An atoll called French Frigate Shoals—our destination. Waves are breaking lacily on a ring of reef about eighteen miles in diameter. From the air, the swells breaking themselves on the fringing reef look like a white pearl necklace dressing a turquoise throat. Dominating the Shoals' central lagoon stands a spectacular rock rampart an eighth of a mile long and seven hundred feet high, sharpened on both ends like an ax. This is La Pérouse Pinnacle, remnant neck of this ancient atoll's parent volcano.

We're descending. The surrounding Pacific, in its gentle swell and subsidence, looks as calm as a napping cat. The forereef comes up quickly from true abyss, miles deep, taking the water from deep cobalt to jade green, then to white breakers. On the surf-scoured reef crest, the corals look beige. They're broken into tongue-and-groove formations, as though the waves in their perpetual thrusting and withdrawing have raked their fingernails across the reef.

Just inside the corals corralling the lagoon, the bottom lightens to lime-green flats, dotted by a few dark lava-rock patches. In places the shallows rise in low little islands. Some have green vegetated centers, surrounded by bright coral-sand beaches. Others, too flat and washed over for any growth of green, are all dazzling white.

As WE NEAR the airstrip on one of the atoll's islands—Tern Island—copilot Ron Lum dons a helmet. "In case a big gooney bird comes through the windshield," he says as he tightens the strap. "Or," Lum laughs, "in case the pilot gets killed while we're landing." For me and my traveling companion, the seabird scientist Dr. David Anderson, there are no helmets.

Pilot Bob Justman doesn't reply. He's busy concentrating on making the helmet unnecessary.

The coolness aloft changes abruptly as we near the planet's surface and the greenhouse effect takes hold inside our glassed-in passenger compartment. It's an impressive demonstration that just a thin veil of survivable warmth blankets Earth's surface. The thinnest soap bubble holds all known life.

Swiftly approaching the unpaved runway for landing, Justman says, "Uh-oh, birds are taking off from the southeast."

An astonishing swarm of seabirds rises into the air on both sides of us. Because of the crosswind, many are flying over the airstrip.

Suddenly there's a blur and a thud so heavy and direct on the windshield that when my eyes blink open again I'm surprised the bird didn't come crashing through.

Justman curses. "Tell me how I could have avoided *him*." He taxis the plane to a stop.

This is a tiny island; it can't be much more than half a mile long and a tenth of a mile wide. I notice a hand-painted sign reading, WELCOME TO TERN ISLAND INTERNATIONAL AIRPORT. ELEVATION 6 FT. Tern's also an odd little island. During World War II, the U.S. military took an eleven-acre islet, filled it to create a thirty-seven-acre island, and bulkheaded it to a T-squared rectangle, creating a kind of terrestrial aircraft carrier. Most of the "shoreline" is therefore a low wall of rusty metal, though some beach has formed, especially along the lagoon side. The island's middle third is all runway, the outer two-thirds all bird colony and vegetation. At one end, an old military barracks now serves as living quarters and labs for the scientists working here.

But immediately, as the plane door opens, any artificial aspects of Tern Island vanish amid the din and dancing of courting albatrosses and the dazzling action of thousands of other seabirds. The first glance, the first sounds, the first whiff, say that *everything* is different here. Wow.

We all get out, squinting in the sudden glare of bright sun glinting off the reef-powder runway. Amid the creatures, and with water stretching away in all directions, your immediate impression is that you've arrived at the heart of creation. The next impression is that anyone who ever gets the opportunity to stand here as we are is breathtakingly fortunate. We've been here for thirty seconds.

This is a place of chalk pastels, of coral sands and colored waters. The lagoon surrounding this strand of land is glass calm, crystal clear. The clouds, tinted. It is quite as though those clouds are white canvases set up merely to reflect the purples and blues and turquoises of the sea. And everywhere—seabirds.

ABOUT A DOZEN PEOPLE, mostly scientists and aspiring scientists, are already here. They've been spread out along the airstrip, shooing the birds off for our landing. Now they begin converging to meet the two newcomers. A young woman, introducing herself as Melissa—first name only; very informal—says that the bird we hit, a Laysan Albatross, was merely stunned, had lost consciousness briefly, is awake, and miraculously appears unbroken. That's a relief.

Then a twenty-year-old woman wearing a tank top and a faded pair of paint-splattered shorts walks up. This is Karen, carrying a dove-size seabird called a Brown Noddy. Our plane has killed it. Thousands of other birds are already resettling, back into nests in bushes or on the ground. But the inescapable irony of having killed one of the birds we've come so far to see is unsettling.

WE HAVE TRAVELED this long distance to study long-distance seabirds. Only the tiniest sliver of seabirds' lives—on land, when they breed—is accessible for detailed human observation. If seabirds studied us that way, they'd do all their research in our bedrooms. We'd be gone from the "study area" for long periods, but when we returned they'd take detailed notes on how we put on our pajamas, how many times we turn during sleep, and more about our mating habits than might seem proper. That's how it's been with scientific study of many marine animals; we study them on land or haul them onto the decks of boats, because we are incapable of following them where they really live, in the sea. This is changing. By attaching small, highly sophisticated satellite tracking devices to large seabirds, seals, turtles, whales, and giant fishes, a handful of people like David Anderson are discovering where oceanic animals really go.

Until recently, no one could guess where albatrosses went when they took to sea. Now, with these new state-of-the-art technologies, we can finally ask the most fundamental and elementary question: Where do they *go*? In a pilot study Dave discovered that the albatrosses breeding here may fly halfway across the North Pacific to find food for their chick. Now he's come for a deeper look.

THE PLANE HAS BROUGHT everything from scientific supplies to fresh fruit, from liquid nitrogen for preserving blood samples to capers for dinner. While everyone else begins unpacking, Dave and I remain dazzled by the seabirds and the setting.

Among the people already here is Dave's graduate student, Patty Fernandez. She is happy to see her professor, and broad smiles blossom. The relationship between adviser and student is almost parental, but—if it's a good one—can carry the uniquely special dynamic only a mentor brings. You immediately see that this relationship is a good one.

An albatross flies in low over our heads like a light aircraft. Patty, with a sweep of her hand, giggles exuberantly. "This is so wonderful, don't you think? I *love* working here."

Dave replies, "It *is* wonderful. It's *surreal.*"

As if to emphasize that Alice is now in Wonderland, that Dorothy has arrived in Oz, a bird called a Masked Booby—sublimely white with jet-black mask and wing tips—walks up on big webbed feet as if to welcome us like the mayor of Munchkin Land. Our odyssey has brought us to his embassy. Dave bows respectfully, as if meeting a foreign diplomat, and in a rather formal tone says, "Hello. Pleased to meet you."

Patty waves a circular motion with her hand and the bird follows it intently with fixed eyes, its head going around in circles. She giggles again. We're all smiling. You almost want to make conversation: "And how long have you been a booby—all your life?"

Birds are nesting on, adjacent to, and underneath the barracks. As we drag our duffels inside, I notice a little white Fairy Tern incubating its precariously balanced egg—no nest—atop the barracks' permanently propped open front door. If you don't like wildlife, this is a bad place to be.

We take a moment for better introductions with the people here. Melissa is Melissa Shaw, a veterinarian studying the health of the endan-

Over our heads like a light aircraft—Laysan Albatross

gered Monk Seals. Her seal-research teammates are Mitch Craig, Mary Donohue, and Jason Baker. The volunteer bird-research interns include Karen Fischer, Frans Juola, and Laura Carsten. Anthony Viggiano is a graduate student. Soft-spoken, bespectacled, thirty-something Brian Allen is the manager of this station, and curly-haired Mark Defley is assistant manager.

Everyone—volunteer and veterinarian alike—helps unpack. When the cargo is unloaded, everyone goes for the mail, taking a spontaneous break to devour letters from lovers and loved ones, and to otherwise check the pulse of the distant world.

Among cards and letters, the mail yields treats. From headquarters, Dr. Beth Flint has sent some home-taped TV shows and movies.

"Who do I know in Bryan, Texas?"

"Trashy fashion magazines to lighten the workload."

"Bills—for later."

"Junk mail. Even here."

"My grandmother loves me! She's sent me a two-pound box of chocolates!"

"Has sent you? Or has sent *us*?"

Like the island itself, the barracks is a military hand-me-down (my door bears the words SICK BAY) from the days before satellite spying and long-distance atomic weapons of mass destruction made such installations obsolete. The U-shaped barracks consists of two parallel dormitory corridors joined by a large central room with a dining table, living-room chairs arranged for reading or video viewing, shelves holding hundreds of paperback books, and a large kitchen.

Living on Tern Island entails shared meals and shared bathrooms— just like family. Most people have the luxury of their own bedroom, but during the day almost everyone leaves their door open to the breezes. Many rooms are decorated college-style, with posters of animals or a teddy bear on the bed.

This outpost of the U.S. Fish and Wildlife Service does not enjoy lush funding. The plain interior is in some disrepair. Most bedrooms now lack electricity. Some toilets don't work. But the available budget is wisely focused on the part of the operation that gets the work done. Supplies for scientific work and medical emergencies are well stocked and highly organized. The computer room is modern and air-conditioned, and communications with the mainland function flawlessly. Silent, clean solar panels have replaced the roaring generators that so afflict most field stations. One theme runs through everything here: devotion to the wildlife.

ONCE WE GET SETTLED, Patty leads Dave and me on a brief tour. Energetic Anthony, dark-eyed, with short, dark hair, comes with us. Patty's been here for a month, scoping out albatrosses to carry the tracking devices that will let us follow their at-sea travels. This is Patty's first big research project, and she knows that if she pays attention and works hard, it will earn her a master's degree and launch a career. Patty and Dave make a contrasting duo: Dave, in his early forties, is tall. Patty is a compact young woman. He's clearly of European ancestry. Patty's facial features speak strongly of Native South American roots. Dave is bearded; he's wearing his Wake Forest University cap to ward the tropic sun from his otherwise bare head. Patty's hair is long and Inca-thick and midnight-black. Dave is much the professor, careful of word and clear of pronunciation. Patty, having studied in the United States only about a year, retains enough of her native Ecuadorian accent to make the simplest things she says sound charming.

Though it's just after New Year's, it's hot here. But this great city of birds provides ample distraction from the heat. Over the barracks, Red-tailed Tropicbirds so pearly they seem to glow are hovering and backing up in the breeze, displaying their superb tail streamers to each other, shifting them first to one side then the other, calling attention to their slender, exquisite elegance. These displays are supposed to look sexy, and, well, all I can say is—it works for me. On the ground you can see that their gleaming white bodies are infused with a peachy bloom, offset by striking black feet and a black stripe that passes through their eyes and then curls to a stunning comma, as if the Red-tail is some mythic Egyptian creature.

We walk along the airstrip—the only place on the island reserved for people. Sleek, flit-fluttering, dove-sized Black Noddies create perpetual-motion commuter air traffic at eye level, carrying seaweed for new nests. They crowd the leathery-leaved Beach Heliotrope and Naupaka bushes like big figs, making the branches seem fruit-laden. Upon landing, they invariably open their mouths to flash their bright red-orange tongues and oral interiors. How very odd. The gesture must convey something important enough to say constantly. They let you close enough to admire their ashy crown and the white eyeliner around the trailing edge of their eyes.

While Black Noddies nest in bushes, barely bigger Brown Noddies nest on the ground. While Blacks are hyper, Browns seem quiet, reserved, going along and getting along. All these subtle differences and little puzzles that mark the boundaries of closely related species offer abundant delights for eye and mind.

Most bushes are rimmed with crow-sized Red-footed Boobies atop their stick nests. Their most common colors—they vary a bit—include red-webbed feet, black wing tips, and powder-blue bills. A few Red-foots are a lovely creamy café-au-lait morph. If you move in close—but stay out of pecking range—you can see the subtle pink pastels at the base of their bills and the pink eye-shadow skin around their eyes.

Masked Boobies hail us from little pebble nests on the ground. These guys are incredibly handsome: immaculate white body, tail tip and outer wing feathers night-black, black mask, bright yellow eye with black-dot pupil, bright yellow matching bill. Their stares seem quizzical, a little apprehensive.

What's in a name? Plenty. Names—especially a name like *boobies*—impart bias. Temperate-region members of the same family are called gannets, and everyone thinks they're oh-so-graceful—which they are—and that their diving skill is wow-how-spectacular. Which it is. Tropical members of the family—equally graceful and spectacular—are called boobies, and everyone titters and thinks they're amusing. These birds misnamed boobies are hard-driving, plunge-diving, weapon-tipped missiles built to kill. Their stout, straight, sharp, serrated bills inflict real damage to any flesh, be it a flyingfish or a hand. Around here, boobies get respect.

All the animals here are tame, because—present company excluded—the place lacks land mammals. So the animals' minds lack the pawprint of fear. "Tame" means unafraid, but not friendly. They either ignore or scold you as you pass. Extend a hand to see whether a noddy is incubating an egg, and rather than flee it vigorously bites. No serious harm from its tweezery bill, but you get the point: this is *their* place, and they're not scared of *you*.

Their fearlessness makes this seem like paradise without predators. But watch closely. A tern chick is vulnerable to a frigatebird. Rummaging Ruddy Turnstones and Bristle-thighed Curlews will happily peck open an egg if granted a chance. And each of the seemingly pacifist seabirds turns predator at sea. Paradise depends on which side of an appetite you find yourself.

Great whirling clouds of Sooty Terns are gathering overhead, and they will stay aloft all day, not landing until about sunset. They are patterned striking black above and white below, with elegant forked tails and a white forehead. Their squeeze-toy call sounds like they're saying, *Wide awake, wide awake.* About ten thousand of them have returned so far. These constitute only the vanguard—perhaps a tenth—of the eventual breeders, merely the first breath of a living hurricane that will nest several months hence. The rest remain at sea. You would think the birds flying overhead would be more anxious to land, because all the while they are at sea they apparently fly nonstop and never rest. They land only to breed. Juveniles appear to *fly continuously for up to five years* before they touch down for their first nesting attempt. No wonder landing seems like a big deal for them. Dave admits awe: "These birds still have me knocked back on my heels."

HERE IN THE EXTREME OCEAN, many of the birds are built for ultimate flight efficiency. Land is almost an afterthought in their design. Tropicbirds are so aerial they're crippled on the ground. To reduce wing loading for travel far offshore, they have traded away leg muscle. They cannot stand. Shoving along the ground with both feet, they push themselves forward piteously, thudding their breast with each "step." Strange and severe. Their close neighbors and distant relatives the frigatebirds have enormous wings for their size—quite possibly the greatest sail-area-to-body-weight ratio of any birds. For a bird with a six-foot wingspan, Great Frigatebirds are extraordinarily light: three pounds, a mere kilogram and a half. Their feathers reputedly weigh more than their skeletons. Frigatebirds' feet are nearly as useless as tropicbirds'. Frigatebirds can't land on water. Can't swim. Can't *walk.* Their sharp-clawed toes are strictly designed as clamps for holding branches when they land. Frigatebirds are built to fly and geared to snatch food, and that's it.

But what frigates do, they do devastatingly well. At sea frigatebirds make a living chasing and robbing other birds, threatening them with their hooked bills until they drop or disgorge the fish they've caught. Most birds are smart to distrust them—and to not leave chicks unguarded.

Look up at these dark frigatebirds, their forked tails streaming, their long crooked wings recurved. Flying crossbows, they evince a grace most sinister. A dozen of them are cruising back and forth in the uplifting cushion of breeze on the windward side of the island. A booby commits the mistake of returning to the island right here. One frigate immediately makes chase, and a pack quickly follows. The booby attempts evasions, but the frigate twists expertly, locked in like a heat-seeking missile. Now other frigates close in, and the booby cuts its losses, coughing up its tithing. The falling fish is immediately snatched by Frigate One.

I catch a blur out of the corner of my eye and put my head down just in time for a Masked Booby to slam into me so hard that it slaps the reinforced brim of my cap against my face, then falls dazed to the ground— its penalty for not watching where it was going. It must have had its eye on the frigates. Had I not been wearing a hard-brimmed cap, I might have gotten skewered in the face by its carrot-sized bill. The bird picks itself up from the ground and flies off again.

Frigatebirds not airborne crowd the highest bushes. It's their mating season, and the dark-bodied males have their erotic, heart-shaped, scarlet throat sacks inflated, hoping to attract a female. With those swollen throats tautly distended, they sit shockingly unashamed, overtly sexual, falsely nonchalant, quiet and smug in the knowledge of their own sexiness—yet always a little insecure about whether they're attractive enough, and whether they have what it will take to make it in the fierce competition for a mate. One female on a mere flyby immediately sets all the males a-quiver. Now she lands among one group of blooming males like a thorn among roses—and the inflated admirers are going mad with lust, shaking their outstretched wings, rocking their heads side to side jiggling those big swollen balloons, and uttering spooky, wavering howls. Despite the scarlet intensity of the males' desire, the female looks utterly disinterested. But she's landed for a reason, and she's making her calculations: Who seems strongest? Who looks oldest and has survived longest? Who has won the best spot on this bush? Is anyone here good enough for me? She sizes up the suitors. Then—she simply departs, leaving a wake of shaking, rattling, howling males.

Along the beach berm, sleeping like yellow logs under the bushes, lie several Hawaiian Monk Seals, rare and endangered animals that inhabit only these islands. And on the wet lower sand, lapped and lulled by wavelets from the lagoon, naps a male Green Turtle of impressive heft— perhaps three hundred pounds. This chain of islands is one of the very few places remaining on Earth where non-nesting sea turtles still regularly bask on beaches during daylight.

One Sooty Tern is lying on the dry sand. Life has left it. I pick it up by its picklike bill and run my fingers along its soft, feathered contours. It is an immaculate death. Bright. Sleek. So lovely that its corpse invites contact, offers assurance that close admiration will not disturb. It seems in excellent health, save that it's dead. We envision collision with another tern during darkness, with fatal consequence. Patty asks to see it and takes it gently from my hands. Stroking the dead tern, Patty says, "I know there are many important reasons for conservation, but I think mainly we care about nature because of its beauty."

ALBATROSSES AREN'T the most numerous birds here, but on wings spanning seven feet, they get your attention. Two species of albatross breed here: the Laysan Albatross and the Black-footed. Every few minutes a bird who's been at sea crosses the pale tropical flats. Some arrive over your head on their immense bowed wings. Others come low, almost touching the sand. The tips of their long wings curve down conspicuously, like the head of a pickax. At this close range, they seem on the far side of enormous.

One Laysan Albatross is coursing airily up and down the island's shore, zooming half a mile with each directional change. It does this for many minutes on end. We can speculate on the costs of this seeming waste of energy, but this bird challenges us to explain the *benefits*. I sense the exertion of a joy so sheer and light it embodies the most time-tested truths.

Some albatrosses land awkwardly, coming a little too fast, having trouble arresting their momentum, hitting the vegetation and rolling forward on their chests. But usually they land skillfully; impressive if you consider they haven't touched firm ground for weeks.

No welcoming committee awaits. No fanfare. Just a mate at the nest, who has sat incubating throughout the time the arriving bird wandered at sea. At this reunion and relief, no rejoicing ensues. The mate actually seems reluctant to yield custody. That's surprising. After three weeks of incubation, you'd think hunger and prolonged endurance—and sheer boredom—would grow unbearable and they'd veritably spring from the nest at first sight of their mate. But no. Old habits die hard, and arriving birds sometimes have to shove their spouses off the nest.

Patty, Dave, Anthony, and I are watching one such homecoming albatross trying to relieve its mate. Anthony interprets: "A lot of times, it takes them half an hour to switch. It can take hours, one trying to walk onto the egg and the other trying to stay put—like they're in a trance to incubate."

When an albatross finally departs, it needs a lot of running room. Some run the width of the runway—about forty yards—before getting airborne. They run along with their outstretched wings waving, waving,

waving—always into the wind if there is any breeze at all—and patter along with their feet loudly slapping the ground. Eventually the job of defying gravity shifts from their feet to their wings, and they are off and magnificent.

➤ ➤ ➤

*I*N THE SIEGE of space-time that is jet travel, it's easy to forget just how much water separates Hawaii from the continents. The Hawaiian chain comprises the most isolated islands on Earth. No other islands are so far from any mainland. And consider this: the Hawaiian chain is so disconnected from the rest of the *ocean* that one-third of its reef fish species are found nowhere else on Earth. Of the hundreds of Pacific coral species, fewer than 10 percent have ever reached the Hawaiian Islands. No land mammal (and only one bat) ever reached the islands. So few birds reached Hawaii that most of its native land birds actually evolved on the islands, adapted descendants of those stray fragments of flying DNA that were the few birds blown so far off course.

Even by Hawaiian standards, the remotest part of the Hawaiian archipelago is this string of islands and atolls called the Northwestern Hawaiian Islands. They stretch more than a thousand miles west from what you usually think of as Hawaii. They include a series of isolated dots and dabs in the wide sea, rocks and atolls and other shards of barely emergent land you may never have heard of: Nihoa Island, Necker, French Frigate Shoals, Gardner Pinnacles, Maro Reef, Laysan Island, Lisianski Island, Pearl and Hermes Reef, Midway Atoll (the only famous member, flashpoint of the pivotal World War II sea battle), and Kure Atoll. These ten little exiled lands range in size from Maro Reef's single emergent rock and Gardner Pinnacles' three dry acres to Midway's 2.3 square miles. Anchored in a deep sea yet adrift in deep time on Earth's floating crust, these islands have become terra firma's tiny outposts to the northwest, far from surfboards, bikinis, packaged tours, June honeymoons, and the rest.

Though little and remote, they're crammed with seabirds—*six million breeding seabirds,* of eighteen species. If you count juveniles and non-breeders, the number balloons to fourteen million. Having just 0.1 percent of Hawaii's land area, they provide breeding ground for 95 percent of its seabirds. This includes some 600,000 breeding *pairs* of

Laysan Albatross, and 60,000 Black-footed Albatross pairs—virtually their entire world populations. The sheer concentration of birds makes the density of life here hugely impressive.

Tern Island, where we are, is among this holy group of isles. Its parent atoll, French Frigate Shoals, is a roughly circular rock and coral platform nearly twenty miles wide, dotted with scarcely dry land. Though it is the largest of the chain's atolls, most of French Frigate is the underwater lagoon. Tern Island, though less than a mile long, is the largest island here. Most of the others are too small for a long stroll, and often get washed over.

But these tiny sites are the reproductive generators of wildife inhabiting many millions of square miles of ocean—including U.S. waters, other nations' territories, and the high seas. In other words, without these safe havens, wildlife populations throughout the North Pacific would shrivel. So although the area of these dollops of land is a trivially tiny fraction of the ocean's total realm, the ecological "footprint" of the islands is enormous, vast as the sea itself.

IN THE LATE 1800s, fortune-seeking plume hunters began hammering away at the birds and their islands. Feathers became high fashion in America and Europe, so wildly popular that the hunting soon threatened to exterminate numerous bird species. Only a small number of people cared that certain birds were headed for extinction, but one of them happened to be president of the United States. Teddy Roosevelt had a soft spot for seabirds, and he put his boot down. Wielding his big stick—the privilege of executive order—in 1909 he created the Hawaiian Islands Bird Reservation, now the Northwestern Hawaiian Islands National Wildlife Refuge. National wildlife refuges had been his idea, and this was the second such refuge ever established. French Frigate Shoals and most of the other Northwestern Hawaiian Islands are included (only Kure Atoll, at the chain's end, is not a designated refuge). It is fitting tribute to the greatness of Theodore Roosevelt's vision and compassion that a century later we remain grateful for his wildlife refuges, national forests, and national parks.

Roosevelt's vision seems even more remarkable when you consider that seabirds breeding on other islands of the tropical Pacific have suffered widespread losses. The U.S. Fish and Wildlife Service's Dr. Beth Flint recently reviewed seabird status in twenty-six countries throughout the tropical Pacific. Of these countries, she wrote, "perhaps only eight

Hawaiian Archipelago

still have healthy colonies of the most vulnerable species, and only six of these have legal protection for sites, and management plans. Just a subset of these countries are actually implementing management for their seabird colonies." More than 90 percent of the birds that have gone extinct over the last few centuries have been island nesters, including both sea- and land birds. Birds have a hard time when humans and their domestic animals arrive on isolated islands.

WE STOP TO LOOK at one albatross alone on its nest just a few paces from the porch steps. Patty is planning to include this bird among the first in her satellite tracking study. I decide to give this scientific pioneer of the air a name: Amelia.

The bird I'm trying to admire is, I have to say, not the most engaging bird I've ever met. Amelia's been sitting on her single egg nearly two weeks during this shift, oblivious to the world. Like Dr. Seuss's Horton the elephant, an incubating albatross is faithful to its egg—100 percent. On their nests—and there are nests on the ground all around us—they seem detached from reality. They make no eye contact. Day upon week they sit dazed with broodiness, mostly dozing with bill tucked under wing and eyes closed, now and then opening a lid to see whether the world has gone away. They're not interested in you. Even if they're watching with one eye, they usually don't bother taking their bill from under their feathers as you walk by.

They're not interested, but I am. I'm lagging behind the others so I can look enough to begin actually seeing. The albatrosses seem to maintain a certain grace despite themselves; a beauty unselfconscious as a child's.

Black-footed Albatrosses appear chocolate-dipped. They're the color of double-fudge brownies; they're that dark. They support their brownish-black bodies upon black legs and eponymous black feet. Their faces feature ashy gray detailing at the bill's base, and subtly contrasting light highlighting just below their dark eyes. They walk with their necks low and outstretched, their heads going from side to side, giving them an exaggerated, hunched, Groucho Marx air, a comically sinister gangster look.

The Laysan Albatrosses, conversely, tend to take a high-stepping, high-headed waddle with their pink legs and feet. The Laysans bear a blackish cape upon a white body. The head is finely airbrushed. The basic black eyes are rimmed with white-lined lids, set into a lovely dark pastel eye-shadow mask that is black just ahead of the eye and blends to a fine powder-gray dust on the cheeks. Their bill is light pumpkin-orange or pinkish, grading to a light gray tip.

An albatross bill is a heavily constructed weapon made of a dozen or so separate plates connected as though welded, ending with a nail-like hook. It means business, and most everyone who works with albatrosses has scars to attest. Hard, tubed-shaped nostrils lie along each side of the bill, indicating the albatrosses' membership in a large family called the tube-nosed seabirds.

The softness in albatrosses is not in their feathers, which are stiff, but in the powdered gradations of color. Shade and tone. And in the bits of skin exposed to air. Albatrosses' scaly feet and legs—the most reptilian parts—are most surprising. The scales are embedded in supple skin, and the webbing between the long toes is as soft as fine buckskin or chamois. The albatrosses' feathers form a dense and surprisingly stiff armoring against the cold sea, the blasting wind, and the beating sun.

These birds live all their lives out in open weather. They know no sense of cover. Not only do they take no shelter, but they're exposed to some of the harshest extremes of heat, cold, water, and wind the world can hurl. These are sturdy beings.

. . .

THE NAME *albatross* stems from the Arabic word for pelican, *al-qadous,* derived from the Greek word *kados,* for the leather scoop on ancient water wheels (thus referring to the pelican's capacious bill-pouch as a water bucket). Spanish and Portuguese sailors corrupted this name for pelican to *algatraz* or *alcatraz.* Mediterranean mariners exploring farther into the Atlantic and Caribbean began using familiar names for unfamiliar birds, widening *alcatraz* to include pelicans' relatives, like gannets, boobies, and frigatebirds. In the 1500s, south-venturing mariners began describing enormous seabirds never before seen by Europeans.

In 1593 Sir Richard Hawkins, newly confronted by the great albatrosses, observed, "During this storme, certain great fowles . . . soared about us . . . and from the poynt of one wing to the poynt of the other, both stretched out, was about two fathomes" (twelve feet). By the 1600s English mariners had adopted the Spanish name. Sailing toward Madagascar in 1638, Peter Mundy noted, "Allcatrazes is againe the biggest of any Seaffowle I have yett seene . . . hee seemeth not to Move att all as hee Flyeth leisurely and close to the Rymme of the water." English accents began softening the hard Arabic *c* to *g* or *b.* And so in 1673 John Fryer referred to "Albetrosses" while rounding the Cape of Good Hope on a passage to India, and the highly traveled William Dampier remarked on the extreme size of "Algatrosses" in 1697. On a circumnavigating voyage between 1719 and 1722, George Shelvocke was impressed by "the largest sort of sea-fowls . . . extending their wings 12 or 13 foot," and he called them "Albitroses."

Shelvocke's journal described a storm near Cape Horn, during which a "disconsolate" black albatross "accompanied us for several days, hovering about us as if he had lost himself." One of Shelvocke's officers, "observing, in one of his melancholy fits, that this bird was always hovering near us, imagined, from his colour, that it might be some ill omen. . . . The more to encourage his superstition, was the continued series of contrary tempestuous winds, which had oppress'd us ever since we had got into this sea." The man shot the albatross, "not doubting (perhaps) that we should have a fair wind after it." What actually followed were winds so severe it took them six weeks to sight the coast of Chile. By the late 1760s, Captain Cook's naturalist Joseph Banks began using the modern form *albatross,* and this word, with its Greek and Arabic roots, is now understood worldwide.

In 1797 William Wordsworth had been reading Shelvocke's account when he took a long, moonlit night walk with Samuel Taylor Coleridge.

During their passage on moorland paths from Alfoxden to the fishing village of Watchet, Wordsworth described the incident to Coleridge, thus providing the seed of inspiration that in 1798 blossomed into "The Rime of the Ancient Mariner." That epic poem gave us, of course, the image of the albatross around one's neck. Any belief among seamen that killing albatrosses would bring bad luck dates from Coleridge's poem. (A more genuine notion actually borne by some mariners—if perhaps tongue in cheek—was that when old sailors died they returned as albatrosses.)

Coleridge's poem turned the albatross into a metaphor from which the bird has never escaped. But the metaphor has been distorted and is often misapplied. "An albatross" has become an icon of unshakably burdensome responsibility, psychological distress, or social baggage. We hear people say things like "That project has been an albatross around her neck." Somehow the albatross has been made the villain, the bad thing. But an albatross is not the same as a white elephant (some physical thing too big to manage and that no one else wants, like a huge, inherited run-down house that won't sell) or a ball and chain (an acquired burden that is a constant emotional drag). Only if the dilemma you have is your own fault, if your suffering is deserved, is it, metaphorically speaking, your "albatross." In the original poem, the crewman is made to wear around his neck the albatross he killed. The burden of his own deed is his just punishment and reminder for his offense.

> *And I had done a hellish thing,*
> *And it would work 'em woe:*
> *For all averred, I had killed the bird*
> *That made the breeze to blow.*

In the windless calm that follows, the sailing ship lies helplessly stranded under "a hot and copper sky," beneath "the bloody Sun." Eventually afflicted by horrible thirst—"Water, water, every where, / Nor any drop to drink. . . . /And every tongue, through utter drought, / Was withered at the root. . . . / With throats unslaked, with black lips baked, / We could nor laugh nor wail"—everyone on the ship, except the Mariner, dies. Thus by its authorship of the wind the bird plays a critical role in atmospheric nature and human survival, which is unrecognized and unappreciated until the bird is killed, whereupon all share the unforeseen consequence of its destruction.

When the Mariner finally recognizes the beauty of *all* nature—in a sight no one else would likely declare beautiful—the encumbrance around his neck disappears. The revelation comes to him while watching sea snakes swimming alongside the ship by moonlight, leaving tracks in the phosphorescence of the ocean:

> *Beyond the shadow of the ship,*
> *I watched the water-snakes:*
> *They moved in tracks of shining white,*
> . . . .
> *I watched their rich attire:*
> *Blue, glossy green, and shining black,*
> *. . . and every track*
> *Was a flash of golden fire.*
>
> *O happy living things! no tongue*
> *Their beauty might declare:*
> *A spring of love gushed from my heart,*
> *And I blessed them unaware:*
> . . . .
> *And I blessed them unaware.*
>
> *The self-same moment I could pray;*
> *And from my neck so free*
> *The Albatross fell off, and sank*
> *Like lead into the sea.*

Thus the Mariner, having opened to appreciate all creatures, is relieved from the curse and burden of having destroyed a benign being and thus having brought disaster to his fellow men. A wind comes up and the ship is magically propelled homeward. Coleridge seemed concerned with our crimes against nature, seeing nature as God's work and thus closely tied to humanity. And so those resonant lines

> *The spirit who bideth by himself*
> *In the land of mist and snow,*
> *He loved the bird that loved the man*
> *Who shot him with his bow.*

And later in the poem,

He prayeth best, who loveth best
All things both great and small;
For the dear God, who loveth us,
He made and loveth all.

This idea of the connection of all living beings through God was a major theme. And in 1817, Coleridge evoked an even more direct and intimate connection within the family of life by writing, "Every Thing has a Life of its own, & . . . we are all *one Life.*"

Coleridge was not the only person who felt the attractive power of albatrosses. Even in scientific nomenclature, people repeatedly freighted the birds with metaphor and meaning, draping them with everything from heroic virtue to fear and foreboding. Thus the genus name scientifically denoting most albatrosses is the Latin *Diomedea.* Diomedes was one of Homer's war heroes. During one campaign he so offended the goddess of wisdom, Athene, that in retribution she beset his fleet with a terrifying storm. When, rather than acting contrite, some of his crew further taunted the goddess, she transformed them into large white birds, "gentle and virtuous." The genus of dark-plumaged Sooty Albatrosses, *Phoebetria,* derives from the Latin *phoebetron,* an object of terror, and the Greek *phoibetria,* a prophetess or soothsayer. *Exulans,* the Wandering Albatross's specific name, means "out of one's country," or to live in exile. That may be how the mariners and naturalists who saw them felt on multiyear voyages—but the albatrosses themselves were always quite at home on the wild, wide ocean.

In the metaphors we make of the creatures of the heavens and the deep, we often project our imagery, imbuing them with our own reflection. But the world is more than a coloring book of shapes for us to fill in. When we perceive metaphor in reality we enhance our understanding of ourselves, but when we install meanings *instead* of seeing reality, we miss all the true texture and inherent value, like a child doodling over a great painting. Loading up an animal like an albatross with our own fears and symbols is a bit unfair—unfair to the animal, who suffers the bias or false impressions we've created, and unfair to us. We miss the expansive opportunity of knowing other creatures. Why force albatrosses to wear humans around their necks? Sometimes an albatross is simply a bird. When we see that, worlds open—and even the metaphors that find us become more interesting.

. . .

AND SO WE'VE COME to meet the albatrosses and all the other creatures on their own terms, in their own time. This year, as usual, most albatrosses arrived in November and by December had laid their eggs. Males began arriving first, perhaps a week before females. When previously mated albatrosses reconnect, they generally skip the elaborate dancing of their youthful past. With little preliminary courtship formality, older, well-acquainted mates copulate within as little as an hour of their reunion.

They then go to sea on a "honeymoon" averaging ten days, while the female acquires bodily resources for building an egg. No one knows whether they feed each other chocolates out there during this time—or even stay together at all—but they often return to the island within a few hours of each other. Upon arrival back at the colony, the female usually lays her egg within a day.

None of this orderly progression is apparent here on the island. Your main impression is bewildering busyness, birds constantly coming and going.

After the female lays, she leaves in a hurry—usually the same day. Her need to immediately get back to sea for food reflects how expensive egg laying is. Probably because of the inequitable cost to her body condition of constructing that large egg, the male takes a larger overall share of incubation, sitting about a week longer than the female when you sum all their time. When the male takes the first incubation shift, he sits, sits, sits three solid weeks on the egg, until she returns. Then she takes possession of the egg, and *he* goes to sea two or three weeks. After that, the spells grow shorter: something like a couple weeks back on the egg for the male, then a week or so for Mom, maybe followed by a few more days for Dad.

With all that alternating activity and inactivity, their bodily condition fluctuates dramatically. Albatrosses first arrive plump and sassy, with thick layers of fat under their skin and around their organs. Laysan males show up weighing nearly seven and a half pounds and females close to seven. For the first ten days or so, the male doesn't eat enough to maintain his weight, and loses mass until he weighs about the same as the female. He regains much of this during the "honeymoon" at sea. When the honeymoon is over, the female instantly loses 10 to 12 percent of her body weight laying that big egg. She gains it back at sea during the male's first incubation shift. Meanwhile, *he's* incubating without food or water, getting lighter again. During the long bouts of incubation, they fluctuate inversely, each in turn losing roughly 20 percent of their weight on the nest, while their mate out at sea is regaining much of its condition.

During normal incubation, after about five or six parental shifts and an elapsed time of over two months, the male has sat for about thirty-six days and the female for twenty-nine. Those are averages for Laysan Albatrosses; they vary. (One whose mate was killed just after she laid her egg sat for thirty-two days—instead of the usual *single* day.) After about sixty-five days of incubation, the chick stages its grueling, slow-motion breakout. In the twenty-four hours—or sometimes several days—during which the chick struggles to emerge, the adult will render only abundant moral support and no physical or material assistance—a model of perfect parenting.

Albatrosses are good at staying alive. About 65 percent of eggs, on average, result in chicks that survive to fledging age. About 10 percent die at the perilous transition to first flight. Of those that survive fledging, annual survival is often an extraordinary 93 to 98 percent through at least age twenty. Many albatrosses live much longer. Scientists aren't sure exactly how long yet, because a lot of albatrosses still living have been wearing leg bands for forty years, outlasting some of the original researchers who wished to know.

MOST ALBATROSSES HERE are incubating solitarily, but some have company sitting or standing inches away. Some sit touching bill to bill. The companions might be mates just returned from sea, waiting their turn at incubating. Or they might be visitors. Albatross social relationships are complicated, poorly understood.

"Look," says Dave. "This bird is sitting on an egg, and somebody else just walked up to it and started preening it around the head, and it accepted the preening. What does *that* mean? The bird is almost certainly not its mate. But they may have long-term relationships that are very cryptic to us." As we watch the interaction, Dave continues, "The birds may know each other. One might be the offspring of the other, hatched here years ago. Or they could be acquaintances, and they might become mates at some time in the future if something bad happens to the mate of the bird that's on the egg. That kind of stuff is very obscure to us. The only way you can get at it is long-term, by watching season after season—trying to see how these relationships are developing. But that's really hard to do. With long-lived seabirds, I think a lot of it is about relationships." Dave adds that a student of his just finished a long study of divorce in Masked Boobies. "He learned that if you're a booby and you and your mate split up, you're much less likely to breed next year." Dave says biologists tend to collect data on the number of eggs, number of chicks hatching, number surviving in the nest, that sort of thing, but not very much on relationships. "Virtually everything about human society is about relationships," Dave says, "and I think we are missing a lot by not putting more effort into trying to understand relationships in societies of other animals."

Though most albatrosses have spent the last months incubating, many are still courting. These are probably nonbreeders, but it's not always clear what their status is. As you walk along, you see them engaged in different kinds of courtship, from quiet mutual preening to raucous, reckless dancing. Watching them is delightful and intellectually challenging. Dave, observing that some of the birds here are nonbreeding adults, wonders aloud how adults decide whether to breed in a given year.

Anthony, explaining the main emerging finding of his developing research, says that these albatrosses can't raise a chick *and* regrow all their feathers in the same year, because each task requires almost as much energy as an albatross can earn by foraging. Trying to do both would result in energetic bankruptcy—starvation. So after one or more years of breeding they have to take a year off to molt their feathers. There's an important implication. One of the most important things that will decide what will happen to these albatrosses is how many chicks a bird can produce during its life. Most people have assumed they breed every year, from when they first mature to when they die. Anthony says, "But skipping breeding in years when they're molting will really affect total lifetime reproduction. Understanding this is important for calculating whether or not albatross populations will grow or decline in response to things like the numbers of birds being killed by fishing boats." Anthony gestures to the birds around us and continues, "Albatrosses themselves have to know when their mate needs to skip a year, and when their mate is ready to breed. Otherwise the pairs will get out of phase with each other."

How can they communicate such information to each other? Dave and Anthony both agree that there are many things we don't understand about the lives of animals that live a long time.

LETTING THE OTHERS WALK AHEAD, I sit—albatross eye level—at the edge of the coral-powder runway and watch something so strange it

With extraordinary gentleness and trust—Black-footed Albatrosses

seems familiarly human. This pair has been sitting next to each other for many long minutes, nibbling tenderly around each other's faces, taking turns preening each other with extraordinary gentleness, each bird soaking it up as though this is the greatest luxury. Right now one bird is working the small feathers right around the other's eye. The recipient turns its head sideways so the first bird can reach its cheek. Its throat. Watching them preening so delicately, enjoying it with eyes closed, you sense this is as immensely pleasurable for them as it would be for us—something anyone who has ever been tenderly touched would recognize.

Not all the courting implies partnership intentions. Some birds are preening in threesomes. And several little clubs of up to half a dozen adolescents or non-nesting birds are displaying or interacting together. Many of the courting birds are immature. Juveniles remain at sea for several years, then visit the breeding island for several additional years of courtship before acquiring a mate and themselves breeding. Laysans first breed at eight to nine years of age, usually. So these displaying birds may be adolescents just practicing, or maturing birds getting serious about the future. If the latter, they are forming a true bond that will bring them back next year to mate and invest in the months-long struggle of raising their first chick.

I resume walking. Every few steps brings a new sight that expands my appreciation of albatrosses' unusually complex behaviors. Two non-breeders are playing house with a cold, abandoned egg. One attempts awkwardly to sit on it, perhaps getting a feel for being grown-up. I've done a lot of research with seabirds, but I've never heard of anything quite like this apparent role-playing with a found egg.

By far the most complicated part of albatross courtship is the elaborate and prolonged dancing that goes on for months. Quite a few birds that aren't breeding are dancing. One albatross waddlingly approaches another with its neck outstretched and its head pointed down, its throat quivering out a high wavering whistle. The other responds in kind. They engage in a bout of beak-to-beak touching, shaking their heads back and forth as if saying no but meaning yes. They begin to dance, their movements together intensifying in speed and emphasis.

Albatross shake-rattle-and-roll dances look like a game of Simon Says, but with everything done so fast, it's often impossible to tell who's leading. Simon says head up. Simon says head down. Simon says vigorously pump your head. Simon says bray like a donkey. Simon says throw your bill straight upward to the sky and scream your wavering whistle. Simon says suddenly get on your tippytoes while your bill is up, and moo. Simon says clack your bill like somebody snapping closed a wooden jewelry box. Simon says clack so fast it sounds like a rolling *r*. Clack while shaking your head side to side and wailing. Simon says lay your head against your partner's neck and clack so fast you drum-roll like a castanet; Simon says switch sides instantly. Simon says snap your bill to your wrist and flare one wing. Flare both gorgeous wings. Alternate flared wings and head pumping. Alternate now with bill drumming. Faster. Simon says walk slowly, high-stepping, with head going up and down. Simon says strut in a circle around each other, take deep bows, now point skyward. Simon says pump your body. Simon says wing out sideways. Flare wings and moo!—ooh how beautiful. Nice new *feathers*!

And they're not just going through the steps. During these dances they can seem truly carried away, like holy rollers, whirling dervishes. These birds are globe-trotting athletes, and they dance with Olympian energy. Everything in the dancing is about displaying quality, paying close attention to each other's motions, instantly matching their partner's movements. Speed, coordination, synchrony. They may be saying in effect, "I'm healthy and vigorous; look at how fast I can do this," or "Look at me; the sleek, strong feathers I have for flying make me a reliable food getter." It's all about showing and assessing health, vigor, and prime condition. Can you keep up with me? Are you fast? Can you cut it with me? Can I cut it with you? Are you worthy of my offspring and the best years of my long life?

Laysan and Black-footed Albatrosses are more varied and faster dancers than all other albatrosses. Dances may last fifteen minutes. They are highly dynamic performances; unlike the stereotyped courtship in many birds, no two albatross dances are the same. Most dances end with slowing pace followed by bowing, and then the female wandering off. After the dance they may sit quietly together for a while, then dance with another bird. Most dances are between a male and a female. Some—less than 10 percent—involve threesomes or small groups, and two females will dance together occasionally; two males, rarely. Prospecting females may spend a third of their time ashore dancing. Wandering and Royal Albatross dances involve full extension and display of both enormous wings, something not done by smaller albatrosses with lesser spans to boast. Sooty and Light-mantled Sooty Albatrosses (which have been called the Siamese cats of the bird world for their lovely shading) do much of their courtship aloft, during beautifully synchronized flights. They are gracile and exquisitely elegant birds; even among albatrosses, superb forms of life.

ALBATROSS COURTSHIP IS almost certainly the most intricate courtship of any nonhuman being. The reason is that there's a lot at stake. The pair-bond and relationship must last years. The commitment implied is immense. Compared to other animals, an albatross does not get very many chances to breed, and each breeding attempt, each egg, is highly valuable and expensive. Albatrosses can lay only one egg in a season, and many cannot nest every year. Unless your mate invests extraordinary effort, your chick dies. If you're going to put your only egg in somebody else's basket and sit there for weeks waiting for them to return, you want confidence that they're committed. If you want them to come from thousands of miles away, after weeks at sea, and feed your chick, you want to know they're committed. If you're considering a marriage that may last several decades, you want to feel sure they're committed.

So albatross courtship is highly complex. It involves both sexes very actively rather than just a male doing most of the displaying. And they don't rush into anything. The mutual wooing may last months or years.

Females want to be sure males will feel invested enough to return; males want to be sure the chicks they invest in are their own. But consider this: all males in a sense care for young that are not their own, because all males incubate eggs produced by a female, not by them. This trivial truism has repercussions that wrap the ends of the Earth: the great dilemma of being male is uncertainty of paternity. Result: much of male psychology is geared toward aggressiveness designed ultimately to accumulate rank and territory necessary to attract mates, depose rivals, and ensure fertilization of females and creation of genetic heirs. This is true across species, order, class, and phylum. It's true among tropicbirds, verifiable among vultures, beheld among beetles, done among dolphins. Perhaps this is the root of male insecurity, and the deepest taproot of male aggression and violence the world over. But consider also: among these albatrosses, nesting in these densities, it's perhaps most surprising that most males do in fact incubate eggs of their own parentage, in the right nest, in the right place. For that, of course, they can thank females. Females do have a choice. And they use it. Here's the dirty little secret of the many-splendored monogamy of most kinds of birds that "mate for life": quite a few of them color outside the lines. In most species, females often try to get fertilized by males who are older and better established and hold higher status than their "mates," because a proven survivor is the best indication of the high-quality genes you want your child to inherit. These same patterns and tendencies function throughout the animal kingdom; many birds—even some albatrosses—aren't really very different from many people in this regard.

Thus, elaborate, prolonged dancing is in a sense the albatrosses' search for reassurance, their quest for a promise. At the beginning of courtship, females may respond aggressively ("Is this male serious?"). But after displaying with the same male for some time, they allow closer proximity, mutual preening, and eventually—years later—mating. Lance Tickell, who studied albatrosses for half a century, has written, "Over several years, the number of different birds with which an individual communicates will steadily decline until it is perfecting the language of . . . one partnership, distinguishable from all others. This synthesis of language unique to one pair is, through repetition, synchronised in that pair. The paradox of these events is that once . . . mutual language is so perfected that breeding can take place, much of it ceases to be used. Breeding pairs no longer employ the full vigour of their language because they recognise each other and continually reinforce their close relationship by contact and preening." With the development of intimate familiarity, the dancing ends. Between experienced breeders, mating is usually a quiet act carried out on the pair's territory with little or no preliminary display. Experienced pairs often breed together over many years, until one dies. Divorce is unusual. Most albatross species display exceptional fidelity; albatross pairs sometimes remain together for longer than two decades.

We have only a comparatively short time to get to know these animals. Already our first day is nearly spent. The sun is nuzzling the horizon, throwing long shadows. It's a calming light. No machinery, no mechanical sound, no running motors rack this air. We await no loudspeaker announcements. No one gets paged. No phones ring. For virtually all of human history, this is how the whole world felt. The distant surf and even the din of birds frame a great overwhelming, underlying quiet now found only in remotest nature.

Within this musical silence beats the rhythm eternal. The sea rolls in, piles up, crashes, withdraws, rolls in. The great living tides of migratory animals render their own seasonal rhythms. The various seabirds, seals, turtles—feathered, furred, scaled—each perform a different theme upon these shifting shores. Each reads its score, enters on its cue, and takes its turn as featured soloist, playing a well-rehearsed part with vigor and intensity enough to render the music of the spheres. What you see and hear is a perfected performance born of millions of years of concerted practice in the most competitive environment imaginable.

It's a perilous paradise. The vast majority of hatchlings and newborns of most species, perhaps 90 percent, never see their first birthday. But those that win a chair onstage succeed to remarkable degrees. Many of the nesting terns are rather old, into their thirties. Great Frigatebirds and even these little Fairy Terns may survive well past the four-decade mark. Albatrosses—they can live a *long* time; no wonder they seem to be looking at you wisely.

Sunset is pulling the curtain down on this day. And so this enveloping quiet imparts a deceptive sense of peace, while each animal is pressing its limits to keep living against the odds. The calm that comes over you derives, perhaps, from the intuitive recognition that this is a scene that has endured, that underlying the frantic scramble for survival is stability and a long wave of slow change. The feeling this imparts is an overwhelming sense of things gone right. It's difficult to comprehend the long lineages that have put us all here, what elder beings we all are upon Earth. But this atoll, this wildlife, these remarkable albatrosses, all provide a visceral sense of continuity from deep, deep time. Here you can feel that our intertwined stories began far into the distant past, and that—as Coleridge's ancient Mariner implied—we are kin.

> ➤ ➤ ➤

BONDING

*E*VEN BEFORE the horizon began so slowly to lighten, Dave and Patty were already in the main room, prepping the ten high-tech "tags" Dave has brought.

Patty asks me how I slept. I was awake a lot, enjoying the constant murmurs, purring, and chattering from the hundreds of noddies and the Fairy Terns nesting just outside the dorm windows, and from thousands of Sooty Terns who came in after sunset and overnighted on the runway. Now, rather than having singing birds as dawn's alarm clock, the island is the quietest it's been all night, because the Sooties have already departed to search their fishing grounds. Still tired from yesterday's travel and the nocturne chorus, I could have used another hour's sleep. But being awake here is better. Sometimes a dream feels real. Here, reality feels like dreaming.

Dave shows me one of the transmitters. It looks like a robotic mouse, with a mouse-sized body and a long wire tail. A pricey little unit—$2,900—it communicates with satellites that zoom around Earth in under an hour. It's the biggest advance in seabird tracking in over 150 years.

On December 30, 1847, off the Chilean coast, Captain Hiram Luther of the whaler *Cachalot* shot an enormous albatross. Tied around its neck was a vial containing this message:

8 December. Ship "Euphrates," Edwards, 16 months out. 2300 barrels of oil, 150 of it sperm [whale]. I have not seen a whale for 4 months. Lat. 43° S., long. 148° 40'. Thick fog, with rain.

The bird had flown 3,394 miles (5,466 kilometers) in twenty-two days. For a century and a half, this fatal fix remained the best record of albatross flight over distance—until the advent of satellite tracking in the 1990s.

A transmitter weighs about an ounce, 1 percent or so of an albatross's body mass, a tenth the weight of an albatross's egg, a twentieth of the bird's usual weight fluctuations during breeding. Dave remarks, "The birds seem relatively comfortable; they don't try to take them off."

OUR MORNING PLAN CALLS for putting transmitters on several albatrosses. Our crew assembled on the porch includes Dave, Patty, Laura Carsten, and Frans Juola. Frans has already worked with hawks in California, Nevada, and Montana, and has volunteered here to get experience with seabirds. Laura, from Boulder, Colorado, feels inspired by nature and desires to teach biology—"to give something back." A willowy young woman with lengthy blond hair, she too has come for experience working with wild animals. Her parents, who were never able to get a higher education, always wanted Laura to attend college. Now Laura has made them proud with a new master's degree.

I ask Patty how she discovered her interest in biology. Patty, now twenty-seven, says her father died when she was twenty, and a year later she started on the winding path of higher education that has led all the way here. In nearly perfect English she explains, "In Ecuador, to do anything, you need your parents' approval. My father believed to study biology was crazy. He said to me, 'Bad idea.' He believed I should simply get married. No study. But my mom is really different. She always said, 'You know right from wrong, now it's your *choice* what you do.' My mother is a really smart woman, and always wishing she had gone to college." Patty has only one sibling, unusual in Ecuador. "My mother always said: 'I want to take care of two children really well, and not more than that.'" She continues, "In the Ecuadorian system you must choose your specialization when you're fifteen years old. I wanted to be a medical doctor since when I was little. But in high school we went to the place where they open the bodies. And it's like a *meat* place, you know—really gross. I decide: medicine is no for me. In the university, I meet a girl doing her thesis on Indian use of plants for medicine and food. So for three months I go work with her, going to different tribal villages." Patty went to villages so remote that getting in required a three-week boat trip. She ate tapir meat and monkeys killed with blow pipes and drank *chicha*, made from yuca plants. She learned that the Huaroni people have one word that incorporates everything positive, from "thank you" to "that's beautiful." She also learned that a woman like her—early twenties—

might be a mother of five and considered middle-aged. It was, she says, "the most incredible experience of my life." After Patty's jungle adventures, her sights narrowed on field biology, leading her to Dave Anderson's ongoing seabird work in Ecuador's Galápagos Islands. Among other things, she learned that "working in the field is hard. It's not like Monday through Friday and weekends off. You have to *work;* you have to commit yourself—but I like that."

THE MORNING SEEMS almost too cool for a T-shirt and shorts, but that's what we're all wearing. And collectively, we're quite the fashion show: Laura's shorts are spotted with paint. Frans's faded blue cap is streaked stylishly with tern droppings. Dave's unique shirt says BIOLOGY REEKS. Attention to the raunchier, uncouth, and unpleasant side of nature—which abounds—is one category of what passes as humor afield. (Advice: never dine with parasitologists.) There is attention to the fascinating too, which also abounds, and the surrounding beauty. I think this outwardly focused attention largely accounts for the way field scientists dress and look; they're too enthralled with the world—too in love, actually—to worry about a smudged T-shirt. As we descend the porch steps, Frans says to me from under his filthy cap, "I think you'll like being here at Tern Island. It's the middle of nowhere, but this place is a little miracle."

The idea this morning is for Dave to supervise, Patty to affix transmitters, and Laura and Frans to learn how it's done so they can assist later. Patty wants to choose birds nesting near the barracks, so she can keep an eye on them. And because this will be a study of the travels of adults who are caring for chicks, we need birds whose eggs will hatch. One way to check an egg is to "candle" it, to ascertain that an embryo is indeed alive. But Dave thinks these shells are too thick to shine a light through. Anthony, who has just joined us, says he's used a slide-projector bulb to "candle" albatross eggs.

So that's what we do.

The first bird whose egg we check is Amelia, the Laysan Albatross nesting just a few feet from the barracks steps. Her eyes are dark and deep-looking. She regards us as though skeptical, first with one eye, then the other. While I'm captured by the mysterious beauty in the eye of my beholder, Frans says, "When I look at an albatross I try to imagine what it's seen and what it's been through. I often think, 'That bird may be twice as old as I am.'"

These elder birds' eyes shine with a knowledge of experience unfathomable to us. Even the broadest strokes of their lives have long remained the albatrosses' secret. But we're here to peer into that secret a little bit, to start peeling the layers of mystery. We're not here to invade their privacy; we want to better appreciate them. And knowing about these albatrosses will also help us understand their exposure to human-made hazards, which may help us aid their survival. A third reason we want to know them better is to put the shimmering diversity of the living world in slightly clearer context, to gain a better sense of similarities and differences among us all.

Frans steps over to the nest, crouches, gently pushes Amelia aside, and lifts her soda-can-sized egg. It measures nearly five inches long, three inches wide—too big to fit easily in your palm. As Frans stands, Dave instructs him to keep the egg in the same orientation and avoid rolling it.

Amelia, who'd been sitting placidly, is now perturbed. She keeps getting up, fluffing out her belly feathers, and sitting back down. Feeling no egg, she keeps shifting. Her discomfort makes me uncomfortable, even though I know it's only momentary.

Frans holds the egg to the projector and puts a blanket over us. We can see the illuminated interior. It shows an embryo; we can see all the blood vessels. We can see the embryonic chick moving. Frans says to Dave, "This one's a kicker."

In under a minute, Frans returns the egg to Amelia, who gets on it before Frans is even off his knees.

Frans checks two more eggs. The third egg brings a moment of doubt. He says from beneath the blanket, "Hmm, can't see much on this one." Pause. "O.K., there are some blood vessels; this one's alive."

Dave announces that we'll put transmitters on these three birds this morning. As he approaches Amelia, she rises partway off her egg and opens her bill slightly. Patty, with an index finger over her lips, is watching Dave intently. Wary of being bitten, Dave puts a hand above Amelia's head and wiggles his fingers to distract her, then wraps his other hand around her bill and deftly scoops the great bird up, whisking her from the nest. Frans immediately shrouds Amelia's egg in a towel to keep it from getting pecked open by a hungry Ruddy Turnstone or overheated by the sun.

Carefully walking around other nests, Dave brings Amelia to the shaded barracks steps, where the transmitter awaits. He safely closes her bill with a rubber band but gives her a small stick to bite, thus keeping the bill open and aiding her breathing.

A man's whole thumb can easily disappear in her thick breast feathers. These albatrosses are nesting in the tropics, but they're not really tropical animals; they're heavily insulated against cold water. Dave shows us her brood patch, a bare bit of warm belly skin surrounded by thick downy feathers. If you were a chick, it would be a nice, cozy place to take a nap.

Dave sits, situating the big albatross in his lap, facing her toward him. Amelia struggles a little and tries scratching with her feet. She succeeds, leaving the inside of Dave's bare thighs painfully bleeding. Frans moves to steady her wings and feet.

With an index card, Dave lifts several of the outer feathers on Amelia's upper back. Patty takes special waterproof tape and lays a short piece across the underside of these feathers, then lays another short piece across their topside, so that the tape firmly sandwiches those feathers. Dave explains, "You want feathers that will remain in their normal position after the transmitter is on, so it won't bother the bird."

Into the tape Patty punches several holes, then carefully ties the transmitter to the tape with Teflon ribbon. A spot of instant glue fixes the knots. The process is repeated in the aft section of the transmitter. This effort is all concentration. It involves no idle chitchat, no jokes. Because of this, all goes smoothly. In a few minutes the transmitter is rather elegantly attached to the albatross's feathers. Patty smooths and preens Amelia's plumage. Her new antenna sticks out.

When we're ready to release Amelia, Laura carefully unwraps her egg. Dave puts Amelia near her nest. We all back away. Amelia takes a step toward the egg, stretches, and waves her great wings a few times. She stands over the nest, then bends down, talking to the egg in low and confiding tones. Then Amelia rises tall, flares her feathers to expose her brood patch, settles down, stretches her bill to the sky, and moos like a contented cow. She spends a few minutes preening but never fusses with the transmitter.

Laura walks to the next Laysan Albatross we've chosen. The bird is dozing. Laura places her hand gently over the bird's bill, then smoothly and competently sweeps it up with her other arm and carries it to the barracks porch. This bird struggles a bit more than Amelia did. When we're done transmittering the bird, Dave places it a few feet from its egg. It seems so broody, so programmed to incubate without moving, that it doesn't want to take a single step. Dave kneels next to it, and it backs away from him into the nest, but sits *beside* the egg. It seems wobbly on its feet; perhaps because it's been sitting for days, possibly weeks.

It takes six long minutes—a seeming eternity to us but probably a mere moment to a bird in this meditative mind-set—before it stands and takes the final step, flares its brood patch, and sits squarely on the oval egg.

Our third bird is a Black-footed Albatross, a large male. As Dave lifts it, it defecates directly on his T-shirt, making the shirt's sentiment, "Biology reeks," true in a literal sense. "Ow!" Dave says after an unsuccessful attempt to get the rubber band around the agitated bird's bill. These birds can *bite*."

Bite they do. Laura's got numerous scars on her arms, and Patty shows off her own recent marks. Like sailors' tattoos, the scars all come with stories. "They'll bite anywhere: fingers, arms—. Nipple bites are the *worst*."

The bird shakes his head and kicks. Dave says, "This guy is a handful. Jeez, it's fierce."

Laura, hair loose over her shoulders, concentrates on holding the albatross's wings and feet. When the bird struggles, Laura offers a silent "shhh" with her lips. She says, "It's really interesting, the different personalities they have."

The rambunctious bird utters three short grunting bellows and spits out the stick he had been biting. Dave resituates the albatross in his lap.

Patty concentrates on putting on the transmitter.

Dave observes that the feathers on Black-foots are shorter and denser than on Laysans. That suggests they might go to different parts of the ocean. I guess we'll see.

Until now, we've all been focused entirely on the birds and the transmittering. But as Dave watches Patty finish up, I suddenly notice about fifty bird lice well on their way to exploring Dave's shirt and shorts, reinforced by about twenty more lice just beginning their heroic trek from the present albatross to Dave's body. In fact, at least four species of lice and blood-sucking flies are moving up Dave's chest.

"Excuse me, Dave," I say. "You're covered in parasites."

"Am I?" He looks down for confirmation. Patty looks up for confirmation.

Still holding the albatross, Dave begins pulling the lice off with one hand. Patty, dedicated student that she is, helps.

Dave mumbles jokingly, "I hope I don't get any on the birds."

This would be full-on gross if there were any chance at all that these bird parasites would bite or infest a human—even a biologist. That they won't is one of the practical glories of evolutionary adaptation on a small scale; the parasites are so finely adapted to the seabirds that they aren't interested in people.

Dave says, "Well, that's one good thing we've done for the albatrosses—they have a lot fewer lice than before we handled them."

Patty continues helping Dave pull the invaders from his shirt. Dave chuckles as he pauses to pinch a louse from Patty's face. The moment of mutual nit-picking—perhaps the most ancient, time-honored social-bonding institution among primates—provides a rare opportunity for Patty to tease her adviser, and she says to Dave, "You don't need to worry too much about the lice, because you have no hair."

Dave responds, "That's really *nice*, Patty. Are there any other *lousy* things you'd like to say?"

When we're done with science and hygiene—and the lowbrow slap-stick that passes for high parasite-comedy in the mid-Pacific—Dave takes the big dark albatross to his nest and places him directly on his egg. He doesn't fluff, rouse, settle, or shake. Just sits down tight.

Dave says, "Well, that went quite well." He's pleased with the birds, and he's proud of Patty. As Patty and the others gather the equipment, Dave remarks to me, "Patty has done great. Three years ago she was just like many other girls in Ecuador, but since then her horizons have really broadened. She has worked in the Galápagos on research, come to North Carolina on her first trip abroad, entered our master's program, learned to speak English *well*, come to Hawaii, begun her own research, and met an English guy and gone to visit him in the U.K. That's a big three years for any young woman. The only thing is—and this is proba-bly cultural—I want her to learn not to defer to me so much. For a young Ecuadorian woman, deference to male authority is the norm. I'd like to see her more comfortable with questioning my decisions and dis-agreeing with me."

AT TEN O'CLOCK we take a moment's rest on the porch. Amelia is dozing just a few feet away. Her transmitter is hidden by feathers, its antenna barely showing. A noddy lands on the porch rail near my arm.

The weather has been unseasonably warm—abnormally hot, actu-ally—the air unusually still. More typically, continuous winds blow here. But now the heat is intense, and the sitting birds are showing the strain. They are clearly uncomfortable under the pressing tropic sun. Many have raised the feathers on their backs like louvers, trying to radiate heat. Some albatrosses have recently deserted. Either the mate's dead, or the heat has gotten to them.

Dave doesn't want to put on any more transmitters or handle any more albatrosses until the weather changes. He asks Patty's opinion. Patty says, in recently acquired English, "Well, because albatrosses lay only one egg, and they seem they don't breed every year, you have to try to make sure you don't cause more problems to any bird. So let's wait."

While everyone goes inside to eat, I linger on the porch, savoring existence. Beyond the lagoon and reef, the ocean rolls placid and eternal, pacific as ever. Until it meets the reef. Right now the swell on the north side of the island is piling a ten-foot surf. You can see but not feel the violence, because the breakers exhaust their energy by pounding the resolutely resisting reef. Each rolling swell that has wrinkled the sea surface for thousands of miles unfurls itself here, becoming a breaker for a moment or two, taking everything that went before and turning it into something new, different, spectacular, and brief. Ah yes, brief. As Virgil said, "Death plucks my ear and says, 'Live!—I am coming.'"

LUNCHTIME. Inside the barracks, Patty and Dave are prepping tacos and empanadas. Anthony is having trouble deciding between making pea soup with popcorn in it or veggie chili. He's a vegetarian because, he says, he has ethical objections to how animals are treated in industrial agriculture. "In many cases, the way animals are made to live is worse than how they're made to die." He doesn't usually eat seafood, either. "I don't like what the fishing industry is doing. For instance, you know how, for every pound of shrimp they catch, they often kill and dump about five pounds of small fish? That pains me somehow in my gut, so I don't buy it."

The freckled blonde, Karen Fischer, is a University of Colorado biology undergraduate with a proclivity for multiple earrings. Aged twenty, Karen has already traveled in: "Let's see; Ecuador, Peru, the Galápagos, Belize, and Costa Rica—oh, *and* Europe." After this stint at Tern Island, she'll head to New Zealand for a study-abroad program. Why the travel bug? "When my sister was fifteen she died of cancer. She missed out on so much, I feel I kind of owe it to her to try to do and see as many things as possible." In memory of her sister, Karen has a little forget-me-not flower tattooed on her ankle.

Someone pops Aretha Franklin into the boom box, and everybody starts bobbing while gobbling Karen's fresh muffins and making lunches from leftovers. One thing you quickly sense about the people here: they include more than the average proportion of idealists and self-motivated seekers. But they're all pretty down-to-earth. The work demands a lot of physical and mental effort. Slackers don't make it this far.

➤ ➤ ➤

*E*MERGENT LANDS HAVE COME and gone in the location we call Hawaii for nearly seventy million years. These are islands not so much lost in time as lost *to* time. The Hawaiian Islands and the Northwest Hawaiian Islands have all been moving constantly westward toward the setting sun on an immense conveyor belt of rock, drifting on the moving Pacific Plate like puffs of smoke in a breeze. Most are in late senescence and on the way out. Beyond the Northwestern Hawaiian Islands, in fact, lie ancient drowned former islands known as the Emperor Seamount chain. Those deposed Emperors, many tens of millions of years old, lie so stooped and eroded they no longer graze or grace the sea surface.

All Hawaiian islands past and present trace their parentage to the same volcanic hot spot, a deep, stationary point in the mantle of the planet that generates heat intense enough to partly melt the overriding Pacific Plate and force magma through it. (Only a handful of similar hot spots exist on Earth, including those beneath the Galápagos Islands and the Azores.) This spot is still giving fire-and-brimstone birth to the Big Island and building the newest future island, which has yet to surface for air. Only about half the volcanoes thus created break the surface. But some, at a total height of thirty thousand feet from sea floor to summit, stand among this planet's most massive mountains.

As they all drown in their slow procession west, they will be "replenished" by the birth of new islands. Kure Atoll, at the end of the island chain, was born about thirty million years ago and is now far from home, roughly 1,500 miles (2,400 kilometers) from the hot place where it was first expelled from Mother Earth. The most distant Emperor seamount has drifted 2,900 miles (4,700 kilometers) and lies near the Aleutians. Seventy-five million years ago, it was born of the same hot spot that conceived the current embryonic member of the family, Lo'ihi, right where Lo'ihi is now. Lo'ihi is growing from the sea floor twelve miles southeast of Hawaii's Big Island. Its birth above the surface—requiring another thousand meters of vertical gestation—would make it the newest baby Hawaiian island. This will likely take somewhere between two thousand years (in which case humans will probably witness it) and twenty thousand years (twice as long as civilization has existed). Lo'ihi is an active little baby, kicking at a rate of one thousand undersea earthquakes per year, and venting water twice the normal boiling temperature.

Long before scientific studies, ancient Hawaiians, by noticing differences in erosion, soils, and vegetation, recognized that the islands to the northwest were older than those to the southeast. Instead of proposing hot spots in the mantle as the underlying cause, they reasoned that Pele, the goddess of volcanoes, had originally lived on the island of Kauai. When her older sister Namakaokahai, goddess of the sea, attacked her, Pele fled to Oahu. When forced to flee again, Pele moved southeast to Maui, then to Hawaii, her current address, where she now abides in the summit of the Kilauea Volcano. Pele's stepwise flight from west to east, and her problems with her watery sister, conjure the continual struggle between the island's volcanic growth and the tearing and wearing of the eternal sea and the rains upon the shores and shoulders of the islands. The mythology remains consistent with geologic knowledge developed centuries later. Preliterate people are often excellent at noticing relationships; science excels at explanations.

WHEN SEA LEVELS WERE at a low point seventeen thousand years ago, during the last Ice Age, high tide was three hundred feet lower than it is today. Some of today's barely drowned shallows and barely emergent atolls, like French Frigate Shoals, would have been substantial islands. Now there's not much margin for error. In fact, if not for the magic of coral, many of the most bird-populated atolls would already have drowned. An atoll is a roughly circular island with a central lagoon, dependent on the upward growth of corals to keep its head above water. Today, many of the Northwestern Hawaiian Islands are atolls. Some North Pacific atolls have been drilled to see how thick their coral cap is—it's thick: thousands of feet at certain atolls.

Charles Darwin, an even greater genius than most people realize, was also first to correctly figure out the evolution of atolls. As magma rises from a hot spot or a plate boundary in Earth's mantle, a volcanic island forms. By the time formation ends (as when the island is conveyored away from the hot spot on a moving plate) the massive mountains have already begun eroding. Those Hawaiian islands that have moved west of the active volcanic zone have begun this process. Over two to five million years, while the mighty island begins subsiding, a ring of corals forms around the island. In five to ten million more years, as the island continues sinking, the coral forms a fringing reef. By ten to thirty million years, the island submerges just below the sea, leaving a ring of upwardly mobile growing coral reef and low islands around the perimeter, and a shallow lagoon in the center.

As long as their corals can grow fast enough to keep pace with island sinkage and sea level rise, these will be islands and atolls. The place where the water becomes too cool for coral reefs' growth to keep pace with sinkage—about 29° north latitude—is called the Darwin point. In the Hawaiian chain, it is no coincidence that Kure Atoll, at the extreme end of the Northwestern Islands, is both the last emergent island and the world's northernmost atoll. This is the last place where coral growth can compensate for island subsidence. The sunken Emperor Seamounts are the drowned islands past this point, whose fossil corals, extinguished by too cool waters, still cap the submerged lands. This fate next awaits Kure, too, on its inexorable journey north, and the sea will eventually reclaim each island as it trips over the Darwin point.

➤ ➤ ➤

THE ALBATROSSES HAVE a deep history too. The earliest known fossil albatross is about twenty-five million years old. Albatross species similar to those now flying were coursing the seas sixteen million years ago. Albatrosses, and all the tube-nosed seabirds, descended from a common ancestor. That ancestor's other descendants branched off to become different highly specialized families of aquatic birds. While one extreme line of seabird adaptation became the penguins, who entirely sacrificed flight for deep-diving ability (and turned their wings into finlike flippers that can no longer be folded), the tube-nosed seabirds invested everything in the ability to fly as far as possible over the oceans of Earth. Though they range almost limitlessly in any direction, the vertical lives of tube-nosed birds are severely compressed, seldom rising more than about fifty feet from the surface. While they travel distances unimaginable to us, altitude never occurs to an albatross. It's as though by collapsing their world into just two dimensions—true Flatlanders—they maximize the spread of distance.

In the eighteenth century the great biologist Carolus Linnaeus gave the tube-nosed seabird group its scientific name, Procellaria, from the Latin for storm or tempest. The group comprises roughly half of all seabirds, well over a hundred species, in several subgroupings. In size order: the storm-petrels (the smallest weighs under an ounce), diving-petrels, prions, larger petrels and shearwaters, giant petrels, and albatroses. The largest albatross is about 350 times the size of the smallest storm-petrel. The easiest way to remember what distinguishes albatrosses is that while other tube-nosed birds' nostrils are fused atop the bill, albatrosses' nostrils lie separated alongside their bill. And among tubenoses only the Giant Petrels rival some albatrosses in size. Albatrosses are *big*.

Today albatrosses inhabit every open ocean except the North Atlantic. (Fossils from eastern North America and Europe show that albatrosses lived even there five million years ago.) Rare vagrant albatrosses do occasionally turn up in the North Atlantic. Two Black-browed Albatrosses appeared annually in Northern Gannet colonies in the Faroes and in Shetland for twenty-five years. Yellow-nosed Albatrosses are sighted from time to time off North America and Europe. But any Atlantic sighting north of the equator is extremely rare. Most bizarrely, a Wandering Albatross slipped through the Strait of Gibraltar, crashed onto the coast of Sicily, and was hit by a car and killed.

Virtually all albatrosses spend most of their foraging time in seas between latitudes 30° and 55°. These are the great, windy regions of the oceans. The sole exception to this latitude rule is the Galápagos Albatross, which breeds near the equator and forages where the Humboldt Current streams cold water into the tropics off Peru and Ecuador. But it too relies on wind. Twenty of the twenty-four species of albatross live and breed in the Southern Ocean's middle latitudes—including the "roaring forties" and "furious fifties." That's precisely because the sweeping gales that gust and bluster around the open seas at the bottom of the world energize these giants' journeys. Wind, more than anything, defines where albatrosses live and go. All albatrosses are tied to remote islands for breeding, but between nesting they span long stretches of space and time, often years, at sea—propelled by that wind.

LIVING ALBATROSSES FALL into four groups: the great albatrosses, several smaller Southern Hemisphere albatrosses, the sooty albatrosses, and the North Pacific species.

Scientists long considered those four groups to comprise thirteen species: two gigantic "great" albatrosses (the Wandering and the Royal); five other Southern Hemisphere types (Black-browed, Gray-headed, Buller's, Yellow-nosed, and Shy); the Sooty and Light-mantled Sooty Albatrosses; the Galápagos, or Waved, Albatross (for their wavy markings); and the North Pacific's Laysan, Black-footed, and Short-tailed (or Steller's) Albatrosses.

Many Southern Hemisphere albatross forms vary from island to island, with slight differences in plumage, eye color, and size. These variants were long considered races or subspecies within the same species, but DNA analysis indicates that some of these varieties are actually different species—depending on your view of how much differentiation constitutes speciation. If you accept this analysis, the Campbell Island Black-browed is a separate species; the Yellow-nosed comprises two species (Atlantic Yellow-nosed and Indian Ocean); the Buller's and Royal each comprise Northern and Southern species; the Shy is actually a complex of four species (Tasmanian Shy, Auckland Shy, Salvin's, and Chatham Albatrosses); the Wandering actually includes five species (*Diomedea exulans* plus Gough, Amsterdam, Auckland, and Antipodes Albatrosses). In all, eleven races have been newly recognized as species by most scientists, bringing the total number of albatross species to two dozen.

We like to say that among animals, forms that cannot freely interbreed are separate species. That's a good and useful definition for *most* animals. But because evolution is a gradual process, some varieties— caught present-day in the act of change—are neither clearly the same nor clearly different species. For example, in New Zealand a mixed pair of Northern and Southern Royal Albatrosses produced four fertile offspring over several years. The crisp definition of "species" smudges and blurs at such margins. In nature there is no exact moment of speciation, only accumulated change—degrees of relationship, degrees of separation. Darwin came to his insight on evolution through the differences in very similar Galápagos birds from nearby islands—as though they'd started from a common ancestor and their isolation on different islands had provided time for differing local environments to modify the separate populations' characteristics. Then he reasoned that the same process of selective breeding used by farmers for centuries was essentially at work in nature; most animals died young, and the individuals best suited for survival under local conditions left more surviving offspring who'd inherited the winning characteristics. He wondered about it, then concluded that, eventually, the birds could accumulate change enough that the different populations would in some cases become no longer mere varieties but actually different species. Because some of the Galápagos finches differed only slightly while others showed considerable change, Darwin perceived the whole process in various stages of progress. It was perhaps the most important insight ever granted a human mind.

Albatrosses' taxonomy is confusing because albatrosses are Darwin's finches writ large. Albatrosses have undergone a course of change similar to the finches', but albatrosses' islands are separated by hundreds, sometimes thousands of miles. Though they roam extraordinary distances and often mix at sea, they almost always *breed* on the island they hatched on. For instance, researchers discovered that more than 90 percent of Gray-headed Albatrosses breed within 250 meters of where they'd hatched years earlier. On Midway Atoll, albatrosses breed an average of 22 meters from the nest they were born in. This makes any albatross nesting ground a neighborhood for extended family, where, over the years, parents and their offspring and their grandchildren may all breed in rather close proximity. But for evolutionary purposes, the birds' strong tendency to breed at their place of birth keeps the populations almost as isolated as Darwin's famous finches—isolated enough to evolve different forms on different islands. The isolation of breeding on the world's remotest islands is continually shaping albatrosses in slow, dynamic change.

➤ ➤ ➤

*T*HE BREEZE IN MY BEDROOM is the first sign that this morning is different. After days of dead calm, newly moving air has passed its kinetic energy along to the heat-stressed birds. You can feel their excitement in their increased activity.

Patty is doing the day's first round of her nest checks, looking for any mates of transmittered albatrosses that may have arrived and switched incubation duties. We walk among the incubating birds like grape growers among vineyards. So far all the incubating birds in the study area are familiar, Amelia and the others. No new arrivals. But there has been one premature departure, probably forced by the just-ended heat wave; its abandoned egg is now cool to the touch.

Patty, several yards ahead, suddenly calls and waves.

Has one of the transmittered adults departed? No. But when we walk up, Patty gestures to a Black-footed Albatross standing over an eggshell with a gaping hole at one end and a downy chick beside it. Karen arrives eagerly, and immediately volunteers to guard the chick as we give its parent a transmitter.

Karen gushes, "Oh my *God*. It's *so* cute!" Its head is wobbly. Its little black decurved bill seems proportionally larger than an adult's. The little wing stubs offer scant hint of the flying power that may come. The chick's black down, frosted light gray at the tips, is so thick and long and matted that the nestling looks rather oddly like a large fluffy pinecone. It probably weighs about seven ounces. "Oh my gosh, look at its fat little legs!"

The chick stands shakily and stretches its wings, pulling all heart-strings within ten yards. Before the mind had a name for beauty, the heart had a response. The chick instinctively starts digging a scrape for itself with its feet. When it yawns a teetering little yawn, Karen's hand goes to her face in delight and astonishment. To the chick she says, "I'll take care of *you* anytime."

Her job right now—a tough job if ever there was one—is protecting this chick from possible frigatebird attack and the sun. Karen is con-cerned that the chick is too exposed. "It's not used to being out in the sun," she says. I offer her my hat to shade it, but she's transfixed.

The chick begins preening, nibbling at its down. The effort seems to tire it, and it rests its head and closes its eyes. When the chick begins to shiver, Karen takes off her sweatshirt and lightly covers it, saying ten-derly, "It's a rough life."

That it is. But with luck and all odds vanquished, this unsteady little new life may go forward—and outlive us.

A Laysan Albatross walks by, pausing to stare at the chick like an admiring passerby. A nearby nester stands up, looks at its own egg, and starts talking to it. As hatching nears, parents commonly vocalize to their upcoming offspring. And as soon as a chick "holes" or "pips" the egg, it begins talking back. As Dr. Seuss might summarize: Horton finally hears a Who. Parent and child keep the conversation going through the hole in the eggshell during the many hours it takes for the chick inside to painstakingly chisel out.

When our crew has affixed the transmitter, we take the adult back toward Karen and its chick. We place the bird near its nest. It stands there until the chick begins calling, then suddenly runs to it. Laura turns to Karen and says, "Well, Karen, anytime you'd like to help out with the albatrosses—."

With what might be termed enthusiasm, Karen interrupts. "I would *love* to help."

BY OUR FOURTH DAY, ten albatrosses wear transmitters. Now, oddly, the fieldwork is largely done, and most of the data accrual will happen almost passively as technology takes over, reporting the birds' positions.

(So far the data are less than interesting, because none of the birds has moved.) Now we ourselves will also wait faithfully like Horton the elephant, attached by effort and scientific curiosity to the patiently sitting birds.

Each day we check. Each day, the faithful birds at their nests remain.

> ➤ ➤ ➤

*P*ATTY IS EXCITED. Halfway through a new day's morning nest check, she's just discovered the mate of one of our birds sitting on the nest. The transmitter-bearing bird is *gone!*

Dave rides up slowly on his bicycle. Even though the new bird arrived just last night from weeks at sea, it sits here as though nothing is unusual. Amelia and her neighbors, sitting as always, appear equally indifferent.

But Patty is stoked. "Now," Patty says, "we'll be getting some *data.*" Somewhere between the vast Pacific and outer space, albatross, satellites, and Dave's North Carolina laboratory are already corresponding. Each day the satellites will interrogate the transmitter, and the bird's location will be beamed to Earth.

Amelia couldn't care less; she's still here on her nest near the porch, still broody and dozing.

Patty and Dave set up a laptop computer on a picnic table on the barracks' back porch, and using a solar panel to power it, they link to a communications satellite to download e-mail. With noddies lined up on the porch rail and the computer set up near the laundry lines, information flows into the laptop from outer space. The transmitter data has already been beamed via another satellite to a facility in France, then sent from France to Dave's North Carolina lab, and a student has e-mailed it. Result: we discover that our outbound bird is sixty miles north of Tern Island.

Dave, munching from a bowl of cereal, says, "It's nice to see everything working. It's really remarkable how all this technology is being coordinated to solve the question of where they go."

And while most university research data is eventually published years later only in obscurely specialized technical journals, Dave's approach to this albatross work is very different. Every morning when the satellite data from traveling albatrosses arrives, Dave will e-mail it to over five hundred teachers in classrooms in the United States, Canada, Germany,

Estonia, Japan, South Africa, Australia, and elsewhere who have subscribed to Dave's Albatross Project. Students will map the albatrosses' travel tracks as they unfold. "I realized early on," Dave says, "that kids from kindergarten through high school could be discovering what's happening with the birds at the very same time we ourselves are discovering it." He adds, "I'm trying to find ways to communicate effectively about science." Dave believes freedom and democracy require a public that can think critically. "If a scientist has a new idea, his or her first task is to challenge it against everything else that's known, seeing whether it can be disproved. In most other endeavors, everyone is pushing their own ideas and their own narrow interests. I think that when you teach science, you're teaching people a way of thinking that can help them stay free."

DURING THE NIGHT of January 17–18 another transmittered albatross has left Tern Island. But the albatross I call Amelia resides, remains, and rests upon her nest next to the porch steps. We pause. She waits. We watch. She stands, talks in low tones to her egg, flares her brood patch, and sits back down. For now, that has to count as action.

By the following day, two more of the birds are outbound over the ocean. Things are happening. Patty and Dave are departing too, headed home. Patty will leave her birds and begin the hard work of her master's project in earnest from thousands of miles away.

Getting here has been neither likely nor easy for any of us, biologist or bird. The planning, the traveling, the personal and professional toil, the resolute routes and sheer luck that have led us here—the convergence is quite an improbable one. All of us differ in every detail. All have one thing in common: whether seeking to succeed or striving to breed, we've arrived here as survivors of earlier struggles. Hoping our efforts will meet continued luck, we now stand poised for payoff, ready to see our labors produce.

Mark is checking to make sure the cargo and passengers don't exceed the plane's weight limit. He weighs all the bags, then calls across the room, "Patty, how much do you weigh?" Patty yells back, "One thirty-four," then says to me, "Now *everybody* knows." I say our time has shot by. Dave looks at his watch to remind himself what month it is.

Waving, waving, waving, they are gone. They leave over the ocean, like everything else.

⊱ ⊱ ⊱

WHEN AMELIA STANDS for her next nest check, her egg is gone. Between her massive webbed feet sits a gray ball of spiky fluff. By this time, the sixth of February, many of the other albatross nests already harbor chicks.

Amelia broods her baby three days, providing shade and shelter from heat and high winds. When her mate arrives to relieve her in the early morning of February 9, Dad immediately feeds the little chick. Or tries to.

He crouches so far forward toward the chicklet that his breast is touching the nest's low rim. The hungry chick is eager, pecking shakily at its parent's bill, peeping a shrill call that sounds like "Me, me, me." Dad is trying so hard to begin regurgitating that the effort seems to force his wings partly open. At the same time, he is trying to make contact with the chick's little bill, but the uncoordinated hatchling keeps swinging away at the critical moment.

Eventually, with the kind of persistence that precedes all earned rewards, the male practically swallows the chick's head. In the cavern of its father's gape, the chick opens its wobbly little bill. Dad squirts a concentrated stream of gooey, nutritious, liquefied oil into the chick's throat. Unlike most other birds, albatrosses and their tube-nosed relatives store oil extracted from their food. Albatross stomach oil is so energy rich that its mean caloric value rates just below that of commercial diesel oil.

After wiping its beak, the chick half stands and waves its little wings, then sits back down contentedly. For the moment, all's right with the world.

And so a new phase kicks in. Amelia and her mate must now no longer simply share incubation shifts; the chick's arrival begins a period of increasing strain in an already strenuous life. Bodily reserves will be taxed to the max. Now food is the issue.

Somewhere out on the sea, these birds are finding a food supply that is not at all obvious when you look at the surface of that vast ocean. But find it they do. All together, the seabirds of the Northwestern Hawaiian Islands require an estimated eight hundred million pounds of prey annually, largely fishes, crustaceans, and squids—perhaps two-fifths of the annual production of those animals in the ocean region. Of the amount consumed, albatrosses probably take half. Laysan and Black-footed Albatrosses eat mostly various species of squid, fishes, fish eggs, crustaceans, and anything else living or formerly living that they can hook their bills into. Albatrosses in general eat everything from small fishes to dead seabirds to squid to krill to gelatinous drifting tunicates to jellyfish (including the famously sting-infested Portuguese Man-of-War). If they find a dead whale, their diet will include whale meat. Sometimes they feed on scraps of skin and blubber of whales killed by Killer Whales or by people. What they eat depends on where they happen to be and what they find. Many albatrosses follow ships, because even kitchen scraps can make an albatross happy. They are inveterate scavengers and opportunists. When it comes to eating, albatrosses' motto seems to be "Better full than fussy."

But in practice, almost all albatrosses almost everywhere eat mostly squid. It's even been suggested that albatross evolution and radiation around the world has corresponded to squid evolution as the birds became skilled squid finders. Squids are highly evolved, unusually successful predators in their own right. The Cretaceous mass extinction wiped out not only dinosaurs but also many kinds of marine life that had flourished for an enormity of time. As the disappearance of dinosaurs opened the land to opportunities for birds and mammals, the extinction of marine faunas opened the seas to the radiation and proliferation of modern fishes and squids, with new monarchies of predators. The rapidly spreading new jet-propulsion-bodied animals we know as squids evolved complex behavior, excellent eyesight, and surprising smarts (they have been called "the soft intelligence" and "honorary vertebrates"). Squids have proliferated into over seven hundred species moving throughout the world's seas, from sunlit reefs to the black abyss, from the size of your little finger to the Giant Squid, measuring almost sixty feet.

Enter albatrosses. Albatrosses eat about seventy species of squid. At times the birds catch them live and vigorous. But they also exploit the fact that many kinds of squid die en masse after spawning. About a day after dying in the chilly deep, the carcasses of many species of squid float to the surface, buoyed by increasing ammonia resulting from chemical changes in their livers. Albatrosses rely heavily on this phenomenon, which makes deep food available. In the western Tasman Sea off New South Wales, Australia, a spectacular postnuptial appearance of dead and dying ten-pound Giant Cuttlefish prompts a remarkable convergence of albatrosses. Birds from half a world away—from the South Atlantic, Indian Ocean, and New Zealand—find it worth their while each year to come for the funeral feast. In sum: albatrosses eat a lot of squid. People also eat a lot of squid, and fishing boats remove enormous quantities of the food albatrosses have for millennia relied on. In much of the world, squid fishing is done at night, using bright lights to attract squid to the boat as moths are attracted to porch lights. So great is the fishing pressure now that the lights of squid-fishing fleets are visible to astronauts in space, appearing like cities in the sea.

WITH DAD NOW NESTBOUND, it's Amelia's turn to face the vicissitudes of the ocean, but she's an experienced pro. So far, she has survived all trials of weather, threats of starvation, and hazards of humanity. She launches herself from the runway and strikes immediately northward.

Amelia sails past the island's shore, skims across the lagoon, and rises above the towering breakers beyond the reef, setting her course upon an open ocean, striking out into the wide trance of the sea.

Belly to the sideways breeze, catching the wind for levitation, she climbs. Then turning her back to that same breeze, she uses the wind differently—and adds gravity—to accelerate her forward and downward toward the surface of the ocean. She brushes the water and shifts her body again, transferring the downward momentum to help *lift* her, exploiting the force of gravity to take her *upward*. Having used the wind to take her up, she uses it to take her down; having used gravity to take her down, she uses it to take her up. This gives her a smoothly undulating, rocking flight; each wing alternately pointing skyward, then pointing toward the water's surface, showing you now her dark back, now her bright belly. Wings fixed, she seems magically propelled.

Only as you watch her nearing the vanishing point—only then—do you begin seeing and feeling that these birds muster all their distance-eating achievement with their own effort and the skillful exploitation of their exquisite design. Keep watching as she shrinks to a pinpoint, swooping up and down, swiveling side to side, bounding onward into the boundless Pacific. Just this way, she starts steadily accumulating the great span of a great ocean, mile after mile after mile.

➤ ➤ ➤ ➤

LETTING GO

Aɴ ʜᴏᴜʀ ᴀғᴛᴇʀ Aᴍᴇʟɪᴀ ʟᴇᴀᴠᴇs, the last visual trace of French Frigate Shoals falls away behind her. She makes no note of it, as you make no note of leaving sight of your house when you run an errand. She sees herself neither as heroic nor hardworking. Nor does she have any other abstract concept. She has only purpose—to hunt—and she is keenly aware of that. And like any animal, like us when we travel, she knows where she is relative to home. But she has no visual markers on the ever-shifting ocean. Her mental map is not like yours. Her brain contains a compass—yours doesn't—and a clock as accurate as your internal clock, which she pays more attention to. And of course, she has those wings. Albatrosses usually spend 80 to 90 percent of their time at sea flying, day and night.

The sea swells grow and roll beneath her, and fall away. Amelia's flight follows them as she rises higher, her belly to the wind, the wind in her sails, then arcs into the downsweep of her flight path. Like this she goes for hours, this undulating flight, wings set and quivering against the breeze.

She's averaging fifteen miles an hour, sometimes double or even triple that when the wind blows up. She seems in all ways calm and unflappable. Her broodiness is gone, and now this bird is sharply alert. She is traveling, traveling; and she is foraging.

The transmitter's dialogue with the satellites will tell us where Amelia is. But we can also sketch a plausible picture of what she might be experiencing.

Though Amelia has no landmarks, she has her cues. Most birds have a poor sense of smell, but the tube-nosed birds carry olfactory equipment that's among the most sensitive ever evolved. Amelia is sifting scent as she goes, so she sticks near the ocean surface like a seagoing bloodhound. And the sky is not empty of life. She isn't all that far from home, and she shares the air. Terns and frigatebirds occasionally cross her line of vision. She reads them skillfully: terns going and coming in a low straight line, close to the water, have found a source of fish and are commuting. They're worth following. Terns fifty feet above are searching, like her. They bear watching. A frigatebird flying high, tight circles may be watching a marlin or a school of Mahimahi, waiting out the inevitable sprint for flyingfish. If it's late in the day, a pod of dolphins is worth following; a hunt may erupt, making fish available. Diving flocks of terns and boobies signal tuna; tuna signal eating-sized fish, plus a promising area to linger after dark in search of squid.

A line of weeds or flotsam is a good place to find floating objects with delectable flyingfish eggs adhered to them. These lines mark the friction at the borders of enormous masses of water that differ in temperature, nutrient concentration, productivity (thus color), and flow rate. Living things afloat, adrift, and aloft all strongly tend to collect at these energized boundaries, both because new nutrients get injected into sparser waters and because the friction slows the current edges, concentrating minute drifting organisms that ignite the whole food chain. Such places are a bit like bustling frontier towns of countries in the sea, save that their locations are ever-changing with the winds and moving waters. When the breeze is off such a frontal zone, the scent wafts to Amelia, sometimes telling of an unseen meal miles away.

What to us is trackless blue ocean is to her recognizable territory, a familiar mosaic riddled with scents and signs. As we know that in our town the supermarket will hold food, a train will come along the tracks, children will fill the school yard, and a bus will appear at the stop, she likewise knows the sea's vast and changing neighborhoods, and what to expect. She knows when to keep going, and where patience will turn to profit.

She keeps going.

THE SUN DIES IN SOLITUDE, off to Amelia's left. She flies steadily into the deep night. As best we understand, much of this time, alternating halves of her brain are sleeping. (Once, when a ship in Antarctic waters made an abrupt ninety-degree turn, a Wandering Albatross that had been following for many hours slammed into the vessel and fell to the deck. Apparently that bird had been *totally* asleep.) Near midnight, 110 miles northwest of her nest, Amelia swerves around, turns directly into the wind, then adjusts course and begins flying east. She'd used the breeze blowing from the southeast to shoot her away from French Frigate Shoals, and now she puts it on her right and a little ahead—at the two o'clock angle—so she can both use the cross vector for efficient flying and search the oncoming breeze for scents from upwind. By the look of her straight track, she's found nothing. She continues on.

In the morning Amelia is ninety-four miles north of Tern Island. No sight of land guides her. But in a place that looks no different from any of the surrounding sea, her nose tells her to slow. Amelia is getting whiffs of a faint, earthy smell, a little like the aroma of freshly broken succulent vegetation. If she'd ever smelled a cut cucumber, it would remind her of this smell.

Unseen 220 fathoms below, the slopes of an enormous undersea mountain slump to an ocean floor 2,600 fathoms—three miles—deep (a fathom being six feet, roughly the span of a man's outstretched arms). Amelia doesn't know that a mountain is forcing currents up its slopes toward the surface. She doesn't know that when water streaming up from the dark abyss is struck by sunlight, its untapped nutrients can nourish the single-celled plants that need both sunlight and nutrients. Nor that these plant cells—phytoplankton—give off that faint, earthy-fresh smell. She doesn't know that small animals called zooplankton eat those plant cells, or that zooplankters get eaten by small fish, and the little fish feed squid. She doesn't know that. She doesn't need to. She knows this: the smell means food.

Amelia passes into the scent upwind, and the air goes pure salty again. She turns and the aroma resumes. She weaves along its line of origin. And suddenly she receives a whiff of something different. Very faint. It's the smell of fat. Not blubber, not the kind of feast a whale carcass would mean. This mild aroma is from sea foam—including the whipped fat of minute diatoms whose microscopic bodies have been broken by rough water. The foam has drifted into a very subtle line, a thin, diluted concentration zone, formed at the surface where the current is eddying around water being deflected up the slope.

A few widely scattered groups of terns and several albatrosses affirm that this place might be worth investigating. But their sparseness suggests, "You should have been here yesterday." Amelia searches sunlit waters over the unseen slopes. She searches all day.

She comes up with precious little. Not much more than a few jellyfish this time. The smell that drew her in seems to have grown fainter during the day. Nothing in her experience suggests to her that this area is worth further searching. Her nose tells her that the water temperature's been steady; the air temperature at the surface hasn't changed a whiff. The calm, hot weather hasn't brought enough wind to mix up the deeper water for full benefit; at the surface it's still mostly the same water for miles around. This water is too blue and clear—so clear because it's so empty.

She knows that very far to the right of where the sun will set, the way we call north, is a reliable place for food. But that is a trek for a different frame of mind. Not now. Right now she wants a meal for her chick. She wants food here. Her chick is small; she will settle for small amounts. And something about the newness of her chick begins tugging at her. It may be as simple as an urge to stick close to Tern Island when the days are still this short, but she feels it as a desire not to continue traveling. The evening wind, slacking, does nothing to urge her on. On this trip, there will be no long trek to the right of the setting sun.

She travels ninety miles farther east, and goes dozy in the dark, until past midnight she catches another interesting whiff that rouses her to full wakefulness. She turns south. The scent vanishes in a slight wind shift but she continues in this direction, and after about an hour she briefly gets that weak scent again. She flies another hour. Now the scent strengthens. Amelia slows. She's over a larger but much deeper bulge; this one rises to 1,700 fathoms, in water 2,700 fathoms deep. If there is a drift line, or surface rips in the running tides, or any other visual cues, they're invisible in the dark; but the scent is familiar enough.

In the starlit black waters of a moonless night, she sees lanternfish flickering to each other, blinking the lights along their bodies like scouts with signaling mirrors. They're generally too small for Amelia to catch, but she knows patience here now could mean squid—squid in the dark that have followed the lanternfish up a thousand feet since sunset. In the inky water, those puckering hunters become the hunted. Amelia sees a small pod of squid come and go from her field of view. She wheels and sees other squid rushing small lanternfish. Several squid succeed, and as they maneuver their wriggling victims toward their beaks they blush darker to conceal themselves and their meals from hungry schoolmates. Occupied in their own stealth and mutual mistrust, the squid fail to detect Amelia's night-cloaked, gliding approach.

She plows in heavily, like an unseen truck speeding into a busy intersection. Suddenly among the squid an enemy is jabbing. Puffs of ink explode in the water like bombs in the D-day sky. Narrowly, all the squid scatter safely away.

All but one.

Amelia sits watching for more squid. "Patience, patience, patience, is what the sea teaches," wrote Anne Morrow Lindbergh, "patience and faith." A disturbed jellyfish lights up momentarily, and its glow catches Amelia's attention out of the corner of her eye. Her glance reveals several more squid prowling just under the surface. She paddles toward them—half spreading her wings because she wants to hurry—and extends her neck just in time to reach one at the edge of the withdrawing group. When she is done swallowing, she shakes her head in the cool seawater, cleansing the squid's thick, muddy ink from her fine white face.

At first light, the surface life of night—the lanternfish and their pursuers—drift downward like vampires afraid of daylight. They track the black depth toward another day of deep meditation.

For hours and hours—all day—she searches this thin broth of sustenance in the sparse tropical sea. She courses over the edges of unseen slopes deep below, following her nose and the subtle surface turbulence those slopes create in the streaming currents. A squid floats dead at the surface. Amelia lands and paddles forward, nailing it on her impaling bill.

The more food Amelia finds, the more she feels her chick pulling. She can feel that new chick like a rubber band, like a downy bungee cord. Nearly 156 miles into the ocean from Tern Island, she suddenly sets course directly for home, and the satellites log the route change. For ten hours she sails a straight track as if connected by a taut wire to her unseen nest and her fluffy baby.

The satellite has given us tracks on the map. Using everything else we know, we've filled the map with plausible details. Here at Tern, Amelia is again flesh and blood after two days at sea. It is February 12.

AMELIA AND HER MATE exchange brief greetings and a matter-of-fact farewell. Their chick, unveiled to sunshine, lifts its wobbly, hopeful head and opens its stubby bill to a narrow V. Amelia leans forward, centers her gullet on that V, and fills the chick with gooey food until satisfaction reigns and the world seems a secure and happy place. Meanwhile, Dad is off on his own overnight foraging foray. Amelia settles in to brood their fragile chick.

When Dad returns the next day, Amelia rises into the air again. She heads northwest as she did last time. But this time she tries a different area, one she's visited many times.

Amelia is now following the crest of the undersea range whose widely separated peaks break the sea surface to form several of this chain's islands. She overflies Rogatien Bank, whose unseen slopes rise from a depth of sixteen thousand feet to water as shallow as seventy feet. Here the tide flowing across the steep bottom contours creates swirling stretches of surface turbulence and a rough chop full of whitecaps. Amelia scans the glittering tide rips as she courses along with the greenish shallower water on her left and the deep blue sea on her right. She's looking for anything shoved up by the dark currents. There isn't much today. She finds one deceased lanternfish and sees a few small pumice stones in the drift lines. Pumice is volcanic rock that's often so full of air bubbles it floats. It may be ancient, but today it will be lunch, because flyingfish eggs are stuck to it. She lands, and swallows the eggs and their hard pumice pit. She picks and pokes at a jellyfish here and a few more fish eggs there, at intervals separated by miles, until she has a meager payload. After working her way northwest in a nearly straight line for six hours, she slows.

Amelia is still on the crest of this one long underwater ridge. Fifty miles west of here and unseen, one peak of this mountain creates surf as Gardner Pinnacles. Almost eighty miles to the southeast, we know another peak as French Frigate Shoals.

The lingering memory that equates north with food begins to motivate her. No taste on the breeze hints of more food here, or a new body of water in the near distance, or of any other change—except a change for the worse in the weather. The weather ahead looks bad. She has sailed into plenty of awful weather. But that was when there was food. Nothing here indicates more food. A line of approaching thick clouds and a sudden headwind help her decide. Having flown seventy-seven miles in a straight line to the northwest, Amelia turns abruptly around and zips directly home for Valentine's Day.

It's probably safe to infer that she hasn't been satisfied with the results of her foragings, because on her next launch, only a day after arriving, she goes in the opposite direction, to a place virtually no albatrosses ever go.

Few of the hundreds of thousands of albatrosses from these islands head south, ever. But on this trip, for some reason, Amelia does, flying directly southeast, just under three hundred miles. Ocean-temperature monitoring buoys placed by the U.S. government are telling satellites this story: Amelia has passed into more tropical waters, the temperature rising more than three degrees Celsius, to 24° C (75° Fahrenheit). Here, near dawn, the marbled aroma of colliding currents and the scent of schools of fishes reaches her.

Fishing boats in the tropics read water temperatures assiduously. They travel hundreds of miles while looking for those temperature changes that indicate a water border and the animals it implies. They are guided by satellite-imaged sea-surface-temperature maps faxed or downloaded on board, as well as by onboard temperature instruments. Albatrosses and fishing-boat captains read clues using different methods, but they speak the same language.

Amelia wanders twenty-five miles to the west. She wheels and backtracks: back toward the marbled scents for twenty miles in the searing tropical daylight. She sees fair numbers of flyingfish but catches nothing. If you want to catch flyingfish for a living you have to be either an expert plunge diver, like a Masked Booby, or a master aerialist, like a Red-footed Booby or frigatebird; and you have to hang around predatory fishes like tunas and marlins that will flush the flyingfish for you. That's not in an albatross's job description or list of qualifications; it's not the evolutionary ad they've answered. So they have to limit themselves to taking an occasional dead one. All those seabirds that attack live, agile prey in the daytime are downhill racers. Albatrosses are crosscountry skiers, built for economical travel. Everyone ends up back at the lodge; they just take different routes.

Amelia works back northwest for another sixty miles, until the sun is slanted. There, her track turns back abruptly, following a straight line southeast for forty miles. Likely she's found a fishing boat hunting Bigeye Tuna with a forty-mile longline, sending a thousand hooks into the depths. She is following. And a dangerous game begins: trying to snatch squid from the hooks before they sink, without being hooked and drowned.

She's less effective at grabbing the sinking bait in the dark, so she peels away from the boat. She continues working this area, finding a group of spawning flyingfish vulnerably oblivious in their passion near the surface of the night. For failing to pay attention to how dangerous the world can be, two fish forfeit their lives.

When she feels that chick tugging and her time running short, she puts the trade wind into her wings and sets sail for Tern Island, still over three hundred miles away. Her twenty-hour track home is astonishingly direct. She appears at her nest on February 17. Since leaving two days ago, she's flown a total of 917 miles.

AMELIA'S ARRIVAL and her feeding of the chick has prompted her mate to leave. Their chick is almost two weeks old. In average weather it no longer needs brooding. Barring extreme heat or prolonged chilling from soaking rains, it can now maintain its body temperature. It can also survive a little longer between feedings. Amelia has been losing weight since her chick hatched. So she plays the averages, gambling that the weather will be normal. On the very same day that she's arrived, Amelia's own hunger launches her on her next hunt. Her chick, for the first time, is home alone.

Flying south didn't pay very well, so this time Amelia strikes energetically northwestward, covering over a hundred miles the first night. She's traveling along the edge of that undersea mountain range where she foraged a few days ago.

In the earliest slanting light Amelia is 156 miles north of Tern, and a little west. Led by a medley of aromas, her track weaving and wavering, she works a farther fifty miles along the submerged slopes by midmorning. Filaments of the wide Pacific currents curling around the island chain have formed drift lines at the surface, and schools of anchovies are eating plankton concentrated in those boundary lines where currents collide with local water masses. A few Sooty Terns and boobies begin hunting in little flocks over sparse schools of hit-and-run Yellowfin Tuna, nabbing the anchovies they're chasing up. This place should produce.

Amelia dallies, first heading northwest, then northeast for a few miles, then swerving north. This isn't her best game, and she awkwardly trails the expert gymnasts, hoping to grab an anchovy or two already injured by a tuna's raking teeth and skittering in hopeless circles at the surface. But the pickings are slim, the profit margin thin. It's a pat economy of scales; the edge of endurance within the limits of survival.

Sudden squalls and unusually hard rain coming from the north churn the drift lines; anything that would be concentrated food gets scattered and dissipated. For an albatross, this is no place to make a living. Neither she nor the chick is benefiting.

Now Amelia abruptly changes course, heading northeast, flying 347 miles in just over twenty-four hours. Her track suggests that she may be torn by two conflicting drives: the urge to stay close and forage in tropical waters for just enough food for her chick, and the desire to go to more productive but much farther northern waters that would keep her away longer.

· · ·

MEANWHILE, BACK AT TERN ISLAND, trouble. Unusually hot weather has forced more albatrosses from their nests. Birds are sitting with mouths agape and feathers erect, trying to radiate heat. They're very uncomfortable. This is not the environment that albatrosses are geared to thrive in. Normally, all would stay and brood the chick until it reaches two or three weeks of age and is capable of withstanding sun and surviving the chilling of drenching rain. Some chicks are already that old. But the heat stress is prompting quite a few adults to leave chicks unattended at earlier ages than normal. Amelia's mate himself had felt relieved at leaving. Their chick, still young, suffers its first two days alone in a near stupor of blinding heat.

AFTER JUST TWO DAYS AWAY, Amelia's mate arrives at dawn. Then on February 19, as the morning swelter climbs to blistering, what occurs must seem like a divine miracle: rain.

Heads tilt skyward as hot adults and dehydrated chicks bite raindrops, letting trickling water please parched throats. Bright droplets roll easily from backs designed to fend off heavy seas. No longer feeling the stress of oppressive heat, Amelia's mate stays and broods their small chick, keeping it dry. Any unattended chicks are having their heavy down coats wetted with warm water. The rain plays a steady beat throughout the day.

Steady rain continues throughout the night. By morning, the bedraggled chicks are chilled. The rain falls throughout a second day.

Again, the rain beats through the night. By dawn, many chicks are moving slowly, their drenched down splattered and matted with fine sand. Most chicks whose parents have left are now shivering, suffering hypothermia.

The overcast had been complete, but now the world further dims. Extreme heat is being followed by extreme rain. The weather seems haywire.

The new, denser clouds are the wings of a water-breathing dragon. That dragon starts spewing a driving cloudburst. And now the sky seems to begin falling from its own weight. As the wind-slanted rain drives harder and harder down, the sea is building higher and higher up.

The ocean swell has breached the reef, and the normally placid lagoon has itself become a battering ram of wind-driven waves and drifting foam. Those waves begin pounding on the seawall like they're knocking at death's door.

Death opens to let the sea in. Salt water slamming over the seawall begins joining ranks with the already wide rainwater puddles, until much of Tern Island is awash. Branches, leaves, and other debris are pushed into windrows, scouring nests, as waves sweep dislodged chunks of coral well up onto the island. Colorful reef fishes, forced ashore, swim in calf-deep murky puddles on the runway. And suddenly the lagoon lobs a waist-high, fifty-foot-long drift log over the seawall. The log begins a slow, grim, wave-driven, rolling death march through part of the nesting area, taking out bushes and killing two young Red-footed Boobies res-olutely clinging to their nests.

Anything feathered that can fly is flying, flying in the water-whitened wind. On the ground—disaster. Chicks are being floated irretrievably far from nests, in water too cold for survival. Youngsters drifted and stranded far from where their food-lugging parents will expect to find them will die there. Drenched baby birds will continue shivering miser-ably until their movements slow to a stop. So many eggs of various kinds are floating in enormous brown puddles, they look like marshmallows in lakes of hot chocolate.

Chaos rains. In this often sun-seared place where a little rain and a sea breeze bestow blessed relief, the birds have drawn too much of a good thing. Two days ago they were dying from the desiccating heat; now they're soaking to a chilling death. Under the gale's blustery gusts, rain plays drumrolls with its fists throughout the day.

Throughout the night, the continuing storm keeps me semicon-scious. I dream the power of thunder energizing birds and driving them in rain over black seas enraged by wind.

THE FITS AND FURIES finish at first light. A third of the albatross chicks are dead. Their sodden carcasses lie scattered, or float drifted into lines along the shores of muddy puddles. They lie amid bits of wood and the innumerable foam drift-net fishing floats that the Pacific seems to be attempting to return to humanity. And while the albatrosses got pummeled, the Masked Boobies got it even worse.

Amelia's nest, just a few feet from the barracks porch, is just a few inches higher than much of the island. Amelia's chick, just a few days younger than most, was small and helpless enough to motivate its pro-tective father to linger longer. A little more resolute than many, Amelia's mate just stuck it out. Amelia's baby, just lucky, is alive when the last rain-drop falls.

Albatrosses that have been working hard to bring back food will come trickling home over the next week expecting to find their chick alive. But many will find instead that for them, this breeding season is history. Most of them will leave and not return here again this year.

The Black-footeds' timing gave them a critical advantage. Being a week or two older, far more Black-foot chicks were able to survive the deluge, and many bedraggled youngsters made it. But the Laysans were precisely timed for disaster when the rains reigned.

Yet all the transmittered birds will find their chicks alive regardless; Laura and Frans rounded up their wetted nestlings antediluvianly, and revived them high and dry inside the barracks. The capricious compassion of science allowed these chicks to pull a lucky number, while at other nests, nature overran its course.

AMELIA, NATURALLY, knows nothing of this. She's been hundreds of miles away while the rains pounded Tern Island. Still at sea, all she knows is that she ran into some bad weather—nothing too unusual.

During her 350-mile trek to the northeast she found too little food to make up for the energy she was spending. That's what she expected. She was not wandering aimlessly; she was investing. Her trek took her across a wide area of very deep water, averaging eighteen thousand feet—some of the deepest ocean wilderness in the world.

With this crossing Amelia has accomplished two things: She's crossed into the subtropical frontal zone, where tropical seas mix with slightly cooler waters of the North Pacific Current flowing from Asia to North America. And she has come now to a vast region where the seafloor lies rumpled and massively corrugated with several dozen deep volcanic seamounts believed to have formed during the Cretaceous period a hundred million years ago from a hot spot beneath the then-young and northward-moving Pacific Plate. They lie north of the main Hawaiian Islands, running northwestward for about eight hundred miles.

The surrounding sea looks simply the same as ever. The mountains below come nowhere near to forming islands. Most lie more than a mile beneath the waves, their peaks too deep even to pierce the darkness that entombs the surrounding seafloor, nearly three and a half miles from the surface. If you were rocking on a ship's deck you'd have no clue about the seamounts far below.

But Amelia does. She smells that earthy smell, but the scent is very faint. She sees that the blue water carries here a trace of green, but only slightly. This area holds more life than she has found in five days, but not by much.

Yet here plays the music of the spheres *almost* literally, because these classic seamounts bear the names of composers: by prerogative of the oceanographers who mapped them in the 1970s, there's the Mozart Seamount, the Tchaikovsky Seamount, the Mahler Seamount, the Verdi, Schubert, the Stravinsky—the Liszt goes on. Like the great composers themselves, the ancient volcanoes now lie silenced, slowly decomposing.

Amelia has just sailed over the Rachmaninoff Seamount to the Debussy Seamount. Debussy's *La Mer* is one of the most wonderfully ocean-inspired works of music ever composed, so it is fitting that Amelia is now in a sense Debussy's guest. He's a good host, and for a while he serves enough hors d'oeuvres to make it worth Amelia's trek. The currents striking the seamounts stream water toward the surface, enriching the region's productivity and serving a nice dead squid every few hours. A connoisseur of calamari, Amelia likes hers chilled, and she isn't disappointed.

At sundown she is coursing the Brahms Seamount. She is not alone, and not everyone is here for the lullaby. Several swordfishing boats, nearly eight hundred miles from their Honolulu homes, are spinning their forty-mile longlines into this weak front of cooler water running over the seamounts. During the night Amelia sees the lights of two of them, many miles apart, but it's already after dark and she does not follow.

In the first sharp-angled sunlight of morning a single, rather hefty Flying Squid spurts from the water in a high-sailing leap, lofted oddly on its improbable fins. (Only a year old, the twenty-pound squid will soon die of old age.) When packs of Albacore Tuna surface briefly, Amelia wheels and follows the streaking blue-gray forms, trying to maneuver in among their white bursts. But they aren't staying up long enough. The young mackerel they're after are too small and evasive for her, and she is wasting energy chasing between schools that seem always to vanish the moment she arrives. Only once, briefly, does a nearby mackerel school, distracted by their fear of the tuna below, press so near the surface that Amelia maneuvers herself perfectly for a slow glide over them. Without landing she plucks a fish before alarming the rest. It's an unusually elegant maneuver for an albatross, and she doesn't get a second opportunity.

She keeps moving, moving, drifting 420 miles east, using a favorable wind to push her along the streaming frontal zone, searching for sharper definition to the front but finding only a broad, faint gradient where the life is less concentrated.

So she turns south, moving two hundred miles the next day and nearly 250 more the following. Now she's heading southwest, shortening the distance between herself and Tern Island for the first time since she left. By the time her big, clockwise trek brings her over the Prokofiev Seamount, she's been at sea a week and she hardly slows at all.

In the last few days, she's been as much as nine hundred miles from her chick. She earns an A for effort, but in terms of food her trip has been only marginally successful. Once more she feels that chick pulling. The urge to get back overwhelms her hunger, but her hunger remains. This trip has not succeeded in putting any weight onto Amelia's ribs. Convinced—but not satisfied—that the time has come, she sprints southwest for a steady thirty-one hours, covering over 460 miles. The smells of land and of the densely nesting seabirds help her to home in off a visually bleak sea long before she can see the islands.

By the time she looms into range, Tern Island has darkened. But there's moon enough to gleam the reef's breakers. She lands amid the usual all-night din and bustle of birds. It's February 25. Eight days ago, when she last fed her chick, it looked distinctly smaller. But its voice removes any doubt of identity, and Amelia delivers her high-calorie liquid diet.

➤ ➤ ➤

*I*MMENSE ISOLATION is typical of the great communities of seabirds breeding in dense concentrations on islands widely scattered throughout the oceans. Breeding remotely as they do, sheer inaccessibility had long been the best defense of such defenseless birds. At virtually every place they bred and in every corner of the world's seas they roamed, for millennia albatrosses enjoyed the comparative calm conveyed by great distance from humanity. The world began closing in on them when coastal peoples started launching primitive but effective crafts against the sea. Beginning then, even their remoteness was insufficient to ensure an insulating peace.

The Maoris arrived in New Zealand several hundred years before the Europeans. Their primitive hunting technology was sufficient to exterminate a group of endemic bird species known as moas, and they quickly noticed the albatrosses. The Maoris decorated their canoes with white albatross feathers, symbolic of rapid skimming over the ocean, and they used such feathers in their burial rites. They also used the albatrosses' long hollow bones for awls, needles, toggles, necklaces, and flutes. With tufts of albatross down they decorated their hair and pierced ears. With hook-and-line they caught foraging albatrosses for food.

When the Moriori people reached the Chatham Islands off New Zealand, about five hundred years ago, they began eating the nesting seabirds. They got a taste of their own medicine when the Maoris from the main New Zealand islands arrived and brought with them their appetites—for human flesh. Modern Maoris on some islands continue to claim a right to take nesting albatrosses.

The first people to reach the Hawaiian Islands were Polynesians who made landfall perhaps as early as 200 A.D. Pacific legends tell of travels undertaken simply to discover the charms of another island's maidens, but getting to Hawaii was no lighthearted outing. We will never know what drove the first human comers to Hawaii. Curiosity? Famine? Adventure? Defeat? And one can scarcely imagine the emotions of people who, after many days at sea in fragile craft, traveling beyond all limits of anyone's known world, sighted the massive jungled coastlines of silent islands that had never before reflected light into a human eye.

Despite their limited technology, the Polynesians developed more raw seafaring ability than any people that have ever lived. More than three thousand years ago, rudimentary craft and advanced skills had gotten people as far into the Pacific as Tonga and Samoa—roughly 2,500 island-hopping miles from the large land masses of New Guinea and Australia.

But the Polynesian expansion was the most dramatic burst of over-water exploration in human history. At about the time William the Conqueror made a big splash in Europe merely by crossing the English Channel, a Tahitian high priest named Pa'ao had already logged three several-thousand-mile voyages to Hawaii and founded the conquering dynasty from which King Kamehameha descended nearly thirty generations later. A thousand years before Columbus screwed together enough logic and courage to sail away from land by surmising that he would not—as everyone in Europe believed—fall off the edge of the world, Polynesians had settled the most remote islands on Earth.

Their spaceship was the voyaging canoe. As traditional navigator Herb Kawainui Kane has written, "Built with tools of stone, bone, and shell, assembled with lashings of braided fiber, and powered by sails of plaited matting, it was the finest product of any culture that knew no metals."

Even James Cook, widely regarded as the most accomplished mariner the world will ever know, was astounded by the Polynesians'

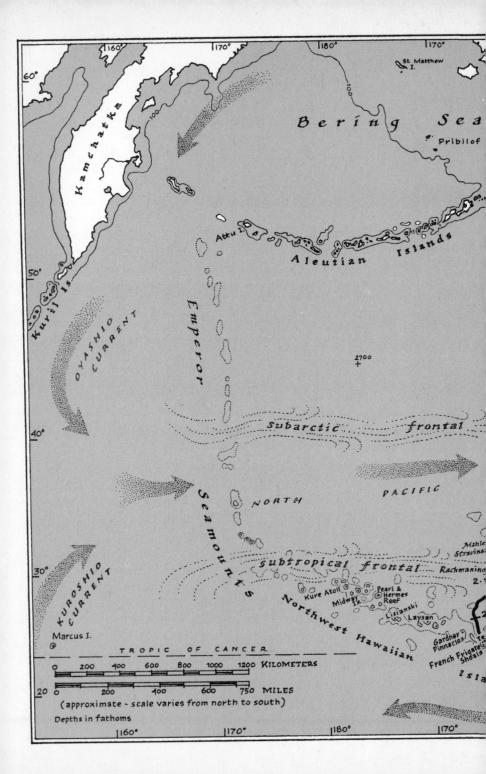

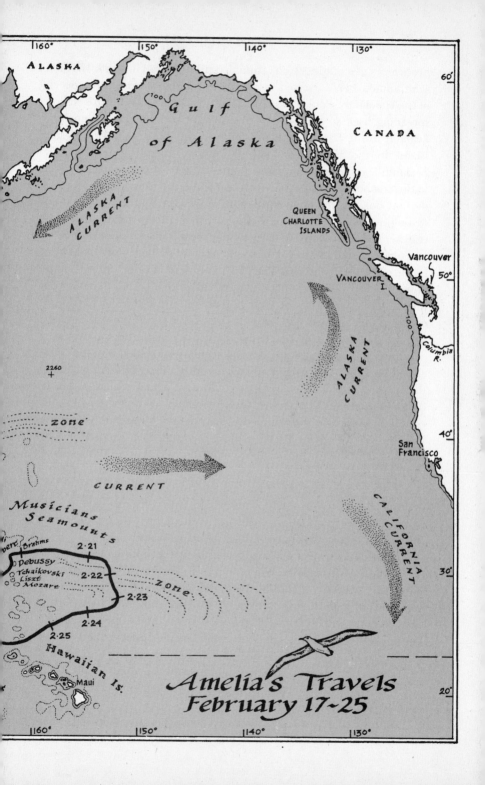

proficiency at seafaring. Cook stumbled upon Hawaii in 1778. His men were immediately surprised to recognize Tahitian words in the speech of the Hawaiians. Cook was awed. "How shall we account for this Nation spreading itself so far over this Vast ocean? We find them from New Zealand to the South, to these islands to the North and from Easter Island to the Hebrides." (The Polynesian triangle spanning New Zealand, Hawaii, and Easter Island encompasses an area roughly equal to the combined surfaces of North and South America.) Most astonishing to Cook was the ability of people with Stone Age technology—no writing, no wheels, not even the pottery that usually defines neolithic culture; *and no compass*—to navigate the ocean's most distant reaches.

Polynesian culture had flourished unknown to the continental world for nearly fifteen centuries. The Hawaiians were in Cook's time so populous that six of the eight main islands had more residents than they do now. (Median estimates of their population at the time of European contact range around 500,000; in a few decades, introduced diseases destroyed more than 90 percent of the people, shattering the dynasty.)

European scholars for the next two centuries wrestled with the "puzzle" of the Hawaiians' origins and routes. Most simply refused to believe that people with their technology could have actually sailed so far. It didn't fit their idea of primitive. One hypothesis was that a great Pacific continent must have suddenly sunk, leaving the Polynesians, who must have *walked* all over the Pacific, suddenly stranded on exposed mountaintops. The dullest Eurocentric conjecture was that the Polynesians were the Lost Tribes of Israel!

We know now that the Hawaiians almost certainly came from the Marquesas and Tahiti—2,300 and 2,600 miles distant—and it *still* strains Western imagination to think of preneolithic sailing canoes venturing over thousands of ocean miles *toward no known lands*.

Polynesian mariners developed skills unmatched in the world, abilities bordering on instinct. When far at sea, Polynesian navigators surmised the existence of land by the flight patterns and directionality of seabirds and migrating shorebirds, or by discerning subtle waves running across the main sea swell, reflected from distant, unseen islands. Large clouds appearing stationary while smaller ones drifted in the wind often betrayed the presence of land well beyond the horizon; the land's effect on the atmosphere generated the standing clouds. Over atolls, clouds tinted green with the lagoon's reflection became visible long before the low-lying sand islands did.

Cook and other explorers remained amazed by the ability of certain

Polynesians traveling aboard their vessels to stay oriented at sea, able to point toward home islands many hundreds of miles away. In 1769, in Tahiti, Cook took aboard the navigator Tupaia, who guided Cook three hundred miles south to the island of Rurutu. Cook then commanded the *Endeavour* westward on various courses to New Zealand, then Australia, then north through the Great Barrier Reef to New Guinea. Throughout the convolutions of these travels, Cook was continually dumbfounded to discover that whenever he asked Tupaia to point toward Tahiti, he could, without access to the ship's charts or compass.

Acute powers of observation and memory were the Polynesian navigator's tools of the trade. Unlike Western systems of fixing position without reference to home port, Polynesians were home-oriented. The navigator mentally logged and integrated all courses steered and all weather and sea phenomena affecting movement of the canoe (requiring him to forgo sleep for long periods). He could trace these backward in his mind, so that at any time he could point in the approximate direction of home and estimate the sailing time required. Departing canoes used a succession of rising and setting positions of familiar stars for steering. During cloudy, dark, starless nights, dominant ocean swells indicated directionality. Upon discovery of a new island, the navigator carefully memorized its location with reference to stars rising, setting, and traveling directly overhead. Thus Polynesians sailed the known universe, and beyond.

If Polynesians differed from Europeans while at sea, on land they were all too similar. Reaching island after island, Polynesians—and the pigs and rats that came with them—eradicated many seabirds by eating adults, eggs, and young. Hawaiians so savored Dark-rumped Petrel chicks that they reserved these only for the nobility. Though the Dark-rumped was the most abundant petrel on Oahu, oncoming appetites consumed the last one there. The Polynesians' pigs rooted out entire colonies of burrow-nesting seabirds. It must have been a time of great horror for birds trapped in their dark burrows, snarfed to oblivion by snuffling snouts from another world. The Polynesians were such a catastrophe for wildlife that at least half of Hawaii's endemic birds were already extinct before Captain Cook's arrival pressed the first European bootprint into Hawaiian sand. (*All* Pacific islands surveyed by archaeologists suffered dramatic declines of land- and seabirds following the arrival of humans and their hitchhiking animals; Easter Island retains only *one* of the twenty-two seabird species that bred there.) Europeans would bring much more trouble.

. . .

MUCH LATER THAN the Pacific peoples, Europeans developed ships capable of traveling into the albatrosses' world. At the end of the 1700s, commercial ships from Europe and America began appearing in the Southern Hemisphere.

From early on, albatrosses saved the lives of many Western mariners—albeit involuntarily. In 1881 a sailor who fell overboard from the ship *Gladstone* grabbed the first albatross that approached him and used it as a living life-buoy to stay afloat until the ship stopped, lowered a lifeboat, and rescued him. Castaways shipwrecked where few vessels ventured survived largely on albatrosses, sometimes for years. One gang of sealers was marooned on Solander Islands, south of New Zealand, from 1808 to 1813. Four men put ashore against their will on the Snares Islands in 1810 (48° S, 166° E) did not see another ship for seven years. Albatrosses helped feed them. When the sealer *Princess of Wales* wrecked on Île de la Possession in 1821, stranding its men for a year, Wandering Albatrosses kept them alive: "Their eggs are very large . . . about a pint. . . . The young . . . excellent for the table, and provided us with a very good dish for a long period, as they did not fly off until December." In 1842 the whaler *Parker* struck Kure Atoll's reef, and in the seven months until rescue, surviving men killed seven thousand seabirds and sixty Monk Seals. In what was surely the first conservation edict in the Northwestern Hawaiian Islands, the captain of the *Saginaw,* which in 1870 also went aground on Kure, limited his crew to twenty birds per day.

In 1875 a woman named Florence Wordsworth was bound from London to New Zealand aboard the *Strathmore* when it wrecked on the Isles of the Apostles in the southern Indian Ocean's Crozet group, drowning nearly half the passengers. She wrote, "I was stunned with cold, and almost fainting . . . till Charlie came with the reeking-hot skins of two albatrosses." During seven months on the island, until they were rescued by an American whaler, they ate birds. After killing an albatross, one of the men wrote, "As is often the case before dying, it vomited up the contents of its bag, and amongst the mess was an eel quite perfect, having the appearance of being cooked. I took it and ate it, and it tasted quite like stewed eel."

In 1916, after drifting sea ice clenched and later crushed his ship *Endurance,* Ernest Shackleton and five companions made landfall at South Georgia Island after a desperate eight-hundred-mile, gale-plagued lifeboat trek to summon rescuers for their marooned crew. "There we found the nests of albatrosses. . . . The nestlings were fat and lusty, and we had no hesitation about deciding that they were destined to die at an early age . . . what a stew it was. . . . The young albatrosses weighed about fourteen pounds each fresh killed. . . . The flesh was white and succulent, and the bones, not fully formed, almost melted in our mouths."

You didn't have to be shipwrecked to develop a taste for the great seabirds. On Captain James Cook's second circumnavigation, in 1772, naturalist George Forster noted both their beauty and their utility: "They skim always on the surface of the sea. . . . When skinned, they afford a good palatable food." George's father, Reinhold, added, "We found them to be extremely curious . . . but they paid with their lives for this curiosity." Cook himself wrote, "Shot some albatrosses and other Birds on which we feasted . . . and found them exceeding good." Another of Cook's naturalists, Joseph Banks, commented that the men "eat heartily of them tho there was fresh pork upon the table."

Explorers and sailors and, later, passengers on commercial ships learned early to catch albatrosses for their own craftwork, food, or amusement. Sealers and whalers made pipe stems of the long, hollow wing bones, tobacco pouches of the big webbed feet, and warm slippers from the downy skins. The egg occasionally found in females at sea was sometimes reserved for ships' captains.

Herman Melville, in *Moby-Dick*, had this impression:

I remember the first albatross I ever saw. It was during a prolonged gale, in waters hard upon the Antarctic seas. From my forenoon watch below, I ascended to the overclouded deck; and there, dashed upon the main hatches, I saw a regal, feathery thing of unspotted whiteness. . . . At intervals, it arched forth its vast archangel wings, as if to embrace some holy ark. Wondrous flutterings and throbbings shook it. . . . It uttered cries, as some king's ghost in supernatural distress. Through its inexpressible, strange eyes, methought I peeped to secrets which took hold of God. . . . I bowed myself; the white thing was so white, its wings so wide, and in those for ever exiled waters, I had lost the miserable warping memories of traditions and of towns. Long I gazed at that prodigy of plumage. . . . How had the mystic thing been caught? Whisper it not, and I will tell; with a treacherous hook and line.

The capture method was hardly secret. In 1594, Sir Richard Hawkins, approaching the Falkland Islands in the *Dainty*, wrote: "I caused a hooke and lyne to be brought to me. . . . One of the fowles being hungry presently seized upon it, and the hooke in his upper beake. . . . By the same manner of fishing, we caught so many of them, as refreshed and recreated all my people for the day."

Such seabird "fishing" became frequent practice throughout the Southern Hemisphere. On passenger vessels, it caught the attention of the leisured class. One enthusiast of fishing for albatrosses from the deck of a ship in the 1860s considered the Wandering Albatross "the crowning triumph of the avian angler." Yet another, singing the praises of "sporting after these noble birds," described his excitement of catching seven Wanderers in one day.

On deck, the birds were often tormented and bullied. One G. Bennett wrote that after being brought on deck, the massive bird "remains the patient, stupid-looking subject of a hundred passing remarks: the ladies give their due share of praise to its large bright eyes, fine sleek and clean plumage; the expansion of wings is duly measured . . . the bird, during the time remaining, sitting . . . very sulky . . . until a few

A morning's catch aboard the *Sobraon* on a voyage to Australia from England, 1890–91. F. D. Green (*courtesy Mitchell Library, Sydney, Australia*)

practical jokes keep its bright eyes on the alert against all personal attacks. After having been admired and pitied . . . by the fair sex . . . it is consigned either . . . to be stuffed; or sometimes regains its liberty."

A slightly kinder pastime involved catching albatrosses, marking them with things like colored ribbons, and releasing them to see how long they would follow the ship. Most followed for only an hour or so, but in 1856 one Wanderer trailed for six days—and a Sooty Albatross followed a ship for 4,645 kilometers (2,880 miles).

Better guns and newer notions of "sport" were advances for the worse, as hook-and-lining fell into obsolescence and shooting albatrosses became popular on passenger ships. Passenger traffic soon grew so heavy that killing at sea for the amusement of ships' passengers significantly affected the numbers of Wandering Albatrosses. In the century between 1780 and 1880, about 1.3 million free immigrants sailed from Europe to Australia. In the year 1875 alone, ninety-three ships took thirty thousand immigrants to New Zealand. By the mid-1800s, a vessel from New York or Boston was arriving in San Francisco every eleven days or so, having traveled by way of the albatross-rich waters around Cape Horn. One nineteenth-century enthusiast noted that an albatross "sails in the most marvellous manner, keeping beautifully even pace with the vessel . . . and it is a curious fact that no amount of noise or close whirr of bullets appears to have the slightest effect on an albatross." (Until it got hit, of course.)

Some onlookers were offended by such shooting. Among them was the Reverend William Scoresby, who during a sea passage in 1859 wrote that the rear deck of the *Royal Charter* "was yesterday occupied with 'sportsmen' . . . firing at the unconscious elegant birds gracefully hovering about . . . I fancy 50 to 100 shots were fired, happily with rare instances of their taking effect; but in one case I saw, on being induced to look astern . . . a poor stricken bird struggling on the surface of the water apparently mortally wounded. This useless infliction of injury and suffering . . . where there was no chance of obtaining them . . . for any use, was to my feelings, and, I believe the feelings of many others, particularly painful." Someone who was not averse to capturing albatrosses with hook and line (because the birds could be used) might be put off by the waste involved in shooting them from the deck of a moving vessel. Another such person wrote, "Often, with broken wings, they are left to linger on the wide expanse of waters . . . until death puts a period to their miseries. It is revolting to the feelings to see these beautiful and perfectly innocent birds destroyed, solely to gratify the inclination to destroy."

One passenger traveling from England to New Zealand in 1841 wrote, "We had an interesting discussion at lunch, whether it was justifiable to shoot those birds merely for wantonness and amusement, when it is impossible to reach them after they are dead. I had only Mr. Otterson and Mr. Barnicoat on my side of the question. . . . It was agreed by the sportsmen that they were justified to continue the sport if only for practice." Killing from ships faded as vessels became too big and fast for hauling in big birds on lines, and safety regulations put an end to passengers discharging firearms. By 1860, the same G. Bennett who had written so sarcastically about the pitying tendencies of the fairer sex felt compelled to admit, "It has been remarked by many voyagers that the large Wandering Albatros [sic] has been during the last few years more rarely seen."

WHEN EUROPEANS WENT ASHORE distant islands, it was usually with the specific purpose of killing the animals. It might be overstatement to say that the highs seas and low islands were soon overrun with people intent on killing albatrosses. But to the birds it might have seemed that way, as people at sea and ashore began taking many thousands of albatrosses and their nestlings for feathers, meat, and oil.

In 1798, Matthew Flinders was aboard the *Norfolk*, exploring the Tasmanian environs. On December 9, the day the crew brought the first boatload of seals off one island, he wrote, "there are vast numbers of albatrosses on the isle to which their name is given, which were tending young . . . and being unacquainted with the power or disposition of man, did not fear him: we taught them their first lesson of experience."

The sealers first exterminated Albatross Island's fur seals, then the "disposition of man" turned its full and terrible attention to the albatrosses for their feathers. They killed 99 percent of the birds (the birds' long periods at sea must have saved the last survivors). Thousands of carcasses rotted, and the birds in their numbers have never recovered.

The misplaced trust shown by the naive albatrosses—the absence of the capacity for fear, really—earned them derisive nicknames from sailors who saw their lack of fright as stupidity. They called the Southern Hemisphere species "mollymawks," probably from the Dutch *mal* (foolish) and *mok* (gull). In the North Pacific they called them "gooney birds"; in Japan, "fool birds." The implication, of course, was that any animal that did not expect the worst from humans was a fool.

Falkland Islands sealers delivered albatross eggs by the thousands to the Stanley markets. On the Tristan da Cunha group in the South

Atlantic, throughout the twentieth century settlers annually took several thousand albatross eggs and chicks for the pot. (As late as 1980 the locals killed penguins for lobster bait.) The birds were finally protected in 1986. By then, the Gough Wandering Albatross had been eliminated from the main island. Two hundred miles southeast, on Gough Island itself, sealers virtually exterminated the fur seals during the 1800s, then boiled penguins for their oil. Likewise, on Australia's Macquarie Island (54° S, 158° E), for three decades hundreds of thousands of nesting penguins were herded up ramps and tumbled into boiling vats for their oil. When you land there nowadays, the ugly giant pots, abandoned in 1919, still stand, rusting. Surrounding the cauldrons live dense crowds of Royal and King Penguins—the survivors' descendants. Their gentle curiosity toward human visitors to this remote shore is so touching that the inhumanity of what was done to them is difficult to fathom.

In the North Pacific, albatrosses have endured several catastrophic periods. Feather hunters killed millions of nesting birds during the late 1800s and early 1900s, eliminating colonies altogether from several islands. That brought the Short-tailed Albatross to extinction's doorstep. After this stopped, North Pacific populations struggled slowly upward. Then for three decades preceding, during, and after World War II, U.S. military operations brought persecution at Midway, the world's largest albatross colony, killing tens of thousands of albatrosses, causing them to decline again there. North Pacific populations generally expanded from the mid-1960s through the 1980s, until the rampant drift-netting in the 1980s and into the 1990s killed roughly a quarter million albatrosses. Now, in the North Pacific and around the world, the miles-long longlines lacing the seas with millions of baited hooks are the main threat.

Even today a few fishermen in some places kill albatrosses as "pests" or for bait, or use their feathers for fishing lures. Australian fishermen were as recently as the 1990s still shooting about six hundred Wandering Albatrosses annually. And the birds also get shot off South Africa, South America, and elsewhere. Uruguayan longline fishers still sometimes decide to float a short line with a baited hook on each end, amusing themselves by the sight of two suddenly doomed birds struggling against each other. Birds unlucky enough to be brought aboard alive on the longline are sometimes killed brutally; the fishers twist their wings and throw them into the water. Those boats catch Swordfish and tuna, destined for a restaurant near you.

> > >

ANTHONY SAYS HE NEEDS to check some of his birds, so I volunteer to assist him. Anthony has worked here for several years, including a stint as manager of the place. He's now thirty, and a graduate student at the University of Washington.

Anthony's research is an attempt to understand the Black-footed Albatrosses' threshold for taking a year off from breeding in order to grow new feathers, and how the members of the pair stay synchronized over skipped years. He's trying to predict who'll return next year by examining how worn out their feathers are.

The large flight feathers of albatross wings bear more microscopic frills on their interlocking barbules than any other known feathers. That toughens them, but they still take an extraordinary beating from punishing winds, sun, and salt water. Anthony explains, "Feathers are either new and shiny chocolate brown; or what I call 'class two,' which are duller brown and slightly worn; or 'class 3,' which are bleached lighter brown and brittle, with edges very frayed. The sixth and seventh primary flight feathers seem to take a beating. They're a strong indicator of where the bird is in its molt process." Anthony can look at a bird's wing and say things like, "Looks like it replaced these four feathers last year and did a full molt the year before that." Ultimately, as he explains, understanding how many years albatrosses actually breed is the only way to understand their lifetime reproductive potential.

Anthony has short black hair, clean-cut features, an earring in each ear. Today, wearing a necklace of small shells, he tells me he grew up in Levittown, Long Island. Levittown was the world's first suburban tract-housing development. It's ironic that such an innovative concept would usher in such a peculiarly homogenized and sterile version of the American Dream. It helped form the modern concept of American suburban life—the manicured lawn, the attached garage, the chain-link fence, the station wagon, isolated "bedroom communities," cultural alienation, the end of Main Street, the death of the Hometown, the decline of family-owned businesses, and the rise of the shopping maul. I grew up a few miles from there. I say, "I know it all too well."

"Exactly," affirms Anthony. The knowing look we exchange bonds us.

Trying to minimize disturbance, we come and go from each nest as quickly as possible. Anthony, checking one band, says, "Oops; got that one already. We didn't need to disturb that bird again." His discomfort with causing disturbance to the birds is further evidence of a new generation of kinder, gentler biologists.

Kinder, gentler—and more physically fit. No beer bellies here. Even after hours of working outdoors, these people run laps, ride a bike, play basketball. One person jumps rope daily for half an hour. Assistant manager Mark even does some gymnastics. After the evening run, they pop in a workout video and the floor gets crowded with young interns following the exercises while the chef du jour prepares dinner for the entire crew.

TONIGHT IS MARK'S TURN to cook. But before dinner he is taking a break, up on the roof, watching the world's slow spin, scanning the ocean, looking for whales through a telescope. I climb the ladder to join him. Mark, thirty-three, has been a national park ranger in the Everglades and in Hawaii. Mark's mother is a social worker, his father a country lawyer. "So I guess I was never destined for business. Who I am all stems from growing up in a tiny town on Mississippi Delta marshes. I love being part of nature; knowing the atoms in my bones are from fish I caught growing up in the Delta. At eleven I had my own boat, and I was free in that Delta wilderness—that joy. We're losing that area now. I wonder what happens to kids living their childhoods there today.

"But *this*," Mark says, opening his arms to include all of French Frigate Shoals, "is fun." He turns to me. "More and more, I realize I want what I had growing up—to be surrounded by wilderness, working outside, my body feeling the pulse of nature. When I worked in the Everglades, if the water dropped a quarter inch, you'd notice the birds' and alligators' behavior changes. I like living where your body and mind are tuned to what's happening. I love cities and fancy restaurants, too, but it's a blast to be in a place like this."

Mark resumes scanning the sea through the telescope, talking as he's searching. "Hey! Breaching whale!" Mark calls down from the roof to some of the others. "I've got the spotting scope on it," he yells as people are coming up the ladder. I swing my binoculars up.

The Humpback's spouts look like a white flag waving truce in the sunset. Soon six people are up on the roof, taking turns at the telescope. The whale lurches out in a half-twisting jump, big explosions erupting as he crashes back into the sea. You don't need a telescope to see *that*. The whale comes for three big breaches. Four. We're all cheering. The whale rolls and slaps the water with its long pectoral fin. Through my binoculars I watch his gigantic head and half his massive body launch in slow motion, turn sideways, and make a big belly flop, detonating tremendous ocean commotion.

From the high tide of the heart, the mouth speaks: Mark shouts to the whole blue universe, "You *are beautiful!*"

Truly this is a gracious place, rife with persistent life, noisy, smelly, all full of the stinking, fluttering, bustling hustle of muscle, corpuscle, and tendon. Let us shout with the pleasure and intensity of it. Behold, the *real* "real world." Four billion years in the making, still trying its best to get it right, brimming with vivid power.

"Not a bad *pau hana,*" Mark adds.

I look at him questioningly.

He explains, "*Pau* means done; *hana* means workday. *Pau hana:* happy hour."

IN LATE AFTERNOON, the Sooty Terns that have for hours been twisting overhead in swelling flocks begin touching down like a broad tornado funnel cloud; a storm of wings, a conflagration of voices building to a screaming white-noise cyclone of sound. By sunset the Sooty Terns' collective voices begin to roar like fierce wind, like some physical force.

The birds begin landing, but time and again, a sudden intensification of their calls accompanies a mass liftoff, as though the birds all decide "Let's not land after all." Perhaps the idea of committing themselves to firm ground after months or years at sea seems so unfamiliar and terrifying a prospect that almost anything can prompt a general alarm. Perhaps there is simply some other sense of liberty or fear in their minds that rejects forsaking the free sea for the arduous ardor of breeding that will leash their lives to land. But land they do. Just after dark, part of the runway is absolutely crammed with Sooties. We're enveloped amid birds and their wall of sound. The sheer volume of their yakkering is absolutely deafening. Painful. You can't take this much noise for long. It's hard to imagine how the birds themselves can stand it.

AS MARK PREPARES to cook dinner, Anthony and Karen volunteer to make an appetizer for everyone. Frans has bread in the oven. The military-sized kitchen is dominated by hanging pots and pans, as well as a big, festively painted ocean mural featuring frolicking stingrays, colorful reef fishes, sea turtles, a Monk Seal, albatrosses, a large Tiger Shark, frigatebirds, and flying fish. Thousands of years ago, cave-dwelling peoples painted images of surrounding wildlife on their walls, and in

A white-noise cyclone of sound—Sooty Terns, with nesting albatrosses

this cavernous kitchen it's clear human nature hasn't changed. We still decorate with reference and reverence to nature; painters, potters, sculptors, and fabric designers do not create decorative images of cell phones and computers. No one paints murals of executives in board meetings discussing votes on mergers. Art tends to reflect what we really care about, our true delights and frights. Art has a fairly good sense of human nature; it's a pretty honest broker of subjective human truths. When new parents anticipate the arrival of a child, they decorate the baby's room with elephants and striped tigers and rainbowed parrots and festive fishes and other animals. This speaks volumes of our wish to welcome our cherished children into a world rich in the company of other beings, of the true, deep importance of animals in our psyche. Of all the many good reasons to defend animals' existence, this alone seems reason enough. If we let the world finally lose its wild elephants and tigers and parrots—as we are doing—wouldn't it be unbearably sad to ever again paint them on the nursery walls?

MARK COOKS a delicious vegetarian meal. Responding to compliments, he reveals his secret: "This recipe was: look only at the date and cook what's oldest."

The salt and pepper shakers on the long dining table are incongruous porcelain snowmen. The oil lamps bring dinner conversation to low and intimate tones. We talk about the day's work and the changes in the animals. With the different stages of reproduction, there's plenty to talk about. Fairy Terns and Red-tailed Tropicbirds hatching; albatrosses with growing chicks; Red-footed and Masked Boobies both hatching and on eggs; Brown and Black Noddies, some with chicks, some still incubating; Great Frigatebirds courting; Sooty Terns now nesting. Turtles on the beach. Someone's seen a large shark near shore.

Missing from mealtime are the Monk Seal researchers. They tend to begin early, work late, and eat together even later.

But we don't lack for extra company. During dinner a Black Noddy flies through one door, across the big room, and out another open door. A little later, as we're cleaning up, a Fairy Tern comes in like the Holy Ghost, fluttering and hovering. Interestingly, its flight is not the mad dash of a bird feeling trapped. Anthony escorts it outside, into the night.

I walk out with him, then linger when he goes inside. The darkness seems to be intensifying the birds' racket into a great, roaring bonfire of voices. The night air carries the guttural grunts and honks of boobies, the brays and bill claps of the albatrosses, the murmurs of the noddies, and the Sooty Terns' squeaky *I'm wide awake, wide awake.* The air also carries the unabated scent of nesting seabirds. A bird colony gives off a certain pungent, powdery sort of smell. It's pleasant to me because it evokes the nostalgia of days working on splendid island beaches with cherished friends and colleagues.

Jason and Mary, two of the seal researchers, appear and join me. While I'm getting sentimental over the eau de guano, Jason confides that he doesn't like the birdy stench. Instead, he loves the stink of seals, because he's studied them for years and has developed a fondness for everything about them. Beauty is in the nostril of the beholder.

We turn our biased noses toward the heavens. The night unlocks, the sky unfolds like a jewelry box. From the diamond expanse of space I pick out Orion, my favorite constellation. A point of reference not only in space but in my life, Orion's presence makes me feel at home no matter where I am.

Why do we think of only the night sky as the heavens, why not the day? And why *heavens,* plural? Jason knows much more about the stars than do I, and he orients us to the sky. There's Orion, yes. The Orion Nebula. Sirius. The Andromeda Galaxy's saucerlike pugmark in far space. The Pleiades (or Makali'i—Little Eyes—who tied all humankind's food in a net and hung it in the heavens until the rat-god gnawed the ropes, letting the food tumble back to Earth). Jupiter, with two of its moons visible through binoculars. Jupiter's moons have lovely names: Io, Europa, Ganymede, Callisto (those are the "Galilean moons," discovered by Galileo himself in 1610 and named after mythological lovers of the god Jupiter), Amalthea, Leda, Himalia, Lysithea, Elara, Ananke, Carme, Pasiphae, and Sinope. What does it say of us that we have not afforded our own lone moon the full acknowledgment of a name? We appreciate the distant more than the close at hand. We see a man in our moon, yet keep him anonymous. No wonder that in his frozen orbit he reflects light with bright intensity, yet maintains a dark side.

Two meteors. And two satellites. Sooty Terns are flying constantly overhead among the immense density of stars. All this noise and noisomeness and vibrancy makes it feel as if the lens of the living Pacific has focused on this dot of sand, and on us.

⊱ ⊱ ⊱ ⊱ ⊱

IN A TURQUOISE
MONASTERY

*B*EFORE DAWN, while the sky is still full of stars, the Monk Seal lab is already casting a glow down the corridor. A day of Monk Seal work can require six hours of preparation. Today's work plan involves actually handling the endangered animals, so all boots, suits, gloves, nets, and sampling instruments must be sterilized or new. Normally, the researchers take great care not to disturb the seals at all, because decades of harassment were a major cause of their current low numbers. But more insidious potential problems with toxic chemicals and possible new viruses now need evaluation, requiring that some seals be biopsied and have their blood sampled. It's for the seals' own good, but the researchers would prefer if it weren't necessary.

Mitch Craig is standing on the porch eating cereal, assessing the impending morning. Mitch takes his empty bowl inside, reappears on the porch with his binoculars and a pair of sandals, and goes to see which seals are on the beach. Though it's light enough now to make out colors well, the sun remains subterranean.

Mitch looks like a rock star: square jaw, pale blue eyes, and frizzy, longish, sun-bleached, dirty-blond hair. You could imagine him up on stage in a white-hot follow spot, wailing away on a guitar. But actually he's very soft-spoken, reflective, thoughtful.

The seal team here consists of Mitch, Melissa Shaw, Mary Donohue, and Jason Baker. Mitch is the field operations leader. He's worked out here for almost fifteen years and has handled hundreds of Monk Seals. Jason is Mitch's superior back at headquarters, but he's new on the job, so he is deferring to Mitch. He's tall, dark, *and* handsome, with wavy hair and several days' growth of beard. Mary, a sweet-voiced biologist with a fresh Ph.D. in physiological ecology, is also new on this job. Mary has her shoulder-length hair pulled into a ponytail while she works out-doors. Melissa—in her early thirties, petite—is an experienced veteri-narian and has worked here several seasons. Her blond hair is also ponytailed, and she's wearing a blue floral bikini and a necklace of small beads.

Mary and Jason are new to the tropics, but they have extensive expe-rience with seals in Alaska. Their partnership extends across the bor-ders of the professional and the intimate, as does Mitch and Melissa's. Jason and Mary met in Alaska's Pribilof Islands, while he was doing a study of Northern Fur Seal foraging and she was studying pup develop-ment. Melissa met Mitch while studying the Monk Seals.

We load all their equipment onto a cart. Much of it is in buckets. For drawing blood samples we have a variety of syringes, needles, and stor-age tubes. For bacterial, viral, and parasite sampling, we have swabs and probes. For biopsy samples for dietary and contaminant analyses, we have large hollow needles. All the team members will be using dispos-able white synthetic overalls in addition to sterilized boots, sterilized calipers, and a sterilized net.

I ask Jason, "Why all the sterility? Don't the seals on the beach spread to each other whatever diseases they have?"

"Maybe, but Monk Seals don't lay all over each other in crowds like some other species. These seals are usually spaced out along the beach. We don't want to take any chance of being an additional disease vector. For instance, when we put a net over a seal's head, against its muzzle, it'll be getting saliva and snot all over it. We don't want to take that to the next seal."

Mary and Melissa are wheeling the piled-up cart down the runway. Mitch is walking ahead, carrying over his shoulder a circular net about three and half feet in diameter. Jason carries the largest pair of calipers I have ever seen—for measuring the length of seals that can weigh up to five hundred pounds—and is carrying another bucket and two small tubs. Still getting his first impressions of this place, Jason is looking around at the boobies, frigatebirds, and albatrosses, commenting, "You come to an otherworldly place like this, where we humans are in the minority, and it's a pretty peculiar feeling. It completely jerks your per-spective. When the Sooty Terns are in full swing, there'll be, like, a thou-sand birds every thirty feet along this one-kilometer strip. It's not that it makes me feel small or appreciate the vastness of the universe or any-thing like that, but the abundance here gives you a sense of what the world used to be like."

The main objective of the team is to resample some seemingly healthy seals that earlier tested marginally positive for morbillivirus. The results were at a level that sometimes gives a false positive, and are considered inconclusive. But the implications of this type of virus are great. Morbilliviruses have caused major die-offs elsewhere, killing half the Harbor Seals in the North Sea, thousands of Caspian Sea seals, and large numbers of dolphins—thousands—in the Mediterranean Sea and other parts of the world. Morbilliviruses have been suspected in multiple mortalities of Mediterranean Monk Seals. They cause measles in humans and distemper in dogs. Sled dogs brought to Antarctica introduced canine distemper to Crabeater Seals, and Siberian dogs passed distemper to Lake Baikal Seals. In the Northwestern Hawaiian Islands, dogs owned by military personnel during recent decades could have harbored seal-deadly viruses, but luckily no dog-to-seal infection seems to have occurred here. There remains the possibility that other infected marine mammals, such as dolphins arriving from elsewhere, might have introduced morbilliviruses to the local Monk Seals. So there's intense interest in seeing and sampling these animals again, to either confirm or rule out the presence of that type of virus in these individuals.

Elsewhere, the deadliness of the viruses seems exacerbated by toxic chemicals like PCBs (which were used by the military here at Tern). Morbillivirus-associated mass mortalities have hit mostly marine mammal populations carrying relatively high contaminant levels. In a European experiment, captive seals were fed herring from either the contaminated Baltic Sea or the much cleaner Atlantic. Those fed the more contaminated herring experienced diminished T-cell function and reduced killer-cell function—both of which are crucial to antivirus defense. Wild European seal populations that suffered mass mortalities had PCB levels higher than those levels found in lab experiments to cause immune problems. So some animals that might otherwise have fought off the viruses are probably getting sick nowadays because PCBs and other chemical pollutants have weakened their immune systems.

We walk farther along the runway, scanning for seals along the lagoon shore. Two large seals and a smaller one that may be a yearling are spaced out on the sand, dozing quietly. Mitch is looking first for the ones they need to retest for exposure to the disease, and secondarily for solitary individuals, to avoid disturbing other seals.

One qualifies. It looks like a large male. Mitch goes to the berm and assesses it from a distance, then comes back. Mitch whispers, "We've jumped this one before. He'll be a little wary. We'll try sneaking up. He's probably not really sleeping. I'll take the net. Mary and Jason, you watch me. Carl, just stay a few feet behind Melissa—and tell her what a great a job she's doing. Get ready to move fast, especially before the drug comes in; if the seal rears back we'll all be coming backward."

I ask if it is wearing an identification tag in its flipper that Mitch can see.

Mitch whispers, "Yeah, but I recognize scars. See that scar on the right rump? Probably an old healed-over shark bite. He's an elder male, looking a little older than last year—a bit more scratched up, not as robust, a bit thinner."

"So you know these animals individually by marks and scars?"

"Mmm-hmm. A lot of adults don't have tags because they're older than our program—twenty or more years old. So for them I use scars. But I know basically all the animals by body marks. This one's seven years old."

Everyone suits up, putting on their white disposable overalls and disinfected boots. Socks go into boots with a little slosh of bleach solution so feet, too, become disinfected. Everyone wears dust masks. Mitch has a pair of goggles. Everyone wears white gloves. Melissa wears rubber examination gloves and pulls out an orange box with sampling and surgical equipment.

We walk slowly through the bird-nesting area, out to the berm. Everybody looks to Mitch for cues. Mitch signals *Forward*. The sounds of the breeze, the birds, and the waves help mask our approach. A low-flying albatross zooms by.

Mitch, Mary, and Jason move to within about fifteen feet of the pungent-smelling seal, then halt. The animal is lying facing the lagoon. A brief powwow ensues, with Mitch indicating by hand movements that he would like Jason and Mary to get between the water and the seal, then come toward it. But before they get into position the seal wakes fully, rears its head, and opens its mouth in threat. Distracted at first by Mary and Jason, the seal suddenly realizes Mitch is coming up quickly behind, and starts hurriedly humping seaward.

As Mitch moves in with the net, the seal rears its head again, opens its mouth, and bellows. It swerves around and makes a lunge, forcing Mitch to nimbly swing his legs away. The seal continues fleeing. Mitch keeps after him. With unexpected agility, the seal rears up surprisingly high, almost jumping into the air—moving much faster than I thought it could. Mitch tries to toss the hoop around it, but the seal deflects by biting the net's rim. Mitch finally gets the hoop most of the way over the seal's head. The seal is struggling, turning onto its back and trying to bite. Mitch skillfully manages to keep his hands safe. As soon as the seal turns onto its belly to try to escape, Mitch pulls the hoop fully around its head and draws the net down along the seal's body. Essentially bagged, the seal continues trying to bite, lunging right and left. Jason leaps aside. Pulling the net up snug, Mitch jumps onto the seal's shoulders, straddling it with his legs. While the seal is still thrashing, Jason and Mary pile on its back. They have it pinned down with the net over its head. The seal snorts and struggles again, waving its head back and forth. Then it settles resignedly.

Melissa comes in behind. She applies Betadine, then alcohol to the animal's rump, soaking the liquids into its dense fur. Then, very carefully, Melissa palpates the seal's hindquarters. She's feeling along the backbones, below where the nerves split (to avoid hitting a nerve), so she can find the right place to deliver an injection to a sinus beneath the vertebrae. She chooses her spot, then inserts and injects, announcing "Valium in, needle out." In half a minute, the animal goes calm, remaining awake. It's not sedated exactly—just no longer worried about us.

Mary goes down to the shoreline for some water. She pours the cooling liquid over the seal's head and pugged face. The water washes some sand off its high forehead. It blinks its big dark eyes.

Next, Melissa reaches for a four-inch needle. Mary affixes a flexible tube to a syringe. Melissa deftly palpates along the lower back again, chooses her place, and inserts half the needle into the seal. She is not satisfied with the flow of blood, and shakes her head. She discards the first needle, then palpates the animal's hips again with her thumb and index finger. She makes another plunge, and the drawing needle hits a good spot. Satisfied this time, she pushes the needle all the way in, then pulls it up just a bit. The seal squirms to the left and gives a loud sneezy bellow. Melissa affixes the needle to the flexible tube connected to the syringe. Mary pulls up on the plunger, and scarlet blood suddenly begins filling the syringe. She takes two 30 cc blood samples. Mary separates the samples into six tubes and two small bottles for different later analyses. There is virtually no talking, only acknowledgment of moving through each procedure.

All this while, the sleek seal lies calmly. He's awake, occasionally moving his head side to side, remaining quiet. We, too, remain quiet. The seal has become so sedated that no one is holding it down, although Mitch is standing by. The seal is breathing evenly. Jason, with a glance, silently inquires of Mitch whether the animal is doing well. Mitch gives the O.K. sign.

Melissa changes her examination gloves again. She applies more disinfectant. By now Melissa's and Mary's white overalls are stained with Betadine. Mary stows the syringe and hands Melissa a small scalpel. Melissa palpates the skin and softly says, "Cutting." She makes a very small incision. Mary takes the scalpel and hands Melissa a biopsy probe, essentially a large hollow needle. As she plunges the probe in about an inch with a turning motion, the seal twists its body to the left. I wince. Mitch grips the back of its neck. Melissa pulls out the probe. A trickle of blood comes to the surface. With tweezers Mary has handed her, Melissa pulls from the instrument a small cylindrical piece of blubber that is the biopsy sample. She drops it into a small vial held by Mary. Melissa makes a second incision for a second biopsy sample; the first is for fatty-acid study of dietary components, the other for toxic-chemical analysis. She plunges the corer in. The animal responds identically, curling its body toward the side that Melissa is on, giving a bubbly snort. Jason pinches the biopsy wounds closed and, amazingly, they almost immediately stop bleeding and stick shut.

Another sleek, water-darkened seal comes ashore only about twenty yards away, looking like a pile of coal against the coral powder. These seals don't use their flippers on land, so it inchworms its body up the beach. Not quite a fish out of water, it makes itself comfortable, resting its head on the shore's soft shoulder, closing its eyes to peaceful slits. It snorts a long, wet snort: a seal of approval. Its color will lighten to dull yellow-brown as it dries in the sleepy squint of the sun. These seals' lives look lazy and peaceful in this open turquoise cathedral, but their rest is well earned. You see them lying on the beach, gliding in the warm shallows, seemingly living a life of leisure. But for a Monk Seal, real life happens outside the reef, out in the ocean, often out of sight of land. Foraging dives often take them down two hundred feet or more on the atoll slopes. A Monk Seal may forage at sea for two or three weeks, then come ashore to rest for just a few days. But some go much deeper, up to fifteen hundred feet, foraging in darkness, in cold water under intense pressure—a world away from the sunlit beaches. Their imperiled numbers attest to their difficulties, their scars to the dangers. Surviving is a matter of hard work, and dying a matter of hard luck.

Melissa changes her gloves again. Next, she raises our animal's stubby tail, inserting a swab into its anus. Mary holds open a jar to receive the tip of the swab, snips off its stem, then screws the jar cap closed. They repeat the process. Next Melissa puts some K-Y Jelly on a longer probe with a loop on the end and inserts it rather far into the anus. This is for parasites. She turns it several times and removes her sample. After one swabbing for viruses, one for salmonella, and another with the looped probe for parasites, they insert a thermometer. The seal sneezes. This animal's internal temperature is 99.6° Fahrenheit.

Melissa brushes more disinfectant onto the animal near its left hip and injects two tiny, coded-wire tags. If it loses its external cattle tags, its identity can be ascertained by merely waving a special wand near its hindquarters.

Mary and Melissa take all the equipment and back away about twenty-five feet. Jason and Mitch get ready and then pull the net away from the seal's head. It turns, flaring its nostrils, looking at us wide-eyed. Soon the sedative will wear off and it can go back to a natural slumber.

We retreat through the bird-nesting area. Gloves and suits are traded for new ones. Boots and net get sterilized again in a big tub of bleach. Everyone relaxes for a moment. Even when all goes well, everyone feels the strain of mixed feelings about working invasively and forcibly on an animal.

A little farther down the beach, a plump young seal is tossing around a plastic soap bottle drifted in from the farther side of our small world. It's a newly weaned pup born earlier this year. About fifty yards past it lies another seal that Mitch says is a yearling. Surprised, I say the yearling looks smaller than the new weaner. Mitch says that the yearlings *are* smaller. "They start out fatter when they wean, and lose a lot of weight in their first year while trying to survive on their own."

As we approach the weaner, it opens its mouth wide and croaks a warning. Mitch confidently takes hold around the neck and straddles it.

It's a female—a precious gift from out of the future. The team repeats all the blood work and swabbing, but does no biopsy for this youngster. It does, however, get ID tags. Melissa takes a hole puncher designed for leather and punctures one rear flipper. There is a snapping sound of metal meeting metal. The animal jerks when she does that. It is clearly not pleased; body piercing is not yet in vogue among Monk Seals. Mitch remains straddling the animal, holding its head the entire time. Melissa punches the other flipper. Mary picks up the numbered yellow plastic tags designed for the ears of cattle. These are numbered YI99. Melissa has a hard time pushing the second tag through the flipper, and the animal bellows. The problem with the tag is conveyed in whispers. Finally it goes in. They measure the seal's length with the calipers, and girth around its chest with a tape. Then we're done for the morning. The team is two seals closer to the fifty animals it needs to sample.

On the bright beach, a black newborn seal is actively nursing, enjoying its first taste of oral gratification. Its mother, sleeping placidly on her side, is plump with bodily reserves, like a big vat of milk and honey. Mitch says of the mother, "She's a fatty, in really good condition."

Another pup loafs nearby. It looks quite healthy but is alone. Mitch says that's a classic example of a pup that's been weaned too soon.

I ask, "How do you know it's been weaned?"

He says, "There's no mother around."

I say, "Does that mean the pup is doomed?"

He hesitates for a second, and then says, "Probably. There's a possibility that it'll go and bug the hell out of another female, possibly even kick off a younger pup and then suckle. But probably it's doomed."

The name Monk Seal derives partly from the animal's relatively solitary habits. So, unlike densely breeding seals and seabirds that have evolved the ability to recognize their own young in crowds, Monk Seals aren't very good at identifying their own offspring. Consequently, pups sometimes get mixed up. Lost pups sometimes get adopted.

But even adoption is not a ticket to survival. Mother's milk translates fat into time—time for the pup to learn. A normally weaned pup can be so fat it doesn't need to eat much for two months, while it is learning how to forage. This has to happen on the right schedule. Pups are born at around thirty pounds. Normally they get nursed for five to six weeks. In those few weeks, they grow to about two hundred pounds. (The mother loses all that weight—and more—and doesn't eat during that time.) At that point, the mother merely leaves, forcing the pup to independence.

Adopted pups have a fighting chance, but only if their timing is lucky. Here's the calculation: You've got to be nursed for at least a month to have any chance of survival. A mother's milk lasts six weeks, maximum. A mother with, say, a five-week-old pup of her own has only a week's worth of milk left. So if she adopts a one-week-old pup, the adopted pup will get only two weeks' milk total (one week from its real mother and one from its adopted mother)—thus dooming it. And sometimes, if an orphan is adopted, the adopting mother may lose her own offspring in the exchange—another route to doom.

· · ·

As WE'RE WALKING OUT, Mitch notices that a young seal that came ashore while we were working has a plastic packing strap stuck around its body, just past its flippers. That's potentially lethal, because it could cut through the skin and flesh as the seal grows. As Mitch pulls a pair of pruning shears with two-foot handles from our cart, he says, "We see maybe one or two entangled seals each year here. But this one had gotten another packing strap stuck on it a few years ago. So that's odd. There was another tangled one the other day, with a loop of rope and some gill net on him."

Monk Seals like to get close to anything lying on the beach, such as logs. This may be one way they get tangled. Indeed, this one was lying snug against a big heap of hawser rope that had been somehow lost or discarded by a ship.

We stay behind, watching from about twenty yards away. Through binoculars I see three big stripes down the seal's flank: probably a Tiger Shark bite, long healed over. Slumber in a world of deadly hazards.

Mitch sneaks up. Just as he's almost there, the seal wakes and rears. In one concentrated expert motion, Mitch deftly jams the shears under the strap, presses them closed, and twists. The strap pops off. Mitch backs away from the seal. It immediately lies down again.

Jason, who has worked a lot on very active fur seals, remarks with surprise, "These Monk Seals *all* seemed drugged. That seal is back *dozing* already!"

Mitch adds that seals that have been handled before do less struggling. "Sometimes they just look at you as if to say, 'Well, O.K.—whatever.'"

Melissa says, "Regardless of anything else—at least we know we did some good for that seal today."

Mitch says, "It was a good morning. Except I really don't like jumping on seals. I'm getting tired of it. You spend so much time trying not to disturb them. Then you go and scare the shit out of them. We tell other people to not even look at them, and yet now we're going around poking them, doing all this disturbance."

Mitch scratches a line in the sand with his toe and adds, "I often wonder if it's really justified. The seal doesn't care what agency you work for, or whether you're a tourist or a scientist, if you happen to be sitting on it. But the bottom line I keep coming down to is—y'know—as long as human factors affect their numbers, I suppose it's important for us to remain involved trying to preserve them. We know that they've persisted here for fifteen million years. But in the last human generation or two they've declined so much they could easily become extinct within a short time."

Mitch gazes out past the beach to the lagoon, then continues, "This study is a hundred and eighty degrees different from our usual approach. It's not our normal work. We try never to handle Monk Seals. We view each one as sacred. The only reason we're handling them again is the possibility of morbillivirus. Because morbillivirus has devastated other marine-mammal populations, we have to take it very seriously. Still, I have mixed feelings about what we're doing. I'm glad this season will be the last time we handle these animals for a while."

Jason, too, views his endangered-species work with perspective. "You feel confident that you can do all the tasks. Yet in the larger picture you wonder whether all the skills we can bring to bear are really enough to get these Monk Seal populations into recovery mode. Most of the stuff that we do—who knows if you're having a positive effect. You hope— you *hope*—it's at least not harmful. You hope that by learning more you'll be able to help the population in the long run. But certainly it's pretty intangible. In Alaska we disentangled hundreds of seals that had netting around their necks. When you cut a piece of net off a seal, or pull some netting off the reef, you know that you're actually helping individual animals. That's one of the few times you can say that with certainty. But *still* you're not sure what difference it makes to the population as a whole. You always have to have some humility. You always have to confront the possibility that if the population does go up, maybe it's because you're lucky."

Using surgical suits, masks, and gloves and carefully washing nets and boots in between each seal minimizes any possibility that the work will add to the animals' troubles. Most everyone has a true affection and a deep commitment to the animals and the work. I don't know a field biologist who isn't concerned about the effect they may be having on the animal they're studying. But neither do I know a field biologist—including me—who has not occasionally shaken his head with disappointment and self-anger at an egg accidentally broken or an animal accidentally hurt. Few researchers take casualties lightly. Particularly among the new generation. Everyone constantly asks: "Is there a better way we could be working?" Techniques continue to improve. It feels good to be among those people, because their dedication is genuine. Ultimately, the work is intended to draw out what the animals cannot tell us. To give words to the wordless, and voice to the voiceless, so that we can try to reach the ones among *us* who so far have been beyond words.

We walk back through the bird colony, and several albatrosses rise to their feet, clacking at us.

APPROACHING THE BARRACKS, we notice that a seal has hauled itself onto the basketball court. It came in through a low break in the fence. There aren't too many places where an endangered seal is likely to show up on the hoop court, but here in Wonderland you never can predict what the day might deliver. In a court of law the endangered animal has status. On this court of basketball a seal cannot appeal. Mitch fears it might be unable to find its way back out. He goes to talk it into leaving. He must shepherd it back to the same fence break. It goes to the brink, then snorts, looks back balefully, and rears up at him. It will make its determined stand right here. Mitch presses. It barks; it will not move. He presses more, using seal psychology: "Too far away and they ignore you, too close and they'll turn to face you." The seal gives up its occupation and humps back through the fence break.

We arrive at the barracks' back entrance. About fifty noddies flush from their nesting bushes as we round the corner to the lab door. Though they return almost immediately, Melissa says, "Ooh, I hate to bother those birds." To a little Fairy Tern chick resting on a concrete window ledge, Melissa calls, "Hi, little chickie."

The seal lab has a microscope, a centrifuge, racks of test tubes, a sink, workbenches, a small seal skeleton, and a couple of lobster shells and various bird feathers for decoration. Even in the lab, the scientists work in bathing suits and bare feet. While Melissa and the others are preparing and storing the morning's samples, she is explaining to me her spiritual perspective on her work as a wild-animal veterinarian. "I believe everyone has inside of them an innate sense of animals as beings. You see it most in children. As we go on in our lives, it gets covered over more and more. Most people have forgotten." Melissa sees the basic nature of animal life as eating, sleeping, mating, and defending. These same things are basic for people, too, she says. "So, while in some ways we are different from other animals, the essence of what we are is the same. Since the great majority of the problems animals are facing are the consequences of human actions, I feel it's our responsibility to be caretakers, to correct these actions, and be more gentle."

A short while later, Melissa decides to take a break, saying, "Today I think we'll actually have time for lunch."

As we rummage through kitchen leftovers, Mary is telling Melissa and me about her studies of Northern Fur Seal pups. Mary says, "Young Fur Seals transform from little puppies, shivering in the rain like ordinary land animals, to fully adapted marine mammals capable of spending nine entire months in a frigid ocean. Very young pups can't maintain their body temperature in water. They can't stay warm. After they molt into their dense fur, their body temperature gets perfectly stable. Their metabolic rate gets stable too, even in the water. In other words, they can stay warm in really cold water without burning any more food to do it. That's incredible when you look at the sea temperatures. A suite of things develop: the dense fur, the thick fat; their red-blood-cell density doubles—. So they really transform from tiny baby land mammals to truly aquatic marine-adapted animals. It's truly amazing. By the first time they are ready to go to sea they don't need to increase their metabolism to stay warm."

"What's the significance of the red-cell doubling—that they can carry more oxygen?"

"Exactly, so they can hold their breath long enough for deep diving. A whole bunch of physiological things prepare these guys for the first day they take to the sea." She pauses for a far-off moment. "Working in the Pribilof Islands was fantastic. There were twenty thousand pups born at my study site. It was really incredible to see the abundance of animals there. Like here; same thing." She adds, "I think people have some kind of need for animals and natural places. Just look where people pay the most money to go—Africa to see the wildlife, or coral reefs to snorkel. People spend a lot of money to see and experience the kinds of places that we would consider worth preserving. Where there hasn't been any conservation, those places tend to be very unpleasant to live in or visit." Mary used to teach at the Orange County Marine Institute, and she offers this possibility: "We had kids coming in from Los Angeles who live within fifteen miles of the ocean and had never seen a starfish. These were troubled kids. While I wouldn't say that not seeing starfish was responsible for the situation they were in, I think it's possible that the lack of open spaces and nature-type experiences contributes to a sense of disconnection, and discontent."

MITCH AND MELISSA HAVE BEEN WORKING with Mary and Jason for just a few days, and they're still getting to know one another. When Melissa asks Jason his age (he's thirty-five), Mitch says, "Let's not talk about age." Rock-star looks notwithstanding, he's closing in on an uneasy forty.

Melissa consoles him: "There was a man who lived to one hundred and twenty-nine. He said his secret was that he never told anyone his age."

"Then how do you know how old he was?" Mitch says. "It's all genetic anyway. You're just destined to get what you get regardless of whether you smoke or are fat or don't exercise."

Jason says, "If it's inherited, I'm destined for either heart disease, cancer, or senile dementia."

"I'd try for the heart disease," opines Mitch. As for him, now that he's ripened toward forty he's given this some thought. *He* wants to go by swimming here in June; he wants his last impression of the world to be a sudden jolt from a big shark.

Melissa says she doesn't think so. "I watched two Galápagos Sharks kill a seal pup at Trig Island." That's just across the channel from Tern. "They took both her rear flippers and a front flipper. When the pup got to shore, you could see the shock in its eyes." One shark dragged it back and they devoured it. "Not the way *I'd* want to go." She shivers at the thought.

The misnamed Galápagos Shark lives in warm seas around the world's midsection, showing a particular fondness for oceanic islands. Mitch remarks to me, "In the last year, more Galápagos Sharks have been preying on pups around Trig island. I've never seen that before. It's always been, if anything, Tiger Sharks." This year the sharks are a real problem for seal pups.

But overall, shark predation is not the root cause of trouble for the Hawaiian Monk Seal. The real threats to their numbers—the things that have landed them on the endangered-species roster—were killing by people in the early years and chronic disturbance by military personnel and their dogs in the latter half of the twentieth century.

Only about thirteen hundred Hawaiian Monk Seals grace the face of Earth at this point in human and planetary history. It's an unlucky number times a hundred. That includes juveniles and the year's pups. That's it. Fifteen million years ago, and for every era, epoch, millennium, and century since, there have been more of them—until the last few decades. Before the Polynesians arrived, the main Hawaiian Islands might have served Monk Seals as breeding areas. Remember, there were no predators on land anywhere in Hawaii—any beach was an absolute safe haven. If the seals had been using the main islands, the Polynesians likely ate most of them and frightened away the rest. Virtually all remaining Hawaiian Monk Seals owe their existence to only six breeding populations in the Northwestern Hawaiian Islands.

But these islands didn't always offer refuge. In the late 1800s, sealers, crews of wrecked vessels, and various fortune hunters nearly snuffed out the Hawaiian Monk Seal. In 1859 one ship took fifteen hundred Monk Seal skins, more than exist today. By the year 1900, seals were missing or nearly gone on several islands. After decades of slow increase, the population halved between the 1950s and the 1970s as military people and their dogs constantly scared females from breeding on the islands.

Now the Hawaiian Monk Seal is one of the most endangered mammals in the world. Now the idea is *E ho'olaulima makou I malama 'ilio o ke kai*—"We must cooperate to take care of our Monk Seals." Endangered means there is still time.

NO ONE KNOWS how many Hawaiian Monk Seals existed before humans first arrived in these islands, but since scientists made the first counts about fifty years ago, their tribe has declined by more than half.

They should consider themselves lucky. Their cousin the Caribbean Monk Seal (noted in 1494 by Christopher Columbus) inhabited a wide and lovely island-and-reef region from Mexico's Yucatán Peninsula through the Bahamas. Europeans went on their usual spree, killing the fatally tame seals wherever they found them. Humanity finally deprived itself of the Caribbean Monk Seal in 1952, when the last handful vanished from Earth. And the Mediterranean Monk Seal now has a sword dangling over its big brown eyes, too; about four hundred exist, in tiny, widely scattered groups. So, holding at an all-time low for the last few years, the Hawaiian Monk Seal is doing the best of a beleaguered lot. And there might be a brighter future just over the horizon.

Virtually the entire historic decline of the Hawaiian Monk Seal was due to disturbance on land. Tern Island's lowest counts coincided with a period of continual harassment by Coast Guard dogs. Disturbance made females move after giving birth, causing pups to get lost or prematurely weaned. Or, rather than pupping on larger islands, badgered females gave birth on sandbars so tiny and low they got washed over while the pup was critically young.

In the late 1980s, humans dealt Hawaiian Monk Seals a new challenge: disturbance at sea. Mitch explains, "That's when long-liners began fishing in Hawaiian waters for Swordfish and tunas." In the late 1980s, over a hundred longline boats, fresh from having depleted Swordfish in the Atlantic, flocked to Hawaii. "They started hooking seals on their longlines. Several seals showed up here with hooks in them. Some had head injuries from being clubbed by fishermen." With unusual haste, federal fishery managers created a fifty-mile no–long-lining zone around the breeding islands. This left the seals with two other issues related to fishing: likely competition with commercial fishing boats for lobsters and octopuses, and entanglement in lost nets. The severity of food competition is uncertain, but nets are a definite problem.

Mitch explains that in the last fifteen years or so, over 150 seals have been *found* entangled in derelict fishnets throughout the Northwestern Hawaiian Islands. Only about half a dozen were dead when found; the rest were tangled and still alive. That means either most tangled seals die and the carcasses disappear, or many tangled seals can get free. No one knows what percentage of tangled seals get free. But the carcasses of seals that die in nets must quickly get eaten by sharks, leaving no trace. The lost nets also tangle many sharks, fishes, and sea turtles.

Seals—especially young ones—also approach floating junk with the inquisitiveness that has always helped them learn how to survive. Now their intelligent curiosity risks entanglement and death. Because of the way the currents gyre around the Hawaiian Islands, derelict, lost, and dumped netting, as well as other fishing gear and debris, can arrive here from just about any country in the North Pacific. Lots of the netting on these islands has drifted in from over a thousand miles distant, off Alaska and Asia. It causes trouble to several kinds of seals, whales, and turtles here, there, and along the way. In the late 1990s, federal researchers found an average density of 230 pieces of lost and discarded netting per square mile at French Frigate Shoals, and estimated that 38,000 net fragments burdened the Shoals. In fact, there's a large pile of derelict netting beside the runway here. I've sat comfortably on that immense pile of netting, contemplating the discomfort it caused to creatures less fortunate. None of it is local in origin; nets like that aren't used around here. But all of it was pulled from the waters and reefs of French Frigate Shoals by the people who work here.

So now, finally, Monk Seals might just possibly be entering an era where, on balance, humans are helping more than hurting them. At least, humans are basically leaving the seals alone, not constantly disturbing them. In fact, in the central part of the chain, places like Laysan and Lisianski Islands, the seals are holding steady. And Monk Seal numbers are actually *climbing* in the northwestern end of the chain—places like Midway and Kure Atolls—where numbers had dropped by as much as 90 percent.

But in the more southeasterly locations, most notably here at French Frigate Shoals, survival has been terrible for more than a decade. This is a troubled population. The many pups produced here—about seventy births per year—just aren't surviving well after weaning. It wasn't always that way. Back in the late 1980s, survival of first-year pups was something like 70 to 80 percent. For older animals, annual survival was commonly 90 percent.

In 1990 pup production fell here—nearly halved—and first-year survival rates began plummeting. By the late 1990s, first-year survival rates had dropped to well under 30 percent. Since 1990 the number of Monk Seals surviving to reproductive maturity has declined to about a tenth of what it was in the 1980s. From the class of 1990, for example, only three animals survived to breed.

French Frigate Shoals still has the biggest population of Monk Seals in this island chain. But the seal population in this atoll has fallen from eight hundred during the late 1980s to about four hundred right now.

Mitch emphasizes the point: "At the rate that we're losing pups in French Frigate Shoals, there won't be enough young animals to maintain the population. Even though we're actually seeing increasing numbers at the northwest end of the island chain at the moment, the problem at French Frigate Shoals has been so dramatic, it's pulling down the total population." Though French Frigate Shoals is still producing about half of all births, 65 percent of those pups are dead within a few months.

Shark predation, adult male aggression, disease, parasites, ciguatera poisoning, entanglement, and even human disturbance have been ruled out as *primary* causes of the most recent French Frigate decline. The new sampling will soon rule out morbilliviruses entirely.

"What's the speculation about what's going on?" I ask.

"Well, the speculation is—" Mitch hesitates. "That they're starving here, mostly. When survival started dropping, you would see animals not doing so well, looking like they might be starving. Then you started seeing them starving earlier in the season. Now, you don't see them starving—they just disappear."

But it's not one factor alone; it's a suite of all the problems, pulling in the same downward direction.

Hawaiian Monk Seals contend with yet another predicament: some islands have developed skewed sex ratios, probably a chance artifact of their populations having been driven to very low levels. At islands with more females than males—Midway Atoll, Kure Atoll, and Pearl and Hermes Reef—seals are increasing. But at islands with more males than females, mobs of males have killed females and juveniles in mating attempts. This results in even fewer females, making the problem worse and worse. (At Laysan during the early 1990s, males outnumbered females by two to one, and as many as ten females per year died as a result. Researchers have on several occasions effectively dealt with this by removing males to bachelor exile on other islands, away from breeding colonies. In 1994 they removed twenty-two males from Laysan.)

Mitch sums up by emphasizing the magnitude of recent problems. "So, between starvation, predation, entanglement, and killing by certain problem males, about sixty pups disappeared from this atoll in just the last two years. At that rate, the chances of any surviving long enough to breed . . ."

"That's very sad."

"Very. Actually—it's bizarre."

AFTER LUNCH THE SEAL TEAM goes off to sample more seals on other islands in the Shoals, returning in the late afternoon to the lab.

In the early evening, while the others eat dinner at the far end of the building, the seal team spends two hours sorting, stabilizing, preserving, and analyzing blood and biopsy samples. They check blood glucose levels. They make slides of blood samples for microscopic analysis. They freeze samples in liquid nitrogen for later transport and analysis. Melissa counts white blood cells to get a sense of whether a seal is fighting off an infection. Jason takes a centrifuge-spun capillary tube of blood and compares the fraction of the blood that is red cells—"packed red-cell volume"—against a printed scale. This is to determine hematocrit level, which is an indicator of hydration and anemia. Mary looks at blood urea nitrogen (Melissa says, "We call it BUN, for fun") by testing a drop of blood on a reactive litmus-like strip; this gives her information about protein metabolism and kidney function.

Jason says, "Basically, what we're doing here is keeping track of stuff." The team is spinning most of the blood and the plasma, parceling it into tubes, and packing it in liquid nitrogen. Jason explains, "If somebody needs some serum for screening at a later date, we don't have to thaw blood; we just pull out one little tube." The blubber gets frozen for further analysis, and bacteria samples will be placed into a culturing medium.

Mitch, wearing a T-shirt that says LOVE MAKES THE WORLD ONE, explains that here at French Frigate Shoals the seals seem to mature at later ages and stop growing at smaller sizes than elsewhere. This may be further evidence of the suspected food scarcity. Melissa says, "New ways of analyzing fatty acids in the blubber can identify parts of their diet. It may show us, for instance, whether juvenile seals rely on lobsters. If so, competition with commercial lobster fishing may underlie their nutrition problems—or maybe we'll find their food problems really have very little to do with commercial fishing."

The question of whether fishing robs Monk Seals of significant food has been hotly debated for years. Fishery managers long ignored the Marine Mammal Commission's repeated pleas that waters within twenty miles of French Frigate be closed to lobstering. The fisheries people wanted proof that commercial fishing for lobsters and octopuses would hurt seals—and the mammal people wanted proof the fishing wouldn't. Who should bear responsibility for the burden of proof? That fight was philosophical, but critically endangered seals were starving.

The mammal commission's director, John Twiss, in what he later referred to as "a series of extraordinarily unrewarding exchanges," pressed fishery managers throughout the 1990s to close the area around French Frigate Shoals to lobster fishing. In one letter he wrote, "The best available information clearly indicates that monk seals at French Frigate Shoals are food-stressed and that lack of food is causing the death of newly weaned pups. It is also clear that monk seals eat lobsters and octopi, . . . that commercial lobster fishermen take both lobsters and octopi, that commercial lobster fishing has occurred at French Frigate Shoals and neighboring banks, and that declines in monk seals at French Frigate Shoals occurred concurrent with declines in abundance of exploitable lobsters." The following year, Twiss felt compelled to write, "The current status of the population is critical . . . due almost entirely to an alarming decrease at French Frigate Shoals." One year later he again wrote to the head of the fisheries service: "The National Marine Fisheries Service is not adopting a prudent, precautionary approach to the management of lobster fishing at French Frigate Shoals. . . . Steps must be taken to prevent lobster fishing at that atoll." No steps were taken. So in 2000, the Center for Biological Diversity, Turtle Island Restoration Network, Greenpeace Foundation, and Earthjustice Legal Defense Fund sued to end lobster fishing in the Northwestern Hawaiian Islands. Agreeing with the plaintiffs, a federal judge indefinitely closed the islands to lobster fishing, finding that the National Marine Fisheries Service has "failed to protect the endangered Hawaiian monk seal from the impact of the fishery." So maybe there are fatter times ahead for French Frigate Shoals' skinny seals.

At eight P.M. Melissa asks, "Are we all ready for tomorrow?" Jason says, "Not fully, but I just realized I'm so tired my mind is not even capable of counting the sterile suits."

Melissa says, "Hmm—must be your glucose level. Let's check it, feed you, and check it again."

At nine P.M., after a twelve-hour field day, Melissa is counting white blood cells in the lab. She was wet for a long time in the boat this afternoon after being caught in a squall between islands and fears she is coming down with a cold. I give her some vitamin C, but my talking interferes with her concentration, and she miscounts the white blood cells in the microscope and must start over.

She says, "Boy, I am *beat*. I haven't had enough rest. I get up early to meditate for an hour. It starts my day, it makes everything work right. I used to do two hours, but it's not practical. I think the secret to a good spiritual life is going to bed early. And that's hard out here."

Her eyes are red and tired looking. She's taking samples and putting them into a solution to burst the red cells and dilute the white cells so they can be counted on a slide. She is being very deliberate and paying extra attention because she is so exhausted. She plants herself at the microscope with her feet apart, a steady stance. And counts again.

This time, I keep my mouth shut and don't distract her.

At ten P.M., Melissa is still standing at the bench, her sunglasses still on her head. Mary, who said good night an hour ago, is back in the lab. She has a small puncture in her foot from today's visit to East Island, and she's not sure if there's a glass sliver in there or possibly a piece of coral. She can feel something with a pin, and when she does that I can hear a little scraping sound that makes my stomach woozy. (Some people can't stand the sight of blood; I have a problem with splinters.) She can't dig enough to get it out because it hurts too much.

Melissa, turning her veterinary skills to the primate in all of us, examines Mary's foot carefully with a magnifying glass. Nothing is visible. But soreness and a developing red streak leading from the wound raise concern of possible blood poisoning—way out here. She prescribes a Betadine-and-hot-water solution to soak in. If the red line develops any farther, she'll prescribe antibiotics from her emergency kit. But with a little luck the soaking will loosen the splinter enough for retrieval and everything will be okay.

By now, Melissa is thinking about maybe eating dinner. "But first, I might even get to do a load of clothes for the first time in a week." She asks everyone in the lab if they have clothes that need washing. Mary does. As the Zen saying goes, "After ecstasy, the laundry."

Mitch offers to make some spaghetti for the crew, and I offer to help. We make our way down the quiet corridor to the darkened kitchen, where we light a couple of the oil lamps. Mitch says he spent his freshman year in premed at Duke University, but discovered pretty quickly that premed wasn't for him. He went home and worked in a motorcycle shop for about a year and a half, selling parts and racing, before going back to finish a degree at the University of Maryland. He recalls, "When I first came to Tern Island fifteen years ago, I was a volunteer. I think everyone should have a job they'd volunteer for—y'know? So anyway, I was nervous; anxious to do a good job. As usual, I was being pretty hard on myself. My job at first was to camp over on East Island and document the amount of time different mothers were nursing their pups."

Mitch's superiors were not as hard on him as he was on himself; they hired him to come back. He went to graduate school for about a year but never completed an advanced degree. "I quit. I already had the job I wanted."

For Mitch, this is a labor of deeply ingrained love. He searches for words, then says, "It may be hard for me to explain how I felt about being here that first year. I just absolutely loved watching those mothers nursing those little black pups on the beach. Just sitting, listening to the seals breathing, or hearing the babies sucking—this little *woof-woof* sound that they make. There were fifty-two pups born on that island that year. I learned more about Monk Seals that first season, by just sitting and watching for hours, day after day, than I have since.

"And it wasn't just that—it was the whole thing: you're trying to pay attention, trying to stay focused, trying to do your job. For me it's like, it's—*present*. The birds are all around you, the boobies yelling, the Wedge-tails squabbling; you wrap pillows around your head to stay asleep. And the turtles—the turtles would be coming up scratching, throwing big clouds of sand and stuff. You're just smack in the middle of it *all*. You're one of the wildlife beings. Seals would come up and sleep next to the tent. You're lying *this* far away"—he shows with his fingers—"from a snoring seal. And then you wake up in the morning, and *every-thing* is beautiful. Waking up, getting your stuff together, making your little lunch, going out and setting up, seeing what new pups were born at night—. It's just mind-boggling. I just—I don't know how to put it."

After a momentary reflection, he continues translating these deep feelings into a flow of words. "You're sort of in your own world, and you have to confront your own thoughts. You have a lot of time to think. That could be nerve-racking at times. You have a lot of thoughts running through your mind about events in your life. Things I wish I might have handled differently—. Sometimes you think of something you wish you'd said to somebody." He falls silent, then adds, "Is it odd to have those kinds of thoughts in a place so remote and beautiful?"

I say it's not odd at all, that the same kinds of thoughts occur to me.

"So anyway," he continues, "you're seeing creatures being born all around you, things living, things dying. Once I was watching a pup that'd been born just that day; the mom was finally catching some sleep and a wave came up and grabbed the pup, and the pup was swept away in the current before the mother even woke. You might be sitting there so long that suddenly you feel a thump, and it's a tropicbird that's just come to be right next to you.

"When you first come here you're sort of overwhelmed with how lovely and beautiful it is. The colors. The fact that half your view is the sky and the other half is the water. The wildlife everywhere. It's very soothing. After a while it becomes the background that you accept. But it's always wonderful."

Now a typical year for Mitch and Melissa includes being here from April to September. Mitch adds, "Each year when you come back it's very exciting at the beginning. Then you realize again, 'Wow this is a lot of *work*.'"

He checks to see how the spaghetti is doing, then says, "It's very important to me to try to excel at a job, and this job has a lot to it. It's pretty complicated. And the fact that it means something for an endangered species—. To have my work affect something in the world that needs a lot of attention is really the best thing to be involved in. This job fills something for me. It makes my life feel worth living."

In the soft light of the oil lamps, I sense there's something darker lurking just at the periphery of this joyous conversation. I don't press it. But Mitch tentatively reveals a little more, saying, "This job takes me out of myself, too. If I didn't have this, I might choose not to live, or get off into something that was pretty distracting. Like—" He stops himself. "I could name all kinds of things. So this is sort of a saving grace for me."

I nod, not really clear about what he is hinting at, but not feeling entitled to ask.

"I think," Mitch says slowly, almost as if talking to himself, "I would disintegrate otherwise. I have my demons. Drugs. Beer. It's a little too easy." He brightens a bit and looks at me again. "But when I'm here I can do something tangible. I can move a lost pup back to where its mother is. Or, you feel good at the end of the day if you've removed two hundred pounds of lost fishing netting and ropes out of an area with seals."

Mitch opens a container with some salad and offers me a bite. He says that when he sits on these beaches looking out at the lagoon and reefs, he gets the sense this has all been here forever, and will be here forever.

I tell him that to me these shelly beaches and sandbars look so changeable, seem so transient, that I sense these islands will one day vanish. But I also know that the species are so ancient, that these creatures have moved in these waters for millions of years. So the animals prove the timelessness of a place that seems ephemeral.

Time seems to be happening here at different rates, on different scales. But we can only see it through the lens of our own experience, our own time. Mitch says, "I've known many of these animals from birth. I've seen them growing up, having pups of their own. So these are the friends that I have. They are the people that are my family. I've come to recognize their behavior and their nuances of expression, and whether they're comfortable. I recognize a lot of them by sight. I wonder if they recognize me. I don't suppose they do."

➤ ➤ ➤ ➤ ➤ ➤

MOVING ON

*I*N THESE FIRST FOUR TRIPS since her egg hatched beneath her belly, Amelia has logged round-trip distances of 506, 199, 917, and 2,388 miles.

The girl's just warming up.

Amelia is a workaholic. Though she's just returned from an eight-day trip of over two thousand miles, she seems to think there are better things to do than sit around brooding. After a short nest rest—just a few minutes—she walks slowly to the runway, turns into the southerly breeze, and cranks herself into the wind. Once airborne she wheels and puts the wind behind her. It's a good start, because this will be an even longer trip.

In the last couple of weeks Amelia has spent a lot of time foraging in the meager tropics. Her devotion shows; her chick has grown vigorous and healthy. But she has put all her surplus energy into her chick, and she herself has been losing weight steadily while scouring thousands of miles of ocean slipping beneath her.

Despite her hunger, the small size of her chick urges her to begin this trip as she began the last: looking for food nearby, trying not to stray too terribly far from Tern, searching the trackless, crystalline tropic sea.

At sunset the shining sea stretches away and around the world like a gold-threaded tablecloth. Her hunger briefly pulls her in the direction of reliable food she knows lies far north. She swings northward but then swerves east, into the night, then into dawn. After flying 360 miles Amelia is back in the concert hall, foraging among the Musicians Seamounts. Without slowing perceptibly she flies the length of the Chopin Seamount, then swings up across the Haydn and skirts the Handel, turning northwest. Measure by measure, mile after mile, she waltzes along.

Though the sea is wide as ever and she is hundreds of miles from any land or visual marker, she travels along the seamount province as though able by magic to divine the lay of the seafloor miles below. She swings past Tchaikovsky, performs a thirty-mile loop like a ballerina dancing *Swan Lake* on the world stage, and swoops back up to Debussy.

Her grace and style are breathtaking, but she is repeating her last, marginal trip. That trip worked well enough for the chick. But what worked well enough then does not work well enough now. It's a week later, a week further into her hunger, into her loss of weight and body condition. Her devotion to home wavers. Her blood chemistry is signaling her brain. The long averaging process of evolution steps in, as though whispering, "I am crucially hungry. No chick benefits from a mother starved to death." So the seesaw between maternity and hunger tips—and now hunger wins.

Amelia has decided: she will go for food. Real food. Much food. She'll ignore the sight of a few flyingfish, and she'll ignore every faint cue the tropically warm ocean gives her about small snacks or some fish eggs here or there. She is no longer foraging. Now she is truly traveling. And she knows exactly where she's headed. She strikes north. Directly north. Absolutely north. Straight as an arrow: north.

She'll leave the boobies and frigatebirds and terns far behind her. She is headed to the edge of cold water. She burns past Stravinsky Seamount like a firebird and hurries past Schubert as if she has unfinished business. For the first time in months, Amelia will fully unfurl. Like an Olympic runner just stepping onto the track, she will now be what an albatross is all about: traveling to the limits of any sea. No ocean stretches far enough to outdistance an albatross. They seem to bend the laws of physics; in this magic realm space collapses and single birds command whole ocean basins, and time's arrow becomes elliptic, cyclic, as the birds become consumed with going and returning.

On a favoring wind, Amelia sails nearly six hundred miles in thirty hours. Much of that time, she flies in half-sleep, on and on. In a 1926 poem the South African Roy Campbell imagined himself an albatross,

> *Stretching white wings in strenuous repose,*
> *Sleeving them in the silver frills of sleep,*
> *As I was carried, far from other foes,*
> *To shear the long horizons of the deep*
> *. . . I floated like a seed with silken sails*
> *Out of the sleepy thistle of the sun.*

Over the miles, the sea temperature begins dropping slowly. Eventually, Amelia reaches the southern edge of a broad frontal zone that blends warmer and colder water. Nine hundred miles now from Tern Island, Amelia slows along this edge. The broad boundary she is working flows across the entire North Pacific in a slow but highly dynamic current that wavers like an unmanned fire hose. This fountain of change separates the warm-hearted central Pacific from the chill subarctic. All things referenced as "tropical" now lie far behind her.

Amelia hesitates, turning toward the northeast a ways, following a hundred-mile meander in the flowing current. This front constitutes the northern border of the six-hundred-mile-wide North Pacific Current. The current's broad northern and southern margins, undulating across the ocean at roughly 30° and 40° N, are known respectively as the subtropical and subarctic frontal zones.

The wide North Pacific Current and its frontal borders separate higher-salinity tropical southern water from the cooler and fresher subarctic water to the north; they separate two enormous regions of the North Pacific, distinct biological realms inhabited by very different groups of animals. The tropical side is the sparsely populated solar realm of frigate-birds, flying fish, and tunas. The cold side, near where Amelia is now, is the richer polar kingdom of fulmars, herring, and salmon. Two worlds.

The North Pacific Current itself originates in the western Pacific, spawned where the warm Kuroshio ("Dark Blue Current" in Japanese), coming north along Japan's coast, collides with the cold Oyashio ("Mother Current") flowing down from the Bering Sea. This tangled mass of enriched water then heads eastward as the North Pacific Current.

Where the North Pacific Current crashes into North America, the portion deflected north becomes the Alaska Current, flowing up along British Columbia and then curling west along the Gulf of Alaska and the Aleutian Islands. The part turning southward becomes the California Current, a meandering jet of water flowing south, shedding eddies and cool filaments. It keeps the coastal ocean chilly all the way down past San Francisco. Near the equator, the water turns back westward, recrossing the Pacific Ocean, and when it hits Asia the part of it that turns north along the coast becomes the Kuroshio all over again. The round-trip takes about five years.

IN SIX DAYS AT SEA Amelia has flown from latitude 23° north to 40°. This is like traveling from southern Baja, Mexico, to the Oregon border, or from the Bahamas to central New Jersey.

She is now foraging the border waters of the subarctic frontal zone. She's hunting intently, scrutinizing the greener water here. When the scent of a school of fish wafts to her, she flies a mile or so until the scent dissipates, then doubles back until it gets stronger, then passes it until it again grows faint. Once more she wheels and doubles back, until she's found the perimeter of the densest scent and has some sense of the school's direction of travel. Now she searches intently over the thickest aroma, flying mile-long patterns for a couple of hours, waiting for the light to weaken and the fish to rise.

Packs of fish called sauries, elegantly thin and about six to eight inches long, come up into view. She lands near a dense group, and they scatter. She lifts off again, resuming her large oval flight patterns. Amelia finds one dying saury, then a dead squid. Glimpses of fishes in the closing dusk are followed by squid rising under cover of the gathering dark. With eyes nearly as well-adapted to the dark as an owl's, Amelia begins seeing more squid here and there as the sunset melts away to the shine of midocean starlight.

But she is still working hard and traveling many miles between mouthfuls. Hungering still, she breaks off her search. Again she swings straight north, skimming over piling swells that roll like dark marching hills, and white-capped seas whipped by blustery new winds that have come to oppose the current, until another 180 miles of water separate her from Tern Island. Well over a thousand miles from her chick, Amelia is now on the northern edge of that broad subarctic frontal zone, bordering the cold water.

Amelia zigs and zags this boundary. The weather isn't so nice, but to Amelia the chilly air feels refreshing, brisk, bracing. The water slipping beneath her now is plain cold, as low as $54°$ F ($12°$ C). The single-celled drifting planktonic plants at the bottom rung of the sea's larder like it cool, so this cooler water is greener, cloudier with plankton. It has lost its tropical clarity. With that lost clarity and the new chill, the water has also lost its tuna, and with the tuna have gone the tuna-dependent tropical seabirds: the boobies, tropical terns, and frigates. Those birds are much better than Amelia at making a living among the ballistic beasts of the tropic seas, but they can't make a living out here at all. This is the advantage of albatrosses: to make a modest living yet be able to do so over most of the ocean. Laysan Albatrosses can feel at home anywhere in all this vast realm, and that's why there are so many of them.

The subarctic in early March isn't exactly the same sunny, warm climate that Amelia left at her nest. It is gales and sleet, freezing and dark

and terrible. Few marine animals can withstand both extremes. But albatrosses do. How does she handle that kind of climate shift? Dave Anderson, looking at the satellite track Amelia is sending to his lab, has this
answer: "I don't know. I don't have any idea how an albatross can do
that. Most animals would freak out. This bird in a few days went from
basically a tropical climate to basically an arctic climate. I don't know
how it can handle such abrupt change. When I first saw what this bird is
doing—it was quite a moment."

Albatrosses belong in cold waters like these, along these fronts and
gradients, in this chilly air, where the wind seems to have an appetite of
its own. Here in the chill, Amelia feels fully at home and comfortable for
the first time since she went to Tern Island months ago to start the breeding season.

Amelia works this zone four days, sometimes in the flowing front,
then drifting beyond, then back along the front. She searches for concentrated scents, sharp sea-color changes, and other signs of concentrated life. She moves west into the current for 225 miles one day, 250
the next.

Then she finds the life she's looking for. And the death that accompanies it.

The frontal boundary is distinct here, the sea-surface temperature
gradient sharp. Certain patches along this front suddenly seem almost
to be squirting with squid. This is part of the area, in fact, where during
the 1980s and into the '90s the squid boats of Taiwan, Japan, and Korea
set tens of thousands of miles of drift nets each night. Pacific albatrosses
had been recovering from the feather hunting of the early 1900s and
the disruption of World War II and Cold War military presences at major
breeding sites when drift nets began infesting their foraging areas. With
something like forty thousand miles of nylon webbing spun into the
blue Pacific each night, hungry albatrosses found a lot of dead fish and
squid tangled in those nets. But the drift nets served dangerous dinners.
Before the United Nations finally banned them in the early 1990s (they'd
originally promoted the same nets), each year roughly twenty-two thousand Hawaiian albatrosses attempting to wine and dine got wound and
drowned. Their populations again declined. Drift-net crews sometimes
fashioned earrings from albatross leg bands. Those nets also killed
much higher numbers of other seabirds. The estimated kill of Sooty
Shearwaters ran to half a million *annually* for over a decade. Tens of
thousands of dolphins, whales, and seals also drowned, and tens of millions of unwanted fish died in the nets and were shoveled overboard.

The level of collateral mortality doesn't begin to speak to the millions and millions of tunas, marlins, Swordfish, salmon, and Neon Flying Squid that the nets removed from the oceans.

Amelia is now a recipient of the United Nations' belated wisdom and the banned boats' departure. Not only did so many albatrosses die annually in those nets, but now more squid again slide through the waters here for Amelia, and for the famished, feathered nations whose culinary traditions were set long before the seas were etched by a million wakes.

Amelia is also benefiting from the predations of pods of dolphins. From time to time they stage well-coordinated attacks, streaming up under the squid from below in tight, streaking packs, sending them fleeing into the atmosphere. Packs of squid are jetting around here and there, appearing and disappearing, everywhere and nowhere. Stimulated by the activity, aware of the opportunities, keenly alert, Amelia wheels in among the streaking mammals and swift fleets of fleeing squid. She lands and takes off repeatedly, trying to keep up with the speeding dolphins. She splashes in among their bubble trails and deep boils and the spraying squid, paddling around excitedly, sometimes clumsily, trying to exploit the possibilities that keep coming and going around her. Her snapping bill mostly misses, registering a loud empty clack. But once, there's the satisfying feel and heft of writhing flesh impaled with the nail of her bill tip. The squid wraps its resisting arms around her bill, and she shakes and worries the life from it. It goes coolly into her belly, and for a while it squirms a little as it warms. She likes the feeling of food inside.

But the main thing, for Amelia, is that the squid are here spawning. And after they spawn they die. And after they die, many float to the surface. And beautiful fresh, floating squid are what makes this trek north worth all the effort. She begins loading up on nice, ice-cold squid. She's finally putting back a little weight and storing extra food.

Here in this rich, cold water, Amelia has company: many other Laysan Albatrosses, a few Black-footed Albatrosses (most of them are much farther east, nearer the continental coast), and very occasionally a rare Short-tailed Albatross from Japan. Amelia doesn't pay much attention to any of them—except when they're zooming in on the same meal.

With her belly feeling full for the first time in weeks, Amelia sails west for a day or so, outside the current edge and into the 48° F (9° C) sub-arctic watermass, until she's fourteen hundred miles from Tern Island. The seesaw between maternity and hunger tips again—and this time maternity easily wins. As if by magic, Amelia lights out on a heading that

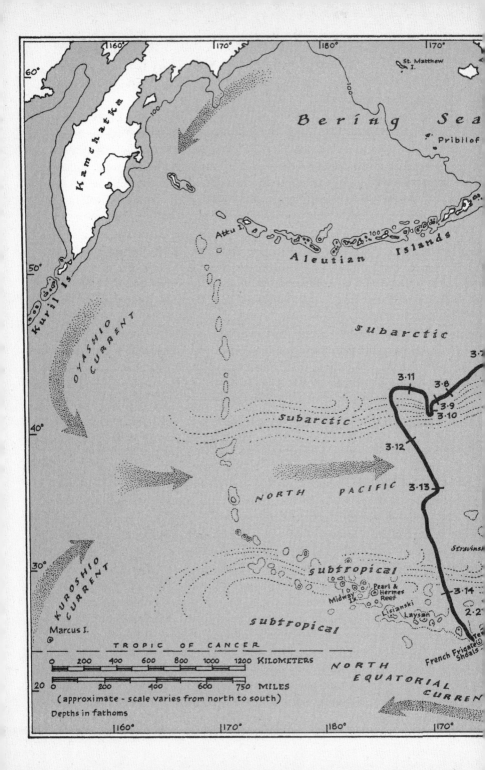

60°

160°   170°   180°   170°

St. Matthew I.

B e r i n g   S e a

Pribilof

100

Kamchatka

100

Kuril is.

50°

Attu I.

100

A l e u t i a n   I s l a n d s

OYASHIO CURRENT

s u b a r c t i c

3.7

40°

s u b a r c t i c

3·11   3·8
                  3·9
                  3·10

3·12

N O R T H   P A C I F I C   3·13

Strevinsk

subtropical

30°

KUROSHIO CURRENT

Midway
Pearl & Hermes Reef
Lisianski
Laysan   3·14

2·2

subtropical

Marcus I.

T R O P I C   O F   C A N C E R

French Frigate Shoals

0   200   400   600   800   1000   1200 KILOMETERS

N O R T H

0   200   400   600   750 MILES

E Q U A T O R I A L   C U R R E N

20°

(approximate - scale varies from north to south)

Depths in fathoms

160°   170°   180°   170°

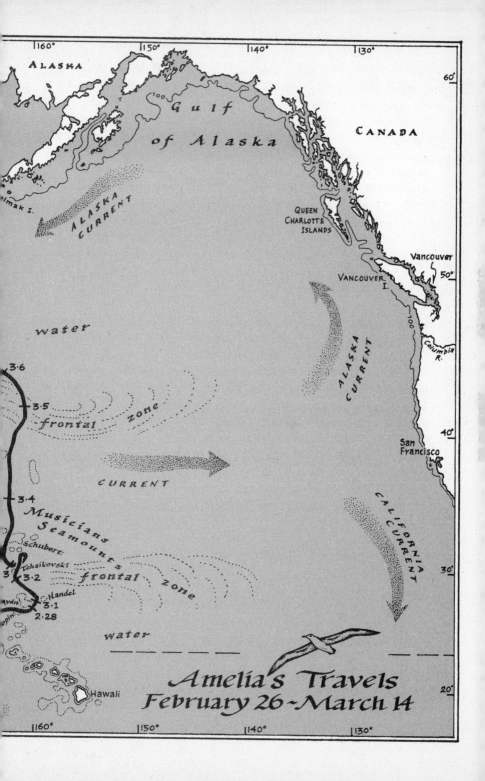

ALASKA

160°   150°   140°   130°

60°

Gulf

of Alaska

100

CANADA

ALASKA
CURRENT

Uimak I.

Queen
Charlotte
Islands

Vancouver

50°

Vancouver I.

water

100

Columbia R.

ALASKA CURRENT

3·6

3·5

frontal   zone

40°

San
Francisco

CURRENT

3·4

CALIFORNIA CURRENT

Musicians
Seamounts

Schubert

30°

3   Tchaikovski   3·2   frontal   zone

aydn   Handel   3·1

2·28

pin

water

20°

Hawaii

Amelia's Travels
February 26 ~ March 14

160°   150°   140°   130°

will take her directly home, and flies for another thirty-two hours, covering 560 miles in a straight line on a strong sidewind, crossing back into subtropical water. During a stormy, gusty, squally, rain-pelting night she drifts a hundred miles to the southwest. Then she streaks straight toward Tern Island again, this time aided by a strong tailwind from a fresh high-pressure weather front. She smells the air growing saltier and warmer as she bores back into tropical waters, back to the domain of terns and boobies and frigatebirds and tunas and tropicbirds. It's all so different and it's all so familiar. After another 730 nonstop miles and thirty hours of straight flying, she again crosses French Frigate Shoals' thundering reef and lands clumsily on Tern Island. It is March 14. After sixteen days at sea, the ground seems oddly unyielding. She still feels as though her body is gliding with gusts and swaying to swells.

On legs that have grown unaccustomed to supporting her weight, she waddles over and calls to a surprisingly large chick. "That you?" To which the chick immediately responds. "Me. Alive." Amelia hasn't seen her mate in weeks, but by the looks of the chick, Dad too has been faithful to his duties, working as hard as Amelia.

Amelia has just returned from a forty-two-hundred-mile odyssey, but does her chick appreciate it? Does she get a moment's rest? Her chick is big enough now to be aggressive, and hasn't been fed in about a week. He practically attacks Amelia, whining and battering her bill with his own hooked beak. This ritual stimulation makes her retch on cue. And the chick scissors his bill into her gullet to catch her presents. Amelia barfs a sizable whole squid and several meaty chunks in the first payload. This immediately goes a long way toward filling the chick, which suddenly pauses to swallow, mucusy strings of goo dangling from the corners of his mouth. Mmm.

No chick could ask for more. But this one does. In maternal devotion, Amelia pours her heart out. On Amelia's next retch, the meal comes as liquefied high-calorie oil, stored from food she caught at the beginning of her journey. Oil squirts from her in a strong brown stream, as though from a pressurized hose. The chick takes all of it, reveling in the satisfaction of liquefaction. About a minute later Amelia leans forward again. Her babe sticks his bill way up into her gullet. Another stream of liquefied matter comes forward. The chick sits back, swallowing. Amelia resumes her upright position. The urgency seems gone; the chick seems finally satisfied. About a minute later, Amelia leans forward one more time. When she steps back, a gooey string stretches between her bill and the chick's, then parts. The chick spends a few minutes wiping its bill in the sand. Then it dozes, a fat little child, healthy and vigorous, content as any youngster could ever be.

Her parental duties discharged, Amelia walks away. She surveys the noisy island, the birds of so many species crisscrossing overhead, the younger albatrosses courting and dancing with the passionate fervor of youth (and no adult responsibilities). Amelia has seen it all before. She's a hardworking mom, and the youthful crowd holds no fascination for her. Amelia registers only that her chick is alive and vigorous, and this means one thing: it will need more food. In a mere ten minutes she's on the runway, good for takeoff.

➤ ➤ ➤

Seabirds are the avian world's undisputed champions of long-range navigation, but nobody knows for sure how they navigate. Unlike land birds, seabirds remain oriented over open ocean, where— to us at least—there are no landmarks; and they do so over *extremely* great distances. Behold one of Amelia's lovely smaller cousins, the Sooty Shearwater. Sooties are long-distance travelers in the Atlantic, but New Zealand's Sooty Shearwaters are most amazing. After being abandoned by their parents a month before they can fly, the young ones make a fifteen-thousand-mile migration—perhaps the longest annual migration in the world—on their first attempt. They head out into the Pacific toward Japan, spend the summer off Alaska and in the Bering Sea, then go down the west coast of North America. Where the ocean is widest, they fly west across the entire Pacific and travel back to New Zealand, to the same island they left. They make that long migration, including its complex directional changes and equator crossings, without any contact with older, experienced birds. If you're following your parents, you don't really need a good navigational system. But if you have to go it alone, like a young Sooty Shearwater, the demands are much, much higher.

We know from experiments that migratory songbirds have two compasses: magnetic and celestial. Seabirds probably do too, but they have hardly been studied because of the difficulties both of keeping them in captivity and of performing good experiments in the wild. Much of what has been learned about the orientation capabilities of songbirds probably applies to seabirds, though. The celestial and magnetic compasses are not as you would imagine. For their celestial compass, young birds are born only with instructions to look for rotating light dots in the night sky and to orient their first migration away from the center of rotation—away from the pole. In other words, they start their migration using just the rotational point of the heavens over Earth's poles. During that first migration, though, they learn star constellations. After they've learned the star map, when the rotational point is covered by clouds they need only to see a few stars and can extrapolate where the rotational point is.

A bird's magnetic compass is even more counterintuitive. After decades of studying navigation, we still don't understand the mechanism by which birds perceive and orient to magnetic fields. We know that they do so, because experiments clearly demonstrate that changing the magnetic field in a laboratory changes the orientation activity of wild-caught birds during the migration season. But we haven't found a magnetic sensory organ. Many kinds of animals have magnetite in their bodies, including birds. Some fishes have magnetite in their nasal region, in close association with nerves and in proximity to the brain, suggesting strongly that these fish can navigate with a magnetic-polarity compass like the ones people use on boats and in airplanes. But in birds magnetite is usually found in bones, not consistently in association with nervous tissue or the brain, as you'd expect if they are using it for navigation. Nonmigratory birds also have magnetite, suggesting it's not there for navigation. Further, birds have an inclination compass, not a polarity compass. That means they can't distinguish between north and south across the equator. Their magnetic-orientation ability allows them to understand only whether they are headed toward the equator or toward the pole. Near the equator, where our mechanical magnetic-polarity compasses work perfectly, a bird is unable to orient magnetically; it can't sense the polarity of the magnetic field. (Birds migrating across the equator probably switch to celestial navigation, using the sun and stars until they can get magnetically oriented again.) If they were using the magnetite for navigating, they should have a polarity compass like the mechanical compasses we use, and they should not have the inclination compass they actually have. So why do they have magnetite at all? Dr. Henrik Mouritsen, who has worked on Waved (Galápagos) Albatross navigation with Dave Anderson, believes that birds use magnetite simply to get rid of excess iron; it has nothing to do with navigating or orienting.

Dr. Mouritsen has another idea that he is testing. One evening at Dave's field camp on the Galápagos island of Española, while an albatross that had just returned from a foraging trip sat under our table with its chick, Dr. Mouritsen explained to us: "A very fascinating thing about birds' magnetic orientation is that they can't do it in total darkness. In white light as faint as starlight, but with no view of stars, they move in the right direction using purely magnetic cues. Now the thing is: if you then test them under green light, they're fine. If you do it in blue light, they're fine. If you give them red light, they're equally active—but unoriented. They see—they're jumping around—but they cannot orient to a magnetic field in red light." Drawing on these clues, Dr. Mouritsen has theoretically worked out a mechanism by which birds might *see* Earth's magnetic field. He says, "The theorized visual mechanism could not give information on north and south, only on equator versus pole— exactly the information the birds are actually somehow acquiring." If, after several years of experimentation, he turns out to be right, his discovery of a mechanism by which birds see magnetic fields could make him famous. Meanwhile, the mystery remains. We know that seabirds use the sun and stars, that they have a magnetic compass of some kind, and that they rely on their unusually sensitive sense of smell. But nobody really understands how seabirds accomplish their great feats of navigational magic. Yet navigate they surely do, over vast, seemingly bleak distances.

ALBATROSSES FLY SO FAR for one reason: to get to where food is. But another way of looking at it is that they fly so far because they have no way of getting their chicks closer to the better foraging zones. These albatrosses' tropical breeding sites, so far from abundant food, are just an accident of island formation. If suitable islands existed closer to these food-filled frontal zones, they would be graced by nesting albatrosses. The Aleutians are too ironclad with cold during late fall and winter and early spring, while the birds are laying, incubating, and hatching fragile chicks. No islands lie closer to the food and also have eight months of weather eggs and chicks can survive in. And weather aside, most islands closer to the food in this ocean—off Alaska and British Columbia—have things like eagles, bears, and otters. You don't leave a fattened chick alone on places like that and expect to see it again. So there seems no suitable real estate that would afford a shorter commute.

It seems hardly to matter. Albatrosses are well forged to endure long trips. Their high-efficiency long-distance dynamic soaring, ability to store liquefied food as high-energy oil for fueling, and their chicks' ability to survive prolonged fasting all indicate long accommodation to tough conditions necessitating extreme travel. For albatrosses, sparse times and long trips are nothing new. Albatrosses wield distance as their weapon against deprivation.

Albatross travels are everywhere prodigious. Light-mantled Sooty Albatrosses forage an average of a thousand miles from their nests. One Wandering Albatross with a chick in the nest logged a jaw-dropping single round-trip of nine thousand miles between feedings.

After breeding, unchained from the need to feed a chick, albatrosses begin roaming enormously. On July 2, 1992, one Wanderer that had lost its chick left the subantarctic island of South Georgia (the large, glacier-crusted island twelve hundred miles east of the southern tip of South America) for the edge of the continental shelf off central Argentina. It then flew east, crossing the Atlantic to spend nine days foraging in waters well off South Africa. From there the bird lit east again, and by August 9, when its transmitter's battery failed, it was within a few days' travel of Australia. In under five weeks, it had traveled fifteen thousand miles from its nest.

Northern Royal, Chatham, and Buller's Albatrosses from New Zealand cross the entire South Pacific in as little as seven to ten days to spend their nonbreeding time foraging in the Humboldt Current off Chile and Peru. Some New Zealand birds, including the Northern Royal Albatross, pass the tip of South America and continue through the Drake Passage into the Atlantic, where they forage over the Patagonian Shelf east of Argentina. (One arrived off the Falkland Islands, over eight thousand miles away, eight days after leaving New Zealand.) Some Northern Royals continue to the east, completing a circumpolar route.

Albatrosses making global circumnavigations must share Albert Einstein's view of the universe: that if you go far enough in a straight line you will eventually come back to the place you started. Or perhaps they are inspired by T. S. Eliot:

> *We shall not cease from exploration*
> *And the end of all our exploring*
> *Will be to arrive where we started*
> *And know the place for the first time.*

Check the odometer of an albatross half a century old: Albatrosses spend 95 percent of their lives at sea. They fly up to 90 percent of the time they're over water, and the smallest fraction of time any tracked albatross spent flying was 60 percent. Their slowest average flying speed

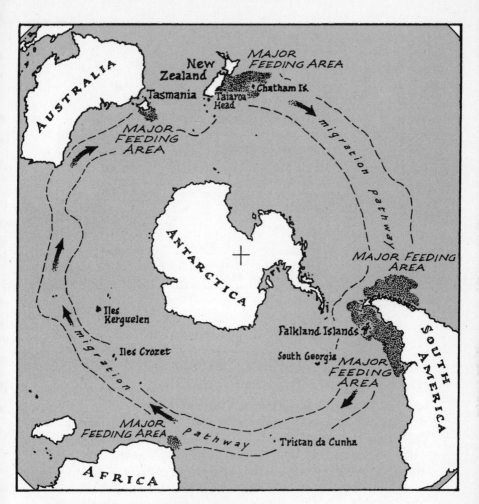

Circumnavigation Routes
of Royal Albatrosses *from New Zealand*

is about fifteen miles an hour. So here's some conservative arithmetic: 95 percent of 365 days is 347 days; over fifty years, that's 17,350 days at sea. Sixty percent of each day is 14.4 hours; flying at fifteen miles per hour gives 216 miles for each day at sea. That yields an extraordinary low-end estimate: 3,747,600 miles.

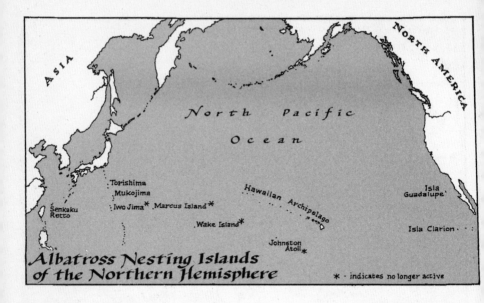

Albatross Nesting Islands of the Northern Hemisphere

* - indicates no longer active

⊱ ⊱ ⊱

ABOUT 1.8 MILLION ALBATROSS PAIRS breed around the world each year. (Albatross numbers worldwide have fluctuated widely since they began finding people in their world; there were many more until the mid-1800s, and probably far fewer in the early 1900s, than today.) Of the current total, two species—Amelia's species, the Laysan Albatross; and the Southern Hemisphere's Black-browed Albatross—contribute a disproportionate share: 1.3 million breeding pairs.

Most albatross species exist in surprisingly low numbers. Of the twenty-four species, four species have annual worldwide breeding populations of 5,000 or fewer pairs; ten have between 5,000 and 20,000 pairs; four have 20,000 to 50,000 pairs; four between 50,000 and 100,000 pairs. No species currently has a population numbering between 100,000 and 500,000 breeding pairs. The Laysan and Black-browed Albatrosses have each had more than half a million breeding pairs in recent years.

The number of pairs breeding annually is only part of the census, because many adults don't breed every year, and the seas harbor many nonbreeding juveniles in their first years of life. For example, though the Laysan Albatross has annual breeding numbers in the vicinity of half

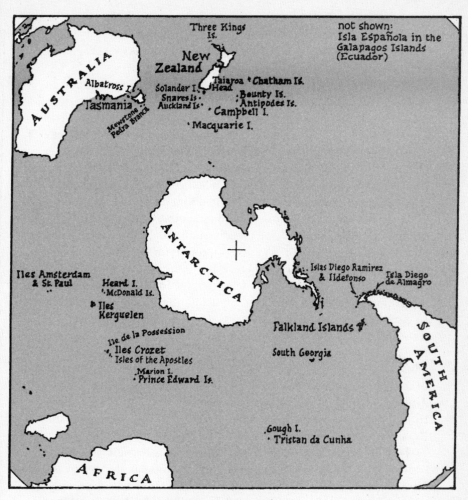

Albatross Nesting Islands of the Southern Hemisphere

a million nesting pairs, the total population of adults and juveniles is currently about 2.4 million birds. Amelia's neighbors the Black-footeds nest with about 60,000 breeding pairs annually, but roughly 300,000 individuals in total roam the North Pacific.

Albatrosses breed on only twenty-two islands or island groups in the entire Southern Hemisphere, and only six islands or island groups in the North Pacific. Between roughly the mid-1700s and the early 1900s sealers, whalers, settlers, and especially feather hunters exterminated albatrosses from about a dozen or so islands.

Despite the vast sea regions they roam, each albatross species puts all its eggs in surprisingly few baskets. Of the twenty-four species, fourteen species breed on only one or two islands or island groups. Ten species breed only on New Zealand islands. Another six likewise breed only on islands of single nations. All the albatrosses in the world breed on islands under the claim of only ten nations (Australia, New Zealand, the United States, South Africa, Mexico, Chile, Ecuador, Japan, and Southern Hemisphere possessions of the United Kingdom and France).

The Black-browed Albatross—the only southern albatross currently maintaining more than a million breeding individuals (there are 700,000 breeding pairs, plus juveniles at sea)—accounts for over half of all albatrosses in the Southern Hemisphere. While it breeds on a dozen islands or island groups, three-quarters of its population breeds on just two islands in the Falklands, and that population has recently dropped by 17 percent. The Wandering Albatross, *Diomedea exulans,* nests on only six island groups spread throughout the whole Southern Hemisphere. Ninety-nine percent of the Northern Royal Albatross population (8,500 pairs) breeds on New Zealand's Chatham Islands. Ninety-nine percent of the Southern Royal Albatross population (8,000 pairs) breeds on New Zealand's Campbell Island. Virtually all Galápagos (or Waved) Albatrosses breed on one small scrubby island devoid of freshwater, Isla Española, in the Galápagos Islands.

Two-thirds of the world's Laysan Albatross pairs nest on Midway Atoll, making up the world's single largest albatross colony. Midway and Laysan Island combined host over 90 percent of the species' world population. Small numbers of Laysan Albatrosses breed on other scattered islands: a few dozen pairs on two widely distant Mexican islands, a handful at Wake, a few dozen in the Bonin Islands, several hundred pairs on Torishima, possibly several pairs on other islands. But this little chain—the Northwestern Hawaiian Islands—is the nesting ground for about 99 percent of the world's Laysan Albatrosses and 97 percent of the global population of Black-footed Albatrosses. That's why I say it's a lot of eggs in very few baskets.

>‒ >‒ >‒ >‒ >‒ >‒ >‒

A SMALL WORLD

BY MARCH, those youngsters still alive at Tern Island have grown quite a bit. Sitting upright, the chunky chicklets look like dark, downy pineapples. This is very interesting, but I've been invited to travel a little farther along this island chain, to fabled Laysan Island. You don't turn down that kind of invitation. Laysan has been praised by Smithsonian Institution scientists as having "the most remarkable biota of any island in the Northwestern Hawaiian Islands." Ornithologist Craig S. Harrison has written that Laysan presents "one of the finest remaining wildlife spectacles on earth." If someone asks if you want to go, you don't say you'll check your calendar and get back to them. You immediately answer, "Yes."

Laysan has no airstrip. Access is by ship only, a week from Honolulu; even from here at French Frigate Shoals, Laysan lies days distant.

Though Laysan is the second largest single island in this chain, it's small anyway: under a mile by two, just 1.4 square miles in area. Only the skimpiest skeleton crew—three to six people—is maintained there to work on seals, ducks, seabirds, and habitat restoration. Now it's time for the five-month rotation, time to take out the "survivors" and bring in the fresh team. And so the bow of the U.S. scientific ship *Townsend Cromwell* is pointed west, following the afternoon sun.

I'm assigned to share a small, windowless cabin with George Grigorovitch, a large man with a weight lifter's build, a shaved head, and a down-curving mustache. He works the night shift in the engine room. The cabin is about ten feet square, crowded with lockers and drawers and some storage boxes. It's a cramped, dark space, part storage unit, part prison cell. Grigorovitch has no other home. "Seven years in that bunk," he woofs in his husky voice. He says he doesn't like the work here anymore, doesn't like the sea, but needs the paycheck. Says, "I can't afford to live ashore." He means that financially, but it's an odd remark in a world where a lot of people with skinny paychecks manage somehow to live on land. I wonder what his comment fails to reveal.

I WAKE IN THE COOL blackness of the windowless cabin after a span of hours rich in dreaming, my wristwatch the only real proof that the dreamtime has run out. I come into the blinding sunshine and warmth of the deck of the traveling ship, where sea and sky rim a round horizon. Here's a thought: you can gaze upon any type of terra firma—from savannahs to deep jungles to the highest mountains—and presume that your legs could get you there. But stand on any boat's deck, or upon any shore staring seaward, and you are reminded that legs are useless on three-quarters of Earth's surface. Whales and dolphins, descendants of quadrupeds, came to resemble fish so they could triple the size of their world. Their farewell to legs took ages, but if you're a person, to get anywhere at sea you need a vessel. And that's what makes boats special; they're the magic carpets of most of the planet's surface. Boats carry us to visit those strangely alien creatures of the vast watery reaches where we were never meant to go, the off-limits spaces and limitless faces of the Deep. A plane can get you over an ocean, but only a boat can really get you in. Boats are unmatched cheating devices.

A large flyingfish has flown aboard during the night and expired on deck. I pull open its big, lacy, cellophaney, dragonfly-like wings. The first albatross—a speck on the horizon rendered unmistakable by that wind-stiffened, bounding progress—appears briefly, then is lost among the rippled blue distances of the sea. Then, for hours, sailing albatrosses are our constant companions. Soon they're joined by a frigatebird and several boobies. It's easy to imagine the solace and excitement explorers felt at the sight of increasing numbers of birds. Birds meant they were again in the company of creatures like themselves—ocean roamers who needed land occasionally—and that an island or continent must surely lie just beyond the blue horizon.

An unsettled breeze has made the sea a wind-roughened, grizzled white. The boat is rocking a bit, but at the moment I find the effect soothing and pleasant.

A brief exposition on swaying: Everything on a ship sways, even in superlatively benign weather. Everything hanging becomes a pendulum. Everyone uses a lot of energy just standing upright. Because of this, you eat twice as much as usual, yet maintain your weight. Putting your leg into a pair of pants while standing becomes a game of skill and peril. You shower leaning hard against the stall or hanging on to the pipes. Cups hanging in the galley become little metronomes of the sea's rhythm. In your bunk you must put a leg at an angle to the rest of your body, to check your motion. Otherwise, you end up rolling like a log all night, rather than sleeping like one. A crew member says, "I can tell who'll get seasick as I watch newcomers climb aboard. The stiff-walking ones are going to have trouble. Those who seem springy and at ease will do better." You can't cruise away if you ain't got that sway.

On a ship, time seems to thicken and coagulate. Events stretch out. Because of the motion of the boat, everything from traveling a flight of stairs to getting out of bed takes longer. There is hardly anywhere to go; your options for walking are reduced to the confines within a couple of hundred feet. The inactivity has a strong soporific effect on anyone who doesn't have immediate work to do. Even attempting to read on deck usually triggers a nap. Eating and sleeping expands to dominate the days. The drone and vibration of the engine, the constant rolling, and the confinement lead to lethargy.

The biologists and a couple of crew members and I have gravitated indolently to the rear deck, where we're watching the world wave by. The new biology crew for Laysan consists of two Monk Seal people, plus two interns whose respective jobs are to continue studies of the endangered Laysan Duck and to help eradicate an introduced grass called sandbur that destroys bird-nesting habitat. A second team is headed farther, to Lisianski Island.

A significant aspect of working on Laysan or Lisianski entails being dropped on an island for a span of several months, hundreds of miles from other people and days from rescue in even the best conditions. It's too far to be reached by helicopter. Any rescue or evacuation would have to be done by ship—minimum cost: $80,000 (so you'd better be dying).

It's not for everyone.

But some people return again and again. Petra Bertilsson, blond, mid-thirties, is sitting with a blue shirt shielding her legs from the sun. She's from Sweden, where she was a newspaper and magazine writer. She'd long been interested in ocean conservation, but, she says, "I was always afraid of the sciences." Yet she took a deep breath and made a major life change, moving from Sweden to the University of Hawaii. "Moving entailed selling an apartment and breaking up with my fiancé and committing to five years of schooling for a bachelor's in zoology. Ja, it was a big commitment. But I've never been happier than I am out here. Here you can focus. You're always in the moment here. It is very satisfying."

Brenda Becker, the lead Monk Seal biologist for Laysan, agrees that the commitment isn't for everyone. Tall and thin, with wavy brown hair, she was raised in Nevada and studied forestry at the University of Nevada. "Until," she says, "I found out that 'forestry' meant cutting down trees." So she got a dual bachelor's degree in range management and wildlife, and has worked in coal-mine reclamation, goose management, caribou ecology, endangered-tortoise management, Bighorn Sheep reintroduction, and even on the U.S. congressional staff. Brenda is coming for her twelfth season. "Mainly," she says, "I come back because I know the seals and I want to see how their lives have progressed and unfolded. It's like soap opera, but better than TV. And for five months, you have beachfront property. I like the simplicity. I'm glad we don't have a phone. I like that you can get immersed in your work. And you're surrounded by wildlife. Of course, some people decide it's not for them. Mind-set is important. And it's hard on relationships." (Brenda's boyfriend, Walter Machado, had been at the wharf to see her off the morning the *Cromwell* left Honolulu. When he kissed Brenda for the last time for the next five months, he made it count.)

Amber Pairis, a veteran here who will be working on Lisianski Island this year, adds, "The flies and ants can be annoying, but the benefits are *so* overwhelming. The islands are just magical. You fall asleep with the sound of the terns and you wake to the most breathtaking view of the ocean. When you walk on the beach the footsteps are yours alone. You're doing something most people will never get a chance to do. So a few flies and ants"—she shrugs—"they're insignificant."

Petra, with a slight challenge in her voice, says, "Not always just a *few* ants, ja?" To me she explains, "Sometimes ants are everywhere. Whenever you were trying to eat, or drink a cup of tea, or anything, there were ants all over the place. If it's a hot night and you're sweating in your tent, you'll wake and there will be ants stuck in the sweat on your body."

"How many?" I ask. "Two? Three? Dozens?"

She says, "Oh no. More."

"Hundreds?"

"*Thousands*. Ja, stuck on your body. It was pretty impressive there for a while. Another night I woke up because there was a spider on my neck. I started looking around with a flashlight and saw there were about twenty spiders in my bed. I had to carry the spiders outside the tent, one by one. I'm sure they came right back in. But I won't kill any animal."

"So are you a vegetarian?"

"I started eating chicken last year. I would eat fish, but I object to fishing practices. If I knew that it was from a truly sustainable fishery with good fishing practices, I might feel differently. I just don't want to be part of any kind of mass-produced fish from large-scale fisheries. When you see big, ocean-roaming fish free-swimming, they're so beautiful. You know the Moonfish? That was my favorite fish to eat, until I saw them alive."

The two greenhorns—not counting myself—are Rebecca Woodward and Alex Wegmann. Rebecca is a very young looking twenty-four-year-old with straight, light brown hair and lots of freckles. She's eager, a little bit nervous. "Hopefully it'll look good on my résumé, but I also want to see whether I can live so remotely for five months." Pretty soon she'll know the answer.

Alex is twenty-two years old and on the move. In his sophomore year he spent a month in Nicaragua, studying coffee farming in a village with no electricity, no running water, no hospital. "There, if your automobile breaks, you fix it by taking parts from the chicken coop." He then spent six months in Australia studying aboriginal society and linguistics. He was shocked to learn that well into the twentieth century ranchers could legally shoot aboriginal people for "trespassing" on land that for forty thousand years had been theirs.

I'm sure Rebecca and Alex will thrive on Laysan, then be ready for new challenges elsewhere. It's an unforgettable sojourn to an unheard-of nook of the world. Somehow, the people coming here have slipped the noose of the usual bind and grind.

There are career downsides, though. Some people seem to get marooned. As one person observed, "This work is a paid ticket to adventure, but I've seen it put people far behind professionally. Doing this for more than a couple of years tends not to be a winning strategy if you're interested in a conventional career eventually, such as in academia or running a research program." Still, convention is not for everyone.

Clouds move in, their big shadows turning the sea surface from cobalt to a mottled blue-black. Ray Bolland comes aft and joins us. Born and raised in Hawaii, Ray says he's "a local kid who has made it into the big field of science." He's leading a survey of the lost and discarded fishing netting hung up on the reefs—a constant danger to the wildlife. A later cruise with a larger crew of divers will return to try, for the first time, to systematically remove lost fishing nets from the entire island chain. So far, Ray has led localized cleanups on several islands.

One method of locating lost nets is for the ship to circle an island slowly while towing a snorkeler who scans the reef below. Dr. John Lamkin, the ship's commander, says, "Hey, Ray, tell Carl about how you like to be towed behind the boat nude."

"Not since the jellyfish incident, I don't."

Brenda says, "Remember Theresa being followed by the Tiger Shark while she was getting towed?"

Lamkin says, "No Tiger Shark in the Pacific is mean enough to take on Theresa."

When talk turns to Alaska's endangered Steller Sea Lion, Lamkin loses his levity. "In 1986 I was up in international waters between Alaska and Russia—that area called the Donut Hole—and the fishing vessels were stacked up like lawn mowers about to cut a whole lawn in one pass. I don't see how *any* fish survived. We caught a lot of Steller Sea Lions even in short tows of our research net. How many the commercial fleet caught, no one would admit. Most sea lions caught alive got shot by fishermen. I'm sure they killed a *bunch*. I'm not surprised they're endangered."

The Steller Sea Lion remains imperiled, and now food shortages seem to be a problem (for unclear reasons possibly related to fishing or climate change—or both). But the struggle to secure their future isn't over. In 1993, the United States, China, South Korea, Poland, and the Russian Federation agreed to stop fishing in the area where Captain Lamkin witnessed such excess. Under 1992 amendments to the Marine Mammal Protection Act, it is illegal for U.S. fishers to shoot marine mammals. And in the eastern Bering Sea, all boats over sixty-five feet (the vast majority) must now carry a government observer. Things change. Some things improve. When they do, we can usually thank a few idealistic people who worked very, very hard.

A Black-footed Albatross circumnavigates the ship on fixed wings, crossing a rainbow on the horizon. It's a good-luck omen if ever there was. The bird and the surrounding sea seem right and comforting, fused and eternal. But the fleeting rainbow makes a more apt metaphor for how rapidly the sea can change. For the moment, though, I'm satisfied to realize that any day one can squeeze metaphors from clouds and ponder eternity in rainbows is a day well lived.

. . .

By MIDAFTERNOON the birds have thinned. The sea seems again devoid and elemental. Time slows and gets syrupy. The ship's crew hammers and paints and scrapes rust. The afternoon fades. In the inactivity the mind can wander to worries at home, but I fix my attention on the waves until I am free of thought and the world acquires a feeling dreamier even than sleep.

At SUNSET SOME OF US are on the bridge for the best view, watching the sun give itself to the sea, savoring the day's blushing afterglow. As the pilothouse goes dark, the officers place transparent red plastic over the instrument screens to dim them. Outside at the rail, we look down at the glowing bioluminescence in the bow waves—tiny living things making mysterious light. We look up at Venus, Saturn, and Jupiter, arrayed in a line ascending from the horizon, embedded in very dense stars. The boat is rocking gently, the forecast mild. The overall effect becomes hypnotic and calming.

By SUNRISE, LAYSAN ISLAND is in view. Today the new biology crew is getting dropped off for five months. But for the next five days the old crew will remain on the island, training the newcomers. Meanwhile, the ship will leave to go farther west to Lisianski Island, where it will drop off that crew for their five months. When the ship returns here on its way home, it will pick up the old crew and me, and take us out.

We are still a few miles away, plowing toward a little bulge of land. Laysan keeps a low, sandy profile, partially clad with windswept vegetation. Black-rock reefs armor the island's surfy perimeter. A central saline lake, unseen from offshore, occupies a fifth of Laysan's area, holding water much saltier than the sea. The sky over Laysan is impressively dusted with seabirds. The ocean here crawls with albatrosses. Within view, hundreds—perhaps thousands—are converging from millions of square miles. Sweep the calm ocean with your binoculars and your eyes reveal birds almost everywhere you look. A hundred or so albatrosses are bobbing in a big "raft" about a mile and a half offshore, as if exchanging stories about their recent journeys. But actually no person knows what they're doing.

Standing at the rail looking shoreward, I say, "It's absolutely lovely."

Petra responds, "I think you'll like it. A lot, I think."

There are rules for going ashore here, and they're unlike anything you've ever heard of. Any clothing—*all* clothing—must be brand-new. New shoes, new socks, new shoelaces. New underwear. New hats. And everything has to be frozen for several days, until the minute before you put it on for shore landing. This leads to the interesting sensation of donning frosted underwear.

Jerry Leinecke of the U.S. Fish and Wildlife Service did a pretty convincing job of explaining the rationale. Jerry has devoted fifteen years to protecting and restoring these islands. He appealed to me: "Please don't think our rules are silly. It's hard to get people to understand why they need new shoes and frozen underwear. But if you're me behind the budgets you realize that introduction of an alien grass may mean crashes in seabird populations or even extinction of a species, and that it will cost a decade and millions of dollars to get a type of grass off an island because somebody had seeds on their socks."

His example is not hypothetical. The grass they've been trying to eradicate was probably introduced to Laysan as a seed on a scientist, perhaps on their shoelace or in their pant cuff. If it seems like a long shot that it arrived here accidentally via scientists' clothing, consider this: I noticed it growing right out of the wharf in Honolulu where the research boat docks.

Leinecke continued, "Something as simple as ants hiding in cardboard boxes can change the ecology of whole islands. The ants now introduced on those islands need moisture, and one of the only moisture sources is hatchling birds. I've seen chicks get eaten alive by introduced ants."

After hearing that, putting on frosted underwear seems the least I can do to help. And hidden in his comments is an interesting point: when, like Petra, you wake up with thousands of ants stuck to the sweat on your body, remember that no ants of any kind occurred naturally in Hawaii. They hitchhiked with people.

These islands are excellent examples of places that exist within a fragile ecological balance. Because of their remoteness, the living things here have evolved specific ways of coexisting. Introductions of new things can threaten long and stable intimate relationships. Prior to people, neither native ants nor earthworms perturbed Hawaiian soils. No amphibians, no land reptiles. No terrestrial snakes. No frogs. No lizards. Nary a mosquito. Prior to the Polynesians, no mammal's foot had ever fallen upon Hawaiian rock. Hawaii's *largest* native land animal was a small goose—now endangered. Since the Polynesians and Europeans arrived, much of Hawaii's native fauna has been driven extinct or to extinction's brink by the rodents, diseases, insects, and plants that tend to round out our luggage.

The alien grass *Cenchrus,* or sandbur, was first noticed on Laysan in the 1960s. It's native to Central America but has spread worldwide, thanks to tenacious little seed burs that cling to everything. As late as the 1980s, its consequences here weren't recognized, and visiting scientists were not directed to even check their socks for seeds.

By the early '90s it was out of control, covering a third of the island with dense mats, displacing the native bunchgrass. Trading one grass for another might not seem problematic. But to wildlife the grasses differ radically. The native grass is needed by birds; the sandbur repels the birds.

Many birds rely on the native bunchgrass for nesting, because its tall blades flop over, forming little hollows that provide critical shade for surface nesters like tropicbirds, Christmas Shearwaters, Laysan Ducks, and the Laysan Finch. The bunchgrass roots also support burrows for underground nesters like Bonin Petrels. Conversely, the sandbur's dense, matlike growth *excludes* surface birds, and its root structure causes burrows to collapse. The combination makes it a real threat to the birds. So the Fish and Wildlife Service decided to control, or possibly eliminate, the evil weed. The project's been a huge success, because it exploits one of humanity's chief talents: a predilection to eradicate living things.

The young interns here are titled "restoration ecologists." That's a glamorous way of saying "weed puller." But the work is critical to hundreds of thousands of birds at risk of losing their nesting habitat and, in the case of the Laysan Finch and Laysan Duck, their last toeholds on existence. The work is even more important because few places like this remain. These islands are, as Dr. Beth Flint of the U.S. Fish and Wildlife Service emphasizes, "essentially the only undisturbed seabird nesting islands left in the Pacific."

That's true now. But Laysan was for decades plagued by problems wrought by the few people who reached here. Ironically, Laysan once had a different vegetation problem: it was devegetated. Rabbits released in 1903 multiplied true to cliché. They had no predators. And the vegetation here had no evolutionary experience with grazers. By 1923 virtually nothing growing remained. When the Tanager Expedition arrived at Laysan in April that year, photographer Donald R. Dickey wrote, "In my wildest pessimism I had not feared such utter extirpation of every living plant. . . . This is a glaring desert . . . the utter lack of green relief makes the drifted coral sand almost unbearable to the eyes." He reported only two small patches of close-cropped weed "that still support a remnant of the cursed host." The Tanager team brought poisoned alfalfa—a kind of Trojan Mr. Greenjeans. All of Laysan's famished rabbits ravaged the ruse, and died.

But by then most land birds were already extinct, or doomed. Seabirds requiring shade—such as tropicbirds—were scarce. Dickey wrote on April 9, 1923, "Not a trace of rail or honeyeater or millerbird could we find." But two days later, one of the party found three honeyeaters in a tobacco patch (which the rabbits, though starving, would not eat). Dickey remarked that "their charming song is out of proportion to their size," adding, "Old age and death now inevitably stalk this childless remnant of a vanishing species." Twelve days after that, a sandstorm finished the last three Laysan Honeyeaters. A few days later, the party saw the last two doomed rails on Laysan. (Some Laysan Rails had been transplanted to Midway a few years earlier, where they thrived until rats arrived.) Somehow the Laysan Finch survived, as did the lovely duck, which was down to fewer than ten individuals. Their future remains uncertain. Some of the problems the ducks now have—such as their chronically poor reproduction—probably result from extreme inbreeding, stemming from that time when they were flickering at the edge of extinction.

WE ANCHOR OFFSHORE and spend several hours loading enough supplies for half a dozen working scientists to survive and thrive until the planet has conveyed us all to the far side of the sun. We transfer hundreds of water jugs and waterproof buckets of food, clothing, equipment, and books over the side of the ship and into inflatable outboard boats.

Eventually it's time for us to crack open our crisply frosted underwear and go ashore ourselves. Stone reefs are piling treacherous breakers where we must land. There's one little opening in the reef; we have to go through it. Our boat pilot, John Sikes, must time our arrival carefully. He maneuvers our boat just ahead of one of the swells, then guns it as the wave is cresting, so that for a minute we're almost surfing. The commander, Dr. Lamkin, is with us, and for a moment we're all yelling like cowboys. Lamkin shouts to Sikes, "And we *pay* you for having fun like this!" With surprising smoothness the craft slides onto a white sandy beach necklaced with a gleaming line of lapping wavelets. All along the shoreline stand little groups of Brown Noddies, sprinkled like handfuls of raisins in the sugary sand.

Sikes says he can't imagine spending five months here. I can. Russ Bradley, who *has* been here for five months—and looks it—is on the beach. He has unruly curly blond hair and a woolly blond beard. He's almost too eager to greet us, instantly super talkative—almost too friendly. "You guys got lucky with the weather for landing. Real lucky. Yesterday we had eight-foot waves where you landed. Last week, forget it—we had fifteen-footers. They were just spectacular. But you couldn't have come in. No way." He abruptly adds, "Excuse me if I'm overly chatty. We've been the only people for four hundred miles."

In fact he's so chatty that he reminds me of a scene from the book *Cry of the Kalahari,* when the two authors realize they are compulsively talkative after emerging from months in the African bush.

Russ suddenly says, "I hope you don't think that I'm talking too much—like that scene in *Cry of the Kalahari* when they come out of the bush and overwhelm everyone."

Michele Reynolds, a biologist who has been working with the endangered ducks, also comes to greet us. There's a lot to do while we talk. Mainly, we have to move about 250 sealed buckets and water jugs from the beach to the tent camp. Some buckets have essential equipment. Some say things like ALEX—BATHING SUITS, FLIP-FLOPS, HATS; or PETRA. COFFEE.

The new gang's all here: Brenda, Petra, Alex, and Rebecca, for the next five-month stint. And Ray Bolland has come ashore briefly.

EVEN COMPARED TO Tern Island, Laysan sets a new standard for remote. Tern Island, with its runway and barracks and administrators and boats and videos and various work teams, seems a booming human metropolis compared to Laysan's castaways living in tents. And while Tern hums with wildlife, Laysan *roars.* The birds are incomparably more abundant—something I could not have imagined. Tern Island has perhaps a hundred thousand Sooty Terns, which seems like a lot when you're trying to shout over them. But Laysan has something like one *million.* Here you feel the heat of life at full burn. Laysan seems like a place we're not meant to see, as if you've put the whole world behind you. The initial impression here is of such stunning island beauty that I almost cannot see—I automatically overlook—the beach debris washed ashore from all points Pacific.

Veils of rain have smudged the western sky awhile, but it's been sunny and hot here. Now I turn and notice a heavy, dark cloud steamrolling our way. Hardly have I finished saying, "It looks like rain," when strike the first drops of a pelting, stinging storm, driven by unruly gusts. The good ship *Cromwell,* big and white as she is, and anchored less than a mile off, disappears behind thick curtains of downpour. The sky behind us darkens to an angry-looking blue-black bruise. But the foreground brightens, and now the light becomes extraordinary. The white Fairy Terns are no longer white—they're glowing like luminous flying pearls.

When the rain clears, we walk up the beach for a wider view. From here we can see albatrosses for acre upon acre, over the dunes and in the swales, over two gently undulating miles. So dense are they that in the distance, the bright breasts of Laysan Albatrosses—their black capes notwithstanding—whiten the ground.

WE GO UP TO THE TENTS. One is the kitchen and headquarters. The others are for sleeping and storing some supplies. Water jugs, equipment barrels, waterproof buckets, and scientific gear surround the tents as if we're all shipwrecked. Tame Laysan Finches that exist nowhere else are poking around the buckets and gear. Take off your sandals to go inside, and a fearless, curious finch or two will immediately investigate your abandoned footwear. They're rather drab looking, but after the honking and wailing and croaking and braying of seabirds, the finches' sweet call provides a startling reminder of the continents, of land—of *home.*

You have to be careful getting out of your tent. You could easily step on a young albatross. One large chick outside my tent is playing with a sock that has fallen from a clothesline, shaking it like a puppy would.

There's no outhouse, just an outdoor seat over a pit latrine, surrounded by bushes on three sides, with a wide view of the sea. The latrine—the loo—is referred to by the Hawaiianized term "the loo'a." One Brown Noddy likes sitting at the loo'a with you, only half an arm's length away, communing at the commode's commanding view.

WHAT'S LIFE LIKE HERE for months on end? We ask Michele Reynolds what they've been eating recently. She answers, "Canned food. We ran out of tofu a few months ago. Then onions. *That* really hurt. Then we ran out of cans of those nicely cut string beans." She turns abruptly to me and says, "So what's happening in the world?"

Considering where I've been recently, I'm not the best person to ask. I punt. Russ is part of the team that's been here, but he got far enough into the outside world today to have an answer, and he's eager to share: he tells everyone here that he went onboard the *Cromwell* in the afternoon and drank orange juice. Everyone in his cohort is so impressed and envious, it's a little spooky.

Brenda comments, "You get inventive here, especially with cooking. We don't just open a can; we make real meals. We are allowed to grow bean sprouts in jars, and we bake bread. We have a good system of fresh sprouts, and we have a good yogurt culture."

Michelle adds, "And a really great sourdough starter that we've made from leftover gravy that went bad in the propane refrigerator."

After five months on Laysan, when the workers returning to civilization glimpse Honolulu's twinkling seaboard from the ship's rail, they say things like, "This is overwhelming." They seem sincerely astonished by all the lights and the buildings. Ashore, they may report that they can't keep pace with the conversation. A little embarrassed, they'll say, "Excuse me, but the conversation seems to be streaming past me."

Petra explains, "The island becomes your *world*. You almost don't *want* to know what's going on outside. Every day is a new adventure to see what's changed with the birds, or what the sea has cast up. You're not tied to house or car payments. Once you live out here, you realize how many of the things we 'can't live without' are really unimportant. Your expectations change in other ways, too. Like, you expect the islands will be pristine because they're so far away. But when you see the washed-up trash, it blows your mind. You'll see it when you get a chance to walk around. Then you realize: *nothing* is really remote."

NEAR SUNSET, Michele, Rebecca, and I walk down long grassy slopes on narrow trails to the shore of the salt lake. Thousands of Laysan Albatrosses line the lake. But the main thing we seek is a look at a lucky duck. These ducks are secretive, hard to see, small. A standing duck could find shade under an albatross's tail.

These ducks were breeding on the nearby island of Lisianski as recently as the mid-1800s. They lived on Maui, Kauai, Oahu, and the Big Island of Hawaii until the Polynesians arrived and found them literally sitting ducks. Now Laysan is the duck's last stand.

The goal of the research is to understand how many ducks exist, and the population trend. The last formal population estimate was ten years ago. Since then, a population crash—caused by drought, food shortages, and parasite infestations—knocked the numbers down by about half. They stand now at around 350. It's Rebecca's job to continue the duck studies and, in a sense, to continue the ducks themselves.

Many are her tasks. She has to count carcasses, to see who died. Because the ducks eat flies, she has to count how many flies land on a sheet of light cloth placed every twenty meters along a transect. She has to count brine shrimp (which the ducks also eat). She has to do observations of individual birds, noting all their behaviors. She has to get samples of duck droppings. She has to do radio tracking. After broods hatch, she has to follow duckling survival.

The only job the ducks have is trying to survive, but it's full-time. Today a frigatebird came down to take a duckling from a brood on the lake. So furiously did the mother duck leap up to defend her baby that the frigatebird, a monster many times the duck's size, gave up the attack and left.

For the moment, the ducks' domain seems placid, and we're fortunate enough to find a brood we can observe through binoculars: a female and her following balls of down, chowing brine flies.

The seething swarms of brine flies here along the shoreline—and at my feet—are matched by the seething swarms of Sooty Terns now in the air overhead. *This* is what something approaching a million birds begins to look like. Alfred Hitchcock got worked up over a few dozen gulls. It didn't take much to scare him.

I come upon a Sooty Tern spread-winged and disabled on the beach. It makes no move while I bend, reach out, and pick it up. Its eyes are bright, its bones are intact, but the keel bone in its breast is sharp with hunger. It has metabolized all its flight muscles as fuel to stay alive and is now emaciated. I place it down and it turns awkwardly tail to the wind, the breeze blowing up through its back feathers. I point it like a weather vane into the wind, to help it with a little comfort, and it manages to scold me—probably the last utterance of its long, wide-awake life. I leave this suffering creature behind, unwilling to do the one thing I could to end its misery.

➤ ➤ ➤

*I*N 1896, HUGO SCHAUINSLAND, a young German scientist exploring the remote world with his young wife as his field assistant, spent three months here. One of the first scientists to see Laysan (his name is lent to the Hawaiian Monk Seal, *Monachus schauinslandi*) he captured the excitement of firstborn adventure in his journal.

A stay on the island offers a rare opportunity, seldom surpassed anywhere else on earth, to closely study its wildlife, and especially, the most intimate behaviors of its birds. In our homeland, which has been dominated for thousands of years by human culture, we are no longer able to observe animals in their natural state, because their original behaviors have become dominated by a justified shyness toward our presence; and therefore, we can only obtain the most superficial impressions of them. In contrast, the animals on Laysan behave as they really are, without any fear. They had not yet learned to consider us their enemy, and therefore, we were constantly in a position to study not only their objective behavior, but also and more specifically, their *emotional life* and their *spiritual character*. We were amazed to discover how much direct comparison to human characteristics we were able to observe in a creature which is generally considered, by the majority, to be a 'lower' form of life. . . . Mated pairs cling together in tender love. This is exemplified by the shearwaters, who are not only constantly side by side, but also face one another, gazing lovingly, for hours at a time, into one another's eyes. From time to time, they will tenderly caress one another's neck feathers, whereupon the fondled one will respond by contentedly lowering its head, visibly communicating its appreciation. They are often seen billing . . . which is comparable to our kissing. It is a sign of tenderness that, in the act, they do not wound or hurt each other with their needle-pointed, hooked bills. And yet, I have often experienced the very opposite: a single bite was quite enough to result in a heavily bleeding wound on my hands. . . . Male and female [Sooty Terns] fly tightly above one another, and together, they carry out each maneuver in such tight precision and with such uniform wing-beats, that it seems as if their two bodies were given life by one spirit, and directed by one will. . . . Would we not find this enraptured, coordinated veering through the air, this delightfully rocking, and stormy, wild flight, comparable to the fiery dance of a lovestruck human couple? And how much more affectionate, how much more graceful it seems when performed by the children of the air!

Though Hugo Schauinsland was a serious German scientist, and an obvious romantic, he had his lighter side. "When we felt unbearably hot, we found pleasure in elaborating upon the inhumane idea of how nice it must have been in the chilly halls of the Löenbräu Cellar in Munich," he wrote. Nonetheless, he was deeply moved by his experiences here.

The esthetic impression which the island commands is quite sober-ing and really very grandiose, perhaps also magnified by the thought of the loneliness and solitude that is this tiny grain of sand island amidst the vast watery desert. . . . Here, we learned to understand anew the language of nature, which rarely rings in our ear amidst the noise of culture and civilization. Here we feel like we are back in our true home, withheld from so many of us during our peregrination through modern life. Everyone who, like me, enjoyed the good fortune of delving for a time in such a solitude . . . would agree that the impressions acquired here would last for a lifetime. The thoughts we had there were more serious, and even perhaps deeper; the pettiness of everyday life disap-peared and the dissonances resolved themselves.

Years after leaving Laysan, Schauinsland wrote, "We still experience in our dreams those extraordinary times. . . . The feelings we have are of a longing, yearning desire to be on that tiny island amidst the imposing solitude of the ocean."

THE BONIN PETRELS, which remain unseen all day beneath Laysan's surface, are now in the air in the gathering sunset, fluttering like bats. A few quick flaps and a glide, flaps and a glide. They lilt and tilt back and forth, zigging their zags over the clumped grass. Everywhere you look you see their little forms: the light belly, the dark back with the light chevron mark. They're most visible against the brighter part of the dark-ening sky, then lost to view beneath the dusk horizon.

About 50,000 to 75,000 Bonin Petrel pairs are breeding here. When walking, you try to step into the footsteps of the person ahead, to mini-mize the chances of going through the surface into one of their many sandy burrows. How they find their own nest among the honeycombed thousands, in the dark shadows—among the dense vegetation—can only leave us wondering. What map of their country they must have, to mem-orize the lay of every clump of grass. Or perhaps it is a scent that they are following. Or both; a navigation system that starts visually and switches to scent in final approach. They obviously know where they're going—or there wouldn't be so many of them. Short-distance homing in sea-birds is extraordinarily accurate but poorly understood. Perhaps the most dumbfounding example of pinpoint accuracy is that of a tiny Antarctic albatross relative, the Dove Prion, which finds its exact nest site even when the entire surrounding area is obliterated by snowdrifts it must dig through.

I'm told that a Bonin Petrel can dig about a foot and a half of burrow per night, that it takes them about four or five days to complete one, and that they always make a grassy nest there, where they lay their single egg. Why dig? Who are they hiding from? Is it the desiccating sun they're avoiding? The frigatebirds? In studies of a shearwater species in which some pairs nest underground and some don't, the underground nesters raise more chicks, and it seems that shade is the main benefit. Christmas Shearwaters don't make burrows and are far less abundant. Is the burrow-nesting tactic the winning ticket that makes the Bonins so numerous here? But if so, how do you explain a million surface-nesting Sooty Terns?

Zooming birds are everywhere. Petrels, terns, albatrosses, frigatebirds, noddies—. Often comes the whoosh of wings close by your ears. The middle distance is thickened with them, and toward the island's far end the air simply swarms, *seethes* with birds. At this spot in so vast a sea, a deep, connecting peace arrives with these wings, the core-warming tranquillity of sharing the movement and sound of so many warm-blooded companions.

IT'S ALMOST DARK when we get back to the kitchen tent. Everyone else is inside, talking. Russ, who plays alto sax, has a Paul Desmond recording playing. Desmond's light-as-a-feather tone is instantly recognizable. The next cut is Desmond playing Joni Mitchell's "Song to a Seagull," which seems to perfectly gift-wrap the evening.

I take a chair outside the cook tent, listening to the best of civilization and watching the best of nature. In addition to listening and seeing I'm also smelling—the ocean, plus supper cooking. When the breeze brushes my cheek, the sense-fest is complete.

It's a good night to go to bed early. The petrels land among the tents squeaking and moaning, growling like two balloons rubbing. The albatrosses moo and clack. Sooty Terns deliver a collective white noise like a stadium full of high-pitched cheering fans. The sounds are continual, but uneven. They come in pulses and waves, arriving on gusts of wind. My mind simplified by tiredness, I lie on my cot, listening with my heart to classical music from nature. Like the work of a minimalist composer confined to a limited palette of notes, there are only a few kinds of sounds here: birds, wind, waves, a rare snort. Of these, the sound of birds is inescapable and eternal. The voices may change with the season, varying in intensity and pitch as different species swell and subside throughout the day and year. Yet for millions of years the chorus of bird voices here, day and night, has never ceased. Alternately all night, the voices bring me in and out of slumber—from my dreamy sleep to this sleepy dream, this world of sound and life.

AFTER A DEEP AZURE SLEEP I awaken in the blue light of a blue-eyed dawn. This morning seems like a good time for an orienting walk, before the sun gets too high and hot.

Some shrubs grow here, including the native Beach Naupaka, which has rosettes of bright green leaves and is favored by frigatebirds and Red-footed Boobies for nesting. As one frigatebird is taking an unwieldy large stick to its nest, a booby tries ripping it away. The frigate hangs on resolutely, and in the war-tug they both lose altitude. The frigate lets go just in time to crash into a bush, and the booby plops on the ground with its prize. The turnabout seems fair play for all the food stealing frigates inflict on boobies. Robbed hit-and-run, the frigate lies spread-eagled in the bush, leveled by larceny. He is having a difficult time recovering even his footing with his nearly useless feet, much less chasing after the booby, who has long since left with his valuable branch. Not to be defeated, the frigate departs, soon returning with an even better piece of vine to line his nest.

Heliotrope grows along the beach near camp. Tropicbirds like nesting under its umbrella-like canopy. Indigenous to most of the Pacific, it has been introduced here. Two vines resembling pumpkin or cucumber grow thickly around the lake. Both are native. The Seaside Morning Glory, *Pohuehue* in Hawaiian ("po-hooey-hooey"), commonly creeps the beaches and sandy spots. Another native morning glory, *Kolai 'Awa,* has no English name. Various other plants have hitchhiked or been escorted here, including Glossy Nightshade, an introduced weed that looks like a tomato plant, and tobacco, introduced for the pleasure of nineteenth-century workers. Then there are the succulents, some with attractive flowers. One Hawaiian native succulent called *Nama* is plentiful here, yet rare elsewhere. The work manual entreats, "This island is special for many forms of life that are not common elsewhere . . . *try not to step on them.*" Laysan is *mostly* grassy. About grasses and sedges, the work manual says this:

> Grasses are always hard but Laysan's species are easy. They are either everywhere or localized. Sometimes one can conveniently

forget about identifying grasses but since you are probably on Laysan to help eradicate *Cenchrus* it is *very important* that you can at least distinguish between *Cenchrus* and *Eragrostis*. This is easy when they are large but a different matter when they are tiny. Wait until you run across six hundred *Eragrostis* seedlings one-half inch high that have three *Cenchrus* of equal size mixed into the patch! It is also a good idea to know the difference between *Cenchrus* and *Sporobolus* so you don't pull all the indigenous *Sporobolus*! *Eragrostis* and *Cenchrus* in their tiny stages at Laysan could also be confused with a similar sized sprout of *Fimbristylis*. The extremely rare endemic sedge *Mariscus* also looks almost exactly the same as the grass *Eragrostis* when not flowering. Check for mid rib in the leaves, not present in *Eragrostis*.

Got that? Not to mention introduced Bermuda grass, native Seashore Rush Grass, a grass called *Lepturus* that has no common name, and the native sedge *Makaloa*. Now you know why the weed pullers are called "restoration ecologists"—there's a lot they need to know. And ironically, the problem now is that there's so little sandbur left that it's hard to train people about what to look for. It seems likely that soon it will be eradicated from Laysan.

FROM NEAR THE TIDE LINE several seals utter uncouth snorts. They lie like slumbering lumber at the terminus of their heavy tracks in the sand. Once hunted on these same beaches, now they again can haul out from the sea and sleep in peace.

Little holes like tiny volcanoes pock the beach, each with a pile of excavated sand outside—crab burrows. These crabs are interesting little packages. Their inch-square bodies are gray-and-purplish. The corners of their stalked eyes have a little elongated art deco projection, like the corners of eyeglass frames that were popular in the 1950s, when automobile fins were "in." Their eyes fold into slots on their faces, making the crabs look like space aliens. They emerge at night to dismember anything formerly living that has been cast up, or chicks that have died. Nocturnal and subterranean, they're the perfect undertakers.

Two pairs of Christmas Shearwaters are sitting on the sand. They seem disinclined to walk. When they do, they appear to be too heavy for their legs. They sit down after only a few steps and moan a long deep *Oooh*.

Just a few yards farther on, fully five little Fairy Terns suddenly hover before me like luminous visiting angels, looking into my face with those huge black eyes. In the air they have an almost intangible quality. Their buzzy, resonant little calls sound somehow electronic, or like the plucking of a jaw harp. Why would Fairy Terns come and hover in my face, and noddies not? What in evolution has produced such personality differences between species? We understand so little.

Laysan's Laysan Albatrosses line this island's interior with about 120,000 nests, while 20,000 pairs of Black-footeds concentrate mostly along the shore. As I've been sitting watching an adult tenderly tending a chick, another Laysan Albatross has approached me quite closely. I feel immediately soothed by the company. I extend my fingers. The bird hesitates, then on its first attempt touches me, giving a tentative nibble. Apparently convinced that I will not harm it and perhaps enthralled itself by the novelty (it has seen far fewer humans than I have seen albatrosses), it begins nibbling my fingers in a way that seems almost affectionate. Anyone who knows anything about courtship can understand a nibble like this.

An albatross chick is sitting on a golf ball—as though it's an egg! It's the closest nonhuman thing I've ever seen to a child with a doll. The little chick nuzzles the golf ball with its bill, then sits on it. Astonishingly, it uses the same motions an adult would use. Who would have thought that these behaviors are already this developed in a chick that will not breed for seven years? More mimicking of grown-ups: two juvenile Black-footed Albatrosses—several years old but not in adult plumage—are courting energetically. One of them makes much ado about a nearby chick as though playing house, pointing down at it with its bill, nuzzling it gently.

The behavior of *adult* albatrosses toward chicks ranges widely. Some adults seem quite tender. Others, for no discernible reason, attack chicks viciously, leaving them bloodied. Sometimes fatally. One adult Laysan Albatross steps away from the chick it is feeding to vigorously peck and shake the neck of a nearby chick that is already injured. That chick looks as if it's going to die. The adult draws its head skyward, wails a high scream, and pecks again. One large albatross—likely male—has a darkly bloodied bill. The chick on the receiving end must have been savaged indeed, almost certainly suffering injury enough to kill it. Humans sometimes abuse even their own children, but what drives such behavior here? The attacks tend to follow a pattern: an adult will often walk from its own chick to an unrelated chick, call, then attack. Possibly they beat up nearby chicks to teach those chicks to be afraid and stay away when they hear their voice—"Don't approach for food." This could reduce the adults' chances of mistakenly feeding precious food to a chick that is not their own, when they return to their nest after two weeks at sea and all the rapidly growing chicks look different. But many chicks continue begging from strangers, and many albatrosses don't seem to attack chicks at all. So it's not clear what's going on. One thing is certain: it's disturbing to watch.

Many of the chicks are so fat that between their footprints you see the tracks of their bellies dragging through the sand. Others seem shaky, small, desiccated, quiet—still hoping to be fed sometime soon. There is no knowing where their parents are, what might have happened, or what a chick's fate is. If a parent is merely late, the chick may live. If one parent is *too* late, the chick may die. If one parent has been killed, the chick sits awaiting only death. One chick lies on its side, breathing hard, gasping. Its swaying head has made a shallow track in the sand, marking the limits of the final distance this chick will travel. The contour of its upturned belly is a planetary surface to orbiting flies. They buzz with buzzardly patience, understanding somehow that this chick is dying. It's an ineffably sad sight.

One of the interns had told me that when she sees a dying chick, "I kneel down, get a finger behind their head where they can't see me, and just scratch them like a parent may do." One way of seeing her action is as silly sentimentalism, pointless and unprofessional. Another way to view it is as the exercise of the most important component of the collective human genius: compassion. The way I see it, there is room in the world for more of it. Especially if you know the human history of this island.

In the late 1800s and early 1900s, several waves of commercial exploiters intent on birds came ashore at Laysan. First, egg gatherers. Then feather hunters. The eggers collected albatross eggs in ore cars for the photographic industry, which used them to make albumen prints. This was a popular process in the mid- to late 1800s. From albatrosses that lay one egg per year and cannot breed every year, they took many thousands of eggs.

But Brenda and Russ tell me that the eggers were here mainly for bird guano. They say that in the 1890s and the first few years of the 1900s, as many as forty resident Japanese hand laborers mined Laysan's guano. They say the miners took off thousands and thousands of years' worth of accumulated bird droppings. They say it was so accumulated, it had formed a kind of rock layer.

From albatrosses that lay one egg, they took many thousands. Laysan Island around 1900. (*W. A. Bryan, courtesy University of Hawaii*)

All of that is a little hard to picture. Seeking clarification, I ask, "When you say 'guano rock formations,' what do you mean exactly?"

Russ replies, "A layer of densely compacted bird manure so thick and heavy that it turns to rock. It's shit happening."

Happening maybe, but happening very slowly. It takes millennia. For most of the time, it's "same stuff, different day."

"You see these big rock piles over there?" Russ points. "That's leftover guano that they didn't take off, left piled there since the early 1900s." They look like piles of light-colored bricks. Mining for phosphate-rich guano fertilizer was big business.

From the beginning, there was no peace. When the guano miners raised a short, signaling mast, an eyewitness wrote, "An albatross returning from the sea and certainly never having seen such a thing before, flew into it with such force that the impact sheared off one of its wings, just as if it had been cut with a knife."

Max Schlemmer, the guano king, also let loose the rabbits that did so much devastating devegetating. But guano mining, egging, and rambunctious bunnies were almost quaint compared to what came next, here and throughout the North Pacific Ocean.

At the end of the 1800s feathers were in demand throughout the Northern Hemisphere for bedding, quilted clothing, and pen quills. Additionally, feathers and birds' wings had become wildly fashionable on women's hats in America and Europe. Paris was the main market for the fashion-crazed millinery trade, and the fad fueled an insatiable demand for feathers from around the Pacific and the world. In the United States, the near elimination of various birds, especially lovely white egrets with their elegant plumes, sparked opposition that coalesced into the Audubon Societies. Then as increasingly now, global markets put catastrophic pressure on wildlife.

At that time, Japanese businessmen were paying particular attention to seabirds, especially albatrosses. Albatrosses' densely insulating body feathers were sold as "swan's down" for soft, comfortable mattresses. Other kinds of birds were killed for just their wings (similar to the way many sharks today are killed for just their fins). Living birds sometimes had their wings cut from them.

In addition to killing adults, feather gatherers also dipped live chicks in boiling water, then stripped their thick down. (As late as the 1990s, Japan proposed to "harvest" Argentina's penguins for their down, for gloves. The government got interested, but the Argentinian locals were duly appalled by the mere thought, and rejected the offer.)

In the early 1900s, on some of the remotest islands in the Pacific, the Japanese "fowlers" killed millions of albatrosses. They devastated the seabirds of the Bonins, Izu Islands, Wake, Marcus, and elsewhere. After snuffing out albatross populations around Japan and the western Pacific, they started moving east like wildfire, igniting chaos wherever they touched. If you were born a seabird, it was a holocaust.

Hawaiian soils had become part of the United States in 1900, but poachers relied on the infrequent patrols in these remote islands. Light as a feather, the Japanese bird killers first touched the Northwestern Hawaiian Islands in 1900, possibly earlier. In 1902 a visitor to Midway Atoll found thousands of seabird bodies. He wrote, "Everywhere on Eastern Island great heaps, waist high, of dead albatrosses were found. Thousands upon thousands of both species had been killed with clubs, the wing and breast feathers stripped off . . . the carcasses thrown in heaps to rot. . . . Bird pirates had worked sad havoc. . . . I was convinced that . . . before long this colony of albatrosses . . . would be wiped out precisely as the one on Marcus Island had been." By the time the poachers were finally evicted from Midway in 1903, they'd taken half a million albatrosses.

In 1904, Japanese schooners landed seventy-seven men farther east, on Lisianski Island. In six months, they killed 284,000 birds. The U.S. cutter *Thetis* arrived in mid-June and arrested the men, who were happy to be taken from the infernal island they must have felt imprisoned on.

Secretary of State John Hay had asked the government of Japan to prohibit Japanese ships from killing seabirds on American islands. Japan's foreign affairs minister immediately agreed to issue a warning but said he "could not guarantee that they would obey." It's unclear whether this was an honest evaluation or a promise to do nothing couched in fine diplomatic niceties. William Dutcher, the president of the new National Association of Audubon Societies, had appealed to Washington to stop the Japanese slaughter. He was taken by Japan's charm offensive. Dutcher gushed, "It is with pardonable pride that I present to the directors and members [that] owing to the cordial cooperation of the Japanese and United States Governments, the large, important, and exceedingly interesting bird colonies are now, it is believed, safe from the ravages of plume hunters." Peace in his time. Later, Dutcher would eat crow.

In 1908, Schlemmer saw the guano running out (he made his last guano shipment in July 1910). In December 1908 he concluded a contract in Tokyo in which, in exchange for giving the Japanese the rights to "guano, and products of whatever nature" (read: feathers), he would receive $150 per month in gold. His legal basis for the agreement was at best debatable.

Meanwhile, continual campaigning by the Audubon Societies prompted Theodore Roosevelt to issue an executive order on 3 February 1909, protecting the islands for seabirds. Laysan was now a federally protected bird sanctuary.

Two months later, a dozen Japanese feather hunters were landed on Laysan, and they worked undetected. In August 1909 their schooner arrived, took away the feathers of 128,000 birds, and left the men to continue their albatrocities.

Rumors eventually reached Honolulu, and the cutter *Thetis* was dispatched. It reached Laysan in January 1910. Captain W. V. E. Jacobs wrote: "One of the buildings was full of breast feathers . . . another was two-thirds full of loose wings, and two other buildings were partly filled with bales of feathers and wings, and . . . on the sand . . . were about two hundred mats . . . under which were laid out masses of birds' wings in various stages of curing. . . . Along the beach and over the island were bodies of dead birds in large numbers, from which emanated obnoxious odors."

They also found cages in which birds had been imprisoned alive. In a dry cistern, hundreds of live albatrosses had been herded to die slowly of starvation, thus reducing the amount of fat beneath the skin, to make skinning and cleaning easier.

The captain arrested the poachers, seized their feather booty, and uncovered 64,000 wings and nearly half a ton of other feathers, leaving them to spoil in the weather. By then, five-sixths of Laysan's albatrosses had been killed.

Moving up the chain to Lisianski, the *Thetis* arrested ten more Japanese feather hunters. The ship returned to Honolulu with something like 200,000 wings and two and a half tons of feathers valued at $130,000—a huge sum in those days.

The Japanese workers produced papers from the American Max Schlemmer, purportedly allowing them to be there to extract guano. (Schlemmer certainly knew what the Japanese were doing, but nothing he had written could nail him directly to the poaching, and the charges against him were dropped.) Legal charges against the Japanese were likewise dismissed, and they got free passage home to Japan.

In 1915—six years after the islands had been declared a refuge—the *Thetis* made another stop at Laysan and found that poachers had been there a couple of months earlier. "Between one hundred and fifty and two hundred thousand birds were found lying in heaps in all parts of the island. All of them were found on their backs with only the breast feathers missing. . . . No portion of the island was spared."

Eventually, the increasing American presence—and diminished numbers of birds—convinced the Japanese ships to stay away. For the next few decades, albatrosses were in great danger from Japanese feather hunters on many islands, but were protected in Hawaii.

The trauma of that time endures. People have probably killed more Laysans than any other albatross, exterminating them from several islands where they once bred. Albatrosses formerly bred in larger numbers on Wake, and "in great numbers" on Iwo Jima before 1900. If the feather hunters had somehow missed a few albatrosses there, the ferocity and famine of World War II put an end to them entirely. The feather hunters did not miss Senkaku Retto (25° N, 123° E), nor did they miss a single bird there. Marcus Island, about 450 miles southeast of Japan, was hit early by Japanese feather killers. Marcus had probably provided nesting grounds for hundreds of thousands of albatrosses, comparable to Laysan Island today. By 1902 all that remained of the birds was large numbers of bones, and the claim by a local that a few years earlier he could kill three hundred albatrosses per day. None nest there today. Their failure to recolonize over an ensuing century probably stems from the island's isolation and the birds' fidelity to their ground of birth, but it's as though the albatrosses have since shunned the place. It had taken six years to kill all the albatrosses on Marcus. It took longer—until the 1930s—to wipe out all three albatross species, including the Short-tailed, on Torishima.

VENTURING TO A PLACE this remote at that time was difficult and dangerous. The work—the slaughter and the splattering blood and screaming birds and thrashing wings—must have been miserable in the heat and isolation. The effort surely entailed the impressive resolution, desperation, determination, insight, curiosity, brutality, and greed that have long been part of the human enterprise. The feather hunters' arduous effort and excess was facilitated by the usual two things: profit potential and consumer apathy.

So here we are now, trying to care, to right past wrongs. That's why, when I see a young intern speaking gently to a starving chick, I don't see it as pointless or silly. I see it as being as far as you can get from boiling chicks alive for their down. And so I applaud the chick soothers, Monk Seal workers, weed pullers, and anyone else who is willing to eat canned food for months just to help heal a place of such beauty, using kindness to benefit other creatures that have suffered at the hands of people who lacked humanity. Let idealism proliferate, let compassion thrive.

➤ ➤ ➤

*P*EOPLE NO LONGER COME ASHORE at Laysan with ill intent. But a measure of human thoughtlessness continually clutters this tiny coast. Laysan's colorful shoreline is a jetsam jubilee, a festival of cast-up trash. Everything from boogie boards to booze bottles. The strand line is a wide band of bottles, floats, shoes, tires, plastic—. If you're on the beach, you're seldom more than a few paces away from something that doesn't belong on beaches. There was debris at French Frigate Shoals, but nothing like this. This shoreline is a beach of burden, staggering under a bright array of mostly plastic rubbish that would look striking on a poster.

A quick scan around confronts your eye with plastic beverage bottles, pieces of plastic pipe, empty containers of everything from laundry detergent to talcum powder to chocolate syrup. And various cast-up foot-wear. Glass bottles abound, too. Here's a bottle saying Coca-Cola in English on one side and in Japanese on the other.

A chick drags its fat belly across the sand and then digs a little divot for itself next to a piece of rusted metal. There are also a lot of coconuts on the beach, and some beautiful shells, like this large, gorgeous spiral snail about twice the size of my fist. Little red shapes sometimes turn out to be shell fragments and sometimes plastic bits. Plastic bottle tops are prominent. There's the desiccated mummy of a unicornfish, its spines fixed and formidable, its eye sockets vacant, its mouth frozen in eternal surprise. It lies amid the cowries, clams, and barnacles—and trash—as though shell-shocked.

Three adult Laysan Albatrosses are resting next to what looks like a glass fishing-net float on the beach. For some reason, the clear, spherical glass floats—many of which have probably bobbed around the Pacific for decades—have universal aesthetic appeal. Like most people, I find them quite attractive. But on closer inspection this turns out to be a bowling ball.

The debris isn't random. It piles up at certain spots. On the south point a hellacious concentration of trash, plastic fishing floats, and bunched-up fishing net stretches for a quarter mile. The northwest side of the island is a postcard of debris of the central Pacific. It's a Monk Seal obstacle course, with seal tracks threading their way among buoys and bottles and balls. The Black-footed Albatrosses here are nesting densely among a psychedelic garden of round plastic fishing-net floats—four inches in diameter to larger than a basketball—colored to be visible on the sea. It's a surreal-looking sight: big dark birds among big colored bubbles on a white sand beach against the blue ocean—like someone's unsettled hallucinatory trip. As Coleridge might say: garbage, garbage everywhere, as nobody thought to think.

You would not guess that dumping plastics into the ocean has been illegal since the early 1990s . Some of the debris is indeed bizarre: Flashlights. A fake-grass welcome mat. A plastic wheel from a child's tricycle. A big coffeepot and a scrub brush. Half a kitchen cutting board, well used. Suddenly there are three umbrella handles within three feet of each other, as though several people had been swept to their death together in a torrential rain and washed far out to sea, with only their umbrellas making the voyage all the way here.

The debris piles up at certain spots—Laysan Island.

Every few steps reveal new types of junk: A golf tee. A small perfume bottle, a plastic folding hairbrush, a toy cowboy, a thread spool, a vacuum tube like one from an old television set. A syringe. A refrigerator door. Small rubber balls. A human skull—of plastic. A toy truck. Toy soldier. A three-inch plastic dinosaur (*Tyrannosaurus rex*). A plastic elephant. Plastic cat. Even some of the fish on this beach are plastic ones.

That warm Kuroshio Current streaming past Japan, whose waters eventually pass Hawaii as the North Pacific Current, is troubled with trash coming from Asia because that's the direction the flow takes it. This stuff, conveniently swept from its sources by the grace of moving water, gets inflicted on the ocean's wildlife. (As you'd guess, the middle of the North Pacific isn't the only place with this problem. In the middle of the South Atlantic, to give just one example, at an island appropriately named Inaccessible—uninhabited, seldom visited—bird researchers Peter Ryan and Coleen Moloney documented "exponentially increasing" accumulations of litter, mostly plastic from South America, two thousand miles distant.)

The most ironic piece of trash ever found on Laysan was a sign in Japanese saying SAVE OUR OCEANS AND RIVERS—DON'T POLLUTE. Here's an insulated beverage container from a brand called Kansai Attaché. It reads: "The power of nature to suit the mind of the city dweller." An exquisitely vacuous example of the marketer's vapid craft. We may find ourselves poetically inspired to answer their slogan with a haiku:

City dwellers' trash
Fouling shores of paradise.
More is on the way.

Laysan's beach also bears multitudes—tens of thousands—of chemical lightsticks used by the millions to attract Swordfish and tuna to baited longlines. Fishing-net floats of oblong foamy plastic are also abundant. They're probably from the superscale "curtains of death" drift nets of the 1980s and early '90s . People here say they've seen adult albatrosses regurgitate these floats and pass them to chicks. That's hard to believe. At fully six inches long and two inches wide, a float would occupy inside an albatross a lot of space that should go to food. Especially in chicks. Likewise, the birds swallow the lightsticks.

These fishing implements begin to hint at pressures untold and uncontrolled on the Pacific's underwater wildlife. We use these implements to empty the oceans, and then the sea itself casts them up to heap

Feeding its pineapple-sized chick

havoc on the remotest shores. From the time this fishing gear is manu-factured, everywhere it goes it's trouble.

I'd noticed several hooks hanging in the cooking tent. One of them looked like a halibut hook. One was a shark hook. The bird crew found them next to bird nests. Two days ago an albatross chick here had a braided plastic cord emerging from its throat. Others have had mono-filament line hanging from their mouths. Russ says, "You pull a fair amount of the line out and suddenly it's tight, like there's a fish hook in the bird, so you just cut the line."

I wonder what happens then. A few steps farther is one small alba-tross chick's carcass with bright bits of plastic sticking through its ribs. You get the feeling the plastic will remain here even after the bones them-selves bleach and pulverize into dust and blow away. A little farther along lies another dead albatross chick, its whole rib cage packed with plas-tic—various shades of blues, pinks, orange, various pieces of bottles, the legs of a toy soldier. And a colored cigarette lighter. Lighters are one of the more horrifying—and more common—things you see in these dead chicks. This fresh carcass seethes with maggots, making the bits of col-ored plastic look woozily alive.

In fact, *every* decomposed chick carcass seems to have plenty of little colored bits of plastic. You can often tell where chicks died last year because piles of colorful plastic particles that used to fill their stomachs mark their graves like Technicolor tombstones.

It is unlikely that any living albatross chick on the island is free of plas-tic. Laysan Albatrosses eat greater volumes and more varieties of plastics than any other seabird. Of 109 identifiable plastic items found inside Laysan Albatrosses in a formal study, 108 had originated in Japan. Plastic can't be good for the birds, and it must kill a few. Large volumes of plas-tics might give a false sensation of satiation and suppress their appetites. This may be enough to starve or fatally dehydrate chicks already in poor condition. Birds may absorb toxic chemicals from plastics and other artificial things they swallow.

One coughed-up bolus contains both natural and unnatural items: a couple dozen squid beaks and several smooth pumice stones light enough to float, plus a couple of plastic bottle caps and a bit of gill net festooned with fish eggs. I hadn't before noticed albatrosses swallowing monofilament gill netting. It seems they're still finding some drift-net pieces that have been floating around—perhaps tangling sea creatures—since before the ban went into effect six years ago. Drift nets up to two and a half miles long (considered "short" compared with the banned nets, sixteen times that length) are still legal. But the net fragments on the ground here are so deteriorated you can easily break them apart with your fingers. They must have been drifting a long time indeed. Imagine the birds trying to clip off bite-sized pieces of netting—how easily it could get looped around their bills or tangled around their heads. Mere eating has turned high-risk for the albatrosses.

On the ground is a lot of pumice that albatrosses have eaten and puked up. We know that in this part of the ocean flyingfish eggs sometimes adhere to floating objects. This might be the best clue to why albatrosses eat hard plastic—they probably eat naturally occurring drifting objects for the attached egg masses and other digestible creatures growing on them. They've been eating pumice for millennia, and it's likely that they've simply transferred the habit to anything swallowable that floats, like cigarette lighters. The pumice the birds disgorge is rounded and worn smooth. But the plastic can break into sharp shards that can block the esophagus or stomach, or cause internal tears or punctures.

I come suddenly upon a strange opaque black bottle in the sand. Its rounded bottom attenuates into an elegant neck with an unusual cap. A genie bottle, certainly. For the world's oceans, the evil debris genie has already been uncorked; mere anarchy loosed upon the world, and it seems there's no putting it back.

RAY BOLLAND IS EXAMINING FISHING NETS cast up onto the beach. One thing we already know: a lot of the fishing nets come from far away and drift great distances before hanging up here. Some fishing gear washes overboard in violent storms. Some is purposely jettisoned because it is easier and cheaper to dump unwanted nets and lines at sea. Those discarded nets sometimes continue to entangle fish, whales, turtles, and seabirds. But Ray is trying to categorize the netting. He wants to know what countries are using it in what locations and in which fisheries. Then, maybe, it can be reduced at the sources. Ray is working toward putting the genie back.

We stop at one pile and Ray takes out a ruler. He kneels and starts to catalog, dictating as I write in his notebook. "Knotted, monofilament, eighty-one and one." We walk over to the next pile. "Knotless, polyethylene, eighty-seven by three." The first number is the mesh size and the second is the twine diameter, in millimeters. "Red knotted, twelve by one.

White knotless, poly-e, two ninety-five by three. Green knotted poly-e, two-fifty by three; this is three-strand with a Z-twist."

Ray tells me that his earlier career, working with fish and marine mammals, was interesting. "But to tell you the truth," he says, "the trash is also very interesting—trying to figure out where it's from and what fisheries it was used in, and how long it takes to get here."

The nets mostly float, and come in shallow before they get grounded. In their recent three-week cleanup cruise, each working day they collected about a ton of derelict nets, line, rope, and other fishing debris. Removing stuck netting is backbreaking, hazardous work. Some balled-up loads of netting weighed a thousand pounds, and took hours to dislodge from the corals. From just 5 percent of the island chain's reefs, they removed twenty-five tons of wildlife-hazardous fishing gear.

"We estimated that to clean up everything in these islands would take about ten years of work," Ray says. "At French Frigate Shoals we found that some of the worst places are right next to where the Monk Seals pup. While we were working we had these little juvenile seals following us around and checking us out. Then we went up to Pearl and Hermes Reef. That place was pretty trashed up. We found the remains of seals, sharks; we found bird bones, dolphin bones—"

Netting hung up on reefs can roll up on the bottom or get caught in the surge, ripping out large pieces of coral; or it can snag and hang like a curtain, waiting in ambush for fish, turtles, seals, and other wildlife. Ray has found seal pups—alive and dead—in some of the nets. Last year, before the seal scientists had returned to start their season here on Laysan, several interns watched helplessly as a seal became tangled in netting. The situation was deemed too dangerous for inexperienced people to go out and try to cut the big panicked animal free. Even people who heard about it secondhand speak as though it was a personally traumatic event. Ray says, "With all my work with animals, I've tried to keep a level head. But one of the saddest things was when we found a four-year-old seal that had drowned in a net, and to realize that somebody's thoughtlessness thousands of miles away did that." Ray adds, however, that it is very satisfying to see results, and to know that he's helping animals.

RUSS AND I DECIDE TO GO snorkeling despite the possibility of encountering a Tiger Shark. (My semilogical risk assessment goes something like this: the chances of getting attacked by a shark are probably less than the chances of getting into an auto accident back home; since there are no automobiles here, we'll take our chances with sharks.) Anyway, I want to see the reef and the fishes, and get a sense of what Ray's been talking about regarding netting.

This will be a casual, unambitious swim. We seek only to have a look around without getting eaten; that's all. With such a clear goal, it will be easy to tell if we succeed. The plan is to simply swim out about a hundred yards from the beach with mask and flippers, go around a shallow lava-rock reef, and come back in through a cut in that reef. The whole swim, start to finish, should be about half a mile.

We enter, put on our flippers, and steadily beat seaward. We're watching the bottom streaming along slowly. It's mostly sandy with occasional black lava rocks. Various corals are growing, though sparsely. And as Hugo Schauinsland wrote in 1896, "Fishes of all wonderful shapes and magnificent patterns pass between the corals. . . . Most pleasing to the eye are the kind that are adorned with lively colors, observed elsewhere only on flowers and butterflies."

Swimming flowers, undersea butterflies. We're seeing big groups of Convict Tangs freely abroad in their striped prison uniforms, and schools of Black Triggerfish with their fine pale-blue outlining stripe. I'm no expert on reef fishes, and this is my first glimpse here, but Russ has been in the area for five months and has developed a good catalog of the underwater fauna and a keen eye. So to help me understand what we're seeing, we stop frequently at the surface and exchange observations. We build up quite a list for a short visit in the sea. There's the native Hawaiian Cleaner Wrasse, who manages to squeeze yellow, blue, black, and purple into a mere four inches. (The species is endemic, meaning it's found only in Hawaii.) We also see several red-and-green Christmas Wrasses and the Gray Chub, whose Hawaiian name is *Nenue*. There's a polka-dotted female endemic Pearl Wrasse (she's female because she's young; as she ages she will change to male and her color will change, as happens in wrasses and certain other fishes). There's a yellow-and-charcoal juvenile Hawaiian Hogfish, and a Yellowstriped Coris, or *Hilu*. It was said that two gods who were brothers each took the form of a *Hilu*. When one was caught by a fisherman and placed on the fire, the other changed to human form to rescue his brother and release him to the sea, but not before he'd been seared with the stripes they all now bear. The Hawaiian name means "well behaved," and pregnant women who ate this fish expected children who were quiet and refined. We pause to enjoy several Bird Wrasses with their comically beaklike snoot. We also notice other kinds of wrasses: a pink and blue-green Surge Wrasse, abundant Saddle Wrasses, and boldly orange-striped Belted Wrasses, plus a Blacktail Wrasse, the latter three endemic. We see Stareye Parrotfish, the larger males with magenta lines radiating from their eyes. Most parrotfishes also transform from female to male as they age, and their colors change radically from juvenile hues to initial-adult shades—some species are initially both sexes simultaneously—to "terminal male" colors. We also notice Bullethead, Spectacled, and Palenosed Parrotfishes—all with their fused, beaklike teeth. It was said that parrotfish behavior told the fisherman what his wife was up to at home: frolicking parrotfishes meant too much levity, and two *uhu* rubbing noses was a sure sign of flirting going on. We see gold-and-black–banded Moorish Idols with their classically exquisite streaming fins; plus Orangeband, Whitebar, and Goldring Surgeonfishes, and Yellow Tangs—all oval-shaped, peaceful grazers, yet all concealing knifelike scalpels at the base of their tail. Bluespine and Orangespine Unicornfishes likewise swim by, the former sporting a mythic-looking horn, the latter trailing graceful tail filaments and using bright orange warning patches to advertise four tail knives. I notice a Barred Filefish tucked into a crevice, and several Keeltailed Needlefish pressing their long silver bodies close to the undulating, light-dappled surface. Fancifully colored butterflyfishes abound, of the Ornate, Threadfin, Teardrop, Bluestripe, and Milletseed varieties; the latter two are endemic. We also notice Manybar and Sidespot Goatfishes smelling and probing the bottom with their odd little fingerlike goatees.

I get alongside a Bluefin Trevally; Hawaiian name: *Omilu*. It's a beautiful fish, green along the head and back, with a golden eye and a silver belly, all trimmed out in fins that start light electric blue at the base and grade to a deep glowing indigo toward the edges. A golden-green keel runs along its side from the aft third to the base of the tail. Blue freckles predominate on the back, grading to black freckles on the belly, head, and face. The pectoral fin ends in a long, streaming point. Blue trim edges the entire dorsal surface, from just behind the head all the way to the tail, then comes along the belly back toward the head. Just your typical everyday super natural miracle.

This crystal-clear liquid display is enough to take your mind off Tiger Sharks. But sharks there are, too. In a lava cave about twenty feet down, half a dozen five-foot White-tipped Reef Sharks lie placidly on the shadowed bottom. Usually scrawny and spindly-looking—and shy—these are particularly beefy and sleek—and grouchy. When we dive for a close look they rise up toward us as if to stress that they are annoyed at being disturbed. Their skin shines in the shafts of sunlight like dark nylon, and we take their point seriously and back away.

The sharks momentarily take our minds off the real danger of the reef: the discarded netting that prompted our swim. Ray and his team have done a good job here, but you can see what they were up against. About every fifty yards you stumble on remnants of another net that they've removed. What's left are some cutoff pieces of rope on the bottom, some anchored remnants of cutaway nets that coral had grown around, and some balled-up monofilament netting that seems anchored in the sand when you dive down and try to tug at it. I'm a bit wary of tugging at nets and ropes. You don't want to be tugging on a cord that conceals a fishhook when you're holding your breath and not wearing a knife.

But, cautious as we are, our most serious error is misjudging the force of the tide draining out through the reef-cut that is our return route. We've gone around a long shallow ledge and are working our way back. The more committed to this route we become, the more insuperable the tide, until Russ is struggling to make progress and I'm struggling just to stay in place. Waves from seaward are breaking on the adjacent reef, precluding our trying to swim over the shallow lava rocks—we'd get pummeled there. It seems too far to go all the way back the way we came. But I feel dangerously winded. I can hear my heart pounding from exertion as I'm sucking deeply through the snorkel. Suddenly two unusually large waves sweep in, and we try to catch their swelling force, paddling and pulling with all our remaining energy, using them to shove us through the draining current. It works, and we find ourselves through the narrow cut, and finally we gain the shore.

On the beach not too far away, a seal pup is waddling toward its mother. They touch noses. The mother scratches herself with a flipper, then plops her head down alongside the pup. The contact seems reassuring to them both.

It's reassuring to me, too, to see a haven for such creatures who were once so vulnerable to rapacious men. This is a place of reconciliation now between humans and these animals. Over the course and coarseness of the last century, devastation has been visited and reversed on Laysan. Between the egg thieves and the murderous feather poachers and the guano miners and their rabbits and the bad grass and the abandoned fishing gear, this whole island—remote as it is—has been transformed from its natural state. Problems remain, but improvement prevails.

Recovery. Restoration. Regeneration. Peace. The change in people's perspective—from exploitation to restoration, from greed to nurturing— is beautiful in a way that is real and profound, and human in the best sense. It makes me feel lucky to have found a place where the program is to set things right, and proud to live in a time when we are also capable—in our best moments—of higher hope, and healing.

➤ ➤ ➤ ➤ ➤ ➤ ➤ ➤

WORKING IN OVERDRIVE

A LOT HAS HAPPENED to Tern Island's albatrosses.

This year's weather has turned deadly. Weather is one of albatrosses' few natural killers. Adults are capable of shrugging off the planet's most god-awful gales, but nests and chicks are more fragile. Winds forty to seventy knots can blow eggs from nests. Adults in their faithful trance of incubation and refusing to abandon nests can get buried by blowing sand. Drifting sand sometimes entombs chicks, or piles so heavily into their thick down that small hatchlings cannot rise normally to beg for food. Grown albatrosses can survive at sea in a world of towering waters and spraying winds, but for small chicks not yet waterproof, cold rains can chill and kill.

The earlier rains left an indelible mark upon this breeding cycle. But the rains are only part of their problem this season. The *Honolulu Advertiser* has run a front-page headline, ALBATROSSES ABANDONING NESTS IN RECORD NUMBERS. It is true.

We're in the hottest, most intense El Niño on record. But this year's intensified heat is just the most recent spike in a longer trend. Before the 1970s, El Niño occurred about once every five years. But since the late '70s, the whole Pacific weather pattern has changed, with El Niño conditions fully five out of every seven years. Instead of recurring El Niños every few years, the tropical ocean has been stuck in a weak warm state, with more frequent and more intense El Niños.

El Niño is the biggest climate variable on Earth, after the yearly four seasons. "El Niño" is the name given to invasions of unusually warm water into the eastern Pacific. What most people know as El Niño, meteorologists call the Southern Oscillation. In simplest terms, here's the oscillation: air pressure is usually high over the eastern Pacific and low over the western, but sometimes that pattern flips, or oscillates. When air pressure is high over the eastern Pacific—as it "normally" is—winds blow from east to west. Winds blowing away from the coast of the Americas drive warm surface water seaward, causing much cooler water to rise to the surface. Think of blowing across a cup of hot coffee. The surfacing of deep, cold water is called upwelling. As we've seen, upwelling deep water brings new nutrients, supporting plankton production in surface waters; and the enhanced productivity ripples up the food chain, supporting squids, fishes, whales, seals, birds, and human fisheries. Every few years the air pressure reverses, and the winds weaken. The warm water comes flooding back, changing the heat balance of the entire ocean. *That's* El Niño.

When that warm water comes sloshing back, it shuts off upwelling. As the winds slacken, the warm surface layer extends deeper and deeper, and the wind becomes even less able to break through the warm water to mix cooler nutrient-rich water up into the sunlit shallow zone, where the plant plankton need it to live. With this undernourishment of the surface waters, ocean productivity crashes. Vast numbers of oceanic creatures starve. (To cite just one example: in one El Niño an estimated twenty million Guanay Cormorants died along Peru's coast.)

Amelia's world feels the flood of warm waters that lower food density throughout the whole eastern ocean. But humans contend with the effects of El Niño in many ways, usually without realizing the connections. El Niño creates floods in some places, droughts in others; it affects billions of animals, influences agriculture over an astonishingly large portion of the landed world, intensifies hurricanes, and brings milder temperatures to places normally cold in winter. Warmer seas have helped cholera incubate inside ocean plankton, facilitating later infectious epidemics in heavily populated coastal places. Some researchers have even linked past El Niños to weather conditions triggering sudden crop failures, outbreaks of influenza, smallpox and malaria, droughts, the blight that caused the Irish potato famine, and the Black Death of the fourteenth century. In one of its most bizarre effects, the intense 1997–98 El Niño brought such mild temperatures to the American Midwest that it prompted unusually active winter retail shopping in Chicago, leading to record sales for January, February, and March.

During the 1997–98 El Niño, the Horn of Africa got as much as forty times the normal rainfall, isolating villages, obliterating roads, and precipitating tens of thousands of cases of disease. In November 1998 Hurricane Mitch, nourished by a warmed Caribbean, killed eleven thousand people, triggered thirty thousand cases of cholera, fanned malaria and dengue-fever outbreaks, and caused $5 billion in damage. Scientists predicted these events five months before they happened—by tracking sea-surface temperature. All around the world, the costs of extreme weather grew exponentially in the 1990s. The 1998 losses alone ($90 billion that year) dwarfed total 1980s losses ($55 billion for the whole decade).

Increasingly frequent warm-water El Niño conditions are among the suite of intensifying climate changes of the last few decades. It's not clear whether El Niño's increasing frequency is related to the overall warming of the planet, but some scientists think it might be. Whether El Niños are intensified by global climate change or not, the conditions caused during El Niño events give us a good idea of what will happen throughout much of the oceans as the world continues warming.

Small temperature changes can have *large* effects. A mere two-degree Celsius increase in temperature in the eastern Pacific Ocean and Gulf of Alaska since about 1980 has caused an 80 percent decline in planktonic animals. Every fish, bird, turtle, and mammal in the ocean feels that as it ripples up the food chain. Many eastern Pacific seabirds are starving or fleeing. Off California, the number of Sooty Shearwaters is down 90 percent, compared to a few years ago. Among other birds, the zooplankton-eating Cassin's Auklet population has crashed by half, and fish-eating Common Murres are starving by the thousands along the west coast of North America. Alaskan salmon have been suffering a tremendous drop in numbers recently, too.

These effects are especially dramatic at the eastern margin of the sea, the waters of California, Oregon, Washington, British Columbia, and Alaska that form the main foraging range of Black-footed Albatrosses. Over the last decade, throughout all the northwest islands, their breeding numbers have been off by 10 percent or so. The number of nesting Laysans has dropped even more, from nearly 600,000 pairs to about 400,000. El Niño probably caused a food crisis for adults, but it doesn't necessarily mean those albatrosses died. Most scientists believe those albatrosses simply skipped breeding because they couldn't bulk up enough fat to come into reproductive condition. Now more than ever, the adults may be relying on their long-distance abilities to get to places in the ocean with food enough to keep them living. But even assuming they are alive, that's a huge decline in eggs laid.

Other creatures are also moving in response to unusual temperature. Marlin that normally live off southern California are venturing as far north as Washington State. Numerous ocean fishes, plus birds and butterflies ashore, are extending their ranges north. They can; but slower-moving animals will have a harder time. Trees will likely have a very difficult time, though their pests and diseases appear more mobile. In the sea, coral reefs that are all dressed up but unable to go anywhere may have the hardest time coping.

Record high sea-surface temperatures are spreading worldwide, not just throughout the eastern Pacific, where the main ocean temperature changes can be pegged to El Niño. During recent years, tropical sea-surface temperatures have been the highest ever recorded, and the weather is causing the worst global coral die-off ever seen. Sixteen percent of the world's coral reefs are suffering extensive mortality. In certain places in the Indian Ocean, nearly all the corals—some of them hundreds of years old—are dying or "bleaching" white, which can be a precursor to death. In lab experiments, a five-degree Celsius increase in water temperature shut off 60 percent of coral reproduction; two additional degrees stopped corals from breeding entirely. The U.S. Department of State says, "The geographic extent, increasing frequency, and regional severity of mass coral-bleaching events are likely a consequence of steadily rising marine temperatures, driven by human-caused global warming."

Albatrosses can't move their nesting islands to a cooler part of the ocean, so they skip breeding to remain alive. But even if it's only temporary, the present reduction in breeding will produce in the population a hole whose effects will ripple through for decades.

In New Zealand, temperatures warmed by about one degree Celsius (about two degrees Fahrenheit) during the twentieth century. Even this seemingly trivial change has killed albatrosses. Adults nesting at a colony called Taiaroa Head have died from extreme heat coupled with lack of wind. Low humidity at hatching dries the egg membranes, making it difficult for chicks to leave their shells. The warmer conditions have allowed a parasitic blowfly to become established, and this fly sometimes kills hatchlings. Even the dried-out soil there now makes it harder for the birds to construct nests. Such are the seemingly subtle yet abundantly troublesome effects of very small climate changes.

New York Times science writer emeritus William K. Stevens has written, "There is no clearer consequence and signal of global warming than rising seas." He calls sea-level rise "the dipstick of climate change." Here at Tern Island and on many of the world's coasts, only a few feet make the difference between land and sea. This was demonstrated back in 1969, when tremendous ocean waves struck French Frigate Shoals in the dark of night, washing completely over Tern Island, demolishing much of the station and its electronic equipment, and sending the desperate military men to the roof, where a New Zealand ship's helicopter rescued them and their three dogs. The best estimate for sea-level rise during this century is twenty inches; the minimum estimate is half a foot. If Earth warms as projected, about three dozen small-island nations will find much of their territory drowned by an increasingly land-hungry ocean. Tens of millions of people in low-lying areas and on islands would likely need to flee. Maybe those people could find other countries. These birds—where would they go? Any higher islands would be increasingly populated by human refugees from lower lands, and thus less available to seabirds than even now. Where *could* they go? Finding the islands unsuitable, albatrosses would likely do what they often do—merely skip breeding. But they would do so in droves. And what will happen to future numbers after too many years of skipped breeding? Hawaii's wonderful seabird colonies and the great nations of albatrosses would mostly be sifted into the sea.

Even for albatrosses on high islands in the most unpeopled expanses of Earth, the implications are great. In the Antarctic, whales, penguins, and many of the Southern Ocean's Black-browed Albatrosses rely heavily on shrimplike krill. Young krill require the underside of sea ice for grazing algae; without it, they starve—their life cycle breaks. But the ice they need is melting at unprecedented rates. Another unexpected consequence: we've seen that with El Niño's heat we also lose a lot of the breezes over vast reaches of ocean. One unexpected surprise of planetary warming is wind change. In coming years some normally windy places may experience less wind, and some normally calmer places may suffer more hurricanes. Five leading albatross researchers have written, "Use of wind by albatrosses has led to the selection of an extreme flight strategy that could only have evolved in the windiest place on earth. The changes in wind regime and variability that are predicted to occur with future changes in the world climate may inevitably impair the foraging ability of species relying so closely on predictable wind." More than two centuries ago, Coleridge had intuited the exceptionally tight relationship between albatrosses and wind by linking the death of "the bird that made the breeze to blow" to a consequent calamity on a sea becalmed. It may be that we will instead harm "the breeze that made the bird to fly." In the greenhouse world, the future of wind itself has fallen into question, and with it, the future of albatrosses.

Most of the world's current warming is being caused by our use of carbon-based fuels. We all cause part of the problems facing albatrosses and corals and other ocean wildlife by the things we burn to fire human survival, industry, and pleasures—our lust for combustion. And, of course, more people means more burning. We've passed the six-billion mark, and all projections indicate that we'll continue to be fruitful until we number ten or eleven billion souls. Ninety million new people join our planet each year. Think of adding over one hundred cities the size of New York each decade.

Earth is already reaching its life-support limits in cropland, fish, water, and atmospheric stability, not to mention what's happening to wildlife habitat. How can we hope to satisfy the needs—and the wants—of all the hopeful people who will soon join us for dinner and who will all aspire to a decent standard of living? So much soil is under human cultivation and so much land under human occupation that agriculture and urbanization now annually take up an estimated 35 to 40 percent of all potential plant growth on land. People already use a tremendous amount of the world's annual production budget. What will happen to wildlife whose land and livelihoods we further usurp?

The single largest effect an ordinary person can exert on nature is to have a child. That's especially true if you're American, because Americans' use of energy and natural resources is extraordinary. Billions of children will be born in other countries, too, both richer and poorer, and they will all also need water to drink, food to eat, fuel to burn, and land to call home. They will also have dreams and aspirations. The most compassionate, hopeful thing we could do for our children and their world would be to ensure they are wanted and loved and provided for and that their numbers will allow them to manage, share, and promote peace in the world they will inherit. But even the loving thoughtfulness of voluntary family planning has proven too much of a challenge—rendered impossible for the most desperate by lack of information and education, turned into a battleground by certain religious and political ideologues, distorted into gender warfare, distrusted as some kind of covertly attempted class genocide. That is a great tragedy and an enormous moral mistake, because the weight of human overpopulation exacerbates virtually every problem people suffer, from health to hostilities. We have just begun to pay for this lack of vision, but the full costs will become increasingly severe and increasingly clear for humanity's next two generations and for the other members of the family of life on Earth.

. . .

BY THE END OF THIS SEASON, only half the Black-footed nests and fewer than one in ten Laysan nests will survive to produce chicks old enough to fly. In a season this deadly, natural selection is applying itself with a vengeance. But is it still really "natural" if human-caused global warming is involved?

At such a time, age and experience count for a lot. Fortunately, Amelia has both abundantly. She knows much of the North Pacific like she knows the tops of her webbed feet. Not all the albatrosses equal her accumulated acumen for survival. By the porch steps where her chick sits, Amelia's nearest neighbors are remembered only by their abandoned egg still in its nest, bleaching in the sun.

But the survivors are miracle enough. Those chicks still alive don't know how lucky they are. They know only their hunger and that they await the mysterious appearance of certain adults who will feed them, whose whereabouts they can scarcely imagine.

Nor can we. But we have the satellites.

AMELIA'S LAST TRIP, by far the longest and most profitable since the chick hatched, stabilized her loss of weight and her condition. This next time she stays at sea only two days, never traveling more than 120 miles from Tern Island.

It's the beginning of a rhythm she'll set up for the rest of the time she's feeding the chick: a very long trip to care for herself, then a very short trip for the chick, while she lets herself lose more weight. Amelia's alternation of short and long trips is a common albatross parenting strategy. When the chicks are very small they can't store a lot of food and must be fed frequently or they'll starve. So the parents make short trips. Then suddenly—often abruptly—they start making much longer trips. Short trips are better for the chicks. Longer ones are better for the parents because they can go to places farther away where food is more abundant and they can regain some of their body weight.

The satellite tracks may also be providing a major clue about why Laysan Albatrosses outnumber Black-footeds by ten to one: they are using the ocean differently, and Laysans are using much *more* of it, foraging over a much larger portion of the Pacific. Most Laysans, like Amelia, are going generally north and west from their Hawaiian breeding grounds. They seem to know how to use the big frontal zones and the edges of oceanic currents and deep seamounts at the most extreme remove from any glimpse of distant land. This gives the Laysans a truly

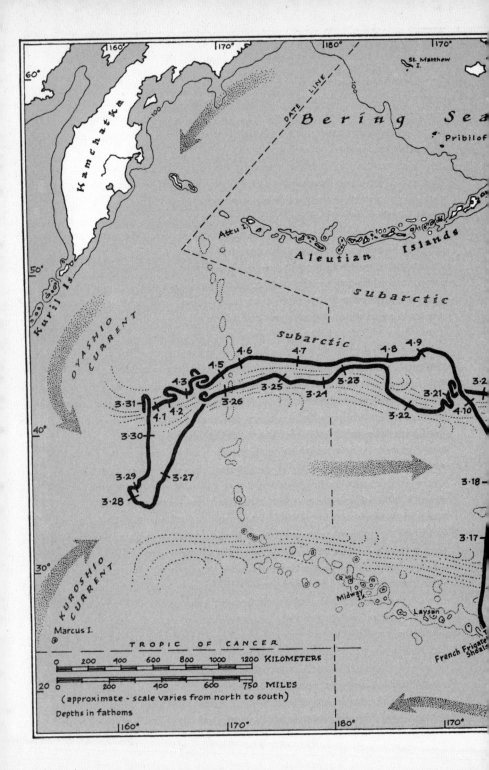

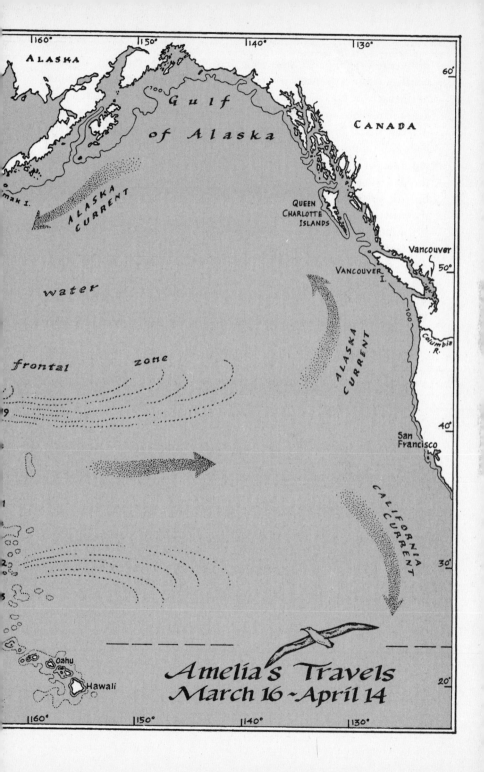

ALASKA

160°   150°   140°   130°

60°

Gulf

of Alaska

CANADA

mak I.

ALASKA
CURRENT

QUEEN
CHARLOTTE
ISLANDS

Vancouver

water

VANCOUVER
I.

50°

ALASKA
CURRENT

100

Columbia
R.

frontal   zone

9

40°

San
Francisco

CALIFORNIA
CURRENT

30°

Oahu

Hawaii

Amelia's Travels
March 16 ~ April 14

20°

160°   150°   140°   130°

vast main foraging area, stretching across the temperate and subarctic North Pacific. The Black-footeds are more specialized, going mainly northeast from Hawaii toward mainland North America. They often slide over the narrow North American continental shelf, prowling the Gulf of Alaska, coastal British Columbia, and the waters off Washington, Oregon, and California. There, the outlines of distant shores and forested mountains come into sight. For people on those shores gazing seaward, the view suggests the immensity of the ocean that stretches over so many horizons. But few people sense the presence of the unseen albatrosses that are usually not very far away.

In fact, one transmittered Black-footed Albatross has gone right to the Golden Gate Bridge and is hanging around San Francisco. Dave Anderson is dumbfounded. He reports, "When I saw where that bird is, the connectedness between these birds from these isolated islands and what we do in urban North America really hit me for the first time. That was another real moment for me; seeing something never understood before—something no one had any idea of."

On March 16 Amelia is off again. She goes only a few miles north, then northwest of Tern Island. At the outset, nothing about the look of this trip suggests it will be a long one. But Amelia is just gathering her courage, or her will. Whatever albatrosses gather, she gathers enough of it to suddenly head north with breathtaking conviction. She flies a nearly straight twelve hundred miles essentially nonstop, until she crosses the subarctic front. She's wasted little time getting back to the region she was in a few days ago, scant time dillydallying on the island slopes or seamounts. Her position is now about 42° north latitude, 166° west longitude. She's in a very chilly place, and it's still a nasty time of year. Near-constant winds whip the sea into fierce gray-green rolling mountains. Her wings, taut as a bow, quiver in the blasting gusts. When the wind blows from the north, the air is so cold it seems hard. Amelia loves this weather and this wind. It's as though she's reminded again that this—not the blistering tropics—feels like home.

Here she begins foraging heavily all day and part of the night, along the cold side of the frontal zone. For a week she continues working upcurrent, looping and meandering westward, to the international date line and way, way past it, performing the squids' aerial burials.

When she needs a break from feeding, she wanders south for a few days into the calmer North Pacific Current, before her appetite takes her back up to Chow Town. Amelia's looping track indicates that her luck has landed her back on Squid Row, and that she is savoring success. This feeding should increase her weight and maintain her health.

Amelia has worked her way deep into the open ocean, very far from Tern Island—she's twenty-one hundred miles from her nest. Again she can feel the pull of that chick, and she breaks out of the front and begins a long, nearly straight sail eastward, continuing in the direction of morning through five dawns and darks.

When she has navigated herself eastward back to a position due north of Tern, she hangs a right and makes a three-day, fourteen-hundred-mile sprint for home. Her return track parallels her outbound route so closely you'd think she was looking at a map.

Altogether, she's spent twenty-nine days at sea, covering seventy-six hundred miles. Finally, on April 14, she and her now much larger chick exchange calls and a major delivery of concentrated food, under Tern Island's tropical sun. The chick, having neither eaten for two weeks nor had any fluid except a little rainwater, is at its limits of health, on the verge of trouble. It takes all the food Amelia has and, feeling a bit stronger because of it, demands more. Somehow the chick's condition makes an impression on Amelia. The last trip was for her health. The next trip will be for the chick.

AMELIA LEAVES AGAIN, the very same day she arrived from her monumental journey to the frigid north. This next trip is perfunctorily short: forty-eight miles to the northwest for a few quick kid's snacks, then home to baby—all the same day.

Amelia's chick must be confused by a mother who can alternately abandon him for a month, then leave and return the very same day. A chick can have no concept of what its parents are doing. The parents are gone, then suddenly they're there with food. The chicks' thoughts probably can't even extend as far as the water that will be their whole world if they're lucky enough to survive. Whatever Amelia's chick thinks, at the moment it feels only one thing: full. No hunger. No thirst. Good.

Satisfied with the chick's health and her own, Amelia rests at Tern Island, dozing in the sun, lulled by the restful racket of the thousands of other seabirds.

SOMETIME AFTER MIDNIGHT, Amelia vanishes—as if half a day's rest was too much. It's April 15, tax day across America. Amelia fits the national work ethic. Once again she hits the North Pacific's major food locker, works her way along the front, then travels even farther north

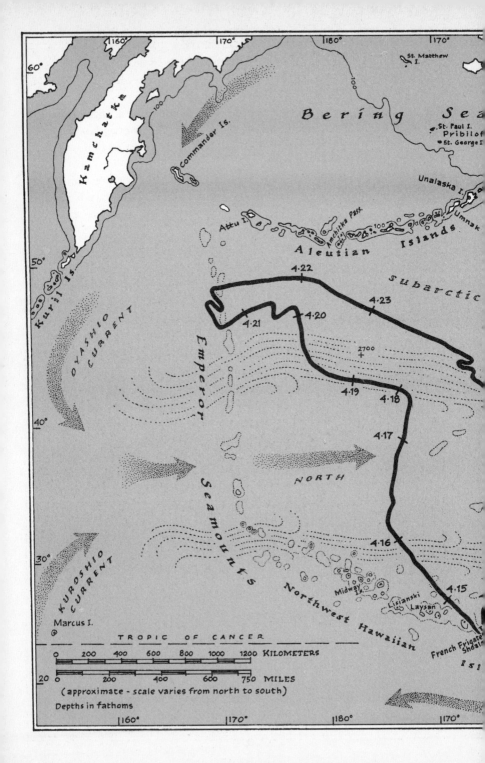

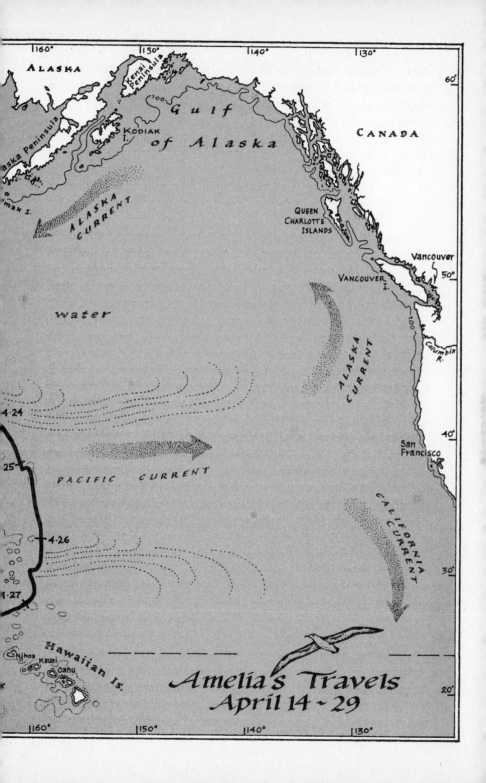

Amelia's Travels
April 14 - 29

than on her last long trip, until she nears the edge of the continental slope south of the Aleutian Islands. Twenty-one hundred miles of ocean separate her from her chick—and she's just gotten here.

Now the cold and storms and buffeting winds are at least compensated by spring's rapidly lengthening days. Daylight spans fourteen hours, and the temperature has lost its bitterest edge, though wet snow squalls roll through repeatedly. The first long-lining boats of the Alaskan spring are venturing into their hazardous work, wrenching Sablefish from their bottom habitats. Export to Japan's lucrative, insatiable market drives this effort, as it does so many others in the sea.

Eventually Amelia penetrates almost far enough north to join the long-liners for a few days. Most of the work is undignified; squabbling with hundreds of fulmars and gulls for heads and guts. But the pay can be good, often worth elbowing her way through the deafening throngs.

Freeloading is not exactly the right word for that sort of thing. There's no free lunch. In the fine-tuned natural world, even free food can cast a curse. Some albatrosses and other seabirds become so preoccupied with following ships for all the free dining that they take longer to return to their nests, causing malnutrition in the chick. But the free food can be a good thing in certain ways; in some populations albatrosses are breeding at younger ages than in the past, and significant increases in breeding success suggest that birds are benefiting from increased food availability from fishing boats. For instance, South Georgia Island's Wanderers breed about a year younger, and have 15 percent better breeding success, than they did in 1970. Yet in this same period the overall breeding *population* plummeted by about 25 percent and is still slowly declining. That's because too many of those birds that have benefited from fishing boats are also getting killed by fishing boats—most on the hooks of longlines.

So there are pluses and minuses and trade-offs. But one thing we know for sure: before humans took to the seas, the world brought forth albatrosses in great abundance. Since then, many albatross populations have declined sharply, some continue declining, and some are recovering from past abuses. None, apparently, have enjoyed a net benefit from having met us. That's a sad thing to have on our résumé.

In the past, when Amelia was following a boat in Alaskan waters or elsewhere, she and many other birds crowded closely as it began setting its line, keenly interested in the hooked baits streaming into the wake. This year, to lessen the chance that critically endangered Short-tailed

Albatrosses will fall victim to the hooks, Alaskan boats are required to drag floats and streamers or "scare lines" while they're setting the baited lines. Older, more experienced birds like Amelia find the new commotion particularly disconcerting, and they hang back.

Amelia has picked baits off longlines in the past. She knows the hook's hardness in soft bait, has felt hooks scrape her bill. But for all the things she has experienced, never has she felt the hook suddenly catching, the line pulling taut, stretching her neck, pulling her under; never has she felt herself biting the stiff ring of the hook, resisting with feet splaying, wings not working in the push of submerging water as the tight line begins slowly sinking; the rapid doubling and doubling again of pressure, the water squeezing all the internal air, the pain in the ears and pain in the hollow bones; the need for breath and how for the first time air is not granted; the light dimming; the twisting and jerking of the head, the pounding heart and the whole body using oxygen rapidly, vision closing in until the slide into unconsciousness and the motion of automatic breathing returns, the rib cage expanding, drawing cold water into the lungs until all is still, except that the trip to the bottom will take a long while.

Amelia has seen other albatrosses, struggling, simply vanish. So in the wake of boats she senses a vague danger and is wary of the situation but does not understand how food can threaten. In all the world before, nothing could be both nurturing and deadly at the same time. Her world, like ours, has gotten more complicated, more perplexing.

When a major storm chases fishing boats from their grounds, Amelia lets its shrieking winds pick her up like a slingshot, shooting her southeast until she turns south again and hooks home.

Amelia returns on April 29. She's logged another fifty-six hundred miles.

Only two weeks have passed this time, and the chick was recently fed by Father. Having survived its trials by weather and a scrape with hunger, the chick looks plump and healthy. But he seems frenzied with hunger, frantically pecking and biting at Amelia's bill. Amelia waves her head back and forth, trying to avoid her own chick, yet standing her ground. Such pestering seems to remind her what she's come all this way for, and it again gets her to regurgitate food. Even immediately after taking several feedings, the chick acts famished, pecking at Amelia's bill, begging, beseeching, *demanding* more, more, more. During six and a half minutes she transfers even more food into the avidly ravenous chick. This

The trip to the bottom will take a while.
(*photograph by Graham Robertson*)

was a pretty big feeding, 15 percent of Amelia's body weight—like a 112-pound woman delivering 17 pounds of groceries and having her adolescent immediately swallow them all.

Amelia stands by for another minute and twenty seconds—no longer. Then, while the chick is still uttering its squealing appeal for food, Amelia turns into the wind, spreads her sails, and with a few running steps is airborne. In less than half a minute she is coursing beyond the reef on the open ocean to the north, and in under two minutes, her bounding shape disappears from vision. After a trip of thousands of miles she senses no time to rest. Exigency enhances survival.

The disappointed chick, looking around as though still hungry, seems disillusioned to be abandoned so quickly. But it should appreciate Amelia's hurry; some die waiting for their parents. Nearby, a Black-footed Albatross chick that was alive this morning has died. Its emaciated carcass has little muscle left on its breast. It consumed itself waiting for a parent that never returned.

Not far away, another adult has just finished feeding its chick. The parent leaves the nesting area and steps up onto the basketball court. Using the concrete court as a runway, it spreads its wings, running forward for take-off. But a wing tip nicks a pole. This brings the bird to the ground again, whereupon it gets stopped by the two-foot fence erected to prevent Monk Seals from coming up onto the court. The albatross runs back and forth along the fence for about five minutes. Nothing in its world or its evolutionary background suggests to it that it try walking back across the court and attempting again. Going backward would not occur to an albatross. For an animal perfectly attuned to a wide-open world where it can cover thousands of miles of rolling ocean on its own power, a chest-high fence becomes an impenetrable barrier.

This bird is taking longer to solve this dilemma than it took to feed the chick it came thousands of miles to nourish. I'm strongly tempted to intercede because of the unnatural injustice of the situation. But I'm also curious to see whether the bird will figure its way out. Finally, after ten minutes, the great bird takes a heroic running leap, waving its wings frantically. It gets airborne just enough for its belly to barely clear the fence. And immediately, it swings directly north, looking as though it intends to go a long, long way.

➤ ➤ ➤

*B*Y EARLY MAY, albatrosses with living chicks awaiting them in Hawaii are strung out on two-thousand-mile commutes to feeding grounds as distant as coastal waters within sight of California, the Pacific Northwest, British Columbia, and southern Alaska. Some of Amelia's transmitter-bearing neighbors are actually in the Aleutians right now.

So I'm in Seward, Alaska, in a May snowstorm, boarding Mark Lundsten's fishing vessel the *Masonic,* to see what some of those birds are doing. Watching a perched eagle hunched against the driving snow on this bone-chilling evening, I'm wondering how birds from sun-seared Hawaii can really be here, in such a polar-opposite corner of the planet.

For tens of millions of years, albatrosses searching for food roamed seas devoid of boats. In the last few decades albatrosses have grown accustomed to sharing their richest feeding grounds with fishing vessels, and sometimes benefiting, but not without serious risks.

Mark Lundsten also knows about serious risks. He earns his living for himself and his family in the seriously risky business of Alaskan Sablefish and Pacific Halibut fishing. Lundsten is a surpassingly thoughtful man, and he spends a lot of his time thinking about ways to avoid three threats shadowing him and his way of life: the weather, accidents, and the well-being of the Short-tailed Albatross.

The Short-tail is the third albatross inhabiting the North Pacific. Even for an albatross, it is a large bird. The name is a misnomer; their tails are not particularly short. Consequently, this albatross is sometimes called Steller's Albatross, after Georg Wilhelm Steller (1709–1746), whose name is commemorated in the Steller's Jay, Steller's Sea Eagle, Steller's Eider, Steller's Sea Cow, and Steller Sea Lion. Three of those six creatures are endangered and one is extinct—further evidence of our hard presence.

Steller was a German naturalist with the Russian Imperial Academy of Sciences who participated in the epic voyage of the *St. Peter* and *St. Paul* commanded by Vitus Bering in 1741–42. During a dreadful return along the Aleutians, the *St. Peter* and its crew were pummeled by gale after gale in an icy sea. The battered, leaking ship wrecked at the Commander Islands, seemingly dooming the men. Bering died, leaving the scurvy-weakened survivors to endure the bleak prospect of so howling a place.

They soon found an immense, slow-moving, previously unknown creature living in the shallows. Essentially a giant Alaskan manatee, it reached the astonishing size of thirty-five feet in length and twenty feet around. These animals plodded through the kelp beds, grazing the brown algae fronds like cows and snorting like horses, unafraid and unsuspecting.

The hungry men fashioned hooks on ropes. With these they attacked one of the placidly pasturing animals. The stricken creature resisted only feebly, possibly due to pain, but its usually slow companions rushed to it. "Some tried to upset the boat with their backs, while others pressed down the rope and endeavored to break it," noted Steller.

Thirty men on shore hauled the giant animal onto the beach. Estimated weight: eight tons. The Sea Cow was perfectly designed for grazing kelp, but it had one fatal flaw: the people who found it thought it delicious. To their amazement, the meat resembled beef—they likened the juveniles' flesh to fine veal—and its fat tasted like "the oil of sweet almonds."

This strange new animal seemed sent by Providence to nurture the sick, shipwrecked men back to health. So inoffensive were these giants that Steller said he could sometimes "stroke their backs with my hand." He further wrote, "In the spring they mate like human beings." After "many amorous preludes" the female, "constantly followed by the male, swims leisurely to and fro until, impatient of further delay, she turns on her back . . . and both give themselves over in mutual embrace."

Led by Steller, the recovered men built another boat from their wreckage and completed the mission. The survivors excitedly told others of the wealth of furs to be had in the Bering Sea and Alaska, and of the immense and gentle Sea Cows, whose meat was succulent and nutritious. For the next two decades, sealers and fur-hunting expeditions— over a hundred men—wintered on Bering Island. And many other vessels heading from Russia to Alaska stopped to kill Sea Cows for meat.

A Russian mining engineer named Jakovleff, sent to investigate copper deposits, saw that the killing couldn't last. His 1755 petition for Sea Cow protection went ignored. Steller had described the animal's internal organs and had weighed one's thirty-six-pound heart. But the heartlessness of humans caused the Sea Cow's final extinction just twenty-seven years after Europeans first saw it. By 1768, Steller's Sea Cow was gone.

As was Steller. During his long, slow overland journey homeward, Steller became ill and died of a fever at age thirty-seven. His journal and collection of natural specimens reached St. Petersburg a year later. Among them were the "large gulls" that naturalists recognized as albatrosses of a kind previously unknown to science.

But long before Steller, Native American peoples of the coastal waterlands had known these big birds well. People frequently encountered this most coastal of albatrosses near shorelines, islands, inlets, even around river mouths. Native Aleutian people speared the huge birds from kayaks while hunting the island passages. And in the far north of the Bering Sea, hunters caught them at the edge of the sea ice. Abundant bones left behind in ancient Aleut and Indian middens on the coasts from Alaska all the way south to California indicate that this albatross was a frequent part of human diets. It was *the* most important bird in Aleutian people's diets. Aleuts still hunted these albatrosses until the late 1800s, until the feather trade swept the breeding islands.

As University of Alaska professor Rick Steiner has so eloquently written, the Short-tailed Albatross is "perhaps the most stunningly beautiful of all the albatrosses." While beauty is in the eye of the beholder, the Short-tail is an animal of superlatives. It is the largest seabird in the North Pacific Ocean. And it has been the most endangered seabird in the world; for years, it was considered extinct. The adult, as Steiner elegantly describes it, bears "a resplendent montage of color, including a distinguishing golden head, brilliant pink bill with a turquoise tip, a black ring around the base of the bill, wings of brown, black, and white, and pink and gray feet. Its feathers, some 15,000 of them on each bird, blow in the wind like thick fur." Like the Wanderer, their plumage whitens with age.

Short-tailed Albatrosses originally ranged all the way from Taiwan around and across the North Pacific, past Japan and Korea and Russia, and from Alaska south along the West Coast all the way to Baja California. In the early nineteenth century, whalers occasionally brought Short-tailed Albatrosses to Edo (now Tokyo), where their meat was often sold as *okino-tsuru* (offshore crane).

At that time, Short-tails bred in legions on a dozen or so islands southeast of Japan's main islands and around Taiwan. Among these, in Japanese territory, were Torishima, about 350 sea miles (650 kilometers) south of Tokyo; Kitanoshima, north of the Bonin Islands; Kita-, Minami-, and Okino-daitojima of the Daito group; Minami-kojima, Kobisho, and Uotsurijima in Japan's Senkaku Retto group in the East China Sea, and perhaps Iwo Jima in the Volcano Islands. Off Taiwan they nested on the Pescadore Islands. In 1894, a visitor to the Pescadores wrote that the Short-tailed Albatrosses "absolutely swarmed" about his ship.

But Torishima (the name translates to Bird Island) hosted the largest Short-tailed Albatross colony of all.

Torishima was first settled in 1887, by about forty men and women put ashore explicitly to kill albatrosses for their feathers. At this grim task they worked diligently each year from October to May, while the albatrosses were nesting. When not so engaged, they eked out their living with a little desultory farming and fishing. The settlement grew during the 1890s, and by 1900 over a hundred settlers were making their living killing the birds. They built a light railway to move the birds for processing. They took their feathers, boiled their carcasses for oil, then dried them for fertilizer. Nothing was wasted—except the albatrosses.

In 1889, in the second season of intensive feather hunting, a man named Toru Hattori visited Torishima for three months. He observed Short-tails in abundance and described the human interactions: "The birds in the reeds have to be surrounded, but the incubating birds are very easily approached. They are killed by striking them on the head with a club, and it is not difficult for a man to kill between 100 and 200 birds daily." He further observed, "At the approach of men they only clack their bills with anger but never leave the nest. We could not make them quit their nests even by lighting a fire in the nearby grasses, and they remained even though their plumage took fire."

Hattori must have had mixed feelings, because the birds clearly touched him. "At a distance the albatrosses might be mistaken for fallen snow. When they fly up in the sky . . . they float in the air like white breaking waves, truly a sight more than wonderful!" He summed up, "After staying in this unique southern island with the albatrosses as my friends, I have felt an intimate feeling of attachment for them, with which I have written this."

Each albatross yielded a quarter pound of feathers. The year Hattori wrote of his albatross friends, 39.2 tons of feathers left the island—representing about 300,000 birds.

The hunters were just getting started.

The Torishima settlement, which relied on albatross killing for virtually its entire economy, swelled to three hundred people. And the feather shipments in some years reportedly totaled 350 tons. That would have been 2,800,000 albatrosses. This was the time when albatrosses were under siege all over the Pacific, and the Short-tail was under brutal pressure in all its colonies. The distinguished Japanese ornithologist Yoshimaro Yamashina estimated that from 1887 to 1902 the plume hunters killed about five million.

To the Buddhist way of thinking, they had been building what Rick Steiner referred to as "a great karmic debt." The debt came due in August 1902. After the breeding season, while all the albatrosses were far at sea, the volcano exploded, killing all the island's humans as they slept. This became known as "the revenge of the albatross."

Heedless of any lesson, and admirably but unfortunately lacking in the superstition that might, in the wake of such seeming revenge, have warded away less practical minds, new settlers and fishermen came and left over the next years. And though the bird population was greatly reduced, when they came they killed more birds.

By this time, the Short-tailed Albatross had apparently been exterminated from all its other breeding islands.

Yoshimaro landed at Torishima in 1929. He saw about two thousand Short-tailed Albatross adults but fewer than a hundred chicks, and noted the people's practice of taking the eggs. He wrote, "I saw with my own eyes the terrific slaughter, which I could hardly bear. Only the word 'slaughter' can express the sight." He recalled Laysan Island's albatrosses having been plundered by "phlegmatic and cold-blooded Japanese

Slaughtered Short-tailed Albatrosses, Bonin Islands circa 1905,
from a postcard (*courtesy Hiroshi Hasegawa*)

laborers" and added, "I hope to prevent any further such unpleasant occurrences in Japan."

Yoshimaro Yamashina was a nobleman, a viscount with some influence. Good to his word, he returned to Tokyo and had Torishima declared a "no-hunting area" for a period of ten years beginning in January 1933. But the very month before protection was scheduled to start, the birds suddenly disappeared. The inhabitants attributed the birds' disappearance to a storm. But a Mr. Fujisawa, the schoolmaster on the island, came forward and reported that during December 1932, in anticipation of the island's soon becoming a bird sanctuary, the people killed over three thousand albatrosses.

Still, a few survived as the bird-protection law went into effect. The people did not like the law. Later that spring, the last adult Short-tailed Albatrosses on Earth saw people approaching, and soon the slopes were still.

The main crater erupted again—violently—in 1939. Though all but two inhabitants escaped this time, one river of lava completely filled the harbor cove, replacing it with "a forbidding, jagged rampart of black volcanic rock." Torishima was now all but inaccessible and uninhabitable by humans.

The last thin hope was that a few chicks that hatched during the years just before that final massacre might have fledged and survived by remaining in the distant, oblivious safety of the wide sea. The youngest chicks should have returned in the 1940s. If they did, instead of finding hundreds of thousands of courting, calling birds, they would have been met by only the silent sweep of the wind on the quiet slopes, and the rhythmic roll of the surf below.

During World War II a Japanese naval garrison occupied Torishima until 1945. During that time, among the three hundred men, one lone albatross was seen. Was this the last one?

Japan established a remote weather station on Torishima in 1946. They reported no albatrosses. But they did note that Fork-tailed Storm-Petrels came to the island at night in enormous numbers, were attracted to bright lights, and that delicious meals of roast bird could be had simply by building a bonfire after dark and letting the petrels fly into it.

In 1949 Oliver Austin Jr., an American ornithologist stationed in Japan, searched in vain for any sign of the Short-tailed Albatross. Failing to find a single individual, he presumed it extinct. He wrote, "The chances that any of these fine birds remain alive today are remote indeed. . . . Hope always remains that in some overlooked corner of the globe the species will once more be found. . . . It seems only too likely that Steller's Albatross has become one of the more recent victims of man's thoughtlessness and greed."

On January 6, 1951, weather station director Shoji Yamamoto had a day off and decided it was a good morning for a long, exploratory walk. Scanning the view of Torishima's ash slopes, he was astonished by the sight of ten large ghostly-white birds. He rushed back to the station to confirm their identity. They were Short-tailed Albatrosses, returned from the dead.

Thirteen Short-tails were photographed in 1954. At the time they reappeared, perhaps forty remained alive, including younger birds at sea. Forty. If there were five million originally, about one out of 125,000 had survived. Of the lowest reasonable estimate of just *one* million original Short-tailed Albatrosses, forty is less than one-half of one-hundredth of 1 percent, a number statistically equivalent to zero. But biologically, the difference between zero and forty is the difference between oblivion and hope, past and future.

When the first known eggs of the Short-tail's literal rebirth—seven of them—were laid in 1954, they were apparently the first Short-tailed Albatross eggs laid in over twenty years. In 1958 Japan designated the

Short-tailed Albatross a "natural monument." The staff of the weather station acted as the albatrosses' benevolent stewards until 1965, when frequent earthquakes and the threat of further eruptions forced the station's abandonment.

Dr. Hiroshi Hasegawa first visited Torishima in 1976. Instead of the sad scene he expected, he was so inspired by the vigor and vitality of the few dozen birds he found that in that moment, he saw his life's work. One may imagine that, like an albatross coming to its breeding ground after wandering many years at sea, he felt he had come at last to the absolute right place.

Hiroshi Hasegawa was raised in the Buddhist tradition. He recognizes Torishima as a place sacred as any shrine; what place could possibly be more sacred than one relied upon by an entire race of living beings? Because Hiroshi senses the island's sanctity, he perceives in it an opportunity. "It is my responsibility to save the species," Hiroshi has said. The fact is, it is the responsibility of all of us, but Hiroshi, far more than any person in Japan or anywhere, has recognized this calling and acted.

So nearly nonexistent had the Short-tail become that between 1940 and 1991 the average number of sightings throughout the entire ocean from Japan to California was *one* per year. Between 1975 and 1992, aerial and ship surveys of fifteen thousand square kilometers of ocean off Alaska—where Native hunters in kayaks had routinely speared the birds—found only *one* Short-tailed Albatross.

Hiroshi has aided and abetted the birds to great effect, engineering what Rick Steiner has called "one of the most extraordinary resurrections in avian history." Because the newly steepened slopes of the volcano were loose with granular ash that caused eggs to roll, Hiroshi replanted clumps of native grass and built dozens of terraces to offer level nest sites for the birds. He built dikes and channels to divert away from the nesting areas the heavy rain runoff and landslides that can wash away eggs and kill chicks. And he set up decoys and recordings of courtship calls in a part of the island where the ground and vegetation offered more secure nesting potential but the birds had not yet recolonized. Before Hasegawa began his life's work in the mid-1970s, only about seventy-five adults nested. By the turn of this century four hundred adults (two hundred pairs) were raising about seventy-five chicks each year. Including juveniles, the population, growing at 7 percent annually, had passed fifteen hundred birds. We salute you, Hiroshi.

In 1987, exactly one hundred years after the first feather hunters climbed ashore among the swarms of giant birds, Hiroshi climbed across the shoulders of the island's volcanic slopes to conduct a short ritual that Rick Steiner characterized as "part apology, part prayer." Collecting some of the numerous albatross bones from the surrounding ground, he placed them gently on a large stone beside two memorial cairns, lit candles and incense, and knelt. As an offering to the spirits of the millions of dead albatrosses, on the stone he poured seawater for their drink, and set out dried squid and flyingfish.

In the Buddhist worldview, each action carries consequence, not just for the acted upon but for the actor as well. If we do not offer reverence and respect to the world, we will receive accordingly. As Hiroshi told Steiner, "It is our job to make a new world." And it is.

For the Short-tail, bets for the future are almost entirely with Torishima (around 1970 a few also returned to the Senkaku Islands near Taiwan, where a small handful now nest). The prevailing odds remain risky. Even with its miraculous resurrection from apparent extinction, the Short-tailed Albatross is hardly in the clear. Torishima is still an active, smoldering, venting volcano, and it may yet again blow. Or, after witnessing a half century of insults, it may look kindly upon Hiroshi and the albatrosses cloaking its own shouldering slopes, and keep its peace awhile.

Hasegawa has written that he is "optimistic that this impressive bird will once again be seen with regularity along the coastlines of its vast marine range," including "the long and beautiful festoon of islands lying along the western edge of the Pacific Ocean." But full recovery will take two centuries. Hiroshi Hasegawa will not be with us all that time. And so here is my wish: that in the great karmic cycle, Hiroshi will return, reincarnated, to see the albatrosses multiply. And as their tribe increases, may the kindred spirits of Hiroshi Hasegawa likewise proliferate; may more like him come forward, for the sake of us all, so that together we may, indeed, make the world new.

SINCE 1981 the occasional Short-tailed Albatross has visited the Northwestern Hawaiian Islands. A female has laid an egg at Midway Atoll, and two birds have been courting there, leading to excited hopes for a new colony.

Nonetheless, the Short-tailed Albatross remains endangered, and the Fish and Wildlife Service has decided that if fishery observers report more than two Short-tails killed by Alaska longline fishing boats this year, they will likely close the year's fishing for the whole fleet. Of all the wildlife problems caused by fisheries, it's ironic that *this* albatross's problems, originating with feather hunting as they did, hang so pointedly over this fleet. In the Southern Ocean's subantarctic, where albatross populations are being driven downward *because* of longline fishing, much of the fishing is not under effective control.

THE IRONY IS NOT LOST on Mark Lundsten, but here in Seward Harbor on the deck of the *Masonic* he's telling me that he "stopped fighting and learned to love the Short-tailed Albatross."

And so the Short-tail has collected one more savior and proselytizer. Lundsten's been in the forefront of efforts by Alaska long-liners to develop not only methods but regulations for minimizing seabird mortality. I'm thankful he has, because a) it makes things a lot better for Short-tailed, Black-footed, and Laysan Albatrosses; b) it makes his fleet the only group of fishing boats in the world actually initiating regulatory efforts to reduce bird "by-kill"; and c) he averted war with the conservation groups. The fleet Lundsten is part of was getting hammered in the press over bird kills. It looked like regulations would be imposed from outside. So Mark helped find solutions that would work for both the birds and the fishing boats. Now Mark wants to show people that longline fishing doesn't have to be dangerous to birds. So he's issued a challenge: anyone willing to observe firsthand the effectiveness of his efforts to help solve the problem can get on his boat and see what the *real* world is like. And here I am.

LONGLINE FISHING BOATS PRACTICE either drift long-lining or bottom long-lining. Both involve lines miles long, armed with thousands of baited hooks. Drift longlines are usually thirty to eighty miles long (the line is stored on an enormous spool on deck). They drift in the current. Their main targets are Swordfish and tunas. They've deeply depleted Atlantic Swordfish and marlins, as well as many shark species worldwide. And they have serious by-kill problems, catching, killing, and largely wasting undersized fish and endangered sea turtles—and birds.

Bottom longlines, which Mark uses, are usually much shorter, and are anchored to the seabed. Their by-kill problems are fewer, and— unlike the bottom dragnets called trawls that scour and degrade bottom habitat—they are relatively friendly to the seafloor as long as there's no branching coral in the area. The main by-kill problem created by bottom longlines is mortality to seabirds trying to snatch the bait before the line sinks.

Two U.S. longline fleets operate in the North Pacific: Hawaiian boats hunt tunas and Swordfish; Alaskan boats like Mark's target bottom fish like Sablefish, Pacific Halibut, and Pacific Cod. The Alaskan boats set an incomprehensible 170 million hooks annually. The Hawaii Swordfish and tuna longline fishery set 15 million hooks annually throughout the 1990s—less than a tenth as many as the Alaskan fleet—but their per-hook albatross kill rate was about twenty-five times that of the Alaska fishery.

That difference occurs because the drift longlines are less heavily weighted and don't sink out of range as rapidly. Until recently Hawaiian long-liners weren't required to use any measures to avoid killing seabirds; they killed about 1,800 Black-footeds and 1,400 Laysans annually. At the turn of the new millennium, conservation groups sued to help protect albatrosses and endangered sea turtles, and federal-court action resulted in fishing-gear restrictions and large areas closed to longlines (in addition to the earlier closure to protect Monk Seals). Some longline boat owners then decided to leave Hawaii and press into California harbors, taking their trouble elsewhere.

Alaskan long-liners each year snag approximately 600 Black-footed Albatrosses and 700 Laysans—some estimates are higher—plus one Short-tailed Albatross (that's what's known; management agencies still don't bother collecting bird data from a part of the halibut fishery that sets about 30 million hooks annually, about 18 percent of the fishery). Alaska boats also drown about 13,000 gulls and fulmars (Hawaiian boats don't, because these birds don't live in the warmer waters toward Hawaii).

U.S. boats work among some of the densest concentrations of albatrosses. But American boats aren't the only ones on the whole ocean. Japanese, Taiwanese, Canadian, Russian, Chinese, and Korean long-liners are out there too. The United States operates about 125 drift long-liners in international waters. China sends a roughly equal number, Korea has about 150, and Japan and Taiwan *each* operate about 1,600 long-liners. No one knows how many birds they kill each year. The best guess—and it's a crude one—is over 30,000. If those numbers are in the right ballpark, and especially if many of those are albatrosses, the kill rate starts to be very significant. Recent calculations indicate that Black-footed Albatrosses cannot withstand losing more than about 10,000 birds per year; more than that will drive a decline. The limited information scientists have suggests that tuna and Swordfish longlines *alone* are killing more than this—even without considering mortality from bottom-longline fisheries for halibut and cod, or natural mortality. From an ocean animal's perspective, longlines are a bit like minefields in the feeding grounds of the sea.

· · ·

AT ONE TIME, albatrosses survived extermination only by being at sea. Today, most albatrosses are safe only on land—where they spend just 5 percent of their lives. Hunting and killing on land in decades past was certain to miss at least some islands and some nests and some birds. But nowadays every albatross, no matter how remote its nest, finds numerous opportunities to die on a longline. If it does and it has a chick in the nest when that happens, the chick starves.

Increasing numbers of long-liners crisscross the ocean the way worry lines turn a face old. Most current longline fisheries first developed after World War II; some, as recently as the 1990s. Today boats mine the Southern Ocean with about 160 million hooks. In the North Pacific, Japan's boats alone annually set 130 million hooks. You've already got some idea that the seafloor off Alaska and Canada's west coast bristles with 200 million hooks each year. Grand worldwide sum: around 1.1 *billion* hooks annually.

All the world's albatrosses of all species and ages total perhaps ten million individuals. Do the math. Only the Galápagos Albatross—which does not seem attracted to boats—shows no evidence or inclination toward trouble with longlines. All the rest are bedeviled by them. Long-lining could catch the last albatross—unless we do a few easy things.

THE THINGS THAT MAKE albatrosses so successful in the natural world are the same that make them so vulnerable in the human-dominated world. Their exceptionally long lives, extremely low natural adult mortality, and long-delayed maturation before they begin breeding carry surprising consequences: a mere 3 percent increase in adult mortality can lead to a 50 percent population decline in just twenty years. You might think albatrosses could perhaps compensate for increased adult mortality by laying more eggs or raising more chicks. But they can't. They don't have the time, and there's not enough food.

Longlines are annually killing perhaps 100,000 albatrosses and many petrels. Work by New Zealand ornithologist Dr. Sandy Bartle and colleagues shows population declines over the last several decades of 50 to 80 percent in some albatross colonies.

Two fisheries causing the most trouble for albatrosses are problematic in other ways. One has severely depleted the Southern Bluefin Tuna it is targeting. Japanese tastes and willingness to pay outlandish sums for giant bluefin tuna make that fish the world's most commercially valued—and biologically undervalued. In the mid-1990s a single 715-pound

Southern Bluefin Tuna sold at auction for $83,500, nearly $117 per pound. But we're into a later, greater millennium, and so on January 5, 2001, a 444-pound Northern Bluefin caught off Japan sold at auction for $173,000. One fish. That's $390 per pound. Wholesale. Jackpots like that create relentless pressure. Each year fishers set over 100 million tuna-intended hooks where the range of Southern Bluefins heavily overlaps that of albatrosses. Worth too much money in Japan to be allowed to live anywhere, bluefins are depleted everywhere they swim: in the Pacific, Atlantic, Mediterranean, Indian, and Southern Oceans. A study by Australian scientist Dr. Rosemary Gales in the mid-1990s showed that the Southern Bluefin fishery alone was already causing population declines in roughly half of the world's albatross species.

Enter the trendy "Chilean seabass" fishery, which started in the mid-1990s. Interestingly, there is no such thing as a "Chilean seabass." The fishery targets two species of big (hundred-pound) fish—the Patagonian Toothfish and the Antarctic Toothfish—that live in cold, deep sub-antarctic waters. They're caught not just near Chile, but all around the bottom of the world—exactly where most albatrosses breed. Many such boats operate illegally—unlicensed, poaching in closed waters, or far exceeding their quota. Poachers in Antarctic waters take *twice* the legal catch. They inflict some of the worst seabird mortality anywhere. Attributing the recent sudden 17 percent decline in the Falkland Islands' enormous Black-browed Albatross population to Patagonian Shelf longline fisheries, Falklands census team leader Dr. Nic Huin said, "Illegal and unregulated fisheries around the world are having a disastrous effect on these birds." And they get a renewed financial boost every time we buy what they've caught.

Illegal fishing boats, often registered in cash-starved countries unconcerned with regulations, are not luxury vessels. Most illegal boats haven't heard of workers' rights. Many such boats are a world apart, crewed by tough, economically strapped people far from home and community. A toothfishing boat might have a Korean fishing master and a Vietnamese, Taiwanese, and Indonesian crew. Crew members are sometimes compelled to spend two years at sea before they can go home, and during that time may be prohibited from going ashore in ports. Often they have only cold-water showers, and must wash their clothes by towing them behind the boat. Fishing masters often use force and humiliation, and will not hesitate to discipline a man they deem to be not working hard enough by slapping him in the face.

When an Australian patrol boat discovered a Spanish-owned, Togoregistered boat with forty-four men fishing in Australian waters, they chased the pirates for ten days, over twenty-two hundred nautical miles. Finally, with the aid of three South African naval ships, they captured the boat off Cape Town with one hundred tons of illegal toothfish, worth over half a million dollars. Another Spanish-owned boat flying the Belize flag, which had earlier been caught fishing illegally in Australian waters, was later discovered off Kerguelen Island by a Greenpeace ship, which pursued it for sixteen days across three thousand miles of ocean. When it put in to Mauritius, the government found 170 tons of illegal toothfish and refused to let it unload. The owners renamed the ship and sent it back to work.

Increasingly, international agreements are trying to drive out illegal fishing by certifying legal catches and closing markets to uncertified fish shipments. But it remains a serious problem, and illegal, unlicensed, or unregistered fishing boats now take a quarter of the world's fish catch.

All the hooks, the tremendous pressure on the oceans, the illegal and uncontrolled boats lead to this: albatrosses have the highest proportion of threatened species of any bird family. The World Conservation Union considers 83 percent of albatross species "threatened," compared to 11 percent of birds overall. Albatrosses' worldwide total population may have declined by about 40 percent since the mid-1960s. The eminent British ornithologist John Croxall, having devoted his life to the pioneering study and conservation of seabirds, felt moved to write, "It is depressing that nearly half the albatross populations with adequate documentation are decreasing, and that most of those currently stable or increasing are recovering from past decreases." The Australian albatross specialist Rosemary Gales wrote, "The future prospects of albatrosses are bleak."

I respectfully disagree.

Here's why: A lot of work is going into changing things. The birds are now reasonably secure on their islands, where once they were hunted mercilessly. The main threat now comes from longline fishing, but where longline fishing pressure has softened, some albatross populations have begun to trend upward. For example, Wanderer populations on Crozet and Kerguelen Islands in the Indian Ocean, which had plunged by more than half between 1960 and 1990, are now increasing, because many longline boats have moved away from these birds' main feeding grounds (after depleting the Southern Bluefin Tuna they'd targeted). Antipodes Albatrosses increased from about eight hundred pairs in the late 1960s to over five thousand pairs by the mid-1990s—by far the largest known increase for any great albatross population. The Short-tailed has been increasing at 7 percent per year. Full recovery of these species could still require well over a century, and others are in trouble, but the point is this: these birds were in very bad shape, yet things have changed for the better. If good people work hard and more people join them, more of these problems can turn to progress, and progress could eventually become success.

When twenty-eight hundred people from 144 countries convened for the global conference of the World Conservation Union in 1996, it became the largest environmental event since the Rio Earth Summit. By adopting a simple resolution calling for countries to take action to reduce longline mortality to seabirds, they took the first coordinated international step toward helping birds stay off longline hooks. Representing Mark Lundsten's fishery, the North Pacific Longline Association announced that it supported the resolution, would modify fishing techniques to help protect seabirds, and would request legal regulations requiring its fleet to use bird-deterrent practices. And after the conference, they did. Approximately seventy-five governments were officially represented and they voted overwhelmingly for the seabird resolution, with the notable exceptions of Japan and Panama. (Japan regularly undermines international conservation institutions by joining as a voting member, then using economic coercion to get other countries—most often small-island nations—to vote with them against proposals for increased protection of wildlife, particularly ocean wildlife. This is most obvious in Japan's efforts to overturn the International Whaling Commission's ban on commercial whaling. Japan has for years killed hundreds of Minke Whales annually despite the ban and has recently begun killing Bryde's Whales and Sperm Whales. Despite the fiction that the whales are killed for "research," all the meat is sold commercially. In 2001 Japan fisheries official Maseyuku Komatsu got quoted in *Time* magazine for saying, "I believe the Minke Whale is a cockroach in the oceans.")

The albatross resolution was the fruit of more than three years of long-labored preparatory negotiations and international meetings spearheaded by Defenders of Wildlife, BirdLife International, Environmental Defense, American Bird Conservancy, Audubon, the Antarctica Project, Greenpeace, and several other conservation groups. Among national governments, New Zealand and Australia proved particularly instrumental. Only about half a dozen key people drafted the resolution, with maybe twenty-five additional players actively promoting it—proving again Margaret Mead's admonition "Never doubt that a small handful of people can change the world; indeed, it's the only thing that ever has." The World Conservation Union resolution led within the next four years to further steps, including a "United Nations Plan of Action for Seabirds," and the "International Agreement on the Conservation of Albatrosses and Petrels." Scientists, conservation groups, and representatives of several government agencies also formed the North Pacific Albatross Working Group, to promote research and rule making toward reducing bird kills on longlines across Amelia's realm. In Antarctic waters, the Commission for the Conservation of Antarctic Marine Living Resources (the commission that sets Antarctic fishing rules) reduced its member nations' bird kills by up to 96 percent by agreeing to delay the start of the fishing season until most birds were nearly finished breeding and to use scare lines and other bird deterrents while fishing. Though that improvement is only for member countries' boats fishing legally, and though the U.N. Plan of Action is voluntary and most countries' responses have been sluggish so far, and though saving birds will always require the cooperation of the people on boats far from shore, the point is: all of this represents recent activity that is still gaining momentum, and there are now lights at the end of this tunnel.

As Mark is explaining, the main threat to albatrosses now, the longlines, could be solved on boats worldwide. All it takes is a willing captain—as I'm here to learn. Soon we will see what success looks like.

BAD WEATHER HAD US STUCK in the harbor for a couple of days, and Mark and his crew are savoring the luxury. Just a few years ago, all the boats competed directly for a very limited catch in a very short season, and everyone was forced to fish regardless of the weather. But now, in the wheelhouse of the *Masonic*, Captain Lundsten is discoursing on the works of Emily Dickinson and Sylvia Plath. Apparently, two decades as a survivor in some of the harshest fishing conditions on Earth have enhanced Mark's ear for poetry.

Last week he was several thousand miles from here, in Massachusetts, shopping for poetry books at the Harvard Coop. He'd been brought to Boston to advise a National Research Council panel evaluating different forms of fisheries management. Mark says, "People from New England can't seem to understand why we have fish left in Alaska. We tell them: 'We just stick to the quota and we leave some for next year.' They act like they can't relate. And look at the disaster they have."

Mark sees his fishery for Sablefish (also called Black Cod) and Pacific

Halibut improving. Meanwhile, Atlantic Cod and Atlantic Halibut are spectacular casualties in the demolition derby that has been New England fishing. Populations of both species, depleted from decades of overfishing, remain on the ropes over most of their Atlantic range, at or near all-time lows off New England, the Canadian Maritimes, and across northern Europe. The human toll is depressed communities, thousands of people in once-proud fishing families who lost the livelihoods that were their means of understanding who they were, and large areas closed to fishing, with only hopes the fish will recover someday.

Mark is a leading proponent of a rather new approach to fishery management called Individual Transferable Quotas, ITQs for short. Some fisheries are still unmanaged, open to all comers and limited only by what a boat can catch. The results are typically disastrous: depletion of fish, dislocation of fishers. More and more, fisheries are managed in some way. In a typically managed commercial fishery, a total catch quota is established as a limit. When the boats collectively reach the quota, the fishery is closed for the season, for all participants. This causes each boat to try to catch as many fish as possible before the overall quota is reached and the fishing stopped. The intense competition this race creates is called a "derby." Because all the boats are competing directly, fishing-industry lobbyists exert political pressure to leave the season open longer or increase the quota, resulting in overfishing and depletion.

New England and the Canadian Maritimes (and a lot of other places) largely destroyed their fisheries through simple greed. As more and more people got in, political pressures prevented fishery managers from accepting the fact that scientists kept flagging: the amount of fish was finite. More and more boats caught more and more fish—until they all started catching fewer and fewer. And finally boats and fishing businesses themselves went belly-up. In Alaska, as more and more people got in, fishery managers fiercely held the line on the number of fish caught—which was very wise—but they did so by reducing the length of open seasons to just a few days. At the most extreme, halibut "seasons" were as short as twenty-four hours, twice a year. Because these managers always understood that a fishery relies on healthy fish populations, Alaska's most important fish populations remain robust. And nowadays, the intense competition and absurdly short seasons are a thing of the past because of the ITQ system.

With ITQs, each boat owns shares of an overall quota that is determined by scientists. Moreover, each boat owner can buy or sell (that is, can transfer) all or some of their shares. Boat owners, boat captains, and crew members can all buy and sell shares. In many other fisheries, unprofitable or marginal boats are often trapped into continued fishing to repay debts, thus continuing the political pressure to keep quotas too high. ITQs allow fishers to either sell their way out of fishing or accumulate shares. For those who stay in, consolidation means less competition, more fish to catch, and more money to earn. They are at liberty and leisure to catch their share as quickly or slowly as they wish; the race for the fish and the derbies become things of the past, memories of the bad old days.

Yet only a few fisheries are managed this way, and proposals for wider application of the approach have met considerable resistance. Critics include some conservation groups and many owner-operators. They fear excessive accumulation of shares, corporate fishing, and the end of smaller, owner-operated boats. Pointing to timber companies that have clear-cut lands they own, destroying forests for the trees—and money—they also say that ownership doesn't intrinsically yield good stewardship. They're right; that *can* happen.

But Mark rebuts their point: "They insist ITQs will lead to corporate dominance, vertical integration, and loss of owner-operators. I'm proof it doesn't *have* to be that way, that it can *work*." Mark says that in his fishery the system has the needed safeguard—a cap on accumulation—that has preserved the small owner-operators. It has stabilized and professionalized the crews by giving them more future security. And it has helped conserve the fish. In New England, where Mark met resistance, crews often change from one trip to the next (sometimes culled from local bars when it's time for the boat to leave) as people drift in and out of the fishery, because the race for fish and depletion have made fishing there so unprofitable. But old habits are dying a hard death. "I can talk about success until I'm blue in the face," Mark says exasperatedly. "They don't listen."

Transferable-quota management in Mark's Alaska fishery has also made fishing much safer for boats and people. His crew members refer often to "the derby days" when fishing pressure was so intense that the fleet could catch its entire six-month quota in twenty-four hours. The competition forced boats to go fishing no matter what kind of weather, with sometimes fatal results. Nowadays, people who survived the derbies—Mark among them—often shudder at the memories. The most common description you hear these men use about the derby days is the word "nightmare." The references are so frequent they seem to serve a therapeutic purpose, as though these men still need to just *talk* about it.

. . .

CLOSING IN ON HIS FIFTIETH BIRTHDAY, Mark has a smooth, full-bodied radio announcer's voice. He's a brown-haired, flannel-and-fleece sort of guy, with sincere, somewhat somber blue-gray eyes. He is also a large, solid man, sized to match the task of wresting a living where the greatest ocean meets the Great Land.

Mark grew up in Colorado and earned a baccalaureate degree in English. "After college, I wanted to go either to the Southwest or Northwest. My girlfriend, Teru, wanted to be near the ocean. So, ocean is what I got. Plus a wife. I started graduate school part-time, and got a job at a Seattle shipyard. But I couldn't handle academic politics, and I couldn't sit and read all day. I didn't drop out or anything, just never showed up for the third quarter.

"I liked the shipyard's manual labor. It was good training for owning a boat like this. Halibut boats had the reputation as the real professionals, the guys who went up to Alaska and really *fished*. While I was doing some welding on a halibut boat I asked the captain for a job, and wound up fishing with him for about six years in the late seventies. During that time, the fishery got real crowded. It turned into hell. It got so miserable and difficult in the derbies, I almost quit four times. I had my little speech to the boss all rehearsed. But I'm glad I didn't.

"By the time I bought this boat, I pretty much knew what I was doing. But no matter how much you know, it's a shock to go from the deck to the wheelhouse. By luck, I bought this boat just as Japanese boats got kicked out of the federal waters. We were one of the first to go after Sablefish, and with the Japanese out, the market just went up like this"—he gestures with his hand—"and so did fish abundance. But guys saw how well we were doing, and after a year or two everybody was fishing Sablefish. The derbies got incredible. *God*, it was horrible."

Mark led the charge for, and finally got, a federally administered transferable quota system for both Sablefish and Pacific Halibut. That put the derby fishing out of its misery.

Mark sees improvement in every aspect of the fishery. In the derby days, almost twice as many boats chased halibut in Alaskan waters as do today. "In the derbies, lots of boats would set their gear in the same area. The first day you'd have great big fish. And the second day you'd get about a third of what you had the first day, and the third day you'd have about a sixth. A lot of the gear was cross-laid, got chafed on each other; a lot of stuff broke off. It was a mess. Everyone lost expensive gear. Sad to say, a lot of hooked fish got left on the bottom.

"Now," Mark continues, "we do everything systematically, with a pattern; it's *way* more efficient. Now we have our fish to ourselves. We don't see anybody else fishing around us, and we have high catch rates all the way through. And we'll actually fish about fifty days between mid-April and mid-August. It's *so* much better now."

For many, it comes down to money. In the last derby year, a crewman earned $25,000 to $40,000. Fast money in a short time, to be sure (very short if you drowned because you felt forced to fish in bad weather), but the pay was declining as competition increased. Nowadays, full-share (a pay level usually attained after a couple of seasons) for a crew member on a union longline boat is usually $80,000 to over $100,000. These guys are the beneficiaries of some of the best, most conservative fisheries management in the world. The system isn't perfect, but it's much better than most.

ALASKA'S SEWARD HARBOR IS RIMMED with snow and mountains slumping steeply into the water. Eagles grip pilings and sailboat masts. Ravens croak from the roofs. Black-legged Kittiwakes and gulls row buoyantly through the heavy air. A couple of swimming seals, several murres, and a Sea Otter all author chevrons upon the misty water. The docks sleep a couple hundred boats, including small-scale commercial vessels and the sailboats of people from Anchorage. And tour boats. It's too cloudy and foggy to see right now, but we are near Kenai Fjords National Park and its gleaming glaciers. In the last decade or so this place has gone from being entirely a fishing town to becoming largely a tourist town, where ice, wildlife, and mountains mean money.

The crew and I walk to a restaurant that has an excellent harbor view, with more eagles coursing outside the windows. The restaurant walls are hung copiously with big fish, including a ten-foot Pacific Halibut that weighed over 360 pounds. Essentially giant predatory flounders, Pacific Halibut get considerably bigger than even this panel-sized monster. Atlantic Halibut once grew bigger still—to 700 pounds.

Half the restaurant customers are tourists, half are fishermen. Fishermen are sitting mostly at the bar, the tourists mostly at tables. We're mostly fishermen, but we sit at a table.

The waitress tells us that the special today is salmon. Mark says, "Hmm—probably the early-spring Kings from Yakutat. They had thirty or forty thousand pounds."

Mark's five-man crew includes Tim Henkel, Callahan McVay, Jim Fitzgerald, Shaun Bailey, and David "Mac" McArthur.

Tim Henkel, the most senior of Mark's crew members at forty-four, has been with Mark twelve years and is capable of skippering if Mark is forced to miss a trip. He is an athletically built man with thinning short hair, a blackish beard, and wire-rimmed glasses.

Tim came of age in Seattle's university district. Seattle—and the world—were a bit different in the late 1960s. Starbuck was just a character in *Moby-Dick;* the words *micro* and *soft* didn't connote enormity, power, and profit; and the term high-tech was almost invariably followed by the word *weapons.* At that time the "U district" was the hippie hotbed, complete with riots, summertime park love-ins, and Vietnam War protests. Tim says, "We had a lot of wild times."

But not necessarily good times. Vietnam was hard on morale, and the U.S. draft was a looming death sentence for thousands of young Americans, and Vietnamese. Faced with being fodder for an unjust war, many found that getting high was a shortcut to a false escape.

Tim admits, "I was a full-blown alcoholic and cocaine addict by the time I was twenty." He'd graduated from high school with a D average; but he *did* graduate—the only one in his family who did. He went to trade school to learn boat building, and developed an admiration for fishermen. Tim was soon fishing himself. He spent six summers netting salmon. He spent winters in one of the most savage fisheries there is: Bering Sea King and Tanner Crab fishing. "That crab fishery," he says, "draws the most brutal people. And some of them—skippers included—are not the sharpest tools in the shed. It's about the most dangerous, ferocious fishing there is."

Jim chimes in, "Almost no one working the deck of a Bering Sea crab boat is over thirty years old."

Eventually Tim got a friend to introduce him to the union long-liners in Seattle, and he has remained in this fleet since. "In five days, I'll be fifteen years clean of cocaine. A lot of my friends never got clean and now are dead." He says he lost ten years to drugs and is still playing catch-up. Tim sees lots to like in fishing. "It's now more serious and safer, no room for alcoholics and druggies. I like the task-oriented work in fishing. I really like coming into the dock with a load of fish. Fishing gives me a culture that I like. A lifestyle. I like the freedom. Some people have lots of time and no money; others have lots of money and no time. Fishing gives me both. Guys in this fleet can actually raise a family while working on the deck of a boat—not just in the pilothouse. And we're some of the last guys that actually *produce* something."

Tim asks if this is my first time in Alaska. When I say it is, Tim says welcomingly, "You'll be schooner trash in no time."

I feel proud to hope he's right.

Callahan, a.k.a. Cal, wears a T-shirt that says SAVE THE ALES. He grew up on Whidbey Island outside Seattle, in Puget Sound. His mother had married a salmon troller, so at age twenty-three, this is his tenth season fishing, his fifth with Mark. In addition to fishing along with the others, he's the boat's cook.

Jim Fitzgerald is the crew's most taciturn member. He grew up in North Dakota and dropped out of college as a senior chemistry major after reading an article about fish canneries that prompted him to sell everything he owned and drive to Alaska. Jim has been here twelve years and is now thirty-four. Jim says that breaking in, "developing the back for it," was difficult.

"Yeah, it's hard breaking in," emphasizes Shaun Bailey, twenty-six, who has worked on long-liners since he was seventeen and has been on the *Masonic* three years. But he also emphasizes that he loves fishing. Shaun came from a troubled family beset by alcohol, and became an alcoholic himself at a young age. He sees this job as his ticket. Mark left him ashore for one trip after he appeared drunk at the boat. Now he is the happiest member of the crew. On this trip, he will also be the luckiest.

Mac is thirty-seven and has been fishing for seventeen years, the last six on the *Masonic*. Mac was drawn to fishing by the challenge of mastering the work. Now he says, "The older I get the more I enjoy the things I did as a kid, like just being around the ocean. I am a visually oriented person, so I like looking at the sea, seeing the changing view."

Most of the younger crew members speak of other jobs and other skills they want to develop in their off time. Cal does glassblowing; others speak of carpentry. In the back of their minds is fear. Fear of the accidents that often befall commercial fishermen, fear of fatal weather, fear of the grim prospect of working as a deckhand in Alaskan waters if you live to be past fifty. Mac says he feels guilty about not working during the off-season (but not *too* guilty, apparently) and keeps himself occupied working on his house in Springfield, Oregon. But he's ready to move to Alaska, saying, "I find Oregon to be pretty used up by my standards." Mac may have another long-term strategy. He excuses himself to go place an order for two hundred shares of stock in an oil-drilling company.

Skipper Mark has shorter-term concerns. He has spent the morning calling buyers in Seattle, Homer, Seward, and Kodiak, developing his fishing plan based on prices. A story is circulating here, of one boat that ran for two weeks all the way down to Seattle for a better price on their fish and ended up getting five cents per pound less there than he could have gotten in Alaska. Weather and fish prices dominate Mark's concerns, and his crew's. "What we will hunt depends on the price." The weather broke last week, giving Canadian boats a good shot at halibut, bringing the price down. Sablefish is a good fish to go for when the halibut price is dropping. So for now, Mark is targeting Sablefish, which entails going to certain places and fishing deeper.

IN THE RESTAURANT other fishermen talk price and weather and locales—and how to keep their fishery open by avoiding bird kills. Mark is saying, "I think it's important to have an indefinitely sustainable fishery as far as the whole ecosystem goes: the fish, the birds, and everything else out here. That's the main reason I don't want to catch albatrosses and other birds. I want to be able to make the claim that we can keep doing this forever. I never *said* it that way before, but it just seems so obvious."

Mark speaks to me of his affection for the fleet. He says he respects and likes the fishing community much more than the academic community he once knew. Mark says these fishermen are not only smart but very thoughtful people. "They live a life in which they are immediately responsible for what they do."

A fisherman comes over to tell Mark about one night from his last trip. "It was one of those nights you see about twice in your life. Flat calm, full moon, and a hundred yards away was a pod of Sperm Whales in a circle, snoring. God," he says almost prayerfully, "it was *neat.*"

Another fisherman from the bar who has just come to sit with us waves his hands and complains about Sperm Whales. He says they eat fish off the hooks, and wouldn't mind seeing a few killed.

Mark hints that if anyone from their fleet started harming whales, "the public boycott of us would happen so fast it would take your breath away."

The fisherman says, "At today's prices, who cares!"

Apparently, not all these guys are reading poetry in the wheelhouse or feeling inspired to find their place as both user and steward of a whole, healthy ecosystem.

Tim says to me that anyway the Sperm Whales are not nearly as problematic as Killer Whales. Mark adds, "In the Aleutians, Killer Whales somehow know when you have found the fish. They somehow get you on their radar. When you finally start catching Sablefish—it takes a while to find them in the Aleutians—you're excited and the fish are coming up on the line, and all of a sudden you look toward the horizon." He mimes a distant look of combined disbelief, recognition, and dread. "And in the distance you see these white puffs—not spouts but these animals bursting through the wave tops as they're rushing for the boat at thirty-five miles an hour. Usually big males lead, with those high dorsal fins slicing through the surface. When they get to the side of the boat they turn and the winch man just helplessly watches them pull, pull, pull; eating those fish off the line like stripping grapes. And they don't take ninety percent; they take *one hundred* percent. Half of your brain is in absolute awe—and the other half of your brain is saying, 'Oh crap.'" Mark suggests that the answer could be to develop fish traps so the fish don't come up on hooks where the whales can get at them. They'd better be strong traps on strong lines. Jim says that in the Bering Sea, Killer Whales sometimes try to bump seals off ice floes. He says that occasionally, trying to get away from Killers, seals would run right up the stern ramps of dragger boats.

Mark emphasizes how tough fishing in the Aleutians is: The way that the currents run so hard. The way that the weather is so cruel. The problems of icing up. The dangers of boats accumulating ice faster than the crews can break it off with baseball bats; how iced-up boats get top-heavy and turn over. The williwaws—capricious, dangerous, swirling gusts of wind that can pick up water. The way the ordeal of fishing the Aleutians is reflected in a nickname for the place that even these men use: "Hardball Hotel."

BUILT NEARLY SEVENTY YEARS AGO, the wooden, seventy-foot *Masonic* was the last of a breed of sail-powered halibut schooners, hybrids between old-style Gloucester cod schooners and Norwegian workboats. Mark has owned the *Masonic* for about fifteen years. He knows who all of the previous owners are, going back to when the boat was built. Mark says this boat is made of "original wood"—old growth. It would be impossible to make this boat today, because fully 95 percent of North America's ancient forests have been cut down.

Nowadays the *Masonic*'s sail masts remain, but rather than sails she is propelled by a 365-horsepower six-cylinder diesel. She carries 4,500 gallons of fuel, enough for twenty days of cruising. Mark says, "We don't run full-tilt. We use under three hundred horsepower to make it last."

On the *Masonic*'s foredeck lie coil after coil after coil of ropes with buoys and anchors, for securing the ends of the longlines to the bottom.

Elsewhere on the boat: coil after coil after coil of fishing lines. And thousands and thousands and thousands of hooks.

The wheelhouse sits up high amidships. It contains the skipper's private bunk, as well as all the navigating electronics—radars, sonars, GPSs—and radios and maps. The boat's aft deck is a large baiting station that can be closed against the weather. The stern rail accommodates a chute for sending the baited lines overboard. The boat's rear deck also has the toilet, or "head." The privileged view from this seagoing outhouse is of a limitless horizon, a great ocean, and some of the world's most magnificent seabirds sweeping by.

The galley occupies the bow of the boat belowdecks. To get to the galley, you step down an almost vertical set of steps that is more ladder than stairs. It contains a diesel-burning stove and oven (for cooking *and* heat), a sink, and a table shaped to fit the wedge-shaped bow. Surrounding the table are hidden storage space and five tiny bunks barely wider than a man's shoulders, tucked into the bow of the boat. Each bunk has a bare bulb and a cramped storage rack. The galley is thus kitchen, dining room, living room, bedroom, and, because it has a television with a video player, entertainment center.

Space is severely scarce, privacy scarcer. People make a particular effort to show excessive politeness while going in and out of their bunks around the table and in moving around the cramped and crowded galley. Stories abound of crewmen on boats getting on one another's nerves, with violent, sometimes fatal consequences. On one Alaskan vessel, one crewman stabbed another more than twenty times because he could no longer tolerate the way the man chewed his breakfast cereal.

Not counting sea spray and rain, there is no shower aboard. A good T-shirt lasts a week, getting stronger with age. On my six days aboard *Masonic*, no comb will part my hair. And I'll quickly outgrow the habit of glancing into a mirror. I will become, in short, schooner trash.

WE'VE WAITED ABOUT A DAY and a half because the weather forecast calls for steady forty-five-mile-an-hour winds. The days in port make the men a bit anxious, because time spent waiting for good weather adds to the weeks until they return home to families or sweethearts. In the derby days, much worse anxiety derived from being forced to fish despite dangerous weather. Time was money. But now with individual fishing quotas, time is merely time and money is merely money. They've paid for their share of the quota, and the only question is how long catching it will take them. And the weather largely dictates that.

It looks like we will leave tomorrow, so today there's plenty of work loading bait and ice. In a misty snow shower that is half drizzle, ninety-six hundred pounds of herring and squid frozen at −20° Fahrenheit come aboard via crane. We move to a different dock for ten tons of ice powdered like snow.

Least of the provisions on the *Masonic,* though with deeper implications for the crew, is *one* pack of cigarettes. All smokers aboard intend to quit during this trip. They do this almost every trip. Mac refers ruefully to "the demon tobacco."

Well over thirteen thousand hooks need a piece of bait, applied by hand. Baiting takes the afternoon. After dinner, it will take much of the evening.

⊱ ⊱ ⊱ ⊱ ⊱ ⊱ ⊱ ⊱ ⊱

DREAMING AND
DREADING ON ALBATROSS
BANK

"*O*NE OF THE FIRST THINGS you'll notice about the place we're going is that it's all wilderness," Mark Lundsten is saying as he starts the *Masonic*'s engine. "And—though it's beautiful—I mean wilderness that swallows people who don't know what they're doing."

Slushy early-May snow covers decks and docks. Midday fog encases the harbor. And the drizzle has turned suddenly to the biggest snowflakes I've ever seen, falling like feathers from a shredded comforter, whiting out Resurrection Bay. But the forecast has improved sufficiently that we loosen the lines and Mark eases *Masonic* from the slip and out toward the unseen mouth of the bay.

The sea turns thick with cold as slush clots the water's surface into pancakes of ice, dampening the light swell. Wet snow frosts the pilothouse glass. We're navigating on instruments. Mark keeps a sharp eye on the radar, which shows the fjords we cannot see, and the GPS navigator, which tracks the boat's position via satellite and gives Mark information for getting where he wants to be.

About the only thing we can actually see is the boat itself. Mark peers out a cracked-open window to watch for drifting logs. Mac is furtively forming a snowball in his gloved hands. Shouts signal the eruption of a full-scale snowball fight on deck. Inside the warmed wheelhouse, Mark comments, "The real job requirement is to have the emotional maturity of a fifteen-year-old. And," he quickly admits, "I'm not exempt."

As the snowfall lightens and visibility opens a little, the toes of fjords become visible on both sides of the bay, showing from under their flannel fog nightgown. The chart shows them rising to twenty-six hundred feet in height. The opaque air forces me to imagine them.

We see light-on-their-wings Arctic Terns (whose Arctic-to-Antarctic annual migrations let them experience more daylight than any other living thing), stocky Herring Gulls, foraging Glaucous-winged Gulls, Mew Gulls.

The crew sets up fish-sorting equipment on deck, then goes back to baiting the hooks, which will take hours more.

At a modest nine and a half knots, we pass Rugged Island, a jagged, snow-dusted saddleback of scree and trees. This is a transition zone where the open ocean, though still some distance away, first makes itself felt on the protected inshore waters (and your stomach). This rich intersection attracts a collection of foraging birds: Forked-tailed Storm-Petrels, impressive numbers of Thick-billed and Common Murres like flying penguins, various dark and diminutive murrelets, pretty kittiwakes, a whale's briefly glimpsed blackish back, and the first of many thousands of Northern Fulmars we will see and see and see. The fulmars look like small, stubby, uncouth albatrosses. Also here, on the rocks, sprawl the tawny forms of half a dozen endangered Steller Sea Lions—the world's largest sea lion, the one whose serious decline is likely due to a combination of getting killed in nets, fishery competition for their food, and food reduction caused by a warming ocean.

MOST OF THE SKIPPERS and crew have experienced seasickness. Many still do. I like knowing that I'm in good company. Not long after we pass Rugged Island, we begin to feel the long rolling swells of the seas that had kept us in port for two days. Soon I don't feel too rugged or swell myself. That is to say, I cannot in all honesty describe the early-May Alaskan sea conditions as calm. I take a seasickness pill. Too late. It— and my last meal—don't stay down long. While I'm on the stern deck puking, a large cold wave hurls itself aboard, soaking me and accenting my momentary misery—but saving me the need to wash off the deck.

> *How long will ye round me be swelling,*
> *O ye blue-tumbling waves of the Sea?*
> —Coleridge, 1793

At this very moment, in fact, the sea is throwing a lot of water, which eagerly covers *Masonic's* deck but only grudgingly finds its way out the scuppers. The running sheets of water swirling around my boots give the sensation of fording a stream, although the analogy to sinking presents itself.

The gray light, flying snow, cold, and lack of visibility—and how I feel—give the place a foreboding dreariness. In the long-lingering light at 9:30 P.M. the first Laysan Albatross crosses our foamy green wake.

> *At length did cross an Albatross,*
> *Thorough the fog it came.*
> —Coleridge, 1798

In the dim Alaskan snowlight the albatross and I both seem to float along together for a minute or two, haunting the edges of each other's worlds.

Meanwhile, Amelia's chick is coping with heat stress in the sun-seared tropics. Hard to imagine. The blinding beaches and gleaming lagoon of French Frigate Shoals seem like a dream vaguely remembered. Does it seem that way to Amelia, too? At the moment, she's wandering east along the northern edge of that North Pacific Current, two thousand miles from Tern Island. Amelia's undulating flight has stitched these worlds together, causing me to experience—perhaps a little too viscerally—how connected the far-flung distances of the great circle of our planet really are. My lofty musings coincide with another bout of seasickness. When I look up again, the albatross has ghosted from sight through the cold, snow-flecked gloam.

> *And now there came both mist and snow,*
> *And it grew wondrous cold.*
> —Coleridge, 1798

In the wheelhouse, Mark is listening to a Vivaldi opera. Water and music are companionable because both are fluid. Music is a highly abstract art, and so is fishing. With only the rhythm of the sea surface as a starting point, all else is orchestration. Like a composer, a fisher inhabits our world but labors in an imagined universe that remains always unseen. Success of a musical score is in the sound it suddenly conjures to your senses. If the skipper succeeds, fish from another dimension appear suddenly on deck, before your eyes.

I join Mark as much for the company as for the fact that I can jump to the deck faster from the wheelhouse than from the galley. Because I can't keep anything down, I resort to trying just a few sips of sugared water, getting increasingly elemental as I'm increasingly out of my element.

Actually, I'm surprised by how off center I feel. The sea is not all that rough. Mark says, "You have what we call 'schooner shock'—immediate, chronic seasickness. It's common here."

Great. I wonder if the old schooner's archaic masts are acting as levers, raising the boat's center of gravity and giving the *Masonic* the woozy roll that seems to accentuate, rather than dampen, the motion of the sea. I hope that's the explanation. I don't want to think I'm simply a light-weight.

The crew continues baiting hooks. They tend to work quietly. They've long ago told most of their stories to each other. Bait and coil. Bait and coil. Bait and coil. Bait and coil. Do that twenty-seven hundred times, and—if your crewmates have each done the same—you're ready for a day of fishing.

We continue along Kodiak Island. Kodiak has massive cliffs, slopes cloaked in deep green timber, a pronounced tree line (all visible), and the world's largest Grizzly Bears (lurking unseen at the moment). The tundra slopes just above the tree line show a tinge of early spring green. The ridges above are sharp, their rocky peaks snow-laced. Several her-ring netters are working along the shore. We pass some clear-cuts—more scars from America's war on forests, even here. No trees grow near Kodiak's south end, not even stumps. It's just too exposed there to the sea and the flying salt spray and the battering winds of winter.

Several Dall's Porpoises come to play with the boat. Unlike most sleek dolphins, they look surprisingly fat and heavy—pudgy-looking, sausage-shaped, starkly black-and-white animals. They soon tire of us.

In the final light of a long, late day, skeins of Sooty Shearwaters fly sil-houetted against the sky. Tilting sideways, they cut a lovely and pictur-esque profile of life.

We continue running while the world turns its curved back away from the sun. We are still running when the world whirls around to face day-light again. We run through a second sunset. And again we continue, well into the night. By the time the propeller has been spinning steadily for thirty-six hours, all shorelines, all peaks and pinnacles, lie far below the dark horizon. With my usual cycle of sleep, activity, and work disrupted by seasickness and inactivity, all normal sense of time and routine is already broken.

In my bunk Mark has placed a book of the poetry of Philip Levine. Levine writes of working-class people in factory towns, but it's surpris-ingly easy to hear his voice out here. One disconcerting aspect of being at sea in a vessel under another person's command is that for many days you have no control of where you are, and no visual sense of being anywhere in particular. As I suspend control of my life, knowing of unknowable dangers, entrusting Mark to take me *somewhere*, I read of workingmen and hear myself forewarned: "Where he is going or who he is, he doesn't ask himself. He doesn't know, and doesn't know it matters." It's too late for warnings; I know it doesn't matter now.

Surrounded always by the potentially life-taking water from which these men take their livings, my sleep on this boat has been afflicted by disquieting dreams. Mark says bad dreams are also common here. It's unsettling to lie in a cramped bunk knowing that the whooshing you hear constantly—just a few inches away on the other side of the aged planks your pillow rests against—is the hiss of a hungry, frigid ocean that will inhale you for a snack if it gets the chance. Into my anxious, swirling sleep, I take a line or two from Levine's poem "My Grave":

> . . . *barefoot and quiet,*
> *[you] leave my side and . . .*
> *. . . return suddenly, your mouth tasting*
> *of cold water.*

In the deep of night we have crossed a place called Albatross Bank. In the days before sonar, birds alone must have marked the dramatic slope where the bottom falls away from thirty fathoms to well over six hundred. They surely find the place by smelling the plankton concentrated in water welling up from the deep to the shallow bank. Unseen below our hull—but well fixed by our navigation gear and profiled on electronic screens glowing in the dark wheelhouse—is a particular indentation where, over a mere two-mile running distance, the bottom has dropped from 240 fathoms to 400. Integrating knowledge in three dimensions, Mark says matter-of-factly, "This is a tide shadow; the fish just mill here because the current doesn't run so hard." That's his learned sense of the area. My sense is merely water, water everywhere.

We seek fish from a place of such crushing pressure and stunning cold and blinding blackness that no person could function even momentarily outside a submarine. Few submarines, in fact, can withstand such depths. No human has ever eyed this place where our hooks will lie in ambush. Other than its grossest physical features, we know almost nothing at all about this environment—or the lives of the creatures here, or what marvels of adaptation make so extreme a place their familiar home.

But the crew does know how to reach into that alien world. At two

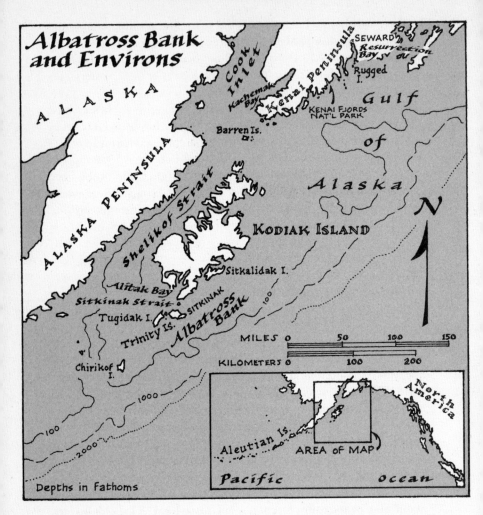

A.M. the engine changes pitch for the first time in a day and a half. Cal shoves a tray of food into the oven. The signal comes to set the long-lines. This is where we will do our hunting. The vessel slows. Here we will act as surrogate and agent for humanity's appetite.

SOME FACTS ABOUT FISHING: These longlines are made of three-eighths-inch nylon line. They're arranged into coiled sections called skates. Each coiled section is stored on a piece of canvas so it can be stacked, or slid—skated—across the deck. For Sablefishing, skates are one hundred fathoms (six hundred feet) long, with a hook on a short leader every thirty-nine inches, about 180 hooks per skate. Depending on conditions, about twenty-five skates in a row are attached to make each "string." Usually Mark and the crew will set and retrieve three strings per day. Under good conditions, they bait about seventy-five skates by hand each day. That can mean hand-baiting about 13,500 hooks. Cutting bait, baiting hooks, setting, hauling, and care of the fish occupies eighteen of every twenty-four hours.

Mac says this fishery uses the same gear it did in the 1500s. "It's archaic, super low-tech, but very effective." That's a romantic exaggeration. In the 1500s they didn't have engines, electricity, line haulers, or synthetic lines and other modern equipment, not to mention things like radar, sonar, and GPS. But the basic fishing gear—a lengthy line with hooks on it, anchored to the bottom—*is* about the same as was used on Atlantic Cod hundreds of years ago.

THE CREWMEN APPEAR on the night-darkened deck wearing rubber boots, orange bib slicker trousers, and waterproof forearm sleeves called "wristers." Inside their orange rubber gloves, their hands are coated with a product called Bag Balm, an antiseptic grease that helps keep hands warm and is actually manufactured for chafed dairy-cow udders.

Mark is in the wheelhouse, visible by the light of his instruments. He's watching the sonar screen and scratching his sleepy face.

A full silver moon burns its cool firefly light through the flickering clouds above. Far, far below, Sablefish swim in frigid darkness. We send the killing gear to take them.

The crew ties the prebaited skates together in the baiting station at the back of the boat, their work harshly illuminated by eight encaged bare industrial light bulbs overhead. The paradox of artificial light outdoors is that it cuts your vision by blinding you to anything outside its radius. But in the short distance that we *can* see, a few birds are already moving in on us, settling down for a long visit. Mostly Northern Fulmars, it looks like. They're fluttering in and out of the short halo of light we're casting over the moving black ocean that's bumping lumpily against our hull. Cal serves warm muffins and coffee, which the crew devours quickly between tasks.

Two of the fishermen set up the buoy lines, which have an anchor to pull one end of the gear down to the bottom, and enough line to let a big orange buoy with a pennant and radar reflector remain on the surface for later retrieval. Each end of the baited longline string will have such a buoy line and anchor.

Tim hurls overboard the heavy anchor and its massive line coils and buoy. The boat is moving slowly forward. The first baited skate of line has been affixed to the sinking anchor. The baited hooks begin whizzing overboard, clicking through an open-topped metal chute. At the rate that the gear whips over the bait chute, it's surprising that most of the bait stays on the hooks. The pretied skates are set to go overboard three in a row. As the last of these three is uncoiling itself and jumping into the chute and over the rail, one man leans in to tie the next set of three waiting skates to it. It looks very dangerous. There is no apparent chance for help if a person gets tangled or hooked, and serious injury would seem inevitable.

Sablefish live mostly on the sloping edge of the continental shelf, often at around 350 fathoms. That's deep—2,100 feet. Sinking at a foot per second, it will take thirty to forty-five minutes for the gear to reach the bottom here. One by one, for over an hour as the *Masonic* continues crawling forward, thousands of whipping hooks continue clicking over the stern, sounding like sneakers in the dryer.

At four A.M. Cal serves a big tray of chicken and rice with salad. I'm not sure if it is dinner or breakfast, but since it's dawn it must be breakfast. It disappears in a hurry. I sample a few tentative mouthfuls. Mac conspicuously engulfs several huge platefuls of rice.

The first pale daylight illuminates the crew's work of setting the next string. Now, just as the fishermen are drawn by their hungers into these deadly waters, the birds are ready to take their chances with our baited hooks. Roughly a hundred fulmars and a dozen albatrosses—mainly Laysans, with two Black-footeds—are already following, crisscrossing our wake. The crow-sized fulmars, relatives of albatrosses, are mostly gray; atop their yellowish bill lie their conspicuously fused little tube-nosed nostrils. Lacking the ease of albatrosses, fulmars pump hard, as though flying is work for them. They seem to have a dour, businesslike approach to life. If Charles Dickens had written about seabirds, fulmars would have populated the uncouth lower classes of his novels. The albatrosses maintain a graceful equanimity, beautiful as ever, pacing effortlessly even when waiting to scavenge a piece of bait or some fish guts.

A hook without bait, or with a drowned bird on it, is a hook that will not catch a fish. So it's fair to say that while the fishermen can be a problem for the birds, the birds can be a problem for the fishermen. Therein lies further incentive for fishers to keep birds off the hooks. This situation has potential for a win-win.

From the mast arm over the bait station, Mark and Tim deploy the "bird lines," two long streamers with vertical lines coming down to the water. The vertical rubber lines dangling from the streamers form a kind of snaking bead curtain of obstruction to flying birds. The streamers stretch about fifty yards astern. At that distance, the baited longline is already too deep for the birds to reach. That's the whole point. Two big buoys on lines tied to the moving boat are also sent astern. They create commotion. The scare lines snake and slither, as though the ocean imparts its own swimming motion to things. The buoys continually splash and startle.

The birds clearly dislike all this folderol. The splashing seems to frighten them, and they appear to fear colliding with the streamer lines. Birds continue following, sometimes landing on the roiled water of the wake, looking longingly at the sinking baited hooks. Few fulmars are coming inside the streamers. Those that do don't stay very long and virtually never attempt a grab at any of the bait. The albatrosses continue following the boat but at a safe distance, staying well clear of the gear. In fact, this year the *Masonic* will achieve zero bird mortality: for the duration of the season neither a fulmar nor an albatross and nary a gull will be drowned on a *Masonic*-set hook.

Mark's system is not unique, but what's unusual is his desire to make it work—for the whole fleet. And as the saying goes: Attitude makes the difference. Similar systems are mandated elsewhere, such as in New Zealand waters. But as one official of New Zealand's Department of Conservation says of the country's regulations that make streamer lines mandatory, "On most boats, the rules are not followed—at all. Regulations alone are a waste of paper. You need education, enforcement, and willing fishermen." The fishermen in Mark's fleet are motivated partly by a fear of being shut down by Short-tailed Albatross kills, partly by the negative publicity they've received, and partly by a genuine desire to fish cleanly and avoid killing birds. The main thing is: they are motivated.

Tim explains that five years ago the fleet did not religiously use bird-avoidance gear.

Mark says, "The regulations did it, and that required heat."

"Like anything else," Tim comments.

Mark, who'd gotten major heartburn from environmental groups, says graciously, "And we need watch-dog groups, certainly."

Tim adds, "Because extinct is for a long time."

So effective is the *Masonic*'s simple system that there is no real reason why albatrosses should be threatened by longline fishing. Few problems of such seriousness have so easy a solution so readily available.

It seems, therefore, all the more heartbreaking, and ultimately unacceptable, that in much of the rest of the world, long-liners don't bother, while birds drown and albatross populations decline.

Mark has proved that where people put a little effort into it, saving albatrosses from death by hook-drowning is possible. It works. Mark explains, "It *is* pretty simple, but it's not just the streamers, it's also how the line is weighted. If you put one big weight on the end of the line it pulls the rest of the gear so taut as you're moving forward that it's strung out along the surface like a buffet lunch before it gets far enough back to begin sinking. But if you put a lot of smaller weights on, it sinks rapidly as it's coming off the boat. The challenge is how to do that and have workable gear at the same time. We've now got quarter-pound weights every sixty feet, and it seems to be working for us." Mark says that the scare lines used to deter the birds would work less well for Swordfishing because those longlines are set shallow—sixty feet from the surface instead of on the bottom hundreds or thousands of feet down—with little weight to get them down quickly. It's less a problem for tuna long-lining because they usually set deeper.

But there's a glitch even here in Alaska: though paired streamers and line weights—just like Mark uses—reduce seabird mortality by over 90 percent, only one out of five captains uses them. Alaska's regulations require fishers to use *one* of the following measures to avoid birds: bird-scaring streamers, a buoy or piece of wood towed on a rope, underwater setting (requiring an expensive and sophisticated machine system), or setting only at night. The easiest thing is to throw a buoy over on a rope, and you're in compliance. So that's what the other 80 percent of skippers simply do. Result: Mark's kill rate has dropped to zero, but the overall rate and number of birds killed hasn't dipped (it's actually *increased* slightly since the regulations took effect). In Australian waters, where boats have been required to use streamer lines since the mid-1990s, albatross kills have taken a 99 percent drop. Why are people in Alaska allowed to do what doesn't work, and not required to do what does work, when what works is so simple and there are champions for success inside the fleet? *Good question.* The answer is that the National Marine Fisheries Service hasn't heard from enough people like you and me, and they're not paying enough attention to people like Mark. (Happily, that situation will change. Because of increasing concern from both the public and industry, Mark's method will eventually become law throughout Alaska, and will also spread to Canada's British Columbia.)

BY THE TIME WE'VE SET the third string, the first line has been deadly in the deep dark for about five hours. We go to pick it up, homing in on the radar reflector and bright orange buoy. Tim places the line into a power-hauler amidships, and for many minutes its wheel turns and turns, dumping the line on deck for the crew to begin coiling and coiling and coiling. At great length, the first hooks begin appearing—empty.

The boat proceeds forward very slowly, with the line coming over the side of the boat as we crawl along its length like a spider running up its own web, summoning our line from the bottom. The boat is a bird magnet. Increasing numbers of winged scavengers are continually arriving. We've already collected a couple of hundred Northern Fulmars. And a couple of Glaucous Gulls, and Glaucous-winged Gulls. They press close to the hull, waiting eagerly. Beyond them, as though proud and aloof, are perhaps fifty Laysan and four Black-footed Albatrosses. Mark says if you go east you see more Black-footeds, until by the time you reach British Columbia there are hardly any Laysans.

I stand shivering, trying to duck the fine bow spray, newly impressed by how comfortable the birds look on this cold sea. Their dense feathers deliver the finest kind of insulation. Their webbed feet, paddling the frigid water, would cost them a lot of heat, but a countercurrent heat-exchanging capillary system takes the warmth from blood leaving the body on its way to the feet and uses it to warm blood coming back into the body from those chilly toes. Cold feet, warm heart. Many of the fulmars are actually sleeping cozily, head tucked under wing. The boat is their chow wagon for a few days, and many of these birds will likely remain with us. The albatrosses, so far from the Hawaiian swelter-skelter, look equally at home. Some are on the water, but many albatrosses are just sweeping around and around the boat as though for the fun of it. It doesn't seem to make much difference to them whether they're sitting or sleeping or in the air, since they expend so little energy while flying. When they do decide to land, they come in with their big feet splayed, stretching the webbing between their toes and skiing onto the heaving surface before settling their great bodies. Bobbing on the swells, two of the Laysans are actually engaged in courtship, with bills clacking, heads shaking side to side and bowing. Don't they ever get enough? I wonder if they have traveled together. Their enthusiasm for each other spreads to two adjacent pairs. On land and at sea, albatrosses—let it be recorded—just love to dance.

WE EAGERLY AWAIT the first fish. The birds practice the refined patience of scavengers. But they know well that the empty hooks are their signal. The fulmars press close, jostling for position. The sky is densely overcast, blue only at the far horizons. Shaun removes a few uneaten pieces of soggy bait from the hooks and flings them to the feathered mob, which rushes forward. Momentary noisy squabbles ensue, and the baits are gone instantly.

Hunger drives everything here: fish, birds, fishermen. Except me. Cal quickly rinses my breakfast off the deck. Embarrassed, I apologize and say again how good his cooking is. Cal says generously, "It happens to all of us. Hardly anybody eats the first night out of port."

Jim opens a beer, and gulps and spits out three quick swigs.

The first Sablefish come swinging aboard, several in a row. They are a sleeker, more graceful-looking fish than you would expect from so deep, from such cold. They are overall a dark charcoal gray with an olive-green tint, their backs a little darker than their bellies. The smaller ones have a mottled pattern on the dorsal surface. The ones we're now catching range to about eighteen pounds, but most are between five and fifteen. Their body narrows to a deeply forked tail, which suggests activity and speed. I wonder if any human eye has ever seen them swim in their natural habitat. They sometimes come up on several hooks consecutively, suggesting that the hooks arrested groups traveling in small packs. After five or ten or fifteen hooks without a fish, there may be three or four or six hooks with Sablefish on each.

Now we're into the Sablefish pretty heavily. The winch brings the line up, and Shaun gaff-hooks the larger fish for security before the line lifts them from the water, to make sure their weight doesn't pull them off the hook and back into the sea. Very occasionally comes up a fish whose mouth is mangled by an old hook scar—two strikes and out. Quite busy now, Shaun pulls most fish off the hook and swings them to his right into a waiting pen on deck. The incoming line goes through a pair of rollers like two kitchen rolling pins, called the "hook stripper" or "crucifier." Any fish Shaun doesn't gaff or remove, and any remaining bait, gets dragged to the paired rollers. When a fish's head hits the rollers, the hook is pulled from its jaws. It then slides into the on-deck bin, called the "checker." The rest of the line then goes around the winch and a person sits methodically coiling each skate of line.

Another crew member cuts the fishes' heads off, removes their entrails, and puts them into the "scraping checker." Fish are picked from that bin, their kidneys are scraped from against the spine in their body cavity, and their next stop is the bed of snowy ice in the hold below-decks. Mark comments, "It's pretty efficient; the fish go from point A to B to C to D."

The fish, some with their faces ripped open, most with gaff wounds, continue arriving in the fish box. If they are in a form of agony, we may feel fortunate that it is a mute agony. They try to do what they know, which is to swim, until, despite their massive shocks and wounds, they simply suffocate in our atmosphere. We hear them slapping around in the checker, a sound we quickly grow accustomed to; a sound that says we are succeeding in the task we have set for ourselves. By the time they've come to the surface, they are fish the way we expect to see them: on a hook, detached from the context of their natural motion and their element, basically dead meat. How could we see these fish on their own terms, how they breed and feed and spawn and migrate? We remain impoverished of the experience of seeing them in their interest and intrigue as wild animals, ranging their natural habitats. There are many aspects of fishing I find interesting. Some I enjoy. But some I lament, even while willingly participating.

We're catching other things besides Sablefish. About 10 percent comprise a variety of other fishes: stingless rays called skates; flatfish called turbot; an occasional cutlass-shaped grenadier; and several species of a group called rockfishes that are long-lived, late-maturing, and rather sensitive to fishing pressure. Of these we see mainly Shortraker Rockfish and Idiotfish (I wonder who the last is named after). These rockfishes are an astonishing Day-Glo orange, the color of the crew's foul-weather gear. They have enormous eyes for navigating their dark world. Many deep-sea fish are orange or red, even though this color is the first to drop out as you go deeper. By the time you're down fifty feet, anything orange or red already looks gray. As the light dims with depth, red looks black. Many deep-living fish are pigmented bright red or orange so they will be gray to black where they live, depending on how much light is penetrating—a passive, self-adjusting form of camouflage.

We discard the skates, turbots, and grenadiers. We keep the rockfishes, the Sablefish of course, and the occasional halibut. Every fishery captures and kills marine life it is not trying to catch, and this by-kill accounts for fully a quarter of the entire world catch—roughly 27 million tons of sea life annually killed and discarded. Some kinds of fishing gear have enormous by-kill. In certain parts of the world shrimp nets kill more than eight pounds of juvenile fish and other marine creatures for every pound of shrimp. Alaska's Sablefish and halibut fleet has relatively less by-kill than many other fisheries.

Masonic's lines are set on the slope so as to lay across a range of depths. Halibut are more common on the shallower end of the miles-long string. These are not large ones as halibut grow, but they are large anyway, up to fifty pounds—the size of a desk top. They live a life of ambush, lying flattened on the bottom, scanning their scant heaven for scarfable prey. They hatch as free-swimming larvae, and as they settle in for a life sentence of lying on one side—like all flounders and soles—one eye migrates until both are on the same side of their head. This doesn't look as strange as it is, because nature bundles grace into all things functional. These are large eyes, to help them gather intelligence in the dark, cold water. With those eyes and their rounded lips, a halibut looks oddly friendly.

The halibut and Sablefish come up quite vigorous. Those few that fall off the hook swim away. That's because they have no internal air bladders for neutralizing buoyancy. Not so the rockfishes, skates, and grenadiers. As they come from the pressure of the great deep to the surface, the rockfishes' internal air bladders expand so much that they push their stomachs out their mouths like bubble gum. Their eyes are often telescoped hideously as well. The skates look stunned from the change in depth. The grenadiers, so unwanted, come up in the worst condition, dead and all beaten up; apparently they're very delicate.

The discarded fishes are immediately beset by the fulmars, who tear at them. They peck and pull their bodies so aggressively they prevent them from sinking. The Sablefish entrails likewise become instant bird food.

The increasingly dense crowd of fulmars—now forming a ferocious feathered rabble—already numbers about a thousand. A boat can attract all the birds for many miles around. They coat the water out to a hundred yards, as though the boat were trailing a long, feathered skirt. They keep up an incessant racket of hostile, competitive whining, whistling, croaking, and yakkering. They lack poise and are devoid of decorum. In dense packs, they churlishly churn the water white around discarded fish, heads, and entrails, screaming, squabbling, pulling gobbets of flesh, and wolfing guts. In appearance and behavior, they seem always just one webbed footstep ahead of starvation. Each fish head or gut bunch that hits the water instantly draws dozens of rushing fulmars—jostling, pecking, pushing, noisily threatening each other. The fighting is fierce, but the ferocity comes from hunger, not anger. They waste no motion on animosity. They merely try to get food—whatever that takes.

Quarreling packs fall behind as the boat moves slowly along the gear, then they come flying back in hungering little flocks and join fresh fish fights. Mark says, "When the birds first arrive in these waters—in April, early May—they seem really ravenous, extremely aggressive, almost frenzied. After June the albatrosses thin out noticeably in numbers, and intensity. But these fulmars are on us all season, always very aggressive. They're so nasty to each other—look at these here, biting each other's necks—it's incredible. When you get a huge pack of fulmars around the boat like this, nothing gets in the middle of them, except other fulmars. No other animal seems able to cope with this kind of frenzy."

The fulmars peck and gouge at the fish heads with such voracity it's a little disconcerting. Floating heads quickly lose their eyes. I say, "It's a jungle out there."

A ferocious feathered rabble

Mark laughs. "It really is," he says. "And these birds are the biggest threat to people lost at sea around here. If you go unconscious, the first thing that'll get you—is the birds."

I turn and look at him with surprise.

"Oh yeah, the *first* thing that'll get you. A few years ago while we were in the Aleutians, the *Majestic,* a boat a lot like this, screwed up a little bit. The crew had loaded the boat badly, and it was unsteady. The wind was blowing only about thirty, but the boat rolled over. I heard their Mayday. It turned out that I was the closest boat. Considering the wind and current, I went to where they should have drifted. As we were approaching, a Coast Guard helicopter got on them. When I saw them come out of the ocean, it had much more of an emotional impact on me than I would have predicted. Anyway, the boat's crew had been in the water in survival suits for eight hours, and they said that when they were starting to pass out, or starting to sleep in the water, they had fulmars all around them, ready to peck out their eyes."

If the fulmars look vicious, almost reptilian, the albatrosses maintain their stateliness as they dine on death. Most of them hang behind the boat, detached from the fulmars' squabbles. Mark says, "The albatrosses don't seem to fight. They don't seem to attack each other."

Churlishly churning the water white

. . .

FLECKED WITH WHITECAPS beneath gray skies, the ocean emanates a cold, uninviting countenance. Yet it proves home to many creatures. Visible through binoculars, across the whole sweep of distant view, are moving seabirds silhouetted against the pewter sea and low clouds. A mile away a large flock of albatrosses has gathered over some feast unseen to us. We can see about a hundred of them wheeling and circling and landing in the water. I wonder what they're eating. Possibly, salmon are attacking herring under those albatrosses. I like seeing them foraging naturally, not mobbed and beggared behind the boat.

Shaun at the rail—gaffing, swinging; gaffing, swinging—suddenly spots a Short-tailed Albatross. It's considerably larger than the Hawaiian albatrosses. Shaun emphasizes to me something I know very well: how fortunate I am to see one.

Someone says, "I hate seeing the Short-tails, 'cause it scares me to think of what they could do to us. It's good to know that they're out here—we just have to make sure nothing ever happens to one."

Shaun, talking to me while watching the hooks coming up—gaffing, swinging—says, "One day last year we had four Short-tailed Albatrosses around the boat. You'd better believe we were towing all kindsa stuff to make sure the Short-tails would get nowhere near the gear."

I ask Mark how he became the spiritual leader and guru of the fleet's efforts to avoid killing seabirds. He laughs and then pauses before saying, "We had never caught very many birds, but a couple of years ago there were so many birds in one area that we were killing several Laysan Albatrosses a day. We'd never done that. We'd killed a fulmar once in a while, but it was really distressing to be killing albatrosses. I felt it was kind of a crime. The Laysan is my favorite. They're just such strikingly beautiful fliers; all the albatrosses are. I don't know—it just seemed like it was bad juju to be doing that. Bad karma.

"On the first halibut schooner I worked on, the *Grant*, we'd towed buoys if we had a lot of birds around. We weren't using them for conserving seabirds; we just didn't want hooks going down without bait. Obviously. So while we were in this spot with so many birds, we spent a few days trying different things to keep them away. We were towing different stuff around. After several days we found a combination that worked really well. Since then we've tried different things, but variations on the Japanese bird line—basically streamers coming off a line towed from the roof of the baiting station—seem to work best.

"Our bird-avoidance experiments seemed to coincide with environmentalists' concerns about the endangered Short-tails being at risk from long-lining. Our fleet had a couple of Short-tailed Albatross kills, so we had to do something here. Plus, the problems faced by other albatrosses in other fisheries—. So we figured out a solution that was working for us, and I published an article in the *Alaska Fisherman's Journal.*"

Tim suddenly announces, "We got about twenty-five hundred pounds from the first string, plus five hundred pounds of halibut." He interprets to me, "Not bad; not great."

We do it all over again.

And again.

Each time we pick up a few miles of fishing gear we rebait thousands of hooks and send the line down and pick up the next miles-long string.

Sometimes hook after hook brings a fish. Sometimes a long series of hooks comes up empty. The men comment repeatedly that the catching is spotty; that the area must have been worked recently by another boat. In this big ocean, where we will see no sign of other humans for days, it seems astonishing that one other boat could have a noticeable effect. But the fish occur in concentrations. They're not just spread everywhere. That's why we ran thirty-six hours to get *here.* Because in the vast sea, there aren't as many fish in as many places as you might first guess.

OVER THE EIGHTEEN-HOUR workdays of this intended two-week trip, we will take no Sabbath. The six-hour night finds us all in our racks—so devoid of humanity is this place that no one stands watch—but the heave of the ocean and the sound of moving water inches from our heads remain incessant. The ocean continually reminds us that this is not our habitat. When the sea is rough, our bodies occasionally leave the mat. A bit uncomfortable. All through the black, moving darkness, we drift unhelmed, trailing our train of seabirds, sleeping fitfully.

While we endure our dreams, Sablefish are committing suicide in the dark.

Daylight means either setting or hauling. Everyone takes shifts at every task, skipper included. Gaffing, swinging, the sound of the winch, the line and coming hooks clicking through the rollers, cutting heads, throwing heads in the water, gutting fish, throwing guts in the water, coiling line as it comes up, baiting and baiting and baiting, coiling more, packing freshly killed fish away on ice, baiting more; it continues and continues—long after the novelty wears off. Always, the boat is rolling, rolling in the long, sweeping swells. Though everything is methodical, there is so much repetition and sameness that any sense of routine dissipates into one prolonged experience. Days begin blending.

LATE AFTERNOON. Hauling. Shaun Bailey is taking another shift at the rollers. Gaffing, swinging. When one rather large fish comes up, it falls off the line before Shaun gets the gaff hook in. A thing measurable in dollars splashes back. Shaun reaches with the long gaff handle.

Cal shouts enthusiasm. "Get it, Bailey!"

Shaun reaches his utmost as the fish slowly begins to sink. As he stretches farther over the rail his feet come off the deck just as a swell rocks the boat, and in the next instant he is over the rail and in the bone-chilling Alaskan ocean wearing boots and heavy clothing.

The fulmars hesitate. Cal leaps over the fish checker and reaches far over the rail, screaming, "Bailey! Grab my *hand*!"

His face showing full knowledge that unless the next move is perfect he is dead, Shaun grasps Cal's hand. But the boat is still sliding slowly forward, and with all his clothing sodden Shaun is so heavy that their grip breaks. Shaun is drifting toward the stern, and in a moment he will be alongside the covered bait deck, and there will be no way to reach over to grab him before the boat slips past him—and by then his clothes could sink him. Mark is already bent over the last inch of rail extending a life ring. Shaun locks his elbow around the ring. Mark and Cal struggle together trying to haul him aboard. Bailey hits the deck uttering a guttural groan that comes from fright and shortness of breath combined. Already cold-stunned, he is having trouble breathing.

When he and the rest of us regain our composure, Shaun goes to warm up and find dry clothes. Warming takes a while. On deck the crew is quieter than usual. Mark comments that no one has fallen overboard in twelve years.

When Shaun reappears, apparently O.K. and smiling sheepishly, the jokes start.

"That is dedication to fishing, man—"

"—when you're willing to go in after them—"

"And it was a *big* one too!"

"Come on, Bailey, it's still your roller turn. Quit slackin'."

"Hey, Bailey, the trip's not over yet. You can't leave us."

Bailey moves back to his place and Cal goes back to cleaning.

Cal says, "Your eyes were about this big. Last time I saw a face like that, it had a hook in it."

Shaun resumes working. Gaff, swing. He says, "I knew those clothes could sink me. I knew that in a minute or two my hands would get useless."

A fish falls off, and Shaun begins to lean over for it, then turns around, flashing a big grin.

Mac says, "Go, Bailey, *get* him."

Still grinning, Shaun waits for the next hook.

MEANWHILE CONTINUES THE CONSTANT BAITING, and the never-abating noise of birds—now several thousand fulmars—and the catching and the incessant toiling and coiling. The deck is such a mess of squid and herring chunks coming off the block that it's surprising no one has slipped and fallen. The guys teach me a new word: *gak*. Gak is crud that involves slime. All the stepped-on squid and creamed herring on deck: gak. I say we call that shmutz. They like it; it catches on. When we get another ton and a half of fish in the boat the crew starts cleaning them by hand again, and birds that have been waiting patiently suddenly move in for another ravenous frenzy. Then the birds wait for more fish; some pass the time bathing and preening.

Every now and then a fishhook leader breaks in the rollers, sending a fish into the checker with a hook remaining in it. Those heads usually go overboard still bearing the hook. Albatrosses swallow some of the smaller heads whole. So the operation may not be 100 percent bird-safe. A Glaucous Gull has been circling the boat with a hook through its nostrils. The hook doesn't seem to be causing that gull much immediate distress, but it looks a little heftier than a nose ring on a college student. I can only wonder what that metal hook will feel like when the weather turns cruelly cold in winter. My guess is that the bird is doomed. In the eastern Gulf of Alaska, Mark says, Sperm Whales are often drawn to the boat, eating fish heads alongside the seabirds. That doesn't sound good.

What happens to an animal that swallows one of these hooks is unclear, because of the hook design. These are "circle hooks"; their points are bent back toward the shank, then down a little. Their shape is based on an ancient Pacific pattern designed to let the hook easily slide into a corner of the fish's jaw and lodge there, so the fish can get hooked without putting much pressure on the point. They are much rounder than standard J-shaped hooks. It seems possible that a bird could regurgitate a hook of this style, or that these hooks could pass through a tube, such as a whale's intestines, without snagging. But it's certain that swallowing hooks can't be good for animals. In some Wandering

Albatross colonies in the Southern Hemisphere, as many as one in five chicks contains a hook received from its parent with its food; and hooks sometimes get stuck in adults, who occasionally die of internal injuries on their nests.

I mention this to Mark, and we agree that after the fishing season we'll work together to add to the seabird-protection regulations a rule requiring that hooks be removed from any heads tossed overboard. Mark instructs the guys to take all hooks out before throwing heads. But I notice that, out of habit and in haste, they sometimes forget.

The working continues—hook after hook until the whole string is done. Then the big buoys and the flag with flasher atop come aboard, then the lengthy line and anchor.

Recounting of Shaun's near-death experience on the wrong side of the element interface continues throughout the long day. By sundown Mark has already received an e-mail reply from Shaun's stepfather, admonishing Shaun that when a man named Spence fell off the *Republic,* he at least got the fish he was after.

That chide notwithstanding, these guys—at least *Masonic*'s crew—are not the macho types I was expecting for such laborious and hazardous fishing. They are inured to hard work without being hardened by it. And they do less swaggering than some sport fishermen I know. Perhaps that's because just being part of the crew proves plenty. Nobody has to fake anything. The work is difficult and dangerous enough to weed out the strutters. Mark's comment: "There's no room for prima donnas. This requires teamwork."

Teamwork and camaraderie. In the cold rain and hard work, the men dream aloud about winter in the Caribbean and Belize. Sportfishing in Baja. Mark talks a lot about outings planned with his wife and daughters. Others will take sweethearts whale watching. After the deep sea there will be hikes in deep ancient forests of old-growth cedars ("What's left of them," as Tim says). Hot springs—and hot tubs.

CAL ANNOUNCES LUNCH: baked halibut. Although Mark had jokingly told me that fishermen's four food groups are alcohol, cholesterol, caffeine, and nicotine, the food on board is hearty and nutritious. Cal pulls his weight on deck and still effortlessly puts together big, delicious meals. Mac wolfs several huge platefuls of rice, then asks Cal whether there'll be any rice at supper. The meal seems altogether too rushed for so fine a feast. But Mark has a different perspective. He says, "During the derby days, instead of having twenty minutes to actually stop and sit down to a nice hot lunch like this, the cook would make three dozen peanut butter and jelly sandwiches and put them out on the hatch. People would just reach for sandwiches as they got hungry."

They're almost always hungry. Watch these guys work for a few hours and the importance of food becomes obvious. Here on deck they drink lots of fruit juice and water and snack on candy bars and chocolate. They need all the hydration and calories they can get their jaws around. They work harder than anyone I've ever seen.

The effort promises big rewards and big hazards. Fishing in Alaska is one of the most dangerous professions anywhere. It's a pain-for-gain, high-risk-for-high-return venture.

Jim comments that his most memorable fishing trip was his first time out for Sablefish. "We caught ninety thousand pounds in six days. And I was in extreme pain the whole time."

Mark's most memorable trip was his first to the Aleutians and the Bering Sea. It was the first week in April. "About five days into the trip," he says, "we hit a horrendous storm. A wave broke over the entire boat. It blew out all the wheelhouse windows. Because I had no experience, it wasn't all that frightening; I just kind of thought, 'I guess this is what we do.' I figured, 'The captain knows what he's doing.'" He grins. "It didn't seem as terrifying then as it would *now*. I didn't realize at the time what I know as an experienced skipper—that the captain was scared witless."

Mark's had other close calls and seen boats with decks swamped in gales. But, he says, "The most memorable trips are the good trips, when we absolutely kill 'em, like the time we loaded the boat in two days."

Tim nods his assent. His most memorable trip was the first time he got a full crew share; the satisfaction.

Mac remembers a four-day halibut trip during derby days—over the entire four days he slept for two hours. "I got really close to hallucinating. At one point I was supposed to cut up a salmon for dinner and I had the meat cleaver in my hand and I realized I couldn't see my hand and I thought, 'This is dumb,' so I put the cleaver down and I picked up a smaller knife and went at it much more carefully. But that was kind of the defining moment in my career, 'cause I realized that with the right attitude, you can do anything. Within reason. And I wouldn't want to do it again."

Mac's most memorable trip was the time every other boat went in because the wind was blowing a steady sixty miles an hour, and for a week they fished in twenty-foot seas while the rest of the fleet was sheltering in port. "We were a pretty wild crew. These were my friends, and we all fit in each other's energy. But I wouldn't want to do it now. No way. It was hard, and it was dangerous, but at the time it was just one of those things—y'know?"

I wryly say it sounds character building.

He says, "We were all characters to begin with. Now I'm boring, boring, boring."

Cal remembers his first trip on the *Masonic* as a very positive experience with guys that were competent and did their job well. Mark adds, "That was a cool trip, wasn't it?" To me he fills in, "We fished right next to the ice pack."

"And then in port that beautiful Coast Guard lady boarded us."

Tim says, "Oh—wasn't *she* nice! What was her name?"

Cal recounts, "We're just returned from a week's fishing, covered in slime, and she steps into the wheelhouse and takes her helmet off—all this blond hair just cascades out, and the smell of her shampoo just filled the place. And we're like, 'Oh God!'"

Tim says, "Yeah, we were like, 'Isn't there something else we're required to do, some other forms or paperwork we need to fill out?'"

We're all laughing.

Shaun Bailey recounts the terror of a January storm when hundred-mile-an-hour winds built deadly, breaking waves forty feet tall. His step-father, Carl Vedo, was behind the wheel of *Masonic*. Mark was not on that trip. "Carl had just woken everybody up to tie stuff down. He had been behind the wheel for ten hours, trying to get us behind some island, out of the wind. I offered to go down and make us some grub. There was water sloshing in the galley; the deck mats had got jammed in the scuppers and plugged them shut, preventing the deck from draining. But I brought up a sandwich anyway, and before he could even get a bite he says, 'Hold on! Hold on!' And he took the boat out of gear. We took a *big* wave. It rolled us way over. As we were still coming back up, another one smashes right on top of us—*Bam!* It put us all the way over, on our side. The pilothouse struck the sea surface and the windows blew out and water was streaming in and alarms started going off everywhere. That was the scaredest I'd ever been." He shakes his head at the flashback and continues, "After what seemed like forever but was probably only a few seconds, the boat rolled slowly upright again. All you can do in conditions like that is to try to keep the bow pointed into the sea. So Carl kept holding the boat into it for hours, until the storm broke." Shaun adds, "It was lucky there was no shoreline behind us; he'd been trying for twenty-four hours to keep us jogging forward, but the wind and waves had driven us backward seventeen miles. So yeah, it was pretty, pretty scary. Our radar had gotten blown out. So then we were coming in at Dutch Harbor without radar. That place is tricky at night. So Carl had us all up on the bow, being lookouts. Human radar." He laughs. "Like the old days."

Tim asks, "What year was that?"

Shaun replies, "That was the last derby year." That last derby year, people drowned rather than miss a day of fishing. Those that lived made half the money they earn now.

At 10:30 P.M. it's not yet fully dark. But the crew quits anyway, because these aren't the derby days. Cal says to me, "During the derby years there was a lot more hurry and less sleep. We called it 'turn and burn.' The operation is very casual now."

Eighteen-hour days of manual labor that start before dawn isn't most people's idea of "casual," but all is relative. We take off our slimy deck outerwear and crowd our scented selves into the galley. After several days I and my clothing are packing a suite of odors that can be masked only by a deckload of cut herring and squid and a putrid peer group. Fortunately, that is no problem. Mark says he'll take a shower when he gets back to port, whether he needs one or not. Tim, in an insightful historical retrospective, informs him that the Roman Empire fell because of warm baths, adding that showers are for sissies.

As the days wear on, a growing collection of filthy, damp, smelly clothing hangs from lines strung among the bunks. Gloves hang on clothespins near the stove. The galley itself is frequently a comedy of gravity. Falling dishes, falling juice bottles—. Cal sweeps from the floor a bowl of fallen potatoes we've cut up, and washes them in the sink. Clambering around the crowded cabin and getting seated at the cramped table for dinner gets increasingly difficult.

But tonight it is so worth the extra effort, because Cal has utterly outdone himself with an extraordinary supper of lamb and Sablefish—complete with mint jelly and gourmet bottled sparkling springwater. Just in time to really enjoy it, my digestive system is functioning again. When you finally stop throwing up, there are some pretty luxurious moments out here in the heaving Gulf of Alaska. Cal usually cooks to perfection on the rocking diesel stove, but this Sablefish is something to go lyrical about. No wonder the Japanese buy every single one this fleet catches; these are the most buttery-fleshed fish I've ever tasted. Most Americans have no idea Sablefish even exist. The fish are bought at princely sums for export as soon as they hit the dock—sometimes sooner.

Mark explains, "In Japan it's one of those presentation fishes. It's made to look beautiful, and people pay for it."

After dinner, because these are not the derby days, we have leisure entertainment: a National Geographic video—*Search for the Giant Squid.*

As the squid video starts, Jim remarks, "They're good eating."

The narrator begins dramatically: "They've been called aliens from inner space. They have been dreaded and feared for centuries. No Giant Squid has ever been seen alive."

Jim says, "I've seen one alive. Sometimes they come up hanging on to a cod."

Tim says, "I've seen two, also."

When an archival scene from *20,000 Leagues Under the Sea* shows a Giant Squid attacking the boat, Mac calls to Captain Nemo, "Smoke the reduction gear!"

Jim says, "Nemo's just trying to hack off an arm for dinner."

Mac says, "For bait!"

Footage of California Squid in their mating aggregations prompts Cal to say, "That's quite an orgy."

"Just like landing in Dutch Harbor."

The narrator warns, "Humboldt Squid have been known to kill people that fall into the water." When the scientist boldly dives into the sea among the hazardous Humboldt Squid, Jim says, "I hope he's wearing Kevlar wristers." Everybody laughs.

The narrator concludes by quoting John Steinbeck: "An ocean without its sea monsters would be like sleep without dreams."

Tim nods thoughtfully and emphatically at this sentiment.

Showtime over. Time for sleep with dreams of sea monsters.

MORNING COMES BRIGHT and—finally!—sunny.

The crew say sunny weather means bad weather is coming.

Well, of course. Bad weather means bad weather is already here, and sunny weather means bad weather will come. In the Gulf of Alaska, nothing means good weather is coming.

Winds are scheduled to increase with a cold front. Ominously, the Coast Guard is on the radio trying to raise a boat whose EPIRB signal they are receiving. EPIRB stands for Emergency Position Indicating Radio Beacon. It's a unit that slides into a holder, usually on the wheelhouse. If it starts floating, it begins transmitting a satellite signal to the Coast Guard, with its position. Usually the only way an EPIRB starts floating is if the boat is no longer floating.

As the wind increases, seas build and the air cools, the crew maintain their pace, their attitude, and their banter. As the day ages, the weather maintains its threatening posture. All day the surface of the sea has been whipped into a tight white-capped chop by a steady twenty-five-mile-per-hour wind. A grim and grizzled sea, ragged and disheveled as an unmade bed.

By midafternoon the weather fax arrives showing a strong air-pressure gradient. A stiff blow is on its way. Mark pensively weighs his options: stay and try to fish through it; or suspend fishing during the blow and try to endure it; or run ahead of it and wait it out in port. The forecast predicts a gale. Options one and two carry the risk of getting trapped; if the storm gets out of hand it may be impossible to run to shelter. We are only eight hours from the nearest port. "Even if we can fish through it, people get battered and worn out. More things sliding across the decks. More strain on the fishing gear. Risk of accident increases. You tend to lose a day," he says, "for every day of fishing like that." He decides that unless the four P.M. forecast changes, we'll fish hard today, then haul aboard all the gear that is out and run for port at about two in the morning.

By late afternoon the fishing improves markedly. To be more accurate, the catching improves markedly. The fishing itself is getting harder, with building winds and waves. But we're getting more and larger fish, and a much cleaner catch of Sablefish, with fewer dead grenadiers to discard. After working twelve hours, everyone wants to stay on the grounds and keep fishing.

We've been resetting after each haul. Right now, the seas are white-capped and building but not huge. All the gear is in the water, fishing, when Mark goes to the wheelhouse to get the updated forecast.

Mark receives word over the radio that the EPIRB whose distress signal the Coast Guard was receiving had gone off by accident. But such a false alarm keeps everyone on edge. Mark listens with concern to the updated forecast. A mechanically generated voice of the government sends its matter-of-fact prognostications: ". . . Gale warnings. Southwest winds, increasing to fifty knots. Seas building, to twenty feet . . ."

Mark shakes his head and says he hates heavy weather. "You never get used to it, and the older you get the more you hate it. The mountains of water, the murderous wind, the driving streaks of foam—"

Cal, who has come in to deliver a sandwich to Mark, adds, "It becomes another world." He lists the only two advantages of heavy weather, and they are: you get to wear all your rain gear, and if the boat sinks you don't have to clean it. He adds, "Fishing has been likened to a prison sentence with the possibility of drowning."

Of course, many things carry risk. Driving a car is risky. But compare: cars crash in a blink; boats in storms sink after hours of desperate effort and terror like a wild animal in the cage of your ribs.

Mark, looking a bit weary, clicks off the radio and says with finality, "We're going in." He sticks his head out of the wheelhouse and announces that we'll run for port after hauling all the gear. Then he sends an e-mail to a fish buyer on Kodiak, saying we should be at their dock in the early afternoon tomorrow.

Now we will pick up everything. This means that the workday that began at four A.M. will stretch to two A.M. tonight. No one grumbles. It's just direction, and everyone takes it matter-of-factly. Faced with a twenty-two-hour workday in worsening conditions, Tim's only comment is, "Hell, we've done it many times before. It's no big deal."

DURING MARK'S TURN at the rollers—gaffing, swinging—he occasionally pulls off an unused piece of bait, tossing it to the waiting birds. A fulmar comes hovering so close in the stiff wind, hanging in midair, that Mark pushes it away with the gaff. Watching the fulmars pace the pilothouse as we move to the next string, I am impressed anew by the shaping forces of hunger and harshness, and by how much the harshness that challenges life is what *causes* the beauty. Birds fly because they must escape predators and search for food. Trees grow skyward because they compete fiercely with other trees for light. Living things need something to push off of. Each of us needs challenges to give us the right shape. The heavenly weightlessness of space weakens the bones of astronauts—a demonstration of the principle that we need grounding to support ourselves, that to achieve and maintain strength we need to conquer forces that tend to hold us down. The weightless, painless paradise that we conjure as "heaven"—where all is given, no thing is contested, nothing carries danger or threatens loss, and no effort can bring gain or cause change—could never create the beauty of a bird, the sleek speed of a dolphin, the love of a child, the compassion, intellect, and inventiveness of the human spirit. We could not exist in paradise. Our minds would unravel and we would wither and dull to nothing, and expire. Blessed are our enemies and challengers. Here is the great paradox of the flesh: without the things that can kill us, we could not survive. Without challenges to our very existence, we could never have come to be.

. . .

SABLEFISH SLEEK AND SUPPLE continue coming aboard as did the first ones, so many thousands of hooks ago. The second-to-last string was the best yet. And the fish are big. The crew and Mark are disappointed that the weather is preventing them from setting the gear again on this spot. Running the boat toward the last string of hooks, Mark in the wheelhouse is listening to Bach's Toccata and Fugue in D Minor as increasing winds orchestrate the shape of the world outside.

The hours slip away. The day slides by. The evening grays with age, then dims and fades. But the work persists. A little before sunset, around ten P.M., we begin hauling the last string. The real becomes surreal as the labor proceeds. The fishermen eat more than their share of ibuprofen pills, ignoring their bodies' warnings that they are exceeding their physical limits.

I'm sure I couldn't hack this work. I just wouldn't have what it takes to labor this hard under these conditions. Most people would jump at the chance to make $100,000 in four months. Most people would be spit out after the first day, or broken after the first week. This is something like climbing Mount Everest. You are drawn by the romance and ambition and the dream, but when you get there you realize that it is all about enduring pain and isolation.

Cal, not yet two dozen years old, says, "It's hard to believe we used to work like this all the time."

Shaun says, "Work twenty, sleep four, work twenty. Jesus, I don't know how I did it."

Cal laughs. "Ha! We're getting t' be old men already."

Elder statesman of the deck crew, Tim says to me, "This kind of work is very hard when you are young, but as you get older, it's also very hard." He adds, "There is less wasted motion as you get older, though." The work takes other things out of you. Tim talks to me about being away from loved ones for months. Missing birthdays and holidays. Not everybody can bear that. His brother, in the Russian crab fishery for the last eight years, barely got home in time to see his child born.

The crew is a perpetual-motion machine. The work grinds on for hours with a kind of industrial monotony. Except that this is not the inside of a factory—we're in the Gulf of Alaska, doing something authentic and suffused with splendor and power. And we're in some danger because anything real entails real risks.

What is it that seems romantic about this kind of difficult, dangerous, repetitive work? Is there a purity that attracts us? If you're not inured to all the killing, it can get to you. And even if you are inured, the work can kill you. This is not so much pure as genuine. This work is what it appears to be. Not long ago, everything was real. Now the real seems too hard, because the fake has come to substitute for real experiences. And so we orbit the genuine because we recognize the value of authenticity, which we call the romantic. But we experience it only vicariously because we are unwilling to shoulder the risk and effort required to really be in it.

THE WIND'S WHISTLING in the riggings intensifies, and the boat is rolling more heavily. Mark has been on this boat in breaking thirty-foot seas. He says the birds scarcely notice such weather. "The birds will just be sitting on the water, paddling into the oncoming seas. When a big breaking comber threatens to smash them, they simply lift off over the white water and plunk down again in the next trough."

Talk of boats in storms reminds Cal of the *Finback*. As Cal and I go into the galley to fix some food, Cal tells of the boat his cousin and a couple of other people outfitted in Honolulu for fishing in Alaska. It was mid-March. About two-thirds of the way from Hawaii to the Aleutians they got into very heavy seas, with confused, high winds from varying directions. "In the middle of the night, the boat—same size as this one—got lifted by a really big wave that broke over it real hard. Collapsed the whole shelter deck. Blew out all of the cabin windows, stripped all the life rafts, took the antennas—completely shredded everything. My cousin Chris got thrown out of his bunk to the far side of the cabin, and another person suddenly landed on top of him in the dark. The other guy wasn't moving, so Chris wasn't even sure who it was. They had cold seawater running over them. And they started getting electrocuted by all the shorts from the wiring. Then floodwater killed all the power. Floating boards in the engine room pinched off the fuel line. Without the engine, they couldn't reposition the boat. They were sort of floating sideways to the oncoming seas, drifting in the pitch dark.

"Wind was howling through the inside of the place, water sloshing all through the boat. The only thing left serviceable was the emergency pump. In chest-deep water in the dark engine room, they tried getting the pump started. They finally got the pump going, and all huddled around, spraying ether in the pump's motor, trying to keep it running." They got the majority of water pumped out, and by daylight they fixed the main power, and got the engine started again. There was so much rope and line drifting back by the propeller they were concerned it might seize the wheel. So at dawn they were out on the deck, trying to cut all the lines to free up the prop so they could get under way.

"When the EPIRB had gotten swept off the boat it started transmitting. So the Coast Guard was notified. But then the boat motored away. When the Coast Guard couldn't find the boat and abandoned the search, they notified the crew's families. They told my cousin's parents that he had been lost at sea. A few days after that, the guys showed up back in Honolulu. They spent a month rebuilding the whole boat, and then turned around for Alaska. They were five weeks late for the beginning of the fishing season."

At midnight Cal and I emerge onto the *Masonic*'s own heaving deck. Now the middle of the boat is almost constantly awash with waves rushing in through the scuppers, sliding across the boards and back out into the other side of night. A dark wind is howling. It's unnerving.

Under the deck lights, we are carrying hot burritos, sandwiches, just-baked apple pie with ice cream, insulated containers of hot coffee and tea, and candy bars. Everyone else chows heartily. The rolling seas, and a touch of foreboding dread, are dampening my appetite. Except for Cal, who has been below to cook, Mac—who came in to put on a dry shirt—is the only crew member who has been off the deck in the last twenty-two hours. No one has had anything that could be called a break. At almost two in the morning, the last hook clicks through the rollers.

The seas have built to a dark and formidable presence, and I realize it's the fish who have caught all of us. The gulls and fulmars have remained alongside, illuminated by the boat's halo, yakkering at us. But the albatrosses have receded into the wailing, tilted night.

Mark consults his tide and current book and considers the wind and wave conditions that will probably accompany our run in. He has two choices; running west of Tugidak Island, which entails slowly quartering into the wind and seas, or running with seas astern—a smoother ride—around Sitkinak Island and into the Sitkinak Strait. But if the predicted gale comes up early, the strait will get very nasty. If the bigger blow holds off, the latter route is shorter and more comfortable. Both routes lead into Alitak Bay, near the remote southern extremity of Kodiak Island. Mark eventually decides on the longer, less comfortable route that is safer in case of worse weather.

The run is about thirty miles to the islands and another thirty miles into Alitak. But in these weather conditions the boat goes slowly; we will make only around seven knots, a veritable crawl.

Mark and the crew will take two-hour turns in the wheelhouse. They draw cards; Mac gets first shift. He has been working for almost twenty-two hours but says he's glad to get the first turn because afterward he can sleep straight through.

Climbing into his bunk, Shaun pronounces, "Oh, my bunk is my *friend*. Yes. My bunk—is my friend." A time for work, a time to dream.

The bow raises a white-noise hiss as it cleaves the heaving seas. During hours in the rack, I feel the sea change when we alter course, from pounding into a quartering sea on our port bow to having the sea following us on our port stern. I finally sleep well for a while.

AT EIGHT A.M. Tim is standing in the galley when I open my own eyes. In the bunk next to mine, Shaun seems to writhe in discomfort, turning fitfully and groaning, twisting and stretching his back in different directions. He wakes briefly, grumbling about leg cramps.

Tim talks to me in whispers as the others sleep in their adjacent bunks. Mainly, he speaks again of missing loved ones for months at a time.

I step into the morning. The sea is considerably lower here. The sky is bright overcast, with enough blue to lend the sea a silver lining in places. We've slipped in under the weather front, ahead of the full gale.

To the starboard, to the east, lies a low, long island, an austere, treeless place. Every now and then we pass thick pieces of drifting Bull Kelp torn from their coastal fastenings and adrift. The occasional piece of floating timber poses a further hazard; Tim knows of one boat that got holed by a floating log.

Shaun comes to take his turn in the wheelhouse, listening to the Rolling Stones singing "It's hard to survive the pain of love." Shaun's nodding head suggests that he relates strongly; he loves fishing.

We've left the albatrosses and most fulmars behind. But other birds replace them: Pelagic Cormorants, Tufted Puffins, a few phalaropes, the lilting, tilting Sooty Shearwaters raking the horizon. All come and pass silently. Philip Levine's poetry speaks again: "No one could score their sense or harmony before they faded in the wind and sun."

We steam back around Tugidak on our way into Alitak Bay. I enjoy the scenery—the sight of land itself seems a novelty—and the strange music of the place-names in this strange place.

When Mark relieves him, Shaun puts his bare feet up in the wheelhouse and sips a mug of tea. He's glad to be coming in safely. Mark admits, "It's a relief to come in. In our last derby it blew fifty. Of the twenty-four hours we could fish, we lost sixteen hours to the weather.

We'd often have to sit in port in nice weather, then hear gale warnings and have to head out into it. It was so destructive to morale." One wonders what the crew looked like in the derby years at the end of a trip. Right now Mark looks like all of us. Like hell. He is unshaven and uncombed, wears dirty clothes, and has bloodshot eyes.

More land appears ahead and to port. Kodiak's brown body shoulders its way into view through the haze. Its famed giant Grizzly Bears fit the persona bestowed by the visage of the land itself: fierce and self-contained. A truly austere wilderness. Though the calendar informs us that this is May's latter half, the brownish monotony of the slopes is just starting to crack the grip of winter with the merest early spring green.

Crab traps, marked by buoys, are set off Kodiak's gray beaches. We now are steaming into a wide bay whose mouth is covered by hundreds and hundreds of Sooty Shearwaters, and various murres and murrelets. Yet just inside the mouth of the bay, all the birds suddenly vanish. For the first time, I see no birds ahead. Instead, the view through binoculars reveals only two fishing boats, a wild beach littered with driftwood, grassland withdrawing hugely into high hills, and beyond them snowcapped peaks brushed by streaming clouds. This place shows the enormousness of terrain at the extremes of human habitation. The span of uncarved land. A place where you can still sense both permanence and potential.

THE FISH-PACKING and -shipping plant is in the first cove inside Alitak Bay, called Lazy Bay. It was built for salmon canning and is very much an outpost beyond the edge of civilization. I don't say that to be melodramatic. The whole island to the north looks unpeopled as far as we can see. No road links this place to anywhere. No town supplies workers. This plant is as isolated and remote as just about anything on land anywhere. Wherever you're headed to, you can't get there from here.

Shaun tells me that fishermen themselves built the plant with their own hands, in the old days. He says that back *then,* fishermen were really tough. He says, "The desolation, the twenty-five-day trips for halibut—I would not have been able to handle it. I would not have been able to cut the cheese."

Gulls (one with a long-liner's hook stuck in its bill) are hanging around the docks, and several eagles grip the pilings. I'm in the boat's baiting station, where the sides and overhead are closed off, and though half the sky is blocked from view I casually count nine Bald Eagles in the air. While I'm standing on the deck in a coat, woolen hat, and gloves, Cal, working to tie the boat up, is shirtless. The wheelhouse window of the only other boat here has a sticker saying I'D RATHER BE FISHING — AND I DON'T EVEN LIKE IT.

The water at the dock is loaded with juvenile herring, the schools moving up and down in the water, toward and away from the surface. The individual moving fish make silvery S-curves. The pilings are festooned with large white anemones on stalks two feet long. They grow below the range of the lowest tide. Packed above them, in the intertidal range, are Blue Mussels. The tidal range is wide, about fifteen feet.

Masonic is carrying twenty-three thousand pounds of Sablefish bodies, about five thousand fish. The boat can hold eighty-five thousand pounds of fish, but Mark says, "Pretty good for three days." We also have about half a ton of gutted Pacific Halibut.

Four men come to unload the boat with a crane and bucket. They are weathered and leathered and all look like Alaskan Natives, perhaps Aleut—but actually these guys are Mexicans and Filipinos. The fish are embedded layer upon layer in fine ice, and the men in the hold have to get to them with shovels, digging them out carefully, as though it is an archaeological expedition into the Ice Age. Watching the men unloading, Tim says, "They come out a lot faster than they go in."

Masonic's crew will spend several hours cleaning up, brushing every possible surface until the blood-splattered, herring-and-squid-smeared decks smell lemon fresh.

Somebody has put a pair of pink flamingos on the hillside next to the plant. They remind me of the two pink plastic flamingos on Tern Island, where at this moment people lathered in sunblock are working in bathing suits and shorts and birds are panting miserably in the heat.

I climb up the hill behind the fish plant. From here the world looks bigger than ever. The land stretches massively to the north with absolutely no hint of human presence. The plant below is the only human structure visible to the far ridges and distant shores. No photograph could capture this scene, because trying to engulf what is visual requires turning yourself through a full circle. An odd sense of desolation suddenly clamps in. I hear breaking surf on the other side of a ridge top, but when I climb the ridge to get a view of the ocean I am surprised that the "surf" sound is instead only the roaring of wind gusting across an even farther ridge. As the saying goes, "Beyond the mountains are more mountains." I think about all of us who've come from so far away; I think of where we're from, of leaving, and of home. To imagine being elsewhere is part of being human—and uniquely enables human beings to both envision the future and squander the moment.

An intermittent drizzle begins as I deny my humanity by forcing my attention to the present, taking my lesson from the sparrows, who are singing their sweet songs of sad exuberance. In the foreshortened spring and summer, they embody all the hope and hopelessness of the universal effort to remain alive. They purge my sense of desolation and keep me in well-connected company. Savannah Sparrow, Golden-crowned Sparrow, Fox Sparrow, and Rosy Finch (I've never seen the Golden-crowned or the Rosy Finch before). Like us, those among sparrows who succeed best will push dying off to the end of their natural life spans, rather than have it interrupt them right in the middle of something special. Bees bumble-buzz the open ground searching out the scant flowers. On a hill I find a burped-up owl pellet with what looks like lemming bones in it, and fur.

Looking down at the isolated packing houses and docks that seem to have sprung up here like a plant growing from a crack in a rock, it seems incredible that anybody came here to establish this outpost. It's hard to imagine getting the building materials and machinery here. It's hard to imagine merely working here. Some people have astonishing nerve. A magpie flits across a nearby slope.

When I come down the hill I remark to Cal about the view and how desolate the place seemed, and before I can tell him of my conversion by sparrows, he interrupts to correct me, saying, "It's remote, but not desolate." That's what I was about to tell him.

THERE'S A GREEN SAILBOAT in the harbor, about a hundred yards from shore. A young man and a woman are jigging Pacific Cod at a furious pace. These don't command near as high a price as the Sablefish that we've been catching on the *Masonic*. But they are worth money, and you can catch them near shore from a much smaller boat. The adventurous couple is working three lines between them. Every time they pull a line up, it has one to three thrashing cod on it. The young man and woman are catching these Pacific Cod like New Englanders caught Atlantic Cod three hundred years ago. New Englanders thought you could never fish them out. And as they did deplete them they insistently denied that fishing boats had anything to do with it; though the scarcity of the 1980s and '90s was unprecedented in the five-hundred-year-old fishery, they blamed "natural cycles" instead. Here, everybody seems quite aware that you can fish them out. In fact, any slow fishing is usually blamed on a boat having been through a little earlier. Their sober pragmatism and conservative approach is a major reason Alaska still has large numbers of fish. Reality breeds contentment.

JOHN JORGERSON, the plant's manager, shows us around. The plant was founded around 1900 as the Alitak Packing Company, has been sold a couple of times, and has grown to house and employ up to two hundred workers during the height of the summer salmon season. The facility's freezer holds just under two million pounds of fish, stored at −38° Fahrenheit. The plant has machines that remove salmon heads, guts, fins, and eggs, or "roe," which is made into caviar. In Jorgerson's office a sticker reads, FRIENDS DON'T LET FRIENDS EAT FARM-RAISED SALMON. But the question of who gets to eat what is a little more complicated, because every Sockeye Salmon that comes here goes to Japan, like every Sablefish. Every single one.

Back at the boat, Cal asks earnestly, "So, what's it like being shown around by the president of the Alitak cannery?" Mark gets a satellite e-mail from Carl Vedo, Shaun's stepdad. Carl is bucking fifty-mile-an-hour winds and still has twenty-five miles farther to crawl to get to shelter. Even at the dock here the wind has come up, driving flying snow and whitecaps across our tiny harbor. Suddenly there is so much wind it begins to bang *Masonic* rhythmically against the dock. All of us are very happy to be safely in port. Outside the harbor the weather must be savage indeed.

Here at this secure outpost of civilization, Mark offers to take Cal's dirty clothes up to the washing machines. When Mark disappears up the steps out of the galley, Cal remarks to me, "*That's* a first!" He's a bit flabbergasted that the captain has just taken his laundry.

Though I've often thought that the perfect antidote for being cold and wet is to be warm and wet, I've been here several hours and still have not bothered to find the hot showers. I guess I have become schooner trash indeed. Mark stops to make a phone call to his wife and daughters from a bank of stand-up plywood phone booths at the top of the dock. I decide to make a couple of calls, including one to my mother, because we've fished through Mother's Day. I'm not the only one with that idea. A crewman from the other boat is in the adjacent booth, talking so noisily I wait for him to finish before I dial. His voice is coming loud and clear through the thin walls of the phone booth, saying, "I didn't realize how much time I spend on women and it's really—you know—super unproductive. . . . Well, I wanted to wish you a happy Mother's Day. . . .

Yeah, Mom. . . . Well yeah, I did meet this girl from Georgia. . . . No, I haven't done anything with her. . . . No, not yet. . . . *Jeez*, Mom. No, just a little kiss for fun. . . . Yeah, I really miss women, but. . . . Yeah, but it's really good to come to a place so different from what I am. You gain a lot of perspective. Okay, Mom, well, happy Mother's Day. I love you."

A dinner whistle sends us and all the workers into the common mess hall, where dinner is chicken, potatoes, rice, string beans, Swiss chard, bread, cookies, lemonade, and water. The workers exchange few words, and the hall remains remarkably quiet—just the clacking of silverware on plates. And although the dinner bell sounded at five o'clock and everyone can eat as much as they want, at 5:20 we are the only people left in the dining hall. Everyone else has returned to work. Mac is engulfing his third helping of rice.

THE FURIOUS GALE CONTINUES kicking the boat against the pilings all night, jarringly enough to make sleep difficult even at the dock. Around midnight Mark gets word that Shaun's stepfather has finally reached safety.

We spend the first layup day loading bait and ice. Mark hoped to get out fishing again tomorrow, but new storm warnings will keep *Masonic* pinned in port. Continued reports of bad weather mean more time away from family and loved ones. And as the crew gets pensive "the demon tobacco" racks new sales, until Mark is smoking heavily again.

We hear a boat while Cal is cooking. Pete Schonberg has just brought the *Equinox* in through very bad weather. He'd been running in ahead of the same weather we were fleeing. But he was about two hundred miles southwest of us, and though he started in earlier, the storm caught him.

He joins us at our sundown dinner aboard *Masonic* but doesn't eat. Where he was a few days ago, he tells us, he saw an amazing thing: twenty-seven Short-tailed Albatrosses around the *Equinox;* 2 percent of the entire world population around one boat at one moment. That wasn't all. "We had just an absolutely humongous amount of every kind of albatrosses. We had a couple of hundred Laysans around the boat at once. They were so hungry they weren't even letting the fulmars get in for the heads." The ravenous albatrosses were disallowing the fulmars their force of number, denying them the popular vote. They were asserting dominance, pulling rank, throwing their weight around, reconfiguring the pecking order. "They were doing things I have never before seen birds do in all my life," Schonberg continues. "They weren't afraid of the bird buoys. And they were cooperating; a couple would pick up the gear and the others would strip a hundred hooks clean. These birds live a long time," he says, "and they've learned what to do. They weren't just engulfing the hook and all, but just trying to pick off the bait. But we killed three of them that did get hooked. I didn't like that," he says, putting up his hands. "It's always been considered bad luck to kill an albatross. And with all the Short-tails around—. So after *that,* our care factor went way up. We posted a guy full-time to scare them. But it was like nothing I've ever seen. They were like they hadn't eaten *all* the way from Hawaii. Just incredible voraciousness. I mean, the *noise*—. I'm telling you: they were not scared of *anything.* So then we decided to set the lines only at night. It's the only way to avoid hooking the albatrosses there right now."

The rest of the talk is about consumer confidence in Japan, the resilience of the Japanese economy, the dollar/yen value. Schonberg says, "Good weather is horrible for the halibut price. Last trip we got a good price because we fished during a storm when no one was delivering. So pray for bad weather, I guess."

Mark chuckles. "No, I'm sorry—I'm not praying for bad weather. I like nice weather." Schonberg gets up to leave and reminds Mark, "Well, I came to give you a warning. Set at night when you get down there toward the Aleutians. And whatever you do—don't kill any Short-tails. That's bad news for us all."

Jim has slept through dinner. At midnight, Mark finally rises from the table and says, "Well, I'm going to turn on to reefer and go to bed."

"Pardon me?" I ask.

He repeats himself, and this time I hear him correctly: "I'm going to turn on the refer"—short for the refrigeration unit in the hold.

"A line like that," I say, "could easily be misquoted."

AN AMPHIBIOUS PLANE LANDS with its pontoons in the choppy bay, and the pilot runs its wheels up the small, smooth, black pebbles of the shore. Mark helps me with my duffels. The pilot turns the craft back into the bay. Through the window I watch Mark, and Cal in his yellow slicker on the black beach, and Tim standing on the dock with his hat fastened tight around his ears and a mug of tea in one hand. All of us waving, waving, waving. The plane lifts off heavily, like an overburdened albatross, thrashing from the water with spray streaking across the windows. We leave the whitecap-salted inlet and rise against the landscape, the great shimmering sweep of pond-pocked tundra and the massive white mountains whose steep snow-robed slopes suddenly rise into our eyes the moment we get above the first low hills.

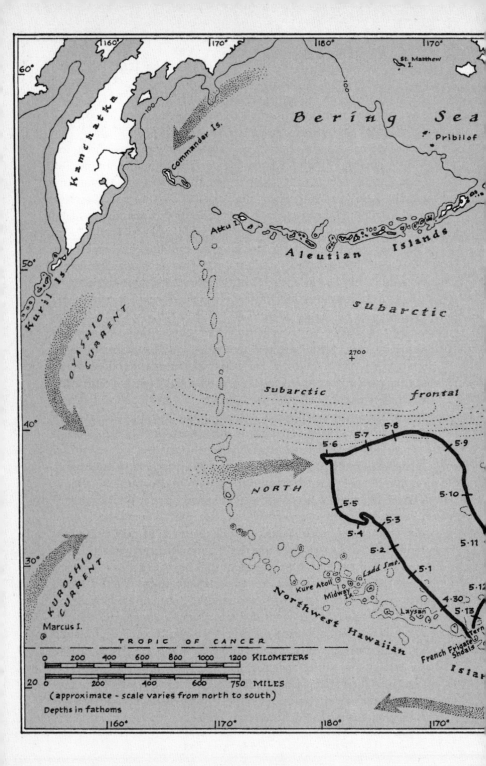

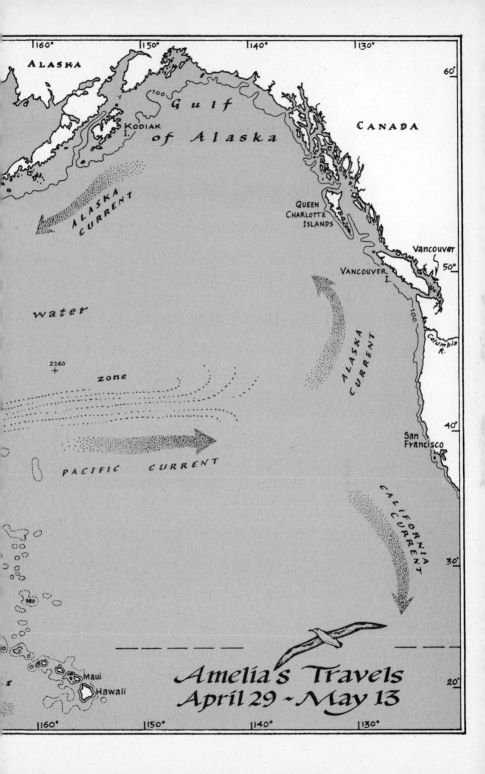

> ➤ ➤ ➤ ➤ ➤ ➤ ➤ ➤ ➤ ➤ ➤

MIDWAY

AMELIA IS DOWN to a lean, athletic weight, fit and tuned. She has invested the last trip—two weeks—in her chick. During this trip Amelia ranged "only" about eleven hundred miles from her nest, to the southern edge of the subarctic frontal zone. She's pursuing an eminently reasonable strategy: intermediate effort for intermediate rewards that will be invested mostly in the large chick's rapid growth. If she stayed close, she wouldn't find as much food; and she needs more food for a chick that's now so big—big enough to wait the extra days. But if she went on month-long trips each time, she'd benefit at the expense of her chick, who would be left to contend with her prolonged absence, disproportionately dependent on Dad. So during this last foraging trip she traveled an immense, clockwise, roughly circular searching flight: northwest up to the frontal zone, a few hundred miles eastward along the front, and then home. The nourishment was spotty and fleeting, and she kept moving. Like a parent working a second job to pay for her kid's college, Amelia doesn't really think much about how hard it is; she just does what she has to do. Amelia's restlessness is contagious, and I'm feeling it. I've kept moving too, this time to the outer reaches of this island chain.

> ➤ ➤ ➤

IN LANGUID LONELINESS at the extreme center of the vast North Pacific Ocean lies Midway Atoll. It's farther from just about everything than just about anywhere. Virtually no island is more distant from the peopled continents. Or more worth the trip.

I've come with the award-winning Canadian nature writer Nancy

Baron to see the world's largest colony of Laysan Albatrosses—several hundred thousand exquisite masters of the art of air, a feathered nation convened to breed, cramming two small islands.

Parts of this island bloom with thousands of chicks per acre. Five-month-old chicks nearly the size of geese so jam the sandy landscape that it resembles a poultry farm. They're at an awkward stage, half puffy down, half feathered.

Midway is a classic Pacific atoll; mostly shallow lagoon clasped by a thin necklace of emergent, broken reef. It has two main islands, Sand and Eastern. The larger, Sand, is about two miles across at its widest. The atoll's lagoon is about five miles across. Midway's emergent lands total a little over two square miles (compared to Laysan's 1.5 square miles and Tern Island's mere thirty-seven acres). Seabirds of fifteen species nest here.

Though exotic, Midway Atoll feels strangely familiar. Midway is like Small Town, U.S.A., plus two million seabirds. The odd *Leave It to Beaver* familiarity derives from the structural remnants of a U.S. military presence that spanned the Second World War through the Cold War. Sand Island's gravel streets connect a network of houses with very American lawns, a very American bowling alley, a tennis court, a small theater, dorms, several small stores, and a workers' bar called the All Hands Club. Energizing the infrastructure is a power-generation station built for up to five thousand military personnel. The power station currently serves only one-twentieth its capacity for the following reason: on June 30, 1997, the last of the navy occupants pulled out, unneeded buildings started coming down, and this became Midway Atoll National Wildlife Refuge.

ON ALL THE LAWNS, and lining the airport, and on every grassy slope are *so many* albatrosses; they are *everywhere* you look. Every few feet on every street or path. Outside every window: albatrosses.

The youngsters are everywhere. You have to walk around them or zigzag your bike to avoid them. Whether you're going to the cafeteria or the beach—*wherever* you're going—you need to get around albatrosses to get there. If you're walking with someone, you must frequently part to step around albatrosses.

At the outdoor Christian chapel—where a round fluorescent bulb serves as Mary's perpetually lit halo—a Fairy Tern drifts by like a tiny moving cloud, seemingly sanctified and blessed in all aspects and regards. It hovers over the statue like a visitation of the Holy Spirit. With appropriate reference and reverence Nancy gasps, "Oh my *God.*" She says the Fairy Terns seem so ethereal they could be the souls of babies. The chapel is surrounded by a low white picket fence, to keep the albatrosses out. The albatrosses don't mind; they get closer to God on their own power.

The albatross chicks have by now grown large, their sleek body feathers mostly in, but their heads still fluffy. They're still unsteady, and you'll sometimes see a big, regal-looking chick suddenly lose its balance like a hiccuping drunk. Nancy and I trade impressions of the big chicks crowded all across the open landscape: "They look like little lions." "Like fuzzy pumpkins." "Like feathered Sphinxes." "Like chocolate poodles."

Nancy squeezes my arm and laughs. "This is the most fun place I've ever seen. We're so lucky to be here." Tourists have been able to come to Midway on commercial flights from Honolulu since the military left. The number of visitors is limited to a hundred. But civilian travel to Midway isn't unprecedented. In 1935, Pan American Airlines began operating the China Clipper, a large flying boat whose island-hopping itinerary—from San Francisco to Honolulu, then to Midway, Wake, Manila, and finally Macao—was the fastest and most luxurious route to the Orient. But a Clipper trip cost three times the average annual American salary. Only the wealthiest industrialists, and luminaries like Ernest Hemingway, had the honor of meeting the "gooney birds" face-to-face. Japan's attack on Pearl Harbor, its first Hawaiian venture since the feather-poaching days, ended the China Clipper era. On Japan's next visit, Japanese forces showered their attention on Midway itself. A monument commemorating the Battle of Midway reads:

> *Where the most decisive naval battle*
> *in military history was fought.*
> *June 4, 1942, the day when the American spirit*
> *reached unparalleled heights and in so doing,*
> *saved democracy for the western world.*

Just as Midway's albatrosses actually spend most of their time on the ocean, most of the Battle of Midway was fought at sea, far over the horizon from the atoll itself, between the attacking Japanese fleet and bombers from an ambushing American flotilla. The American ships were sent from Pearl Harbor after genius cryptanalyst Joseph Rochefort and his team cracked Japan's war code, enabling the Americans to eavesdrop on the attack plan. By the end of the day-long battle nearly four hundred Americans and some three thousand Japanese were dead. Japan lost four aircraft carriers, and its plan to wipe U.S. resistance from the Pacific had turned to a crippling defeat from which Japan's war effort would never recover.

Decades later, President Richard Nixon met Vietnamese leaders here for secret talks to end a dreadful war. Midway's progress from triggering battle to facilitating conciliation was appropriate, because overall, this place is much more suited to peace.

Now bombs and bullets are a distant memory. Noddies line the phone wires like starlings. Instead of sparrows, flocks of introduced yellow canaries flit from tree to lawn. Fairy Terns by the thousands load the lampposts, street signs, and trees. Wildlife, not warfare, is why people come here now. Eight out of ten visitors arrive for the birds; the rest, for fishing and diving. We're here for a little of each.

PETER PYLE IS A NOTED SEABIRD SCIENTIST whose research assistants at Midway are volunteers signed up through the Oceanic Society. Some are seniors participating as part of an Elderhostel group. It's an ideal way for a retiree—or anyone—to become an instant biologist during a vacation's brief duration. Richard, early sixties, a former prison mailroom worker from New York, says, "It's a phenomenal thing to see birds this up close that're not scared." Gordon Bennet, a California retiree, loves the birds and the snorkeling: "The fish are a lot like birds; it's the same kind of beauty." Another senior, Betty, adds, "I like seeing where the sweet Fairy Terns lay their eggs." A high school teacher named Sandy is a bit apprehensive about the albatrosses' snapping bills, noting, "*That* one grabbed Mark in the crotch." Joyce King, here from Florida with the Sierra Club, can't believe all the plastics the albatrosses swallow: "We do all this recycling, but—"

Without these eco-tourists' dollars to keep the planes flying between here and Honolulu, wildlife management and research would be sharply curtailed, and Midway would be like Laysan—a lonely outpost, difficult to reach, many days distant from medical attention.

The volunteers are assisting Peter in applying individually numbered leg bands to the big albatross youngsters. Such identification, fundamental to many wildlife studies, will be appreciated by the next generation of biologists who will come of age during these albatrosses' long lives. Peter selects one large chick after another, applies a band to each chick's leg, closes it with pliers, and checks it to make sure that its ends are smoothly joined and it can rotate freely around the leg without causing abrasion.

At one point we pause, astonished, to watch two downy-headed albatross chicks dancing—as though courting! They're awkwardly head-bobbing, wing-flaring, sky-pointing, bill-fencing, and clacking, but without the usual vocalizations. Their moves are stiff, not fluid; but unmistakably part of the prepackaged courtship program. Like children in their first crush, they seem confused about whether their interaction is aggressive or not, frequently interrupting their shuffle to bite each other. After a few minutes, the love puppies lose interest in the romance dance.

Nancy, enchanted and amused, remarks that the awkwardness of youth seems universal. But while we may delight in their youthful awkwardness, we would err to see them as comedy. Their mere existence is testament to their unlikely success up to now. However "cute" we may think them, everything about them is geared toward one unlikely gamble: surviving.

Mostly, albatross chicks all over the island are sitting passively, shunting all their food to growth, wasting hardly a calorie on movement. At this stage they're both pitifully homely and painfully hungry. Many a chick has been waiting more than a week for a meal, while its parents search the limits of the ocean for food enough to keep it alive. Even through their feathers, many young albatrosses look very thin. This is the beginning of their most difficult period, when food needs are highest and their parents are pressed to their limits trying to find enough for such large youngsters. Not all of them can survive.

Peter points to a bird just ahead of us. "See how scrawny and small this one is? We won't band it because it's not going to make it. I suspect one of its parents died and it's being fed by only one parent."

This very thin chick comes walking by us, pecking at the dirt every few steps. Nancy turns to me, saying, "Once they've died, you can detach. But I hate seeing them on that precipice of death. You feel it."

I say, "There's a lot of pain in paradise."

Why do we discern in nature beauties of sufficient radiance to burn through the veils of such misery and horror? Is it simply that something in us resonates that our little blue planet has won the lottery of Life, and rejoices no matter what agonies that gift entails?

Nancy mentions that a lot of chicks seem to have died in the last couple of days.

Peter says, "El Niño probably caused food shortages that triggered the drop in the number of adults breeding and increased nest abandonment. Plus with El Niño we lost a lot of the breezes. It's been so calm and hot that I think the heat—dehydration—is killing a lot of chicks right now."

Of the birds breeding here, Peter is most concerned about the Black-footed Albatrosses. There are only about one-tenth as many Black-footeds as Laysans to begin with. And in addition to other difficulties, such as oppressive weather and fishing, Black-footeds are having more problems with contaminants. Scientists expected to find the world's most uncontaminated birds at Midway, because of its remoteness. They were astonished to discover albatrosses with contamination levels comparable to eagles and waterbirds around the Great Lakes. Black-footed Albatrosses—but not Laysans—carry enough chemicals to cause low levels of egg breakage and embryo death, reducing their breeding success by around 2 to 3 percent. But Black-footed Albatrosses can't absorb more fatalities without entering long-term decline. Why these contaminant problems for Black-foots and not Laysans? The compounds called PCBs—whose chemistry predisposes them to affect fertility, embryo growth, immune and endocrine system functions, and cell growth—can be ten times more concentrated in sea foam than in seawater, because they bind to the fats in the foam. The flyingfish eggs that Black-foots so relish—they eat far more of them than do the Laysans—are basically bags of fat-rich yolk soaking in parts of the sea surface already enriched with contaminants. One more survival strategy gone awry. Another such example—one of the hardest things to watch—is albatross chicks dragging their long wings behind them, the toxic effect of eating lead-paint chips from the rubble of old buildings. Albatrosses of both species, and other birds, normally eat old eggshells, for the calcium. Yet again a habit that has always aided their survival sometimes turns deadly against them. Fortunately, only a few chicks are so afflicted. But together, these problems begin adding up.

Of the hundreds of thousands of chicks that hatched, each night 300 to 350 of the big chicks die, mostly from starvation and dehydration. Each morning, a white-shrouded worker driving a little tractor and cart makes his rounds, using a sharp-tined pitchfork to garner a harvest of death. As if to affect a sinister anonymity, his face is hidden with a loosely wrapped cloth, his eyes obscured by sunglasses. He's a grim but compassionate reaper, shaking his head as he stops to skewer up a bird that expired the previous night, saying in his Sri Lankan accent, "They get bigger; more now die. Not good."

More will die than will survive to adulthood; so you wonder at times whether the main process of life is dying. Yet survivors by the thousands await their sea trials. Peter tells us that more than a million albatrosses are now using Midway. Ninety percent are Laysan Albatrosses—over 300,000 nesting *pairs* of Laysan adults, plus chicks, plus one subadult nonbreeder for every two breeders. Laysans have proved very resilient over the years. The feather hunters had knocked the Laysans down to as low as perhaps ten to twelve thousand pairs at the beginning of the twentieth century. Then from the 1940s to '60s the military tried to eliminate them from much of Midway. They bulldozed incubating birds, and at one point even used flamethrowers. Before military intelligence figured out that albatrosses won't nest on pavement—and that they could just pave the areas where they didn't want them—they killed 140,000 birds. They finally stopped killing albatrosses in 1965, but another 60,000 died in collisions with Midway's poles, towers, three-hundred-foot antennas with their guy-wire riggings, and barbed wire. Lobbying on behalf of the birds had no effect on the military, but in 1967 satellites made the system obsolete. Only after removal of the antenna system (and final closure of the base in 1993), could the world's largest albatross colony finally nest in peace.

IN THE EVENING Nancy and I introduce ourselves to David Itano, a fish scientist. He, in turn, introduces us to a Fairy Tern chick named Tinkerbell who stands ready to fledge from the backyard bench on which she hatched. On Midway, this is networking.

David Itano has a broad, open face, soft brown eyes, and features that reflect his Japanese-American heritage. Around here, he's often presumed to be local Hawaiian. David's father, a biochemist, put the fishing bug in young Dave during frequent excursions around Chesapeake Bay and Maine. Dave would say, "When I grow up I want a job where they pay me to go *fishing*." Mission accomplished. Dave's current job is research into the populations and movements of tunas in the Pacific. He studies their travels by putting numbered tags into thousands of fish, releasing them, and seeing where other people recapture them.

Dave has generously offered to take us with him for a day of tagging Yellowfin and Bigeye Tuna at a sunken seamount forty miles from Midway. Even at face value, this prospect would rate as sensational. Even more exciting is that these waters have been off-limits to fishing boats for about fifty years, because of the former military base. The place we're going remains as close to untouched as any place in the open ocean can claim to be.

As Robert Frost exclaimed, "May something go always unharvested! / May much stay out of our stated plan." Tapping the same vein, Thoreau observed that a person is rich in proportion to the number of things they can afford to leave alone. A few places should be left to thrive unhindered, so we can have some means to measure the effects we exert everywhere else. How else will we be able to know whether humanity is becoming richer or more impoverished?

Precious few places in the world could apply for the distinction of unspoiled. The place we're headed for qualifies. What we'll get a sense of is this: what a piece of ocean can be like when virtually no one has been there for half a century.

NANCY AND I WALK toward the boat in postmidnight darkness. In the open areas around us, occasional Bonin Petrel chicks are fledging straight from their burrows. These young birds have never seen daylight, never yet flown. A young Bonin Petrel must—in one step—come out into the real world, find the sea, and begin its life-or-death odyssey of living, traveling, and finding food in the ocean—all on its own, all at once.

We meet at the appointed hour and load the boat with the needed fishing rods, lures, and tagging gear. The boat is a cabin cruiser usually used for Midway's sportfishing charters. The captain is Dave Wolfe. Rounding out the crew is mate Mike Meredith. Mike has been here only two weeks, and loves it. "For me, it's the opportunity of a lifetime."

We leave behind the faint, quaint lights of Midway Atoll under a quarter moon, with Mars and Jupiter in uncommonly close consort. Running through the black sea in the ink of night entails the hazard of striking a drifting log or other object, so we will go slowly, giving us about four hours to talk and snooze.

As the boat is running, Dave Itano is telling me how much he loves this ocean. He first saw the Pacific when, as a teenager, his family moved to San Diego. "I knew I was home," Dave remembers. He started fishing Pacific Yellowtail and bonito, and rockfishes in the kelp beds.

We're sitting in the boat's cabin, relaxing with soft drinks. The last I saw of Nancy, she was "racked out" in a bunk. I presume she's catching some much needed rest. Dave and I are forced to talk loudly over the engines, which are noisy enough to mask the pounding that Nancy is doing on the door of the toilet, inside of which she is locked.

When Dave was sixteen, he and his brother fished commercially off La Jolla, California, from a tiny car-top-portable boat. "We located a hole right near shore that was *loaded* with beautiful big Vermilion Rockfish. We made twenty-hook rigs and pulled up full lines every time. We got about eight cents a pound.

"But that lasted less than a year. *We* fished it out! It was my first experience of fishing out a part of the ocean. Whenever I go back to visit my family, I take that little boat and row it through the surf and fire up the kicker and line up the sights and get back to the spot and fish it—and to this day—*thirty years later*—it has never recovered. There were other spots that got fished out too. So that was a lesson.

"In college I stayed out a whole semester just to catch Dungeness Crabs off northern California. Then the price plummeted to nothing. So that was another lesson: booms bust. Third lesson: there's a place along the La Jolla shore that was made a protected park in the early seventies. It didn't take very long for the place to start recovering. Soon you could find lots of small lobsters and Green Abalones in the caves and in the crevices. So that was another interesting lesson: leave it alone *before* you fish it out, and it'll recover."

While Dave was in college, salmon were still a big part of the West Coast scene. "There were hundreds of mom-and-pop salmon boats. It was a very clean fishery. All hook-and-line. Very selective. Very high quality. Especially the big King Salmon—all banquet fish. Then in August we'd go far offshore chasing Albacore. You could roam the whole California-Oregon-Washington coast. I *loved* that fishery.

"So," he continues, "when I returned from college, boy, it was such a shock to learn that the salmon had collapsed and so many of those beautiful rivers I used to know were in such desperate trouble." As a little aside Dave adds, "A while ago I was just hanging around one day in Honolulu's Kewalo basin, just 'talking story.' We discovered that many of us used to fish West Coast salmon in the same years in the same places—we'd all been trolling the Umatilla Reef, and off La Push, or Hecate Bank off Newport, or Point Arena, Fort Bragg, et cetera. We started laughing when we realized that we were all 'old farts,' or old 'futs,' as they say in Hawaiian pidgin. But I'll tell you, it was very bittersweet. It's all a thing of the past, and none of our kids will ever see it like that or understand. The bright, hazy warm afternoons—I'd almost forgotten that they had happened. Sometimes it's hard to remember how it really was. Then I remembered that older guys told me *their* stories, of how it was before my time—and how I'd said, 'Sure, sure.'"

Dave pauses.

I don't say anything.

After college Dave saw the ocean from one of the first really big boats to explore for tuna in the western Pacific. "It was a two-hundred-and-twenty-foot, twelve-hundred-ton superseiner—with a helicopter and everything. Compared to the forty-foot salmon troller I was accustomed to, the seiner was a huge ship." The fishing gear was a purse seine, an enormous curtain of netting dropped around a school of fish in a circle and then pursed together at the bottom. They fished waters off Samoa, New Zealand, New Guinea, Micronesia, and elsewhere. "We had *amazing* fishing power. Some of those schools were incredibly huge back then. We followed one school of Skipjack Tuna that was too big to get a net around, and finally it split in half. And then the half that we were following split in thirds. We wrapped the net around one of those thirds—in other words, one-sixth the original school—and bagged two hundred and eighty *tons* in one set. Most of these guys would set the net regardless of whether there was enough room left in the hold for all the fish. So we would kill, say, ninety tons of Skipjack in one set of the net for the sake of filling up the remaining thirty tons of room on board at the end of a voyage. The rest, we dumped."

Dave sums up: "So all my life I've fished; then seen myself as part of a big problem." Dave figured aquaculture—seafood farming—might be the answer. "But soon after I entered the field I saw that it mostly raises delicacies for high-end markets; it's not an answer to hunger. So after all these experiences, I think well-managed wild fisheries are generally the way to go."

Dave stayed with the tuna boat for three years, married an American schoolteacher he met in Samoa, worked five years as a Samoan government fisheries biologist, and fathered two daughters. "I was perfectly happy there. Nice people. It's an easy place to raise kids. If your kid disappears, it's because some big Samoan lady is giving her treats that you don't want her to have."

But then Dave got offered a job in a large-scale tuna-tagging project based on New Caledonia. The project put serially numbered tags on a couple of hundred thousand tunas in waters of twenty-three island nations and territories over an immense area of the Pacific. "The tagging project showed that the tuna resources were vast, much larger than previously thought. That was before modern purse-seine fishing really got established in that region."

Dave then moved to the University of Hawaii to undertake an

ambitious study of tuna reproduction and travels. By dissecting over ten thousand Yellowfin Tuna he learned that they spawn up to eleven *million* eggs at a time. And they do this every other day for weeks at a stretch. Despite virtually limitless trillions of eggs, the ocean is not overflowing with Yellowfin Tuna because the chances of a baby tuna surviving to adulthood are vanishingly small. In his current project's first year, Dave has tagged nearly twelve thousand Yellowfin and Bigeye Tuna. So far, he has found that individual Bigeye Tuna remain at seamounts longer than Yellowfins. Roughly 9 percent of his tagged tuna have already gotten recaptured in the first twelve months, both in Hawaiian waters and at points north and westward—indicating surprising fishing pressure, even in so seemingly vast an ocean.

This tagging project is what Nancy and I will participate in in the morning. Dave and I have a little while to catch some shut-eye before we get to our intended location. But when we go to turn in, we discover that Nancy is missing—not in her bunk, not on the bridge, not on deck. This raises immediate fears that she's fallen overboard in the boundless black sea. So it is with considerable relief—for all of us—that we finally hear her pounding and discover she has merely spent virtually the entire multihour overnight run locked inside the "head"—where she remains trapped. In her defense we must note that the toilet lock is truly broken, that opening the door requires the combined force and mental effort of two men, a screwdriver, a chisel—and, of course, poor Nancy, who emerges a little bit dazzled with the countervailing sensations of alleviation, annoyance, and fatigue.

AT FIRST LIGHT we're in a different world: all water and one circular horizon. A few Sooty Terns were calling in the darkness when we arrived, and now we can see them flying here and there, and we can see a few Laysan and Black-footed Albatrosses working over the ocean surface. It remains fully impressive that the birds can find and relocate this precise spot within that great circle.

A jetliner's vapor trail provides the only proof of humanity's continuing existence somewhere. Our deck is crowded with coolers, fishing gear, and a big blue plastic barrel. Soon after we left the harbor we discovered a stowaway Bonin Petrel on the back deck, hiding behind some of that gear. It was in a spot we can't reach, and has now disappeared from view. A prepping table is loaded with fishing lures. The lures don't *look* too much like fish; but they're made to *move* like fish when pulled through the water. Nancy is impressed with their garishness—their chrome heads and brightly colored plastic skirts. She says, "Some of these lures look positively lurid."

The quarter moon notwithstanding, we have arrived at our own sea of tranquillity. We're over the Ladd Seamount, a submerged mountain that comes up as close to the surface as thirty-seven fathoms out of water twenty-five-hundred fathoms deep. A few tens of millions of years ago we would have called it Hawaii and sold T-shirts and surfboards, and it would have been about a thousand miles east of here. Now it has a higher purpose.

In the east the clouds are turning gold and pink. The clear sky overhead seems devoid of moisture, but low clouds rim the horizon. Itano checks the instruments and announces what the albatrosses and other birds have already told us: "We're right on the spot."

The air is moving at under ten knots—not quite breeze enough to sail an albatross. They're trying to use the cushion of air between themselves and the water, but they're also doing a fair amount of flapping. I wonder what they've been eating here.

I'm surprised to see so many Fairy Terns this far from land. A couple of Wedge-tailed Shearwaters are also weaving along the ocean surface. At the moment we can see a few dozen birds scattered around. Dave says, "Keep an eye out for some birds to start forming flocks. They should start hunting soon."

Dave has readied two heavy fishing rods with big reels plus two heavy hand lines. All the line is very strong: four-hundred-pound test. To help get fish in quickly, on the back of the boat he's rigged a hydraulic hauler of the kind usually used to pull up strings of lobster traps. He says when he first came to this seamount they weren't able to reel the big fish in fast enough to prevent numerous shark attacks—hence the heavy lines and the hydraulic hauler. That sounds like a lot of sharks. Nearly everywhere in the world you travel, the main story you hear about sharks is how many there *aren't* nowadays, compared to times past. This place, apparently, is different. Either big bold brazen fish abound here in profuse abundance or Dave is employing the most time-honored device in fishing conversation—exaggeration. We'll see if they're really here, and really so hungry.

The rising sun is poised just below the horizon, about to burn its way through a cloud. We haven't slept, but the Sooty Terns are calling, *Wide awake, wide awake.*

"Time to go tuna fishing," announces Dave. He, Mike, and I stream the lures astern. We stop them about fifty to seventy-five feet behind the moving boat and they pop to the surface, skipping and darting like fleeing prey fish. Dave sets the reels' drag brakes at fifty pounds; not an inch of line will budge from the spool until whatever is at the other end exerts at least fifty pounds of pulling power. The two outside lines are run from the tips of the fishing rods to poles called outriggers that hold the lines out away from the boat, helping to prevent tangles. A clothespin-like clip holds the fishing line to the outriggers, and you run the clip up to the end of the outriggers like running a flag up a pole. The two inside hand lines go straight to their lures. So now we're trolling, dragging four lures, watching them skipping in our wake. We're pulling the lures pretty quickly, about ten miles an hour, but we're after fish that can sprint five times that speed. They're the fastest fish in the known universe.

One tern starts hovering excitedly nearby, and a tuna crashes twice through the surface. Immediately, more birds wing speedily toward the spot, streaming in from all directions. Right away you can tell: this is an aerobic place to make a living. This is the big league. Four billion years of product testing and refinement have produced animals at the top of their game: the fastest swimmers, the most exquisite fliers. And—we'd like to think—the best fishers.

A pile of Sooty Terns gathers to our right and starts diving. Dave shouts to Captain Wolfe, up on the bridge, and points to the commotion. Wolfe turns the boat toward the birds. I glance back at our churning wake and the skittering lures.

Nancy suddenly points, "Oh my *God*! Look at all the fish jumping *there*!"

I look forward and see silhouetted fish exploding from the water and sailing through the air like tossed footballs. There's nothing floppy about them. These are projectiles, missiles, bombs.

The starboard lure gets bit but the fish comes off immediately after popping the line from the outrigger clip. Half a minute later the port outrigger snaps and the line shoots tight and begins peeling off the reel. But that fish quickly comes off, too.

The leaping fish vanish. The birds disperse.

A few minutes later, a nice fish yanks a hand line taut and stays on. Itano grabs the line and slips it into the hauler winch. Soon the fish appears beneath our turbulent wake, a life of shining silver, gleaming white, glowing yellow. Dave opens a door in the transom, grabs the line, and slides the fish through, onto a pad on deck. It's a Yellowfin Tuna, *Ahi* in Hawaiian. Gorgeous and bright; a laminated, decorated speed package.

Nancy flashes me a smile. Like nearly everyone on the planet, she's never seen a living tuna. Its great beauty impresses her. She's admiring the dark ocean-blue back, how it blends downward first to electric blue, then into the bronzy burnishing along the side, to the pearly belly; the silver-hard gill plates; the large eyes bearing light blue irises; the lightened vertical flank markings creating stripes and spots; the shape of the fusiform body from nose to the rigid keels along its stiff, crescent-shaped tail; the winglike pectoral fins, and the bright yellow emarginations of the fins; and the rows of little yellow finlets running along the tailward third of both the back and belly, which the fish controls like rudders; the way its larger fins vanish into slots to eliminate friction during streaking bursts of speed.

Dave pops a tag into the fish's back, a nylon dart with a number on it. It sticks out like a little streamer. Each tag says HAWAII TAGGING PROJECT and then the serial number. Dave slides the fish out the door. Into a tape recorder hung in a waterproof bag around his neck he dictates, "Tag number 89, Yellowfin, eighty centimeters—"

He is still saying "centimeters" when another fish hits one of the hand lines and is hooked. Dave slides that fish through the door, disengages the hook, and throws the lure back in so that that line is already fishing again before he even has the tag in the tuna's back.

These fish are small so far, only about fifteen pounds. They're easily manageable. Each fish is on deck for fifteen seconds or less. Itano can handle more action. So he asks Mike to add another hand line. Now we're trolling five lines.

I hear an outrigger clip go *snap!* and the reel near my head starts screaming. This is a really hot fish. I mean, the reel is *shrieking*. Even against the drag brake set at fifty pounds of pressure, this thing is *burning* line off the spool. Dave reaches for the whizzing line and it cuts his glove open. This fish takes out all the four-hundred-pound-test line—intended to be all the line needed for almost any fish out here—and now we're into the 130-pound-test backing.

A much smaller fish hits a hand line—a fifteen-pounder—and Dave tags it. Now I'm charged with keeping the line on the rod tight—which the hot fish does by itself. Dave grabs my line in his damaged glove, slips it into the hauler, and in a few minutes we have a yellowfin weighing sixty pounds coming through the door. This one was incredibly strong for its moderate size; we were expecting a much bigger fish. I'd like to see a two-hundred-pounder pull.

We've been fishing for fifteen minutes and have tagged four tuna. Not bad!

Our stowaway Bonin Petrel makes a sudden appearance from under the bait-prepping table, then goes back into hiding.

Two more fish rise to the lures, sink their hard teeth into the soft plastic, and feel a steely sting. One small Bigeye Tuna, one small Yellowfin. The Bigeye weighs about twenty-five pounds. It's got slight barring on the belly in the rear half, a bigger, stouter head, and a deeper body that got it the Latin name *obesus*. This is a baby; they can grow to be several hundred pounds—if they live long enough.

Captain Wolfe turns the boat toward another group of about a hundred diving birds over breaking fish. Immediately, two more fish rise and strike. This time all the lines tangle. Fish are now spurting and darting through the surface practically alongside us, under a fluttering, diving flock of excited noddies and Sooty Terns, a couple of Wedgies and Fairy terns, and one Laysan Albatross. Except for the albatross, these birds depend almost completely on tuna to drive prey to the surface, where they can get at it. Overfishing threatens even them, because no tuna—or very few—would mean all these birds starve.

About a dozen and a half Sooties swoop in and check themselves over our splashing lures. I'm watching the lures skipping and I see a big splash behind one. A few seconds later, a tuna sucks the lure under, snaps the line from the outrigger clip, and then streaks away. Again all of the heaviest line goes and the fish takes it far into the backing. This fish requires attention. We clear all the other lines out of the water and start backing down on it. I put the reel into low gear. Captain Wolfe yells from the bridge, "C'mon, Carl, crank—reel, *reel!*" I begin putting line back on the reel as the boat backs down farther. Dave gets the line into the hauler, but still the fish is pulling very, very hard. Even with the hydraulic hauler the fish is coming only slowly.

Dave suddenly calls, "Shark!"

A yellowish Galápagos Shark that I estimate at perhaps two hundred pounds and Dave thinks weighs 250 grabs the tuna, engulfing it so thoroughly that it itself gets hooked. The shark corkscrews downward, and the rod swivels violently to meet the arcing movement as it powers away. We work it to the surface. Another very hefty shark appears. "We have a shark coming to eat a shark," says Mike. I not sure he's right about the second shark's intentions. But I'm not sure he's wrong. The first shark suddenly pulls so hard that it breaks open the snap connecting the leader, and gets free.

A minute and a half later, we get blasted by another doubleheader of tuna. The first of them gets seriously raked by a shark. Dave decides not to tag it, and calls it a keeper. It's a hundred-plus pounds, and Dave says it's about four years old.

Nancy says, "How magical that it would grow so big so fast." She adds, "Seeing it come from the ocean strikes me mostly as tragedy."

A sizable school of tuna comes up about fifty yards to our right, our port side. Wolfe turns the boat sharply to meet them. The fish that we're keeping is still on the deck, rapidly drumming its stiff tail. Nancy says, "Look at its rainbow of colors changing as it dies."

It gasps and throws up a flyingfish and a squid. I'm thinking, I'm glad these fish can't scream. Dave comes with a sharp pick and delivers a pithing stab to its brain. The fish shudders, then goes silvery still.

Nancy murmurs to me, "Now that it's dead it looks like a beautiful work of art."

Wolfe says, "Looks like they're smiling when they die."

Nancy turns to him, saying, "Lucky for us."

The cockpit is a mess of blood, lines, and lures. We need to get organized. The shark's abrasive skin did a lot of damage to the line it hit. So Dave cuts off the last few yards and reties the leader. This gives me a moment to ice the damaged tuna, hose the deck, and look around and reorient to the birds' activities. The water is deep clear indigo. The light breezes manage to put whitecaps on the ocean, but there's no swell to speak of.

There is some big stuff swimming around here. I peel down to a T-shirt before we're ready to troll again. I started to really sweat on the last one; when that sun gets up, it is *strong*. Nancy looks around and says, "Man, it's hot for seven o'clock."

A large Wahoo latches on. A cousin of tunas, the Wahoo may be the fastest fish in the ocean, and this one rips out line in a way that leaves that reputation vividly reinforced. Alongside—five feet long and about sixty pounds—it shows a silvery belly and dark back, and its flanks are tiger-marked with broad, wavy, dark-green bars alternating against aquamarine. Very striking. This fish is a painted javelin. Its entire body seems an instrument of speed and impact. It appears more barracuda-like than a barracuda—a hypercuda. It's got lots of teeth, very little patience, and is scary enough that Nancy leaps dancerlike across the cockpit to distance herself even before it comes aboard. Poetry in motion, her verbal reaction is the word *holy* followed by a noun.

Wolfe calls from the bridge, "Nice *Ono*," using its Hawaiian name.

Nancy, registering her new fear of Wahoo with an anglicized name, begins referring to them as *Oh No!* Nancy's never seen fish like this before, and she's awed. "They frighten me," she says with a nervous laugh. She says these creatures *all* seem like implements of war: the Wahoo like spears, the tunas like torpedoes, the sharks like heat-seeking missiles. This version of the battle of Midway has been happening every day for a long, long time, and all these creatures live inside the sea's most sophisticated weaponry.

Dave grunts, "Hefty one" as he leads the Wahoo through the stern door and onto the deck. Meanwhile, a Galápagos Shark that Wolfe says might be the biggest he's ever seen comes and eats a tuna that Mike had just brought alongside. I estimate its weight at over three hundred pounds. Wolfe estimates four hundred. He's a professional fisherman—so he's probably exaggerating. Anyway, it's big. And now it's hooked.

It takes us about fifteen minutes to subdue this shark and work it to the boat. This animal is bulky. Dave reaches over with a knife and makes a slight slice in its lip to free the hook. Nancy says seeing Dave trying to get the hook out of this huge tawny shark reminds her of David against Goliath. Upon release the shark turns a parting shot and *whacks!* the boat with its tail. Dave looks at us with wide eyes, saying, "Whew."

When the next tuna feeds another shark, I start feeling bad about it. Not that I have anything against sharks, obviously, but you want them to catch their own fish for their own moral, psychological, and spiritual well-being. And ours. We decide to go looking elsewhere on the seamount. Of the hundreds of tuna I've caught or witnessed in three oceans, before today I can remember only two getting bitten by a shark while on the line. While big sharks have gotten rare in most places, here they remain so abundant we have to get away from them. I like that part.

Itano says we're not really getting the numbers here anyway. From his perspective, unbelievably, the catching is too slow.

From mine, well, put it this way: there are so many tuna here—so fierce must be the competition among them—that they'll bite on things they wouldn't think of touching elsewhere. While in many places people use increasingly light lines so as not to scare increasingly shy and scarce tuna, here the line is highly visible four-hundred-pound-test nylon, tied to two feet of shiny thick wire. The fish don't seem to have time to think twice about it. If they hesitate to eat something, someone else will beat them to it.

As we're changing locales, Dave hands us chopsticks and breaks out a big plastic bag full of raw fish in lime juice. We pass it around, poking into it and nodding our approval with mouths full.

We go to the north end of the seamount and stream the lines out again.

Interesting move; the fish here are much bigger. The first two Yellowfins—around a hundred pounds each—crash the lures simultaneously like Olympian synchronized swimmers. One of them, on a hand line, comes off the hook right alongside the boat. The other takes a very extended run, then suddenly stops. Although there's weight on the line, we all suspect the fish is no longer alive, and we're right about that. We haul the carcass back. The middle of its body is deeply incised, with huge bites that have left the layered muscles looking like red tree rings of flesh.

Another hundred-pound Yellowfin darts in to snatch a lure and takes a long run. How fast the hunter becomes prey; its struggles summon the sharks.

Wolfe cuts whatever meat he can from the carcasses of both shark-attacked fish. And actually there's plenty of it left; it won't go to waste. But I find myself disturbed by the disruption we are causing to the lives of these creatures. The fisherman in me must be going soft. I wonder if that's a good thing.

Dave says, "We'd better start tagging some numbers here." These big fish are exciting, but for Dave's project a whole bunch of thirty-pounders is better. And, obviously, fish that survive are necessary.

Dave complains again about the fishing being slow, because we have to wait fully five minutes before the next fish. To me it seems red-hot, but I use the few minutes to look at birds again. I don't understand why the albatrosses expend any energy flying here; they don't look like they're feeding. Then again, flying costs them about the same as sitting. Perhaps they're trying to stay on top of the smell of the food until darkness. I'd love to spend the time here it would take to figure that out.

At nine o'clock, not only are the fish still biting every five minutes or so, but they're all big. The next fish is a Wahoo—*Ono; Oh No!*—and as Wolfe grabs the snap holding the leader, the fish tears it open with such force that it gashes his hand. The fish escapes, trailing the lure.

By ten o'clock we've successfully tagged and released about twenty fish, quite a few in the hundred-pound class. Where I come from, that's exceptional fishing of a kind we remember but never seem to experience anymore. Dave is unhappy. He says the fish are winning. Quite a few came off the hooks, broke free, or were taken by sharks. Altogether, about half the fish we hooked did not make it as far as the tags and the measuring pad. That's the bad part.

A ten-foot hammerhead shark appears near the boat, then vanishes.

Our next flurry reinforces the difficulties: Another big *Ono* caught, followed by two Yellowfin Tuna that pull free. A shark takes the next tuna. Dave Itano is shaking his head. His operations usually go much more smoothly, much more productively for both him and the fish.

We find a new group of birds, start circling the edges of them. It's the same few species as earlier, including both albatrosses, which, mysteriously, are always active but never seem to get anything to eat. We hook a tuna that gets the leader wrapped around its tail. It's a plump eighty-pounder, but the wrapped line has cut it in a bad place and it's bleeding profusely. We're bummed.

Dave says we'll keep him. He slices the throat to cut the gills so the blood will drain from the meat. Now the fish begins to panic and thrash, splattering blood everywhere. Dave calls for the spike and he piths the fish. It spasms and stiffens, and stops.

When an identical fish strikes and makes it to the boat intact and is tagged and released—just the way it's supposed to go, the way it *usually* goes for Dave—it seems unusual.

We've been at it five hours. Now we're trolling an area with several dozen spread-out Sooty and Fairy Terns, some shearwaters, four or five Laysan Albatrosses, and a couple of Red-footed Boobies. Suddenly a few dozen birds seem to converge excitedly. Tensed with expectation, we approach.

Nothing happens.

The fish seem to settle down. Lacking sleep, I doze off.

At noon one of the albatrosses happens to fly into our line with its mouth open. This brings it to the water. The line is running through its bill, and we can't believe it can't get rid of the line, even though it's shaking its head vigorously. There's not enough time for us to react, and if it doesn't get away from that line, the hook will probably dig in. Then, sure enough, the end of the line comes through its bill, the lure hits the bird, but the hook misses. The bird is unhurt and untangled.

Over the next while we tag two small Yellowfins and keep two small fish too damaged by the hooks to tag. A much larger fish, unseen, gets bitten off by a shark.

The talk is of heading home. Dave feels the trip hasn't gone well. But he wants to tag one more tuna, to end on an up note. We get a double hookup. We tag one. But during a quick backup maneuver to avoid a shark attack, the second heavy line wraps in a propeller. The shark gets the tuna anyway.

And now we're tangled in one prop. Line this heavy, wound tight, can cause serious damage to the propeller-shaft seal. It has to come off before we can attempt the long run home. While trying to free that line by reversing the propeller, another line that was inadvertently left dangling in the water also gets stuck in the props.

Now we have two lines to cut away from the propeller shafts. That means swimming. The prospect of going overboard with these hungry, agitated sharks seems somehow less than enticing.

Wolfe confirms from the bridge, "There's several big sharks under the boat right now." I climb to the bridge and look down into water so dark it looks blue-black. I can see their lemony-looking shapes slinking along. I count the shapes of seven very *large* sharks. Not only are they large, but over the last few hours they have gotten accustomed to the idea that this boat provides them with opportunities to eat something easy every little while. They *like* our boat. For them our boat is a good thing, perhaps the best thing that's happened in a long time.

Dave says, "Does anybody want to go swimming to get the line out of the props?"

"I'll go," I say.

He says, "I won't let you."

I tell him don't be ridiculous—I'm *kidding.*

He says these sharks are so ferocious—

I say I realize that. And though today is a good day to die, who knows?—tomorrow might be better. I'm curious about that. This scene reminds me of a Gary Larson "Far Side" cartoon showing a terrified guy in a boat, surrounded by sharks who are saying, "Look, why don't you just give yourself up? Otherwise this could turn into a frenzy, and nobody wants that." It seemed funny at the time.

Dave manages to pull one line free. But the other is badly stuck.

A cloud appears overhead from nowhere, as though conjured by our gloomy mood. Nothing dampens the mood of the patiently patrolling sharks. Dave goes into the cabin and reappears with a mask and snorkel.

He says, "I'm just going to poke over and have a look." He says to Mike, "Please hang on to my legs."

I have visions of Mike suddenly pulling back and coming up with *just* Dave's legs.

Dave leans out the transom door on his belly. He's not yet committed to going swimming, but now his torso disappears while Mike holds his ankles. He comes back up to the surface and he says, "It's not bad at all. The line is just around the cotter pin to the nut, and I can see the lure. I can cut it off." He pokes back under with a knife. But then he comes back and says, "It's not as simple as I thought. There's actually a lot wound on." He says, "I need to cut the wire from the lure and then the line. But there are sharks down below."

Somehow that last bit of information takes none of us by surprise.

Nancy whispers to me, "This is nerve-racking."

We limp ahead about two-thirds of a mile, hoping we can leave the sharks behind. I'm skeptical, because we can't go very fast. The sharks have had a very profitable morning following us around. Dave goes over with Mike holding his ankles again. He cuts the lure free and comes back to the surface. But then he says, "It's a scuba job. There's a lot of line wound in. I don't mind doing it, but we need to get off the seamount first because of the sharks."

Wolfe puts the boat in gear. But it makes a bad sound. He's afraid of damage. As captain, he's responsible; plus we're all the way out here alone. So he simply comes down off the bridge, puts a mask on, grabs a knife, and slips over. Mike yells, "Oh, a shark! Bring him back in." Dave takes a pole and taps him on the back. Wolfe scrambles to safety. In a chastened and thoughtful turn of mind, Wolfe says, "Let's just drive off the seamount with one motor. Let's get away from all these sharks."

Good idea. We drive off slowly on one engine.

The atmosphere on deck is part bravado (not mine), part professional responsibility to the boat and the equipment, and part the time pressure of needing to get Dave back to make his airplane flight later.

Now Wolfe is setting up a scuba tank. He goes over.

Mike says, "In addition to the sharks, there's the problem of working right under those propellers with the boat rocking back and forth. A larger wave could land the boat and propellers right on your head, or cut you deep and give you a big problem."

Just being in the water here is bad enough, but *bleeding*!

The problem with running the boat with this heavy line around the shaft is that the monofilament will melt and bind up the shaft itself and cut through a rubber bearing, leading to leakage. Wolfe reports that some of the monofilament is already melted and sucked up into the bearing. That's the bad news. The good: apparently we succeeded in getting away from the sharks.

A school of tuna comes up about a quarter mile away—white explosions under birds against blue water. I'm glad we're not too near them.

Wolfe tries again and comes up and says, "I got it all."

Soon, we're on our way home—all of us, intact.

➤ ➤ ➤

We, THE WILDLIFE, and everyone else here have been enjoying the benefits of a former military base retooled for peace. A lot of research is now getting done—and a lot of people are appreciating the place—because logistics allow personnel, equipment, vacationers, and volunteers to get here safely and efficiently. And that's mostly because of one man. And virtually no one ever meets him.

Meet Mark Thompson, Midway's wizard behind the curtain. A clean-cut, right-stuff-looking, stiff-lipped kind of guy, Mark was born on the early end of the baby boom and raised in Georgia. He comes across as having a tough, taut personality. Perhaps the stiffness comes from an auto-racing accident that left most of his bones broken about a year ago. "When you go from two hundred miles an hour to zero in the distance from here to there along this porch, the effect is *severe*. It wasn't my accident; I just got collected in somebody else's mess. So—"

We're sitting on the porch of his Clipper House Restaurant, talking, overlooking what strikes me as perhaps the most beautiful beach I've ever seen. He has thick dark hair, chiseled angular features. He's wearing a white polo shirt and wraparound sunglasses. Even in the most casual conversations, Mark's cadence and voice seem resolute and determined. "The only thing I ever won in my life," he is saying, "was the draft lottery, in 1969. I had number one. That's right." He spent the next three years as a helicopter pilot in Vietnam—about which he seems decidedly reluctant to say anything further.

But his interest in military aviation continued after the war. For amusement, Mark got heavily into skydiving. For work, he entered an unusual corner of the aviation business: operating specialized aircraft that provide an unusual service to governments of the United States, NATO, Canada, and Japan. "They hire us to be the bad guys," he says. The idea is to help teach tactics to fighter pilots. "For example, one thing we do is electronically degrade their radar, and they have to counter us. We practice electronic countermeasures against warships. We've towed ninety percent of the targets for the U.S. Navy's live-fire and gunnery. We've got four airplanes over Europe right now doing electronic countermeasures for NATO."

That business brought Thompson to Midway a couple of times a year for about fifteen years. "Then, one day a few years ago, I landed here and the guy fueling the planes said, 'This will probably be the last time you'll ever land here; they're going to BRAC us out.' BRAC means base realignment activities. Means close the base. They were going to take a bunch of bulldozers, dig a big hole in the middle of the island, and push everything in. I just couldn't believe it. Then I learned that the Fish and Wildlife Service wanted to keep a presence here, but financially, they didn't see how they could. So we worked out a deal." And here's the deal: the government would take care of the wildlife; Mark's company— the Midway Phoenix Corporation—would run the infrastructure, fuel airplanes, and bring up to one hundred tourist visitors at a time, plus students.

A year later, Mark came out here with the guys that were closing the base. Mark pointed out the buildings he didn't want them to tear down. "That's what's left. They were blowing a lot of stuff up. We had a lot of storage tanks with unknown gases in them. There were about eighty underground fuel tanks, with contaminated soil all around them. They had to clean all that out. They actually steam-cleaned the soil to get the fuel up to the surface, where they could suck it out. And there were old bombs and stuff. They blew all of those underwater. When they'd find one in the lagoon they'd mark it and send a guy down and he'd blow it. Some of them, they didn't know if they had mustard gas. They'd spent decades in the water. We had trucks pumping grout into pipelines underground for a year; if you don't fill them, fuel vapors inside are an explosive hazard. They still find pipelines underground on occasion. Last year they found one still full of aviation fuel. They thought it was a water line—and all of a sudden the guy who was cutting it got a flash. So—"

Over a thousand structures came down. "That big open area had dozens and dozens of officer housing units. We saved the navy ten or fifteen million dollars in demolition costs. But the federal government owns everything, even this restaurant that I built. I don't have a lease, just a cooperative agreement. And operating is expensive all the way out here. If the sportfishing operation needs a seventy-dollar boat part, it costs fifty dollars more just to get it here. They spent seven thousand dollars just this month, just for boat parts. We never throw anything away; eventually it gets cannibalized. We have an unbelievable Filipino machinist who can fabricate just about anything we need."

"What is your desire for the island?" I ask.

"To break even. Period."

"But you can break even by sitting home and—"

He interrupts, saying, "Trust me, I could do a lot better than break even by sitting at home and not getting involved in all this." He adds, "I lost an"—he searches for the right word—"an *inordinate* amount of money on this island. I'm beginning to wear thin. The only reason we did what we did out here was to prevent such a waste. I mean, how would Fish and Wildlife get somebody up here to count seals? And if they did get somebody here in a pup tent, what if they got appendicitis?"

I say, "So your motivation was basically—"

He interrupts me again. "Altruistic? No. My motivation is this: I believe this island will one day be strategically important to the United States. The government doesn't think far enough out into the future to realize this stuff."

"Meaning?"

"Okay. First. The U.S. has fishing rights around this island for two hundred miles in every direction. Right now the Coast Guard is responsible for preventing people from illegally fishing out here. Fifty-mile longlines. Drift nets. All that stuff. If you didn't have this place to refuel, you'd have a C-130 come up from Honolulu, look around for about an hour, then have to turn around and go back for gas. Operating from here, they can stay up for ten hours, patrolling a vast ocean area. One day, America's fish is going to become a big deal, because they're fishing the oceans dry.

"That's one strategic thing. Second: we've been talking to a fiber-optics company who wants to bring a fiber cable from Seattle to Japan, and they want to go through here to clean the static off the fiber-optic lines. Again, that's fairly important."

Mark shifts in his seat and continues, "Also: there are about a dozen people alive today—just since the navy left—that wouldn't be alive if there was no refueling station, no working airport. Picture this: You're on a boat out here. You're twelve hundred miles from Honolulu and twenty-seven hundred miles from Japan. You get injured. What are you going to do if Midway isn't here? You can turn your boat around and go back to Hono; that'll take about five days. If you keep going you'll hit

Japan—in around twelve days. We get about a dozen calls a year from some ship with a crew member who's gotten hurt, gotten appendicitis, gotten all screwed up somehow. We send out a boat with our doctor. They pick the crew member up. Bring him here. Doctor stabilizes him. Several times we've done that, to people who would otherwise have died. O.K.?" He lifts his sunglasses to give me a look that helps his point sink in. He settles back, continuing, "Right now, there's fourteen commercial flights a day between Tokyo and Hawaii. The airlines are changing to twin-engine airplanes, because they're more economical. One day, a twin-engine plane crossing the Pacific will lose an engine. Well— there's not another airport for twelve hundred miles. This is it. You can go north to the Aleutians, southeast to Hawaii. There's nothing between. The entire North Pacific is devoid." He narrows his eyes and adds, "I *assure* you, one day an airplane crossing the Pacific will experience an in-flight emergency. With hundreds of people on board. That *will* happen. And let me tell you: they'll be glad Midway is here to receive them, at this runway."

I say, "All those reasons do sound altruistic, actually."

He says, "I was never out to make money on this island. I *assure* you, I can make money a lot easier doing what I do, operating airplanes."

I ask, "Do you have a particular fondness for this place?"

"It's peaceful," he says without a hint of sentimentality. "It's a challenge to take an island and make it pay for itself. Here's what I mean: we burn seven hundred and fifty thousand gallons of fuel a year to make the lights go on." He pauses for emphasis. "I buy every gallon. I have it shipped here. I have it stored here. And I have mechanics maintaining the generators, maintaining the diesels, storing and transferring the fuel. And that's just the electricity. That doesn't cover the roads. That doesn't cover the water system. I mean, this is a small *city* out here. When you turn on the TV—it works! That's the power system and the television system. When the navy was running the island they had one phone line. Now we have a phone system. You can pick up your cellular phone or go to your room and call home. I *bought* that satellite antenna. I *bought* the cellular system. I bought every bit of that junk. I bought it in Jacksonville, Florida. Had it hauled to Seattle. Loaded on a boat. Brought it all out. Had it all installed. Made it all functional. When I write a check, it comes exactly from that little personal checkbook just like you have. I've written seven figures' worth on this place. So again, *my* only desire for this island is to have it break even. If I make any money here, I'll put it into improvements here."

I ask Mark if he feels appreciated.

He thinks, then says deliberately, "Some people have a solution for every problem and some people have a problem for every solution. Some people have tunnel vision. One person will be overly concerned with the Laysan gooney birds. The other person will be overly concerned with the Black-footed goonies. Another person will be concerned only with Monk Seals. They just kinda don't see the big picture. And the big picture for the wildlife—in my opinion—is that unless we could keep bringing these volunteers out here, within about a year this island would have been overtaken with this introduced plant, *Verbesina*, and the gooney-bird population would have been significantly reduced, and the burrow-nesting seabirds would have been dramatically reduced, because they really can't land or take off in that stuff.

"Also: I believe the American public has the right to see some of this wildlife up close. Fact is, everybody is pretty respectful to the wildlife here. As long as you control the interaction between people and wildlife, I think the sixty-five-year-old woman from Kansas who's been paying taxes for the last forty-five years has the right to come and see those three frigatebirds flying in formation up there." He points overhead. "Or see that gooney feeding its chick. Or that seal over there on the beach. As long as they don't hurt it, as long as they're not interfering. Plus: a million and a half people a year go to Pearl Harbor, which was our greatest naval defeat; but this was our greatest naval victory and hardly anybody knows about it. In 1903 the final round-the-world cable link was made at Midway. I mean, this place is steeped in history.

"So, I think that there's a benefit to people and wildlife to have the island well maintained. I think you have to simply ask, 'What would the island be like if we had not done what we did?' People can come out here to study and appreciate the wildlife, in this setting. I mean, look at this absolutely gorgeous beach and this lagoon. How many places in the world can you go to where you can leave your wallet on your dresser, not worry about anything when you walk the streets in the dark, and see wildlife like this?"

I still disagree with Mark; it sounds altruistic to me.

➤ ➤ ➤

WHAT ELSE HAS CHANGED for the better? Rats.

One of the main reasons seabirds use remote islands in high densities is that in all the ages since the islands formed they've lacked predatory mammals. Consequently, oceanic seabirds have few predator-avoidance skills. Most can't even *recognize* a land mammal as a potential predator—leaving them vulnerable. Rats introduced from ships to oceanic islands are tremendously destructive to ground-nesting seabirds. Rats get into nesting burrows, eat eggs and chicks, and sometimes attack adults.

Rats invaded Midway on military vessels during World War II and did tremendous damage to the birds. In 1891, Laysan Rails had been moved to Midway to prevent their extinction. It worked. On Midway the rails thrived. One observer wrote in 1907, "They must have found the conditions very suitable . . . for they are certainly very abundant now." The exiles outlived their native kin on Laysan Island, who went extinct due to the ravages of the rabbits. Alexander Wetmore wrote in 1923 that on Midway the rails "are alert, self-reliant little fellows. . . . They came frequently to feed with the chickens." In 1945, two years after they arrived here, a rat ate the last Laysan Rail on Earth.

Rats gnawed away 99 percent of Midway's Bonin Petrel population—reducing it from 500,000 to 5,000 in thirty-five years. They *totally* destroyed the atoll's Bulwer's Petrels. They even threatened to wipe out some native plants, like the lovely Beach Naupaka.

Rats usually shy from albatrosses' sheer size. But on Kure Atoll, rats called the albatrosses' bluff. They learned that the big birds were defenseless. During a visit to Kure in the mid-1960s, Cornell University ornithologist Cameron Kepler saw things that shocked him. "I frequently encountered injured Laysan Albatrosses and noticed dying and dead adults with large gaping wounds in their backs . . . sores five to seven inches in diameter. The thoracic cavity was often exposed, and ribs and scapulae, or even lungs, were visible through the gaping hole. The wings drooped when the bird stood or walked, as a result of severed muscles. Birds . . . often limped or were unable to walk. The injuries were often infested with the eggs of flies, and occasionally harbored maggots . . . and the birds' bills were stained from probing into the wound. Birds in these advanced stages rarely survived the night." Determined to find out exactly what was going on with the birds on their nests, he went out at night and confirmed the cause. "As I approached one bird, rats fled from my flashlight beam. The bird had a large wound on its back." He shut off the flashlight, waited a few moments, then turned the light on again. "When I did so, many rats scampered off his back where they had been feeding. Sitting quietly, with the light on, I could see rats approach the live bird, crawl upon his back, and feed on the exposed flesh. Every now and then the bird would twitch, turn back to try to get the rats, and then look forward again. There were over 20 rats feeding on the bird when I left. It was dead the following morning." Another bird was attacked in broad daylight. "Although the albatross turned and seized two rats, throwing them aside, others took their places." That bird, too, later died. As did more than half the adult albatrosses on the island. If you were a chick on Kure, your chances of surviving the rat attack were less than one in three hundred.

Rats have been e-rat-icated from both Kure and Midway. This atoll's last and final rat scurried to rodent heaven in 1997. The birds responded immediately. This year, there are over 100,000 Bonin Petrels.

How do you get rid of *every* rat? Jim Murphy explains: "Real simple: a lot of sweat." Jim, who works for the U.S. Department of Agriculture, ran the operation. "You put poison bait stations out in a fifty-meter grid system, and you set traps between them—and you just stick with it. When I want to start, I go for a real high rat population. I want them at a peak. We waited for the albatrosses to leave after nesting. Then we cleaned up the bodies of all the dead albatrosses. You deny the rats their food, then put the bait out. You don't want big rats in there fending off everyone else from certain areas, so you first do a little bit of trapping to take all of the big boys out. That busts up the whole social hierarchy. Then you go at it heavy. Usually in three to four months you can get 99.99 percent of them. You keep some bait stations going for a couple of years, just to be sure. That's how I do it. It works."

The young birds here have never seen a rat, thanks to Jim. We're walking along talking as Jim recalls his own Midway battle and other wars against alien wildlife-eating rodents on other islands. "Midway was *bad*. But you should've seen Rose Atoll, near American Samoa. The rat population was so heavy that the turtle hatchlings, as they ran to the ocean—the rats would just grab them, *big*-time. *Very* few baby turtles were making it off the island. Want to know how many rats there were? You'd take a walk in the evening, and you'd have maybe fifty rats, in a pack, in front of you. So we'd rat-kick."

"You mean," I ask, "that you were actually kicking rats away?"

"*Oh* yeah. They were scrounging the waterline for food, because the population was so dense. Any island with a lot of seabirds, you get flies from the bird carcasses. But there were no flies, because rats ate every carcass. In fact, they ate almost everything. By the time we got there, there were only four species of plants left. The rats had whacked the others. And anytime a seed would wash ashore, a rat would eat it. It was really extreme. You'd sit on a log to eat your meal and they'd come by and sit next to you. They weren't afraid of us, and we didn't want them afraid of us. We wanted to be able to get them all.

"When we started trapping, there were so many rats that if a trap caught a rat by the snout, that's all that was left: the nose. The rest would be stripped clean. A lot of the rats didn't even have tails, or had bite marks all over them. There was constant fighting. It was intense. It's what I imagine the world will be in the future, as humans become as much of an infesting force—as rats."

➤ ➤ ➤

ANOTHER RATLESS DAY in paradise. This morning we are going diving—on a nice, roomy, modern, rat-free dive boat called the *Spinner D.* One of the divemasters, named Dan, is avid; he's seen 140 species of fishes here. The other divemaster is an athletic young man named Kyoke.

Nancy has just completed her scuba training. She hasn't even gotten her permanent certification card yet. So she prudently asks Dan to bear with her if she's a bit slow.

Five other divers will take the plunge with us today. One's a German with a thick accent, named Uwe. He read about Midway in 1997 in a German dive magazine. He trains German air force pilots for two German air squadrons—at a U.S. Air Force base in New Mexico.

Valerie Ewing and John are also here on their first trip to Midway, also lured by magazine articles. John says, "This is incredibly beautiful here; this is killer." John, thirty-six, works in construction. "I've built a very special niche market: extremely high-end houses—a lot of people in the entertainment business, and financial entrepreneurs—twenty- or thirty-million-dollar homes." He and Valerie each wear a Rolex watch.

The skipper, Drew, eases the boat to a buoy marking our dive site. The permanent mooring eliminates the need to drop a coral-smashing boat anchor for every dive. Kyoke ties the boat to the buoy. We all get suited up and check our gauges, air supply, and instruments. The crystal-clear water here is about thirty-five feet deep; the bottom, patchy coral and rock reefs, and some open sand patches. A variety of reef fish come up almost immediately to check out the boat. They're looking for food; they can't tell the difference between us and the catch-and-release sportfishing boats that throw handouts to attract their quarry. A small Green Turtle swims around the boat just under the surface, then pops its head up for a breath. Valerie likes the turtle and she runs for her camera and takes several snapshots. She says appreciatively, "Isn't that *cool?*" John exclaims, "That's bitchin'!" Valerie, delighted, says, "Look how cute he is, honey; look how pretty his head is." John acknowledges, "That's pretty special."

Also aboard are Alain, the island's chef, and his wife, Laure, who works as both hostess and waitress in the exclusive little Clipper House Restaurant that is the island's only alternative to the cafeteria. Laure is very sweet and has lots of little French mannerisms: a way of opening her eyes big and looking far away to seem wistful, a sweet little pout for mock distress. They spent several years in Honolulu in the restaurant business and then got called for Midway. Laure recalls, "We said 'What ees Meedway?' They say to us, 'It's a distant Hawaiian Island.' And you know for French people a distant Hawaiian island—it ees like *dream*." She's pouting as she struggles to get her booties and fins on. Alain is wearing sunglasses and a blue kerchief on his head.

Several dozen chubs, called *nenue* in Hawaiian, gather behind the boat's swim platform. They're soon joined by one, two, make that *four* Galápagos Sharks. These are smallish, about four feet. Alain says, "I don' like zees." But he is fascinated and gets on the swim platform and splashes water at them with his hand.

Dan assures Alain the sharks are "no problem."

I'm not afraid they'll attack—they're small and accustomed to divers— but a shark is capable of biting in a way an angelfish is not. And the trustworthiness of these sleek comrades is no insurance that a huge, naively famished, voracious, rapacious, predacious, greedy, insatiable, starved, gluttonous, unappeasable monster might appear. Tiger Sharks are a distinct possibility, and they *are* potentially dangerous. But most Tiger sightings during the last couple of weeks have been inside the lagoon, not out here on the reef. Anyway, the odds of getting eaten are vanishingly small; gastronomically small, you might say. As far as I'm concerned, today is a good day to dive.

Suddenly the sharks part nervously. They make way for a charcoal-gray fish, maybe eighty pounds, that strides and glides confidently into view. It's the biggest member of the jack family, a Giant Trevally, called *Ulua* in Hawaiian. Among sportfishers, the "G.T." is the most formidable opponent on these reefs, a fish of legendary strength and toughness. The sharks, who deal with *Ulua*s professionally rather than for sport, maintain a reverential distance. Drew says, "Up at Kure Atoll, a state biologist speared an *Ulua* about that size, and it turned and hit him so hard in the ribs it knocked him unconscious. I've seen *Ulua* head-butt sharks in the side and shove them away. They'll attack the mop we use to clean the boat."

I tell him I've seen husky *Ulua*s swallow whole pork chops, bone and all, in one flashing gulp. When this *Ulua* passes, the sharks reconvene, more numerous than before, as if trying to patch their hurt pride by force of numbers. Alain gazes off the swim platform with trepidation. "I don't like zees. I will not like zee sharks."

Skipper Drew says, "Don't worry; they will like *you*." He gives me a wink.

Nancy fires me a skeptical look, and says quietly, "Do I need to worry?"

I shake my head no as I pull my mask in place and bite my mouthpiece. She doesn't *need* to worry. Worry is optional at no extra charge.

We drop ourselves in among the ever-gathering sharks. But it's the chubs that come to nibble our fins. Thank heaven for small flavors. The water is chilly up at this end of the chain. The wet suits were a good idea.

We descend. The ocean locks around us like a sphere of glass. Nancy is doing well, but having a little difficulty adjusting her buoyancy. As pressure increases and you get squeezed, you sink faster. The trick is to keep shooting small amounts of air into your vest to remain neutrally buoyant. It takes a little practice. As we continue downward I have to clear my ears by pinching my nose and blowing several times to equalize the pressure; I always have a little trouble with this.

The bottom is sharp, deeply pitted lava. A strong back-and-forth wave surge alternately propels us forward a few feet, then holds us in place despite our continuous kicking. Visibility is about forty feet, backed by the blue-gray beyond. The sea surface is rolling overhead like a billowing tent on a summer's day. Our bubbles float up like silver prayers.

The special fish we're looking for on this dive is the long-finned endemic Hawaiian Anthias, which is quite uncommon and usually found deeper than we plan to go. They start life female and become males with harems. We're told that some people suspect they might at times have "cheater males" who look like females but are functionally male and can get in on spawning without triggering a territorial response by the resident male—like a man dressing as a woman to sneak into the palace harem.

We're seeing surgeonfish with orange pectoral slashes, two-inch neon-blue damselfish with bright yellow dorsal fins, Black Surgeonfish with their emarginated fins. A school of uniformly colored unicornfishes with tail streamers flows past; and there's a black parrotfish with brick-red fins and white on the base of the tail, and blue-green wrasses with yellow saddle markings. I need to try to remember these so I can look them up later.

The international sign for sharks is to put your flattened hand at the crown of your head, fingers uppermost, like a fin. And while some people look more like roosters when they do it, there's never a doubt what the signal means. Nobody points out every parrotfish, but on every dive the first shark is indicated without fail. And unless the sharks are many, every shark gets pointed out. Today, nobody is pointing out every shark. Today, hands on head simply means "Turn around; there's a shark coming up right behind you." The sharks, slit-pupiled, catlike, are silky, matte silver, pewter colored. I see Dan pivoting his body slowly, counting the sharks. I do the same. Thirteen. Unlucky number.

But the sharks seem to lose interest in us before we do them. It's a little disappointing. We thought we were more special. We explore through grottoes and under lava arches, looking for fishes in fissures, turning our attention to closer companions, like the moray eel that wears a court jester's forced, toothy smile, and the Forceps Butterflyfish with their tweezery snoots, and barrel-chested groupers with long ventral fins. On the bottom in one area, hand-sized Sergeant Majors are guarding their purple egg masses. There are lots of red, big-eyed squirrelfishes in the lava shadows, including the Yellowfin Soldierfish, which is usually found deeper than one hundred feet but is often seen shallower up here in Midway because the water's cooler. I notice small triggerfishes with a blue back line and yellow margins to the second dorsal and anal fins—they're Gilded Triggerfish males. And along a rock wall swim polka-dotted Hawaiian Domino Damsels and a white-bodied, black-striped, high-backed fish that I think is a Morwong, rare elsewhere and common here. We see purple and lavender Spectacled Parrotfish with strongly etched rear scales; these are "terminal males," the last stage in the cycle wherein everyone starts life female. And I notice a Cross-hatch Triggerfish with blue lines on a bluer head and a red-rimmed tail. In the main Hawaiian Islands they, too, usually live much deeper than we are. And near the end of the dive, a big Amberjack strides boldly in and out of view. All these beautiful things we've named are a great delight to that inexplicable mind-body-spirit mystery we've named "ourselves." Awe begets awe, and it makes for a good day.

We come up slowly, slowly. I silently chant the safety mantra "Never come up faster than your smallest bubbles." Now that we are suspended in midwater like hung hams, the sharks have renewed their inquisitiveness. Several pass very close under my fins.

Near the surface, jellyfish are suddenly everywhere. They weren't here an hour ago. In the current, thousands of small, pulsing Thimble Jellyfish drift like paratroopers. There's also an incredible gelatinous creature unlike anything I've ever seen; a clear, silvery ribbon of light about two feet long and about two inches wide, with rolled ends. Kyoke writes *Ctenophore* on his slate. If it is, it's a bizarre one. I've never seen a life-form like it. Fine, threadlike jellyfish tentacles begin sticking on our air hoses and heads and hair and across our mouths, but their stings are so mild they're hardly noticeable; even on our lips it's more like a tingle than a sting.

We never saw a Hawaiian Anthias. But no matter. Nancy is astonished with her first open-water dive, and quite deservedly pleased with herself. I'm very happy she had a good dive. The sharks brought her no harm, only the fear and fascination they bring to most of us.

Nancy is going back to Canada soon. Shaking out her hair and toweling down, she's saying, "Well, I've just had one of the best weeks of my life. I think what's so remarkable is all the different dimensions—the tuna and sharks and reef and the whole underwater world, the burrow-nesting birds living beneath your feet, the albatrosses on the surface, the Fairy Terns cozying next to their chicks in the trees—it's a layer cake of life. It reminds me of those pictures for children where you have to pick out all the creatures and almost everywhere you focus your eyes, something materializes. It's a Dr. Dolittle world of all these animals that don't seem the least bit disturbed by you. It's such a giving experience."

ALL VERY TRUE, but we are soon reminded that living remains difficult. On the sidewalk is a large albatross chick that appears dead—stretched out contortedly. The Grim Reaper comes along, the tines of his pitchfork shining in the pitiless sun. He hardly glances at the bird on the sidewalk as he passes by like a motor-powered apparition. I was expecting him to fork it into the pile of dead albatross chicks his cart is toting. But the Grim Reaper is a professional, with a vulture's practiced eye for death. He knows when it's time to get off his cart and when patience must prevail. And sure enough, as we walk by, the poor chick gives a final kick.

On our walk home we watch one of life's lottery winners—a sleek adult Laysan Albatross—gliding in low over a fire hydrant on seven-foot wings. It has probably flown continually for days to get here. Its sudden arrival out of nowhere is a momentous event for the chick, whose survival now is entirely a matter of being fed in time to keep living.

The adult lands on the grass next to a paved road. She settles her dark wings over her snowy back for the first time in days. Her feet have not touched anything solid, nor have her legs supported her weight, for perhaps two weeks. She surveys the scene through lovely, dark, pastel-shadowed eyes, then calls a rusty-gate-hinge *Eh eh eh*. A chick immediately comes over, calling. But she knows it's not her own chick's voice, and waddles and weaves along. Another chick calls as she passes, also hoping to con her into misplacing her precious cargo into its crucial belly. What can a desperately hungry chick think or feel while awaiting its own parents yet seeing all these big albatrosses walking by? One by one, five more chicks come begging and calling as the albatross continues walking along. Any other chick fool or famished enough to rush forward gets a sharp rebuke from her hooked bill. Except one.

The adult begins directly approaching the last of this line of hungering hopefuls. But she veers away from it at the last moment. (Perhaps the voice seemed familiar, but the scent was wrong?) Another youngster, much more developed, comes hopping, jumping, and flapping across the road. But the adult ignores it.

Our adult walks about thirty yards farther, then crosses the street. Why did the albatross cross the road? Because a chick over there had just started calling. And at that call, this adult is responding, calling softly, matter-of-factly, with little excitement or energy. It simply walks directly to the chick.

Parent and youngster meet and greet, the adult acting confident that this is the right child. People often seem incredulous that seabirds can recognize each other among thousands. But give them a little credit. We recognize voices on the telephone. We can recognize each other in cities among millions. And we do so without the sense of smell so well developed in other mammals and in albatrosses. Considering the life-or-death stakes involved in recognizing your own chick or parent or mate, animals certainly evolved proficiency for recognizing individuals a long, long time ago. We've merely inherited that capability from much earlier ancestors. But bubble-wrapped within our estrangement from our extended family, we fail to appreciate other animals' competencies. We withhold recognition of their cognitive abilities. Blinded to stark evidence of our relatedness to other living beings, we heap praise on ourselves for supposedly "unique" abilities, whose origins are so plain in birds and bees.

The whining chick begins eagerly nibbling the adult's bill with its own clattering mandibles. Its ravenous aggression seems nearly to overwhelm the adult, which at first tries to duck the advances. But the bill-battering builds, and this necessary food foreplay works as usual to stimulate her into regurgitating her delivery load. The adult hunches forward, neck stretching, retching. The chick, with sudden frenzied expectation, thrusts its bill up tight to the adult's gaping mouth, forcing her wider and wider open.

Nancy remarks that the interaction has an almost sexual intensity.

The adult abruptly pumps out several thick boluses of food: semi-liquefied squid and purplish fish eggs, which the chick bolts down. Both pause. This adult is not Amelia, of course, but she could as well be. Then the chick renews its drive for more. The adult arches her neck and is retching, retching. Nothing comes. More retching. We whisper, "Is something wrong?"

Slowly, the tip—just the tip—of a green plastic toothbrush emerges in the bird's throat. The sight is surreal—so out of place, so *wrong,* that my racing mind interrogates my eyes over and over: Are you *sure* that's a *toothbrush?* Nancy is having the same slightly disorienting reaction of incredulity. The chick, oblivious in a flurry of furious hunger, presses.

With her neck arched, the mother cannot pass the straight toothbrush. She reswallows it and several times repeats the attempt to puke it up. Each time, she cannot pass it fully out. Nancy and I can barely handle the sight of this. It's one thing to find plastic items on the ground and know the birds have carried them, but seeing this bird in distress, this vital mother-child interaction interrupted, is very hard to watch. It's one of the most piercing things I've ever experienced. The parent albatross reswallows a final time, and with the toothbrush stuck inside her, wanders away from her chick.

IN THE WORLD THAT SHAPED albatrosses, the ocean could be trusted to provide only food, parents to provide only nourishment. Through the care bond between parent and offspring passes the continuity of life itself. That the flow of this intimate exchange now includes our chemicals and our trash indicates a world wounded and out of round, its most fundamental relationships disfigured.

The main message from the albatross is this: every watery point on the compass is now conscripted into our all-consuming culture, whether intended or not. No matter what coordinates you choose, from waters polar, to solar coral reefs, to the remotest turquoise atoll—no place, no creature remains apart from you and me.

Many of these albatrosses had already ranged the vast and open ocean for years when, holding my mother's hand, I walked to my first day of kindergarten. Many were feeding chicks while I was fed the fiction that limitless oceans would feed humanity when we exhausted land's limits. Many of these birds flew and knew the sea before it so filled with plastic bottle caps and cigarette lighters; before the strain of drift nets, before boats with multimile longlines laced their feeding grounds with hundreds of millions of tantalizing hooks.

To share close quarters among creatures that mastered a world so different—within their lifetime and your own—is to realize how abruptly we've changed even the farthest reaches of the planet. Unlike deforested or urbanized landscapes whose alterations plainly show, the ocean rolls on as always. But once you perceive the message of the albatross, the ocean's deceptively constant surface no longer fools you. Once you see and feel the disparity between what animals learned to expect and what they now get—when you see over and over how traits and habits fine-tuned for survival seem turned against so many living beings—the world seems on fire.

Seeing a parent albatross gagging up a toothbrush changed my worldview. In my mental map, society no longer stops at the borders of shorelines, or of species. The world is no longer large enough for that. We've woven the albatross and the other creatures into our society. That creates a certain moral obligation. Fortunately, it's an obligation that calls forth the most elevating and uniquely human qualities: empathy, foresight, compassion, generosity of spirit. The implication of finiteness is not merely of limits but also of potential, and the opportunity to create a better world.

In the oceans, less is truly more: less trash, less destruction of habitat, less contamination, less atmospheric disturbance, less overfishing would mean more life and more material and general well-being for us all—humanity and other creatures—in years to come. A rising tide floats all boats. Diminishment creates hardship for everyone. The oceans make our planet habitable, and the vast, multifaceted wealth of oceans spans biological, climatological, aesthetic, nutritional, spiritual, and ethical realms. We need the birds and the seas more than they need us. We need the life and stability and context they provide us. Will we understand this well enough to reap all the riches that a little restraint would engender?

Nothing could prepare albatrosses for changes that have come in the flash of one long lifetime. Our calling cards, in waters and upon the winds, cycle through all living things. In all the far reaches of the wide, wide seas, every single bird, fish, mammal, and turtle carries the trademark of human chemical manufacturing within its cellular tapestry. Antarctic penguins, who'll never suspect that the world contains so many people, carry the imprint of humanity in their flesh; in the Arctic, among polar bears, some now suffer the deformity of having both male and female sex organs, the result of hormone-mimicking contaminants acquired in the womb from their mother's food—from us.

But don't pity just them. Quite a few scientists believe that endocrine-mimicking chemicals and other toxics cause various sexual and developmental problems in people, too, including the 400 percent increase in ectopic pregnancies in the United States between 1970 and 1990, the doubling in cases of abnormal testicle development, the increase in breast cancer, reduced sperm motility and lowered sperm counts, and low birth weight. And so at the dawn of the twenty-first century, 121 nations unveiled a treaty to phase out the "dirty dozen" of the world's worst pollutants, exceptionally toxic chemicals that even at low doses trigger cancers and damage the reproductive, nervous, and immune systems of laboratory animals (including the pesticides DDT, aldrin, chlordane, dieldrin, endrin, heptachlor, hexachlorobenzene, mirex, and toxaphene, plus PCBs, furans, and dioxins, many already banned in the United States and some other countries but still used in Latin America, Africa, India, China, and elsewhere). Some scientists *still* doubt that humans are much at risk, but can anyone remain satisfied with having no choice in being part of this new experiment? No less than a mother albatross delivering cigarette lighters and toothbrushes, a human mother has no evolutionary experience with—and so no sense of detecting or avoiding—the pesticides, food additives, hormones, hormone mimics, antibiotics, PAHs, POPs, and other unsavory alpha-bits spelling trouble and signaling SOS to a world newly transformed by modern manufacturing and chemical agriculture. Like toothbrushes—but invisible—this hazardous soup comes between every mother and child. No nursing woman can avoid pumping industrial by-products into the pure new life at her breast. No less than in the sea, no less than to the birds, many of the new things affecting us arrive unrecognized for what they are. And so the albatross speaks to us of how much the world is changing, and how little difference exists between us—and of what it means to be kin and sibling in the net of time and events that enmeshes us all.

Four centuries ago, John Donne posited that "no man is an island, entire of itself." Donne changed our self concept by weaving individuals into a social fabric. Four hundred years later on Midway, the albatross expanded upon this. Not only is no person an island, no *island* is an island any longer. Albatrossess inhabit only a few islands. Humans inhabit only one island, a blue and white orb of pumice surrounded by a soap bubble, afloat the great dark universal sea.

A STRONG WIND and intermittent rain has the albatrosses flapping, their wings waving, waving, waving. Some are preparing to leave, as are we. As we all must. They are reminding us there are other skies to fly in.

＞ ＞ ＞ ＞ ＞ ＞ ＞ ＞ ＞ ＞ ＞ ＞

GOING TO EXTREMES

On May 27 Amelia returns from a two-week trip after logging twenty-seven hundred miles. This trip was similar to the last in duration, distance, and course of travel. It's the only time all year Amelia will seem to repeat herself. She'd sprinted rather directly to the southern edge of that subarctic front, taking only a couple of days to get there. At that point she slowed dramatically, her speed over distance dropping to one-quarter of her traveling speed. She began foraging the blended waters of the current's frontier, working slowly eastward in the streaming edge over about five days, covering "only" about six hundred miles in that time, stopping frequently, lingering and looping around productive patches, and feeding well. Then she shot home in a long, multiday arc.

Now her big chick seems crazed with hunger. This is his last major growth spurt. His bones are a-building. And he needs enough reserves to make thousands upon thousands of thick, insulating, waterproof feathers tough enough to last a couple of years' punishment in the salt and sun and wind and water.

The chick batters Amelia's bill so aggressively that she almost wants to flee. But again his tantrum stimulates her to disgorge. The chick scissors in, quivering with excitement. Out comes the usual menu: squid, a flyingfish, finally a stream of oil, until Amelia is cleaned out.

She rests a few hours. For the moment, life is thick. Amelia's chick is well past its most vulnerable time. If it survives the next few weeks—and everything suggests it will—it'll be flying on its own. Graduation is just over the horizon.

But Amelia will not be attending. She'll be over the horizon herself.

Parents are forced to make choices. A chick's gain comes at its parents' expense, and eventually that price must receive its compensation. By mid-May, the porky youngsters weighed as much as adult males weighed back in November when they first arrived to breed. In late May, the chicks are 25 percent *heavier* than their own overworked fathers. For the beleaguered parents, this marks their low point in bodily condition. They've put a lot into their youngster, and it shows. At this stage, they've vaporized 25 percent of their weight compared to when they first appeared here for the season. Their reserves are tapped out, and they are within about 5 percent of their abandonment threshold. It's time for them to take care of themselves.

Starting soon, Amelia will concentrate on bulking up again, until she weighs about what she did at egg laying. When Amelia leaves tomorrow, May 28, her departure will end her final visit for the season. As far as she's concerned, her parenting is finished. In caring for her chick the last few months, she's traveled over twenty-five thousand miles—the distance around the world at the equator.

AMELIA'S CHICK will receive another visit from his father. Then the youngster will face whatever lies ahead alone. His weight has risen more or less steadily since hatching, and now he's at his heaviest. All that high-calorie squid and fish oil sits in him like high-octane fuel. He'll continue living off it until he fledges.

With his parents gone for the season to restock their own depleted bodily reserves, the chick's weight begins its first prolonged steady drop. His hunger pangs are his sharp taste of life's no-free-lunch severity. It's a harsh lesson toward harsher realities.

Even the healthy chicks are showing signs of intense hunger. One chick is trying to work on a Bonin Petrel carcass, pulling at the feathers in sharp tugs. It doesn't seem equipped with the skill or know-how to rip the carcass open to get at the scant meat, or to place a foot on the corpse while pulling with its beak like a vulture. Yet its inept attempt indicates willingness to try eating just about anything. I see one nibble even the bare feet of a dead albatross chick.

Amelia's chick spends a lot of time hunkering quietly, conserving energy and water, growing in place like a melon, all his new feathers pushing through his skin. In a couple of weeks when he begins really exercising his wings, he'll need to be at the right weight, neither too heavy nor light. His weight loss is a finely timed free fall.

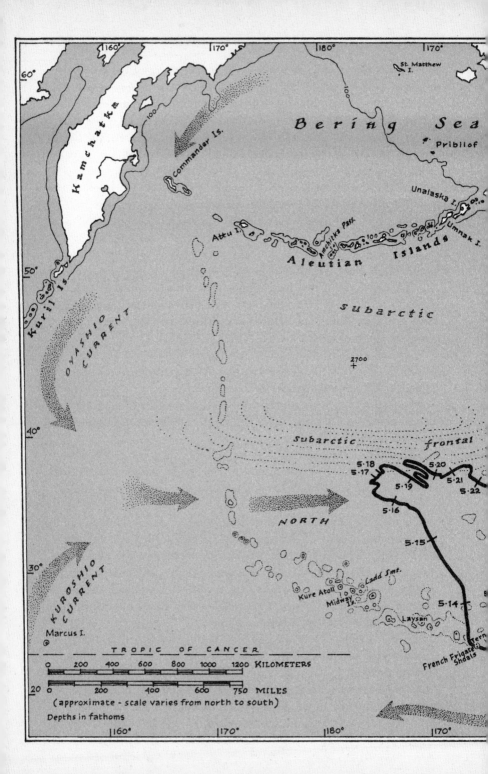

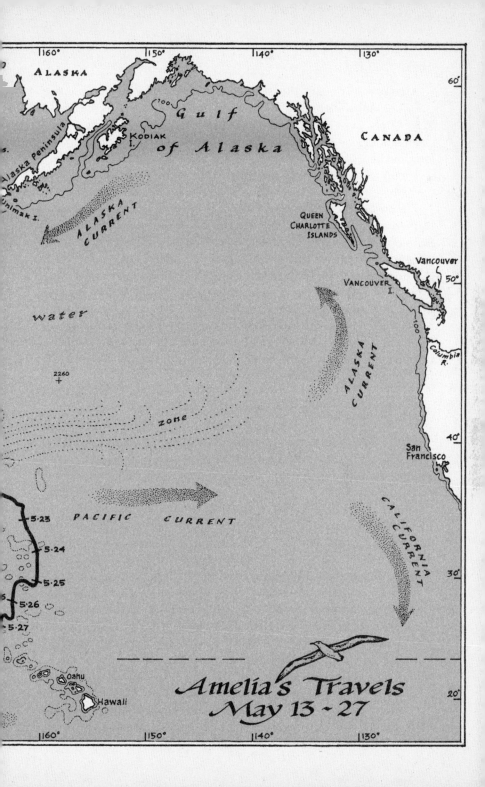

ALASKA

160°   150°   140°   130°

60°

Gulf

100

Kodiak
I.

of Alaska

CANADA

Alaska peninsula

Unimak I.

ALASKA
CURRENT

QUEEN
CHARLOTTE
ISLANDS

Vancouver

VANCOUVER
I.

50°

water

ALASKA
CURRENT

100

Columbia
R.

2260
+

zone

40°

San
Francisco

5·23

PACIFIC   CURRENT

CALIFORNIA
CURRENT

5·24

5·25

30°

5·26

5·27

20°

Oahu

Hawaii

Amelia's Travels
May 13 ~ 27

160°   150°   140°   130°

. . .

AMELIA FLIES about a thousand miles north, and by the first couple of days of June she's back in the subarctic front. Unhurried by the need to feed her chick—an empty nester by her own design—our long-range champion lingers a *week* within just a sixty-mile radius, thinking only of food and herself. For an albatross, this is practically loitering. For Amelia, it's simply a little well-earned and much-needed time for Mom. She likes the eating, and she likes the feeling of putting on weight.

Eleven hundred miles away, Amelia's chick is sleeking down and feathering out handsomely. Hoping to hear one of his parents' voices, he interrogates every adult who lands within earshot of the nest. None gives him more than a sharp peck.

Over the next few days Amelia pushes away from the banquet and drifts about fourteen hundred miles farther away, into the western Pacific, then cuts sharply north, blowing past the subarctic front and pushing well into the Oyashio Current. Amelia penetrates the northern limits of the Pacific, into an ocean nearly devoid of night, pressing into the burgeoning spring like an early flower, following the warming weather up over the rim of the world.

➤ ➤ ➤

WHILE AMELIA IS WANDERING like an albatross, in mid-June I'm back at Tern Island to see the end of the usual miracle. Everything looks different. At sunset you notice how much farther north the sun has swung compared to January. It quenches into the sea far enough poleward to silhouette birds bound for northern waters. You sense that the world not only spins but pivots. Only an ocean view seems to grant so planetary a sense of space. As always, birds make this a place utterly without stillness. Yet it's full of the kind of grace that derives from a sense of time stretched into beauty.

EVERYWHERE DIFFERENCES, everywhere contrasts. Diversity and redundancy, tranquillity—and terror to come. Masked Boobies' well-grown chicks sprawl so fluffy-white they look like little snow piles in the tropics, like big cotton candy—seemingly larger than their parents. Shearwaters and petrels of four species are breeding now. And the Sooty Terns are nesting—in, under, around, and between just about everything. Some Sooties are yet to lay, but so many have already hatched that the nesting areas harbor droves of chicks ranging in age from newly hatched to newly flying. Some Sooty chicks, left unattended, are sitting upright, but some lie on their sides with their heads curled around them, like little sleeping dinosaurs.

One albatross walks from its nest through a group of Sooty Terns so dense it seems impossible it could put a webbed foot down without stepping on them. It's hard for us to avoid them, too. The Sooties stand ground with courage a lion would wish for, biting your pant cuffs, greeting with derision your mortal sole. Or, arising, they screamingly whack your head, setting your hat sideways.

Fewer than ten adult albatrosses are on the whole island at the moment. The rest are spread around the North Pacific. Surviving albatross chicks also seem sparse, compared to the numbers of nests six months ago. But at the size of big barnyard geese, the "chicks" still get your attention. Just a week ago they could barely stand upright. Now their legs are toned, tried, and true. They look so big and grown-up; day by day more and more lustrous feathers replace their woolly down.

THE PEOPLE HERE HAVE likewise changed. The bird crew now consists of two young women—Shiway Wang and Catherine Tredick—plus solidly built, curly-haired Brendan Courtot. Brendan has been here a few months, Shiway has previous field experience, and Catherine could be called green if she weren't so acutely sunburned. Because this is turtle-nesting season, a crew of turtle researchers has also arrived. And because turtles nest at night, the researchers remain unseen during the day, emerging mysteriously after dark like nocturnal creatures, like the ghost crabs that also haunt the night-black beach.

In a few days two shark researchers are scheduled to come. Waiting to work with them are National Geographic film producer Greg Marshall and his crew. And at the moment I am sitting at the end of the island watching Japan's greatest wildlife photographer, Mitsuaki Iwago, and his support team. Best known internationally for his book *Serengeti,* Iwago is waiting so patiently for a Monk Seal to appear that a Sooty Tern has landed on his head. The presence of Iwago and the National Geographic crew emphasizes the world-class importance of this place to a much larger audience of people—underscoring that the wildlife are protected here not only in sacred trust but in a very *public* trust.

Hope is what we have to give, and work is how we show our hopefulness. This is in *many* ways an ocean monastery. All the animals coming here to breed are showing their devotion to the future. And the people are showing the same, trying by their devoted efforts to ensure survival for times to come.

OUR REVERENTIAL, almost prayerful presence finds no cosmic reflection in the meteorological conditions. The weather has turned manic and fickle.

Curtains of rain smudge the horizon even as the June sun has drilled a hole through the clouds. This sun no longer shines—it punishes. It's infernal. Yesterday I walked the length of the island, less than a mile, and got a burn—a bad one—on the side of my neck that faced the sun. The outline of my sandal tops is sun-stenciled on my feet. As a result of her *first day* in the sun here, Catherine's arms are brutally blistered and weeping, and wrapped in gauze.

Yet this morning the unrelenting wind has wound itself into a steady thirty knots with stronger gusts. The lagoon, wild with whitecaps, is conveying waves built to eight feet. The outer reef, where yesterday you could safely have paddled a canoe, is now a madly confused and snaggle-toothed line of surf. The curling waves are continuously getting their heads blown off, the winds sending up twenty-foot curtains of smoking spindrift. The sky, darkly angry, is all astream with dismal, scudding clouds, and rain spitting like an angry cat.

The wind begins gusting anew, and albatross chicks respond with vigorous wing waving and hopping. About two dozen young albies are on the runway, facing into the wind, flapping, as though awaiting their clearance from air-traffic control. One big Black-footed Albatross chick, the most advanced on the island—only a few wisps of down left here and there on its otherwise glossy new body—loves this weather. It stands wide-winged into the buffeting blast. These wings are long now, long enough to resist the air. A few steps forward, and one foot leaves the ground. This could be it—first flight! But as though the strangeness of near liftoff has sent a chastening chill into its adventurous soul, it folds up and resumes its vigil as if resigned to staying earthbound. Another starts running with open wings, very professional and adult-looking. Just as it tries to get airborne, it belly flops. A sudden slight gust catches another, swiveling it sideways. The youngster seems surprised by the invisible capriciousness of the world. But it gamely resumes hopping and running, letting the wind twist it this way and that, taxiing along the runway, turned suddenly left, suddenly right, like an aircraft with a drunken pilot.

A Black-foot with remnants of a down collar jumps into the wind—and for the first time, for a mere moment, the wind lofts its wings, and its feet levitate from the ground a few inches. Exhaustion comes quickly from such new exertion, but this chick seems very stimulated—the newness of these sensations must feel thrilling.

Fully functioning wings complete the physical bird, but there must come more exercising: toning tendons and breast muscles until they are tight on the sternum, capable of pulling those wings or locking them out rigidly in the wind for minute upon hour, tireless for a hundred—a thousand—miles. Getting to *that* will require more play. But by now the Rubicon of flight is a mere matter of time, and patience is an albatross chick's best-practiced virtue.

VISIBILITY CLOSES TO a few hundred feet, and sudden thick rain drives down upon us. The pelting raindrops sting, as though it's raining frozen peas. The albatrosses turn their faces up into the rain, biting at the air, gulping at the raindrops, swallowing precious freshwater that they've been losing for weeks.

Iwago and his crew make their retreat from the rain at about the same time I do. Inside, sitting down to a breakfast of rice and an egg fried sunny-side up, he gestures toward the open door with a toss of his head and says approvingly, "Best light. Dramatic. Lots of contrast."

The old barracks seems suddenly porous. Puddles are forming under windows and in people's bedrooms. And now the roof in the computer room—the most secure room in the place—has begun leaking.

During the day, as the storm pins us into the barracks, the Americans play Outburst and Trivial Pursuit, between mopping floors. The Japanese play Monopoly, Jenga, and chess.

Shiway calls, "Brendan, you want to play Trivial Pursuit? We'll kick your ass." Brendan, ever the athlete, stops skipping rope and prepares to engage in competition. Shiway mentions, "I just learned a new word: peripatetic. It means wandering with no permanent home. We're all peripatetic." Their game consumes two and a half hours, a bag of chips, and a jar of salsa.

Outside meanwhile, something like chaos. Waves in the lagoon slam constant white explosions against the bulkheaded shore. Suddenly part of the boat dock tears loose under the strain. It cracks to bits and washes away before anyone can react. The Gray-backed Terns, which are all nesting on the ground near the dock, are getting pounded by waves breaking over the sea wall. *All* their nests and chicks get swept away.

Black Noddy eggs are blowing off their platform nests, onto the ground. A few Red-footed Booby chicks also get blown from their nests. Their certain fate: starvation. The rain continues all day, and steadily through the night.

THE NEW MORNING's air remains filled with a dense overcast and heavy mist at eight A.M. But the wind is down under ten knots. The front has stalled, on top of us. All the birds look bedraggled. Brian, the manager, looks bedraggled too. He got flooded from his leaky bedroom and slept on the floor in the communications room.

The rain returns. The warm rainwater puddles become a thin guano soup, intensifying the colony's rank stink. Brian and Mitch begin rebuilding a temporary dock in the downpour.

The Sooty Terns' smallest chicks—tiny enough to get under their parents and stay there—have so far survived the rain. The oldest chicks look healthy; even many of the soggy ones seem vigorous. But there is an in-between size: those fluffballs too big for sheltering beneath a parent but too small to be weatherproof. And today is fluffball hell.

I expect lots of dead birds, and that expectation is met. Dead or violently shivering little soggy Sooty Tern chicks are everywhere you look. And the frigatebirds are indeed looking. Near vigorous dry hatchlings that have been well brooded (and stick close to good cover) stagger soaked, chilled, abandoned chicks, for whom death can now be the briefest suffering of their brief lives. One chick, soaked and upside down, is kicking in a struggle to right itself. With each attempt at standing it topples over, tiny legs scratching the air, little wing stubs quivering. Sooty chicks have brown-speckled antifrigate camouflage, but in the pelting rain the disarray among the terns enhances the chances for foraging frigates.

The big frigatebirds are air-patrolling the colony, steadily snatching up Sooty chicks, terminating their short, unhappy lives with a quick-snapping final horror. For the Sooties, the frigates are hell from the heavens. But for the hungering frigates, the terns are a godsend.

A frigatebird pauses and hovers near the edge of a bush. A Sooty Tern adult protests, and soon a flurry of wings ensues. With a dip of its head, the frigatebird plucks the tern's chick like a plum from the earth. The chick vanishes in one frigate-pleasing swallow. For the parent tern, a year's reproduction is gone in a gulp. Imagine a monster with a thirty-foot wingspan hovering overhead then tossing you aside as you try in vain to save your child.

In just the hundred-foot section of tern colony I'm watching, frigates are lofting Sooty chicks to aerial grief at a rate of one every three to four minutes. Over the whole island, the Sooty chick population must be declining by hundreds per hour.

The long, narrow, almost spindly cut of the frigate's dark sails and their extravagantly notched forked tails seem almost designed to strike fear by mere startling appearance, like a pirate flag suddenly run up the mast of a rapidly approaching vessel.

Now the frigates start stealing even from one another, suspending all pretense of professional courtesy. Any frigate mounting skyward with a chick too large for a quick swallow immediately becomes a target for a pack of thieves. Two frigatebirds lock onto a tern chick in midair, trying to pull it apart. One breaks free with the entire chick and immediately gets body-slammed by another swooping competitor. The one with the chick maintains its grip, but is driven to the ground in a confusion of tangled wings. The chick is at the upper end of bite-sized, and the frigate laboriously chugs it down on the ground while other frigates hover. The victor leaps back into action. In the next aerial fight the contested chick plummets into the sea beyond the wall, and a third frigate checks, wheels, dips, plucks.

Another frigatebird takes a chick that struggles so vigorously it breaks free, falling thirty feet. It hits the ground unhurt. Yet now, 150 feet from its nest, this small chick is irretrievably lost, and the longest it can hope to live is a few days, doomed to starvation. But the following frigate, which has seen it fall and rushes in to take it, now commits an act less of pure predation than of euthanasia—saving the chick from a death worse than fate. Zooming in, it dips its head to snatch and swings up to the gulp. One fluid motion of terror and grace.

In nature, things that to us seem good and bad are often two aspects of the same. But who would identify more with the frigatebirds than with the tern chicks? They say everyone loves a winner; but we root for underdogs. And here's something I find odd: that among the weak we offer compassion, but among the strong we deride any weakness.

Paradoxes: Shivering Sooty chicks who wander too near adults who are not their parents get swift pecks from sharp bills, but one adult closely regards a small disoriented chick, extending its bill to the chick's nape in gentle contact. Many Sooty Tern chicks stand vulnerably under an open bush while several frigatebirds rest in the branches just overhead, showing no interest. At one point a bite-sized chick wanders into the middle of the runway. Utterly exposed, it has placed itself in easy sight of several hundred loafing frigates. It goes unmolested.

Perhaps they are already too full to care, stuffed enough to forbear. Spectacular as the frigates' plunderings are, only a small fraction of the frigatebirds—perhaps ten out of hundreds here—are actively hunting tern chicks. And though the density of frigates looks adequate to eat all the tern chicks, in reality the frigatebirds consume only a small percentage.

Far more chicks are moribund from the rain. The weather is a greater and more wasteful killer. I see pipped eggs full of water, the bill of the dead chick visible through the hole it had pecked, which let in the water that killed it. Living is difficult, surviving is often a matter of luck. Those Sooty Tern chicks that will hatch just after this rain abates will not appreciate the luck of their timing.

You wonder again how life can be maintained amid such abundant misery, such universal hostility coming from every dimension. Yet you *see* again that the grace, the acuity, the exquisite tuning of these animals all derive from so merciless a struggle.

By LATE AFTERNOON there is sun enough to throw the first shadow in two days. But the sun is fleeting, and soon the pattering rain again sogs in. Nighttime settles uncomfortably on us like a soaked blanket.

In the darkness, an intense round of howling from the shearwaters startles me from a dream set outside a tiny church, amid the woodlands that as a boy I had loved and seen destroyed. But here on Tern Island I've found again that sense of spiritual home amid natural richness—not destroyed this time, but cherished and protected. The places for me that come closest to holy, that provide that sense of connection to something large and eternal, are places still capable of bringing forth an abundance of creation. These are not Edens. Here amid the profusion of life, the profusion of death remains always in view. Nests fail. Chicks starve. Adults vanish. Competition intensifies. Violence lurks. The animals are hunters all, sometimes of each other. Predation is the common currency; chicks are legal and tender. Here as always: the struggle to be alive again at dawn. But here too—and this is the point—enough balance and enough nurturing exist that species can maintain their presence in great abundance for millions of years, even as they are continually hammered and shaped in the stern, unmerciful forge of natural selection. The net effect, the final verdict, the balance of proof is the triumphant vitality, the bewildering plentitude. If anything can be considered "right," this turbulent throng of life seems right because it works, durably and enduringly.

RAIN AGAIN ALL DAY. Fieldwork canceled. The assignment board now says simply,

Clean UP!

Everybody does. The kitchen gets cleaner and more orderly than I've ever seen it. The entire living and dining area is crisscrossed with clotheslines that seem to grow like a spiderweb as load after load of long-overdue laundry emerges. Soon it's hard to get from the kitchen counter to the dining table without numerous sheets and hanging underwear dragging across your face.

Outside, the wind breathes not a whisper. In fact, there's been no wind in the last two out of three rainy days. This weather system is still just sitting on us.

Adult albatrosses, so hurried to leave in days past, are lingering today. At one point I count six Black-footed Albatrosses and one Laysan within a hundred-foot radius, more than I saw on the whole island when I first returned. They'd rather give the weather time to move than risk flying into dense rain and no wind. One Laysan Albatross seems torn between waiting and leaving. After feeding its chick, it spends seventeen minutes merely standing at the nest, then walks toward the shore. It opens and closes its wings slowly several times as though undecided, walks several steps with wings open, then folds up. It walks over to one of the other adults, sits, and accepts a few minutes' neck-preening. But it quickly becomes restless, walking along the bulkhead, raising a ruckus from the Sooty Terns whose colony it is walking through. As if the protests and jabs from the Sooties are just too much hassle in this unpleasantly crowded neighborhood of strangers, the bird runs forward with open wings, and in a few quick flaps launches northward. It has spent twenty-three minutes ashore. In a few moments the albatross vanishes into an approaching curtain of fine rain.

I hunch as I feel my T-shirt soaking through, then splatter and slop my way through the runway puddles. The albatross chicks look bedraggled but all seem old enough to have survived. They're preening a lot. Rainwater rolls down their backs and wings, while the absurdly matted down on their heads and necks drips like soaked and matted moss.

Inside the barracks, with all the laundry and cleaning done, the biology staffers are writing copious letters home. By afternoon, Shiway says,

"I feel like I've written to everyone I've ever known and everyone I'll ever meet."

There's nothing left to do but cut hair. Before dinner, National Geographic producer Greg Marshall prepares to give his soundwoman (and wife) Birget Buhleier a haircut. She says, "Make it short." But she's a little shocked to see how well Greg follows her instructions. Birget's hair had been down to her elbows. Now it barely touches her ears. Brendan receives a haircut so radical that people greet him by rubbing his head.

The mealtime music tonight consists of the Gipsy Kings followed by Jimi Hendrix's "Manic Depression." Now it's *The Gentle Side of John Coltrane,* including "My One and Only Love," with Johnny Hartman, surely one of the most soul-saturated recordings ever captured in any musical idiom. While I'm inhaling Coltrane's exhalations, Mitch and Melissa are preparing what Greg is already promoting as "a serious pizza orgy." It's going to be quite a night. A gecko lizard pours itself out of a small hole in the cement-block wall just behind Greg's right ear. One or two geckos remain visible on the kitchen walls throughout the dinner hour.

A Brown Noddy flies in and finds the kitchen counter an appealing resting pad. Its close observation of the food preparations brings little comment; we've all grown *very* accustomed to birds. This noddy's behavior is testimonial to individuality among animals. I imagine that individual distinctions among people are as invisible to them as individual distinctions among wild animals usually are to us—that it seems to them that "all those people look the same."

AFTER DINNER, real blue appears overhead. The evening has gifted us the calmest sea and the most beautiful sunset of the trip. The sun, setting, glorifies the air with color. Billowing clouds are towering into a sky that grades from pale at eye level to a very deep blue at the zenith. The lagoon again tints the soles of the clouds green, while the cloud tops rise rose, peach, and gold caught from the sinking sun. Add a pastel-pink tropicbird as a beauty mark. The colors are all in fluid motion, changing as the sun drops. The visual is so stunning, the beauty so pumped up, it's enough to inspire you to fly two thousand miles in it yourself.

Even the runway—full of sheeted puddles—is reflecting the sky, somehow catching the lagoon's green cast off the clouds as the first evening star appears. Catherine comes out onto the porch, spreads her bandaged, sun-blistered arms wide, and bursts out, "It's so *gorgeous!*"

. . .

MORNING. Storm warning. We wake to more rain. The fine morning that evening promised with a glimpse of blue, dawn has withdrawn. The wind has swung again and blown the cloud system back upon us. After yesterday, no one has much to do, so we talk, getting to know one another a little bit better as the day dreams along.

Catherine, who graduated from college two weeks ago, is saying, "I had *no* idea when I wrote the application letter that it was this remote. I was just thinking about—you know—*Hawaii*. Right before I came out I downloaded pictures from the Web. All my parents' friends and my nonbiology friends said, 'Oh my *God*—what are you doing? You're *crazy!*' So I thought, 'Oh my *God!* What am I doing? I'm *crazy!* But from the minute the plane landed I thought, 'This is going to be great.'"

Shiway Wang, whose black, shoulder-length hair is pulled back in two tight Chinese pigtails, says, "My mother was planting thoughts, waving her finger like this, saying, 'Do you know any of these people you are staying with? Do they have a criminal background?'" She giggles almost convulsively. Shiway graduated with a bachelor's degree in chemical engineering but says, "I didn't want to sit in front of a computer all day." She rediscovered her childhood interest in the oceans while working at the University of Washington's chemical oceanography department. "Suddenly I realized you could do something with the oceans as a career. And I thought, 'You mean be happy *and* have a career?'" After Tern Island she'll be going to Alaska for another seabird project. And she got notified today via satellite telephone that she's been hired to work on penguins in Antarctica this coming winter.

Catherine is now on the satellite phone, telling her mother, "It's *beautiful* here. I've seen seals, turtles; I'm doing nest checks on the birds and stuff. Over."

"That's great! I'm so happy for you. Can I send you anything? Over."

"A little camera would be awesome. Over."

"O.K., will do. I love you. Over."

"Love you too. Over—and out."

Meanwhile, Greg is telling us how he came to produce special films for the National Geographic Society, explaining that he'd become fascinated with fish as a child. "But," he adds, "I was derailed for a lot of years in college. I was convinced I couldn't be a marine biologist. My father had scared me: 'no jobs, no future, no money.' He wanted me to get into law. And I did a prelaw curriculum. But after a couple of years, I just realized: Dammit, I want to do marine biology." So he earned a master's in his desired field. His main invention for animal study has been the "critter cam," a camera that attaches by suction to marine animals. "One day I saw a shark go by with a remora attached to it, and suddenly a light bulb went on: if I built a camera body with a suction attachment like a remora has on its head for hitchhiking on sharks' bodies, we would have access to a new world of underwater time and space." This allows the animal to be the filmmaker, giving us unprecedented views of what creatures do underwater. For instance, Greg says that with the camera, "We were amazed to learn that the Monk Seals here, instead of chasing fish, are overturning rocks on the bottom and rooting around in the sand, eating a lot of eels and octopuses."

Here's something interesting about Monk Seals and sharks: there's a small shark in these waters that lives a kind of parasitic existence. It rushes in to hit a larger animal like a seal or dolphin or whale, and twists out a circular, palm-sized scoop of flesh, leaving a round scar. It's actually called a Cookiecutter Shark. Monk Seals generally don't get bitten by Cookiecutters until they're about two years old. Presumably, until that time they're not in the deeper water where Cookie monsters live. It may take the seals that long to develop the lung capacity and skills to dive to between two hundred and five hundred feet.

Monk Seals appear to do most of their hunting at night—that's where those big eyes come into play—which is when lobsters and octopuses are out. They eat perhaps the widest diet of any marine mammal: roughly forty prey species, from pelagic squid to fish, crabs, and the aforementioned lobsters and octopuses.

Greg concludes, "And so we've found, surprisingly, that these seals aren't foraging in the shallows, which everyone thought was their 'critical habitat.' They're going out deep—where people are fishing."

BEFORE DAWN I REALIZE the rains seem finally to have ended. For the seabirds, it's been a trial by water. The surviving youngsters might as well get used to it. Despite the forays of frigatebirds, so many Sooty Tern chicks remain alive that windrows of them move through the vegetation ahead of me, fanning out of my way. At first light, the eastern half of the runway is cloaked in a carpet of adult Sooties—probably fifty thousand. Birds begin drifting away from the island in the half-light, silhouetted against the morning. As sunlight begins flooding the sky, birds continue peeling off the runway in a great confusion of wings and deafening sound, until terns so fill the sky that the island seems to smoke.

The Sooties are still *so* loud by midmorning that I can't hear the plane approaching. Alarmed, their collective roar is earsplitting. Off the plane comes National Geographic cameraman Bill Mills, and shark researchers Chris Lowe and Brad Wetherbee. They will be collaborating on the Tiger Shark film.

Chris Lowe, age thirty-five, has been studying Hawaiian sharks for seven years. He's thin and supple, wears a mustache and a goatee, is soft-spoken, bespectacled, and thoughtful. He grew up on the New England island of Martha's Vineyard, in a family with a two-hundred-year-old fishing tradition. Chris's uncle operated the last coastal schooner in New England. His grandfather, a commercial fisherman who couldn't swim, lost a son and a brother to drowning in fishing accidents. "When my grandfather started, he made a living fishing with just hand lines, no nets. He can take you to the beach and point and say, 'You see that buoy? We used to catch cod *this* big there.' They used to go just five miles off-shore to harpoon Swordfish. That's all gone now, too."

So Chris's route to fish research was a logical extension of his family background. "On Martha's Vineyard there wasn't a whole lot else for a kid to do besides fishing. I started reading books, one thing led to another, and I ended up doing science." Chris got fascinated with sharks and their relatives the rays. As a graduate student, he studied electric rays in southern California. "Those things are just incredible. Think about an animal that can produce and deliver fifty volts—enough to make a fish contract so violently its spinal column snaps—yet itself is immune to the effects of that kind of power. I studied it, and I can tell you: nobody's ever figured out how they do it." Chris adds that the electric discharge is energetically very expensive for them to produce. (Even rays have high electric bills.) Consequently, the rays are conservative with their power. For defense they use small pulses, just enough to discourage a potential predator. But when catching food they give it all they've got.

Chris says, "Here's what else amazes me: in most ways, sharks and rays are the same as other animals—they eat, mate, give birth. But in other ways they're incredibly unique. They have sensory capabilities no other animals have. They can detect animals hidden in sand by perceiving the weak electrical fields living things produce. Some sharks apparently migrate by orienting to the very weak electrical fields created by the friction of water masses."

Chris's research partner, Brad Wetherbee, thirty-nine, is solidly built and clean-shaven, with close-cropped dark hair. Brad's worked in Hawaii for nine years, including his Ph.D. research at the University of Hawaii. He says, "When I was younger, like most people I thought sharks were fascinating because they were dangerous. Later, I realized sharks are not well studied compared to most fish. As a scientist, you could pretty much pick a topic and gain a huge amount of information that had never been known before. They have unique adaptations for reproduction, internal salt balancing, and sensory perceptions. People think they're primitive, but they're quite remarkable."

For his dissertation, Brad studied adaptations of deep-dwelling sharks, some living as far down as forty-five hundred feet. "Their eyes, and many other parts, are adapted to the specific depths and pressures they live at. This totally fascinates me. Shallow-water sharks keep swimming to avoid sinking. But for deep-sea dwellers, there isn't enough food to be constantly on the go. So deep-sea sharks have to find some other way to avoid sinking. The thing is, the deeper you go, the denser the water is. So the bodies of sharks that live deeper are denser than sharks living shallower. Yet I found that all deep-water sharks are neutrally buoyant—they neither sink nor float—*regardless* of the depth and water pressure. Different sharks accomplish this in different ways. Most use large amounts of oils stored in the liver, but others fill their muscles with oil, and some flood their bodies with water. And young ones achieve neutral buoyancy differently than old ones; and males do it differently than females. In some species males live deeper than females, or young ones live at different depths than older ones. Their physiology is woven into the ecology of the animal. The whole process is amazingly dynamic and complex."

WITH TIME FOR AN EVENING stroll, I hit the runway just before sunset, with Shiway and turtle researcher Julie Rocho. Julie's just awakened from her all-day sleep for her all-night work. She's wearing the unofficial uniform of Tern Island: a loose T-shirt and shorts over a bathing suit, and earrings in the form of her study animals.

Wedge-tailed Shearwaters, newly arriving, are clustered on the runway in two squadrons. I sit and count ninety-two in the first group, wondering where these shearwaters have been, the millions of square oceanic miles represented by the sight of a few dark birds. I know only that they spent the nonbreeding season off Central America then followed the equatorial current westward toward the islands to breed.

Newcomers accrue, gliding in with masterful, shearwatery grace. Fluid though they are in flight, they land with an abrupt halt; their feet seem to stick to the ground immediately upon touchdown, jarringly stopping their forward momentum. After that, they do not seem to walk so much as motor determinedly, head down, with a two-steps-at-a-time waddle. They seem greatly relieved when, after a few steps of progress, they sit back on their pink haunches.

Reticent and awkward though they are in gait, they are avid in ardor. Though most of them sit quietly most of the time, the main activity here is gentle mutual facial preening—and fornication. What the little Wedgies lack in ambulation, they make up in copulation. Most of these birds' forward movement on the ground results from efforts to get to each other for neck nibbles or decidedly more intimate and energetic contact. They're not above loving the one they're with. Watch these two. After perhaps three minutes of vigorous "cloacal kissing" (the polite scientific term for rubbing genitals, which is itself a polite term) followed by a good preen, their bond seems weak. Their passion appears spent only briefly, and when they rejoin the larger flock, they reshuffle the deck. Many copulation attempts degenerate into immediate three-car pileups. Without watching for weeks and knowing the birds as tagged individuals, it would be impossible to understand their complex social dynamics. But at face value, they seem willing to court and preen just about anything that moves. We see presumed males going over to other birds who also seem to be males, judging by who tries getting on top. This is social climbing with a twist. We see a Wedgie preening the face of a Christmas Shearwater. This activity does not appear wrought from strong family values, but you have to admire their lack of bigotry. Between preenings, they sit still for long periods, their long, low, doleful moans rising and drifting on the wind. When I sit and imitate their moaning, four of them come over to me in little hops and pauses. One of them starts "preening" my sandal sole.

Julie, one of those rare people who is always finding something that gets a smile, observes jauntily, "Many people react badly to rejection. But *these* birds, they don't get discouraged. There's a lesson there."

Shiway suddenly interjects, "I think that all the tube-nosed birds— the petrels, shearwaters, and albatrosses—have a musky smell, and that each species smells differently." She continues, "The Bulwer's Petrel has a very strong musky smell that I find very relaxing. I inhale it and it just makes me very happy." She giggles a little nervously.

I say, "You sniff chicks?"

"Sometimes when we go out at night banding young albatrosses, I just inhale them," she answers.

If she was unashamed about sniffing birds at first, talking about it is only emboldening her.

"The Ashy Storm-Petrels I worked with in California—they're really teeny-tiny little birds—have a stronger scent, kind of oily. And," she continues stridently, "I *really* like the way they smell."

I nod.

She adds, "Not that I go around smelling *birds* all the time."

No, no; nothing like *that*!

"I like to sniff the Ashy Storm-Petrels right around their little bellies, and the albatrosses smell best right around their head," she says. "But the Bulwer's Petrel," Shiway adds, "I've never smelled *anything* like them before. Not *ever*."

I'm trying to figure out whether this is a plea for help. But then Shiway says something simple that actually gathers this all together quite sensibly: "Other birds don't smell as distinct to me as the tubenoses."

Suddenly, I get it. Scent is important to bonding and individual recognition in many mammals, of course, and it's important to attraction even in human couples. But tubenoses are among the few birds with a well-developed sense of smell. They use smell to find food, to locate their burrows, and probably to identify each other. Their distinct scents—which Shiway seems unusually sensitive to—help them find the right burrows and identify, and be identified among, their mates and young. It's particularly interesting that Shiway says the albatrosses smell best around the head. They must think so, too; they spend so much time nibbling there. Some scientists have speculated that albatrosses like to preen each other around the head and neck because it helps them remember their individual scents. Lesson taken: when someone says something that seems crazy, listen carefully and search for the truth that might be in it.

ALL NIGHT EVERY NIGHT, I hear those Wedgies' low voices from bed, playing the bass line to the Sooties' frenetic bebop. At times the chorus gathers volume enough to wake me fully. A gecko might announce its presence in my bedroom by uttering an occasional chirp that sounds like a smoke alarm telling me the battery has run low. It can be maddening or pleasant. Choose to make it pleasant; let it blend with the moaning birds outside the window. I almost don't want to sleep too soundly. I want to savor the soothing of all the call-and-response talking. But almost inevitably, I drift into a deep, pleasant, and richly dreamful animal-animated sleep.

> ⊁ ⊱ ⊱ ⊱ ⊱ ⊱ ⊱ ⊱ ⊱ ⊱ ⊱ ⊱ ⊱

TRACKS IN THE SEA

AMELIA HAS RUN OUT of ocean. Now, instead of water in every direction, the snowcapped volcanoes of Kamchatka's heavily timbered continental coast pierce the horizon dead ahead. She swings along the lonely shore of this Russian wilderness frontier, passes through the Commander Islands, where Steller's Sea Cows once grazed, and, on the longest day of the year, she enters the Bering Sea. Her chick, over twenty-five hundred miles away, no longer occurs to her.

Amelia's chick remains here of course, near the porch steps, getting more handsome and grown-up looking every day. He has become a sleek young albatross with just a little ruff of down around his head and neck. When he vigorously exercises his now-long wings, they look like they could carry him. You get the feeling he has merely a psychological barrier to confront: the realization that he can fly. He daily gets closer and closer to cracking the flight code. One morning he begins flapping and hopping, as in the last few days, but then runs forward a little bit. And suddenly he lifts off, seeming *effortless,* and flies slowly, with very shallow wing beats, mostly lofted by wind. He lands about fifty feet away, easily and without ceremony. This is the first powered, forward-moving flight I've seen a youngster accomplish. Even this first little flight seems so graceful and right. He repeats the performance. Now there is no more hopping straight up. Now there is just running into the wind and actually flying forward, though never more than about fifty feet. Other albatrosses are still jumping vertically and flailing. There is a trick to getting purchase, to pitching the wings just right for digging into the air. So far, of the chicks I've noticed, he alone seems to have gotten the idea of how to go forward on those wings. It must be like being on skates the first time, where you simply shuffle your feet back and forth until you learn how to push off.

Amelia's chick is still a few days away from leaving. His hunger is working both as a motivator and a constant reminder that he still can't really *go* anywhere. For the time being we, too, are stranded and abandoned at French Frigate Shoals. But we don't mind, because even by French Frigate Shoals standards, we have a very interesting day to look forward to. Today's plan is to visit East Island in an effort to get a transmitter into a Tiger Shark, and to film it all for Greg Marshall's National Geographic Television documentary.

Greg, Birget, cameraman Bill Mills, shark researchers Chris and Brad, and I—and a *lot* of gear—will crowd into two seventeen-foot outboard-powered skiffs for the crossing to East Island. Helping us ready the boats are albatross researcher Anthony Viggiano and seal researchers Mitch and Melissa.

Just loading the boats takes quite a while. Much of the gear is fragile and expensive. Bill is shooting with a $90,000 camera. He has a $4,000 soft waterproof case for shots shallower than eight feet deep. For deeper shots he has a hard aluminum housing costing $50,000. Meanwhile, everyone is talking sharks. Anthony, counting life preservers, is saying, "From what I've seen, sharks are very deliberate animals. They are very wary and they notice things. Like, if you stand up in a boat they notice that. I don't really see them as mindless feeding machines. We do a lot of snorkeling here, and I've never seen a Tiger Shark in the water with me; but many times when we anchor the boat a shark will come up and circle. So you know that they're in the area. But they keep their distance."

"They're not shy if you're a seal pup," says Mitch. "During the most recent Galápagos Shark attack at Trig Island there were three sharks— five- to six-footers—with fins out and tails thrashing. Seeing it was both exciting and terrible. What got our attention was the mother at the shore, calling. The mother knew exactly what was going on, but there was nothing she could do about it. She went into the water and bit one of the sharks, which swam off a short distance, then came back. And then the pup appeared on the beach, lying very still, with flesh exposed and a pink line of blood running down the sand. The sharks were almost beaching themselves trying to drag it back into the water. One finally succeeded. Then another grabbed its entrails and swam away with them. They consumed the whole pup, and left a big slick of oil and a cloud of blood. The mother kept calling. She sounded pitiful."

Melissa adds, "Another time I saw two sharks come in and the mom make a lunge at one of them and the other immediately try to grab the pup."

That's reminiscent of a time I saw two jackals separate a gazelle from her newborn calf by having one jackal fake an attack to draw the mother away, only to have the other rush in and actually grab the baby. Cooperative and group hunting is normally considered the domain of just a few mammals and birds, but certain fish sometimes do it—for example marlins, whose colored markings often light up to communicate to each other the beginning of an attack, and Bluefin Tuna, which sometimes swim in parabola-shaped hunting formations that probably represent the most organized grouping pattern in any fish. It's interesting that these sharks might at times hunt cooperatively.

By the time we've finished loading, the boat has become the usual expeditional disarray of heavy coolers, cases, wet suits, air tanks, rain slickers, gasoline tanks, and scientific gear. Overhead, it looks as if rain could spoil the shoot. We all pile in anyway, adding Mitch at the last moment, pushing away from the dock just as a brief drizzle begins. We thread our way through the cuts in Tern's reefy barricade, maneuvering our boat through the black pinball-bumper lava heads to the open turquoise lagoon. My binoculars reveal that the bursts of white erupting from a calm sea beyond the reef are Spinner Dolphins in their high-spiraling exuberance. A six-mile lagoon crossing puts us in the green shallows just off East Island.

Everyone tells us dawn is the best time to look for sharks here at East Island. But prepping and getting here has taken until almost eleven. Sharks or not, there's plenty to see anyway. Fully half of all the sea turtles throughout Hawaii come to this *one* island to nest, and here they are. Their dark, lumpy forms are bobbing and gliding in the shallows. The shoreline is tractored and trod with the activities of nesting turtles. Many sets of turtle tracks go straight up the steep beach, where the dry-shelled turtles look like terra-cotta sculptures on the white sand. They're mostly sleeping, heads down, looking dormant. Those just coming ashore, wet and gleaming, look absolutely gorgeous, with starburst shell markings of tan, beige, and dark brown. The island above the beach looks like it's been shelled by artillery, with thigh-deep body pits that the turtles have dug. They must raise havoc with ground-nesting birds as they bulldoze through their colonies each night. At one end of the island, an amazing sight: so thick are the sleeping sea turtles, I count twenty-six in a fifty-yard stretch of beach. Some are coming and going up and down the beach.

There's something inexpressibly melancholy about the way a sea turtle moves on land. Their normal activities seem to require unbearable exertion and forlornly heroic effort. Shove and stop, lurch and pause, they row themselves through the oceans, and they row when they're ashore. They row, row, row themselves through the decades of their long, improbable, ancient life.

East Island is higher than Tern and didn't get flooded or washed over in February, so the albatross chicks are pretty numerous on this island. Big juvenile albatrosses—full-sized, almost fully feathered and nearly flying—line the berm. (In almost all birds, the young are adult-sized by the time they first fly, their skeletons fully grown.) You can see a lot of waving wings, even from a distance. Though occasional gusts unsteady them, they savor the excitement and persist in leaping and flapping.

Seals populate the beach too. A mother and pup doze peacefully. One lone little black-velvet pup, permanently stilled, is a boon to flies. Another mother seal has taken her pup into the water along shore—a risky place. She keeps putting her head in the water, scanning back and forth, probably watching for sharks. Another large seal on the beach has a bloody wound near its tail, perhaps from a shark, perhaps from a fight with another male. One just-weaned seal that came ashore last night has a hideous, gaping wound on one side—and this is certainly a shark

To rest and breed—Green Turtles and Monk Seals

bite. The wide crater it left—about one-third the length of its torso—is through the skin, through the blubber, and well into muscle. It is difficult to comprehend how this seal is still alive, yet it seems alert. Almost certainly, this wound is fatal. Perhaps the best to be hoped is for this seal to experience the onset of shock, to mask its misery until the mercy of death. Evolution breeds majesty and misery in equal proportion, and usually in very close quarters.

Mitch says this pup's mother had left it prematurely weaned. In addition to the loss of parental protection, the weaner's low weight, inexperience, and small size left it ill-equipped for survival, and at high risk of starving. So the question presents itself: Are sharks fully responsible for the death of this seal or—in *this* instance—did sharks attack a seal already doomed to starvation by early separation from its mother?

French Frigate Shoals has more such shark attacks now than, say, ten years ago. But most of the seals they hit are low weight, less likely to survive anyway. More seals are starving now than ten years ago. So is it a shark problem? It depends on your perspective. Bill Gilmartin, a Hawaii-based scientist whose research of Monk Seals spans more than two decades, says, "In my mind it's a food problem, causing seals to be skinny and vulnerable to begin with."

ANY DAY NOW, as soon as the first chicks begin taking their first flights and landing in the lagoon here, Tiger Sharks will turn their attentions on just-fledged albatrosses bobbing on the surface. They will be like trout gulping mayflies, but on a vastly enlarged scale. So, like trout fishermen, we will "match the hatch" by luring Tigers with albatross carcasses. We go ashore, looking for dead birds.

We nudge the boat in close, wading ashore through the turquoise shallows, trying to be vigilant for shadows in the water. The soft coral sand tends to be powdery when dry, a bit sticky when wet. A lot of the sand is bits of pink and purple coral or shell. Keeping our distance from the seals and turtles, we collect the carcasses of several almost-grown albatross chicks that have recently died. A blue plastic laundry basket, washed up on the beach, becomes a bird mini-morgue.

We move off, about a hundred yards offshore. Our anchors travel about fifteen feet to the bottom of the bright aquamarine lagoon. From here you have a nice, commanding view of the beach and surrounding waters. A rocky reef extends from one end of the island. Right beyond the black reef's white breakers, the atoll's lagoon plunges deeper, abruptly turning blue. Beyond that, the pinnacle stands like something from a *Lost World* landscape. Two Eagle Rays come to the surface, splashing and thrashing. This is their breeding season as well. We tie the boats to each other so they will remain just a short distance apart.

Scarcely have our boats come tight on their anchor lines when a large Tiger Shark appears suddenly next to us, its dark form gliding in a tight, taught semicircle. The unexpected sight creates instant commotion. It vanishes, but all of us sense that sighting a shark so soon promises further excitement. After we regain our composure, Brad ties the basket of birds overboard at the stern cleat, to start our shark-attracting slick. The dead birds are in various stages of decomposition, from freshly dead to putrefied. A smelly slick immediately begins forming around the boat, but there's no current to speak of. In my shark-fishing experience, you need either a fast drift or a current. If the slick just forms around your boat rather than streaming away and spreading the scent, your chances of attracting sharks decline. And fresh bait works much better than rotten bait. But we'll see what happens. Obviously, there's at least one monster shark lurking nearby.

To eliminate the trauma of capture, the researchers want the shark to simply swallow a transmitter in a bird carcass. The shark will eventually, after some passage of days, regurgitate the transmitter. Greg expresses to me some uneasiness about using bird carcasses for bait. He feels it could seem disrespectful to the birds. I tell him it's aesthetically ungraceful, but I see no ethical problem with it; it's a natural food for sharks, the birds were already dead, and they're being used by scientists to learn something about sharks.

As Greg considers his first shot, Birget wires Brad and Chris for sound. Then she suits herself up with headphones and microphone boom, and checks all of her sound equipment to make sure everything is working. The first scene will show Chris and Brad setting up by putting a transmitter inside one of the dead birds, putting the bird carcass overboard at the end of a line, and checking the transmitter signal. Chris puts the hydrophone overboard. This is a palm-sized, wedge-shaped metal device. When the ultrasonic signal from a transmitter hits its face, a series of crystal-forming ceramic elements vibrate at a frequency corresponding to the sound. That signal is sent through a wire up to the receiver, shifted into human hearing range, and amplified. The wire runs from the hydrophone through a hollow handle attached by a swivel bracket to the side of the boat. Brad turns on the tracking equipment and tests two transmitters on different channels. The receiver, which is housed in a cooler to keep it shaded and dry, responds with rhythmic chirps. Bill sets up, turns the camera on, focuses, and says he's rolling. Birget turns on the sound tape. Greg snaps his moviemaker's slate to synchronize the sound and the film.

Brad picks up a bird, opens its bill, and with a gloved hand puts the transmitter down its throat. Then he tosses the tethered, transmittered albatross directly toward us. It's a strange sight—the dead albatross flying through the air at us, landing upside down on the water with a heavy splat, its enormous black wings splayed, its breast afloat like a black football. Ironically, this poor dead bird is the first chick in the colony to fly over water.

The bird carcass drifts astern on its line. When the shot is done, Bill says, "Good thing the stink doesn't get captured on film. That bird is definitely not ready for prime time." Brad and Chris, standing wide-legged on the boat's benches, watch expectantly and hopefully, searching the hemisphere of vision astern. Greg says, "Chris, just talk about why you're here."

Bill and Birget get rolling, and Chris launches: "Tiger Sharks have been considered culprits in attacks on Monk Seals here. Monk Seals are endangered, and wildlife managers have actually considered culling or thinning the Tiger Shark population here. But we know nothing of their movements here, or even how many there are. In other places, Tigers seldom visit the same sites two days in a row. Are the sharks here residents? Do they patrol the same areas daily? Brad and I, as shark scientists, would really like to find out. So would Monk Seal scientists. We're hoping to get a shark or two to swallow a transmitter, so we can begin to learn their habits here. If this pilot project is successful, we'll come back with surgically implanted tags, and put out listening stations that can detect sharks' movements over the course of a year or so. Basically, we would like to get a handle on what the sharks' movements are, and whether there are patterns."

Bill keeps rolling a few more seconds, then says, "Very good."

Greg agrees. "Great. O.K., guys—bring the sharks in now."

Chris starts scanning with binoculars, a sign of avid impatience.

Off camera, Brad says, "Everybody's worried about Tiger Sharks eating their study animals; the seals, or the turtles, or the albatrosses. Well, the sharks are *our* study animals. The sharks are out here swimming around trying to survive, trying to have their babies, trying not to get caught and have their fins cut off for soup—"

Chris points to something in the distance. We all look.

It turns out to be "just" a turtle.

. . .

WHEN NOTHING FURTHER happens after quite a while, we move near the end of the island, where runs the long shallow reef with breakers, bordered by a crisp line of blue, deeper water. There's a current here, and the stinky slick from the dead birds immediately begins streaming away. These seem like better conditions for drawing attention.

Within ten minutes, I see a dark shape. I watch it for a few moments to make sure it's not a turtle. Not a seal. The word "shark" snaps everyone to attention.

The imposing shadow of a large Tiger approaches the boat. It is mellow of mood, and everything about its calmness is frightening and charismatic.

Bill gets his camera to his shoulder.

The shark is quite a grand one. It looks ten feet, three very heavy-bodied meters of flexing, flowing muscle. It angles away, goes downcurrent about a hundred yards, and makes a long, lazy circle back. The shark seems indolent and not actively hunting, almost as if we interrupted its afternoon siesta with an interesting scent it felt obliged to investigate.

The shark's confident silhouette, slowly weaving back and forth, begins another long, gradual approach. Death itself could hardly seem less hurried.

A subtle dark form when it first appeared, it now looks utterly striking, its shape and shadow in high contrast against the aquamarine lagoon. It moves in a little closer to the boat, then passes.

Bill is rolling.

The shark makes several wide circles beneath the dead albatross. It moves downtide, just a little, then lines up for a direct approach toward the serenely bobbing corpse. Planing upward, its dorsal fin slices into the atmosphere, then in startling slow motion its enormous square head bursts into our world, pushing a pile of water over the bird like a snowplow. The massive mouth opens for a calm gulp.

But surprisingly, the bait remains untouched as the Tiger passes and continues beyond our bow, its beige-brown body vanishing against the darker reef.

Will it reappear? Hopeful anticipation winds tighter as seconds pass.

Brad points suddenly. The shark appears again against the turquoise bottom, about a hundred and fifty yards astern.

Greg says, "It looks big."

Brad, absorbed in the sight, nods quietly. "It's a decent-sized shark."

Slowly, always slowly, it comes back, its dorsal slitting the surface. I'm not into stereotypes, but this is classic.

The shark slides directly under our boat, swerves around, and heads straight up.

Bill curses that his film's run out. Brad jerks the bird to the side at the last moment, stalling for time to let Bill change film. The shark passes, pivots, and charges back fast. Brad, like a marine matador, pulls the bird up out of the water, and the shark swings past. I have an urge to shout *Olé!*

Bill resumes rolling as the shark comes on again. Brad flips the big bird right where Bill can get the best shot.

The shark glides in. Very close. Right alongside. As it flows past, we can see the faint, blotchy side bars that give the Tiger its name. We can see that it's a female by the configuration of the fins on her belly. Greg says, "Lovely animal."

Between passes, we begin noticing more and more water in the boat. I begin looking around, trying to figure out where the water could be coming in from.

The shark comes back, and Bill continues filming. As the shark turns away, there seems to be *a lot* more water, and Greg announces, "Guys— I think we're sinking." If any time for sinking is better than any other time, this is not the best.

The ten-foot Tiger slides alongside us again as I grab a bucket and begin bailing. And suddenly all three of us realize that every time the shark comes by we all crowd to one rear corner of the boat for the best view, dipping the stern low enough to let water in around the outboard engine.

Abruptly the Tiger comes head-up out of the water. Greg asks excitedly, "Bill, are you in tight?"

"*Real* tight," Bill says. "I've got nostril and eyeball."

The Tiger's protective eyelids close as its mouth covers the albatross. Brad yells, "She's got it now!" The Tiger turns and angles down, stretching the nylon cord tight against Brad's straining grip. Twisting, its white belly flashing, the shark takes the taut line hissing across the water, ripping it through Brad's fingers.

Then the Tiger suddenly thrashes to the surface, its dorsal knifing up, its slashing tail lashing. Working and worrying the carcass, it tears the bird in half.

"Tiger Sharks often seem clumsy," Greg says. "But at other times they can be incredibly dextrous."

Chris agrees. "When they really need to, they can be very"—he searches for a word—"articulate."

The shark circles back immediately, thrashing the water, shaking the carcass, pulling down the second half of the bird. Part of the corpse bobs to the surface again as the Tiger comes directly past our stern. For all the commotion, we get the feeling that it's just fooling around, being dainty compared to what this creature is capable of doing. Up once more, it takes the bird's last remnants in one fluid gulp, leaving a smear of oil and a trail of black feathers.

The shark has vanished. But it has swallowed the transmitter, and Chris has the signal on the hydrophone. He points in the direction of the unseen shark. Chris says tersely, "Gotta boogie; let's go." These transmitters don't work over distances of more than about half a mile. You have to keep following, and the fish can give you the slip pretty easily.

Now it's a race to keep up with the shark. Yet our engine needs to be convinced that we really do need to move. Chris has trouble getting the outboard started, but on the fifth pull it kicks to life. Chris sits hurriedly and hits the throttle to go chasing, and the outboard dies immediately. It's critical now to keep up with the shark, but we can't get the main engine started, and even the spare "kicker" won't cooperate. Chris again pulls the cord on the main engine, and finally it roars.

With Chris at the helm, Brad is swiveling the hydrophone, trying to determine the shark's direction. This requires finesse. It's not easy to hear fine changes in the strength of the chirps coming from the receiver. With Brad pointing, Chris steers.

This is where the science begins. Many months of preparation, coordination, and logistical arrangements are suddenly paying off in this moment. Brad says, "This is exciting, isn't it?"

Chris says, "For me, all the stuff I go through, all the work, grading all the papers, the committee meetings—it's all for one thing: to be here doing this right now. This is why you go through all the other inanity."

"And just think," Brad adds. "We're probably the only people in the world who are tracking a Tiger Shark right now."

"Probably?"

"Scientists always say 'probably.'"

Besides following, we must record the shark's track. Chris gives the tiller to Brad. Sitting with his clipboard on his knees, Chris consults a handheld satellite GPS on the bench beside him and starts mapping exact latitude and longitude positions and directionality every ten minutes. Now Brad has a dual job: one hand on the tiller, and the other on the hydrophone. He turns the hydrophone slightly to get the strongest signal and steers the boat to follow.

The shark—unseen, merely heard by the chirps emitted out of the cooler—is running the rocky reef that extends from East Island. A five-foot swell is breaking energetically on this reef, sending white foam sweeping our way. Brad says, "Looks like a washing machine."

The shark is taking us straight toward the Washing Machine. Now we're headed directly into the whitecaps, and the boat starts pitching. If the Tiger crosses to the other side of the reef, we must either follow into hazardously rough water or lose her.

Fortunately for us, the shark makes an abrupt right turn toward the open, deeper part of the lagoon. We follow a clear signal.

The other boat parallels us for a few minutes, getting shots of Brad and Chris tracking, while I stay out of sight, lying on the deck watching clouds streaming by, listening to the receiver. Birget radios that they've got what they need. I sit up and we wave good-bye as they depart.

The transmitter signal suddenly weakens. Brad's afraid that the shark might be getting too far ahead. But when he swivels the hydrophone, the strongest signal is *behind* us. Brad turns the boat around and pulls the hydrophone up, so he can run faster.

After running about one hundred yards, Brad slows and slides the hydrophone down. He begins swiveling the instrument, and looking quizzical. But then the signal comes in clearly. The shark has made a U-turn, heading back toward the reef that extends from East Island.

About two dozen Sooty Terns suddenly and inexplicably gather directly over us, only about ten or fifteen feet up, calling and hovering. I wonder what they want.

Brad says, "In the ancient legends, it is said that when terns gather overhead, one of them is about to—"

One of the terns poops on Chris's shirt, and they all immediately depart as though they were sharing the prank.

Ten minutes later, the Tiger U-turns again, this time toward open water. Several big clouds sweep over, giving us alternately shade and showers that quickly pass. A Laysan Albatross comes bombing along, sailing straight for the boat, etching the lagoon surface with its long wings, right off our bow, just a few feet away.

Chris says, "Wow, they sure know how to cruise."

Brad, sounding philosophical, says, "You know, Blue Sharks are the albatrosses of the sea. They have long, winglike fins. They wander great distances searching for food. They're probably built on the same strategy: to travel long distances looking for widely separated food sources, using a very small amount of energy."

After traveling out about a mile and turning back, our shark is tight again along the reef, island-bound.

Brad asks, "Can you believe how reef-oriented this shark is? It's really patrolling the reef."

Chris responds, "This is what I *used* to think Tiger Sharks would do, before we did our tracking off Oahu and the main islands."

None of the dozen-plus Tiger Sharks they tracked in the main Hawaiian Islands ever returned to the same place during the same day or on consecutive days. Those sharks revisited areas very irregularly—sometimes a few days later, sometimes a few weeks.

Our Tiger slides onto a green flat only about five feet deep. It runs into a rocky cul-de-sac and turns around. Now we can see it darkly patrolling the edge of the reef, where waves are breaking.

Brad invites me to take over the tracking. One hand on the tiller, one on the swivel to the hydrophone, I do my best to follow.

A big *Ulua* streaks in startlingly. It circles around quickly and then strikes the shiny hydrophone—and vanishes. I track our Tiger Shark for about half an hour, then suddenly lose the signal. On the hunch that it is merely outpacing us without changing direction, I pull up the hydrophone and run up ahead at a higher speed. Brad's silent nod affirms that this is a reasonable action. I'm really hoping to recover the signal; I hate being the one who screws up.

To my surprise and great relief, the chirps return, strong.

Chris says, "Lucky."

"Sheer skill," I explain.

Brad asks, "Did you really expect to get the signal back?"

"Of course," I tease. "Did you doubt me?"

"I wouldn't have bet my life."

I poke, "Well, you're not much of a risk taker."

Brad smirks at me with one eyebrow raised.

The shark goes along the reef line again and angles back toward East Island. Brad says, "This one is *really* staying local."

Chris says, "It may depend on the geographical context. Oahu and the main islands, where we tracked before, is a big area with diverse islands. Here you have this small isolated atoll. And inside this atoll, right at East Island, you have all this fatty, meaty, nutritious food coming here. You've got seal pups. Turtles galore. You've got big fattened-up albatross chicks. If I were a Tiger at this time of year, I'd be stickin' close by, too."

The shark is now heading down along the shore of East Island, cruising by a beach populated by ten seals, including three pups and two weaners. And about thirty-five turtles. Halfway down the island, it turns and begins a long crossing of the wide lagoon.

About two hours later, our Tiger is headed slowly toward Trig Island—still a couple of miles away—where most of the Shoals' Monk Seals give birth. Hour after hour, we and the Tiger remain connected through the chirps, sometimes fainter, sometimes stronger.

Chris says, "Everybody thinks being a shark researcher is exciting. Actually it's long, tedious, boring hours."

I'm thinking, "Compared to what?" but I know he's kidding.

An hour later, at six o'clock, we're close enough to Trig to see that the sandy shore is dotted with seals and turtles. About twenty mom-and-pup pairs are on the beach. One mother utters a long, low bellow. Three or four pups have been attacked or eaten at this island in just the last week. Because of the shape of the bites, Galápagos Sharks are the principle suspects. Tiger Sharks' bite marks are wide and squared off, like their square head.

Suddenly the shark seems to pick up its pace again, and the signal breaks. Chris begins swiveling the hydrophone in its bracket, trying to pick up the signal. He's listening hard, concentrating with eyes closed, saying hopefully, "C'mon, c'mon, c'mon," as he turns the instrument in different directions. Chris runs us quickly forward again. It looks as if the shark has given us the slip. "She can't be moving *that* fast."

But wait; there it is, faintly. Chris gets a direction, then lifts the hydrophone and runs again. Now he's got a faint signal, but steady. We run toward it again, and get it back strong.

"*Nice* recovery," I say.

Brad says, "In ten minutes we'll have a five-hour track. About seven miles."

I ask, "Is that good?"

He huffs, "*Yeah,* that's good! Not as good as *fifty* hours, like we once had, but it's good."

At 6:30, we're out of time. This lagoon is too full of reefs to safely operate a boat in darkness.

Chris says, "I think we learned a lot today. The first track is always the most exciting because you have no idea what to expect. When we tracked the first Waikiki Tiger we figured we'd just be cruising up and down the shore admiring bikinis the whole time. We had no idea we would be leaving the island of Oahu immediately and going about fifty miles straight to Molokai."

Brad says with satisfaction, "Today was *very* interesting. That was unlike any Tiger Shark track ever done before. In the main Hawaiian Islands, they swam in deeper water. But this shark was cruising shallows all day. It's the first Tiger Shark that's been tracked doing anything like that. From my other experience, I'd thought that you would be safe from Tiger Sharks in very shallow water, but this one was right up against the reef."

We need to run home. Chris calls, "O.K., shark, we'll try to catch up with you tomorrow. Don't eat any seals; you'll get a bad reputation."

WE'RE DETERMINED to get an earlier start today, and at a little before eight A.M. we're again off East Island, sitting at anchor, listening for our shark. The National Geographic crew will join us later—perhaps with some fresher bait—hoping to film us getting a second Tiger transmittered.

Brad seems in a sardonic mood. As soon as we anchor, he says, "This might be a long day."

Chris answers, "A bad day at French Frigate Shoals beats a good day in Orange County. The sharks'll be here by noon. Trust me." Ten minutes later, he points. "*There's* something—" He scrutinizes with both hands shading his eyes. "An Eagle Ray."

The receiver is silent, save a faint static hiss. It detects no transmitters. Chris, scanning further with binoculars, says there's something out on the flat. "Right where the really light green meets the slightly darker green. Moving fast, whatever it is—. Never mind; it's a turtle."

Brad states, "Tiger Sharks have had whole sea turtles in their stomachs. There really is a *lot* of food for them here at this time of the year. Maybe the sharks come long distances to be here now, like these other animals. But maybe they're here all the time. So the questions are: Where do the sharks come from? Are they migrants or residents? How many are here? What effects might they have on endangered species and other wildlife?"

A short while later we notice two big turtles mating, attended by two smaller males. The male that is actually mating with the female is by far the largest. With binoculars we can really see how the claw on each front flipper lets him lock onto the female for a tight, sure grip, and how he uses his thick tail to help hold her posterior. He looks old and a bit weather-beaten, with several barnacles growing on his shell.

Picking up on Brad's earlier comment, Chris says, "We analyzed data on Tiger Shark stomach contents collected over two decades of the shark-control program in the main Hawaiian Islands—from thousands of sharks. And compared to what people thought, they had a fairly low percentage of turtles in their stomachs. Over there they eat a lot of lobsters and eels off the bottom; plus needlefish, trumpetfish, and slow-moving things—pufferfish, those kind of things. In Australia they eat lots of sea snakes; in Florida they eat a lot of horseshoe crabs. They have a really varied diet, but it was quite a bit different than what people were saying. Fishermen were saying that they were eating lots of commercially important fish. But they weren't."

"The things we found about their movements, too," Brad adds, "were different from what people had thought. Conventional wisdom was wrong again. In many places people see 'the same shark' day after day on the same beach. But when you tag them, you discover it's not the same shark. Fishermen say, 'Oh yeah—*that* shark—that's the Landlord; we see him all the time.' Then someone kills the Landlord and suddenly next week the Landlord is reincarnated. You realize when you start tagging that there are different sharks. And they're not staying in one place. They're huge animals, and they patrol large areas."

Chris says that their movements don't fit any regular pattern. Among the Tigers Brad and Chris have tracked, some left the capture site for weeks, then returned for a few days, then disappeared for a month, then visited for a couple of days. There was no regular routine. "Before we started our study, if there was a shark attack the state would go out and fish in that area to kill the culprit. So they'd go catch a shark, have it on the newspaper and TV and everything. Viewers could see a dead Tiger Shark and feel safer. The government could say, as a guardian of the people—especially tourists—'We're *doing* something about this!' To some, it hardly matters whether they catch the culprit or not, just as long as it looks like they're responding."

Chris sums up: "Overall, Hawaii's extensive control program did not affect the rate of shark attack. They long-lined around the islands for years, removing thousands of sharks. They spent hundreds of thousands of dollars to kill all of those sharks. Five months after the program ended, in an area where they killed thirty-three Tiger Sharks, there was an attack."

The rate of shark attack remained about the same after the program as it had been before. "In Hawaii," Chris continues, "about two people per year get bitten. But there have been only two confirmed *fatal* shark attacks there in the last forty-plus years: one in 1991, another in 1992. In 1991 there were four attacks, one fatal; a woman taking her daily swim off Maui was attacked by a shark and killed. That was the first fatal attack since 1958.

"After the woman got killed in '91, there was another big call to kill sharks. The tourism industry didn't want people thinking it's dangerous in any way whatsoever to come to Hawaii. They wanted to avoid headlines, but the media went nuts anyway and—"

"Yeah, BLOOD BATH IN PARADISE: *They've tasted human flesh. There's no stopping 'em.*"

Chris continues, "Some people pushed for slaughtering as many sharks as possible. People were saying there was a good chance of catching that specific shark. Of course, our tracking showed Tigers don't stay in one place long at all. So the chances of catching a particular shark that attacks are very low."

"People were saying it's not safe to go into the water. Just like *Jaws.* 'How many people have to die?'"

"Anyway," says Chris, "the native Hawaiians were all up in arms about shark killing because they believe that sharks are guardian spirits. Plus, it was simply too expensive. So they did a limited control program.

"All of this raises two questions: How many sharks do you have to kill to make the water safe? And how safe does it have to be? It would make sense that the more sharks you kill, the lower the risk of shark attack. But apparently, that wasn't true in Hawaii. And in Florida, where heavy fishing drove shark populations to their lowest levels ever, the rate of shark attack has increased—as the human population increases. They mirror each other. So it seems shark attack is more related to the number of *people* in the water than to the number of sharks. But even so, sharks actually kill very few people."

Brad says, "There are constantly people in the water all over Hawaii, like fatted calves. If sharks wanted to eat people, they'd be biting more than just two per year. And like Chris says, most of those are not fatal."

Chris adds, "Meanwhile, there are forty drownings per year in the Hawaiian Islands. No one has suggested a wave-control program. People just figure big waves are part of the danger of being in the water. Well, instead of spending hundred of thousands of dollars killing sharks and probably not saving anybody, how about money for more lifeguards to control the number of drownings?"

"Do you realize how many people get killed by sharks every year, on average, worldwide?" asks Brad. "Ten. In the whole world."

"Think about how many millions of people are in the water. The chances of getting attacked are very low. You can certainly increase your odds of attack if you're out at night, or if you're spearfishing and dragging bleeding fish," adds Chris.

"I wish they reported the number of people killed by pigs. And by bee stings. Or crocodiles. Elephants—one year more people in *Hawaii* were killed by an elephant than by sharks; a circus elephant rampaged and killed three people," Brad says.

Chris adds, "Hundreds of times more people get killed by dogs—"

"Forget dogs; wanna talk *automobiles?*" Brad almost challenges.

"Cigarettes," I offer, since we're listing familiar things that kill more people than sharks.

"The common cold," adds Brad authoritatively.

"Polluted water. Do you realize the *thousands* of children that die of diarrhea because of polluted water?" asks Chris.

I mention that I recently read that every year about a dozen children in America alone strangle to death after getting tangled in window-blind cords.

Chris says, "See—that's more than the number of people killed by sharks worldwide." Even in Florida, the place with the most attacks, sharks bite about one out of every million people that enter the water. "The odds of getting attacked are so low it's a freak accident."

"But psychologically," Brad analyzes, "people just don't like the thought of being bitten in half."

"Things that are actually much more dangerous get less attention," Chris says.

"But with *sharks,*" Brad adds a bit indignantly, "there's primordial fear."

It seems that of all the many things that kill people, sharks probably kill fewer people than anything else. Chris says, "Compare it to the tolerance for other causes of death, like automobiles, like you said, or guns. I mean, the risks people are *willing* to take—"

"Gun control in the United States," Brad picks up. "It's something you can't touch. Your right to bear arms. I read that something like thirty-one thousand people are killed annually by handguns in the United States. It's a *huge* number. You could go out there, collect a bunch of guns, and actually change that death statistic. You could do something about it. But we won't even take a step toward that. Compare it to, like, Britain, where they essentially don't have handguns. There were, like, forty people killed in Britain by handguns last year." Factoring in the difference in population, your chances of getting killed by a gun are 160 times higher in the United States than in Britain. "I don't know how they murder people over there," wonders Brad. "They must stab them or poison them, or beat them or something."

We're accustomed to taking prudent risks against far worse odds than getting in the water. But large predators evoke a response from a very ancient part of our brains. If we were accustomed to living in a place with a lot of predators, we might simply have a prudence and respect for them and a caution around them, like we do for automobile traffic. But we fear the unknown, things lurking in the dark or patrolling unseen below the water's surface. And we fear the unfamiliar—like sharks. Many divers, scientists, and fishers who *are* familiar with sharks feel differently. They recognize them as potentially dangerous but understand that under normal conditions, they're usually safe. They accept responsibility for their own risks, and know ways to avoid dangerous situations.

AT THE MOMENT, we're starting to feel a little *too* safe. Brad, into a candy bar, says, "You can wear yourself out, waiting for a shark." Chris turns the hydrophone all the way around, listening intently. There's only silence and a slight hiss. Chris stands and scans again, saying, "There's another ray. More turtles." The dark shapes of turtles are almost constantly in view and keep us alert, cruising like big green taxis. Any glance at the lagoon usually brings the sight of a big bobbing shell or three, or shadows gliding along like undersea angels. The males jostle for females, the females get swept away in long-lasting couplings.

Brad says, "It's noon. Perhaps we've displeased the spirits."

Brad and Chris explain the traditional Hawaiian concept of guardian spirits called 'aumakua. 'Aumakua are spirits of half-human beings—offspring of a god and a human—who utter counsel through the lips of a medium, usually in the form of an animal like a bird or gecko, whom they possess temporarily. Because 'aumakua often appear in the shape of sharks, many native Hawaiians feel particularly close to sharks. Each family has their 'aumakua. A stillborn child is usually the offspring of an 'aumakua and the woman. If the 'aumakua finds the remains, it adopts the child, who becomes another 'aumakua. (This seems a tender way to instill the child with life.) When the mother goes to bathe in the sea, this 'aumakua, who is her offspring, may come in the form of a shark—only to her—and jump at her breast as if to suckle, letting her know this is her child. Brad and Chris tell of a recently deceased Hawaiian who said his great-grandmother used to walk into the shallows and breast-feed sharks.

'Aumakua may appear in the form of a shark or other animal, but they themselves have no substance. In the late 1800s, one Hawaiian explained to an interviewer, "The 'aumakua has no form. It comes in the shape of a wish into the mother." 'Aumakua act as counselors to their kin, who honor their divinity. They also give fishermen luck and protection; they may cure disease, or even avenge an enemy. In current-day belief the 'aumakua concept often takes the form of a special sense of bond or relationship with a particular kind of animal, like sharks or turtles.

Native Hawaiians' relationships with sharks were complex, ranging from catching them with nooses to worshiping them as half-human spirit-helpers. Shark gods may be *kane* (male) or *wahine* (female). Sharks inhabited by the spirits of relatives will never molest you, and in case of trouble at sea will rescue and carry you safely ashore in their jaws. A shark that was once a man might be rainbow-colored, and might put you under his arm and be like a father to you. Inhabiting specific places were particular patron sharks whose name, history, hideaway, and appearance were well known to all who frequented the area. Their care and worship was the responsibility of a hereditary *kahu* (keeper), a function handed from parent to child. In order that the 'aumakua may be strong enough to act as helper, it must receive offerings of prayer, food, and drink, often directly into the sea. An 'aumakua is faithful to its devotee-keeper; the worship and reciprocal service extends to the devotee's whole family, passing from generation to generation.

That is why there was such an uproar from native Hawaiians when people wanted to kill Tiger Sharks following the attacks in the early 1990s.

Brad explains that the woman killed in 1991 was the wife of a sugar-plantation magnate, and that afterward some native Hawaiians claimed that the shark had attacked because she was a white woman, in retribution for the massacre of several Hawaiians that had occurred at that site over a century earlier. The racial tensions in Hawaii are surprising. They're some of the worst I've experienced anywhere in the States— and that's saying a lot, considering that the United States has some of the worst racial tension in the developed world.

A soft drizzle begins, and a Sooty Tern lands on Chris's head. Another lands on mine—as if they're just sitting out the rain. Despite their non-chalance, it's utterly unlikely they've ever before used a person as a foot-stool. In their world, a human head is a very rare thing. As we're playing statue to their pigeon impersonation, putting them on a pedestal, I gingerly hand Brad my water-resistant camera. Chris and I say, "Sooteee," and the shutter enshrines us as bird-brains.

We watch the lime-green water for signs of a dark shape. Chris says it can't be long now. But it's starting to seem as if there isn't a shark for miles.

Brad chugs a big mouthful of peanuts straight out of the bottle. Cheeks bulging like a chipmunk, he suddenly stands up, pointing. It sounds like he's trying to say "Shark."

It's a turtle.

Time and tide wait for no one, but the sharks are at their leisure; they've got time to kill. We decide to travel along the reef, listening for chirps from the cooler.

The cooler keeps quiet. Chris says, "Suddenly the atoll seems very big. Our shark could be anywhere here. It could be at the pinnacle, it could be at Disappearing Island, down at the Gins, Tern Island, Trig—"

Brad interrupts. "About the only place it can't be is Shark Island. They tell me they never see sharks there."

We go back at anchor, practicing the virtue of patience. In its over-head journey the sun becomes less a companion than a circling oppo-nent. The tops of Brad's thighs are getting red in the sun. Chris now has a blue windbreaker spread over his legs. I've worn my rain jacket this whole sizzling day, to keep the sun off my arms. In an all-day affair here, the sun kisses with hot lips. Even for a Mediterranean olive like myself, the sunshine here can be brutal. Despite the sunblock, my arms have turned mahogany-toned, and today my legs are getting burned. I tuck my knees up under my loose jacket.

While the sun burns upon us at this spot, shower curtains are slither-ing in the distant sky, the clouds trailing rain like jellyfish trail their ten-tacles. Soon dark streaks of rain envelope us, blotting out the horizon. The squall's gusting wind and rain motivate the island's young alba-trosses into a burst of activity. They revel in weather we usually revile. All along the berm you can see them flapping their big dark wings. Today a lot more of the huge chicks are down on the beach. One of them gets up in the air repeatedly. On each flapping leap it is spending longer in the air, getting more lift, more hang time in the wind. So fast is it learning that we're actually watching it getting better and better. Another albatross gets up and a gust of wind blows it over backward. It thrashes upside down in the sand for a good minute, wings splayed, unable to right itself. It sprays sand around until finally it rolls over. Almost immediately it jumps up into the air again.

The National Geographic Television crew arrives at a little past noon. With them is Shiway, who is using her day off in hopes of seeing a Tiger Shark. Bill Mills gets into our boat with his camera gear. Unfortunately, so does the basket of all-too-familiar bird carcasses, with which they are only too happy to part.

"Couldn't you get anything that's slightly less dead?"

"We looked; couldn't find any."

The smell from dead albatrosses that have been in the sun for days overtakes our boat. The stench is truly sickening. They're unbelievably putrid. But putrefaction in itself is interesting; the question is, Why do bacteria *putrefy* a carcass instead of just eating it up without ruining it first? It might be the bacteria's adaptation, whereby bacteria lay claim to the whole thing so other animals don't devour it—and them. Alternative hypothesis: the smell of bacteria-occupied meat is something we perceive as revolting so we won't eat it; it's our *own* adaptation for avoiding eating something containing potentially dangerous microbes.

Counteracting the stink, a rainbow emerges, growing vivid across the sky. One sense recoils, the other delights. Could any possible sky on any possible planet under any other heaven ever feel more like home? Could any hell smell as bad? Brad puts the bird basket over the side, which helps.

Soon two smallish Gray Reef Sharks, about four and a half feet long, come darting around the basket.

Shiway puts on her mask and leans over the side of the boat with just her head in the water. She has a little waterproof camera.

Chris calls over, saying, "You can slip into the water. It's O.K.; they won't bother you."

Shiway is reluctant.

Chris says again, "Go ahead and get some pictures; they won't hurt you." She leans very far over, until her feet are way up in the air, but she can't bring herself to take that final plunge.

Brad slides over the side of our boat wearing a mask. He begins following the sharks as they swim between our boats.

I too slip into the water. Following our example, Shiway enters the sea. The two Gray Reef Sharks are orbiting below, staying near the bottom. We swim above them, admiring their grace and glide. We know we have nothing to fear—probably.

Chris calls, "Don't pester them too much. Watch out for posturing. If you see the pectoral fins drop, the back arch, and they start swimming in exaggerated S-curves, they're saying you're too close. Then you've got about five seconds to back off. That happened to a friend of ours. One bite and a chunk of his forearm was missing."

Brad comes back into the boat about three minutes later.

Chris says, "Did they display at all?"

Brad says, "One of them started to drop its fins and turn on its side until I stopped following it."

Greg calls, "Were you harassing those poor sharks?"

When one shark approaches, Shiway huddles next to the boat. I can hear her giggling nervously through her snorkel. Chris, grinning, says, "That's something she'll write home about."

AFTER ABOUT TWENTY MINUTES the Gray Reef Sharks have vanished. Chris, rolling up his jacket under his head, reclines on the rear bench. Birget calls, "We could shoot a sequence showing the boredom."

Intending to doze for a minute in the bottom of the boat, I fall into the kind of dense sleep from which you awake with no sense of how much time has elapsed. I wake because I hear Brad say, "Here she comes." A Gray Reefer is back around the boat and we watch it awhile.

Then very suddenly the dark shape of a big Tiger Shark appears about fifty yards off our stern. How could such a large, dangerous animal sneak up on all of us so closely? Its capacity for stealth alone makes it dangerous. The receiver's silence informs us that this is a new animal.

Chris says, "Wow—*that's* a big one."

It looks twelve feet. Our mingled tingles of fear, riveted attention, and awed curiosity of large animals can hardly have changed much since before the dawn of human time.

Brad puts a transmitter into a bird and floats it out about fifty yards. Everyone watches expectantly. Shiway, excited, has her little camera ready.

Silent as a cloud shadow, the shark makes one pass about twenty feet behind the bird on the line, then circles out about a hundred yards against the light green flats. It comes with unbelievable slowness, yet inexorably, it does come. The Tiger takes fully five minutes to work its way back up toward the bait. About ten yards behind the bird it turns, slowly going on another wide foray. Even though the underwater visibility is only about twenty-five feet for us, the shark seems somehow to know exactly where the quietly bobbing carcass is from distances of one hundred yards or so. It approaches the tethered bait in unerring straight lines. Again it comes, then turns away. Like a slow-motion dream, the Tiger seems almost to be drifting along, taking minutes to complete each circle.

Chris says, "Most people think Tiger Sharks are always mean and very aggressive. But they're usually quite shy."

This one certainly seems so. It has not come near the boat, hasn't attempted to bite the bait. The closest it comes on the next pass is about thirty yards behind the bait.

On the next approach the somnambulant Tiger comes straight up behind the carcass. Its fin shears the surface and the big square head emerges. And that mouth opens.

Brad pulls the bird. The idea is to draw the shy shark close enough for Bill to get some underwater footage. But it seems reluctant to come nearer. Rather than follow the bird it swings out about forty yards, taking more minutes to come around for another pass, then circles out again.

The waiting is excruciating.

Chris says, "If she comes back, we probably have one last chance for giving her the transmitter."

Approaching at the speed of a drifting log, the shark comes back and bites down firmly on the dead albatross. It shakes its head once, throwing white water. It releases the bird. The surface of the water is now speckled with feathers. Chris says, "She shouldn't be this finicky. Something's bothering her. She's disturbed."

I point out that our bait is rotten.

Now another big shark approaches. Our receiver informs us that this is Shark One, newly arrived. Chris observes, "She's where she was yesterday at this same time." The chirping on the machine intensifies, like the ticking of Captain Hook's clock-eating crocodile. Shark One also shadows the bait and then turns off.

Another large nontransmittered shark appears in the lagoon, headed very slowly in our direction in a zigzagging course.

Chris says enthusiastically, "This is an important finding. It shows that this area is used repeatedly and routinely, and that Tiger Sharks' activity space can be shared, rather than exclusively defended."

Shared, yes; but we sense competition. The last-arrived Tiger takes the bait, swallowing the transmitter. We begin following this shark along the reef. For a while, Shark One joins it, and both sharks move into very shallow water on the north end of the island. With bellies brushing the bottom and fins out into the air, they're investigating a dead turtle on the beach. When Shark One leaves, Shark Two continues prowling the shoreline. She catches the scent of a dead bird that is rolling in the wash, being pushed up on the sand by the lapping waves. Our big shark can't get in shallow enough to make the grab. As she circles back out into deeper water and goes out of sight we continue following the chirps from the transmitter.

Chris, fascinated with the sharks' activities, says, "A lot of people think sharks are stupid. They're not stupid."

Brad winks. "Don't believe him."

Chris persists. "Sharks are like people. They go to enormous lengths to get something they want, and if they find it but can't get it, they keep searching for what they need." He pauses a moment and adds, "It's a shame people don't understand that we're not so different from other animals."

I wonder about the similarity between sharks and us. We name things based on differences, and sometimes similarities go unseen. There is a bird in the stomach of the shark we are following. Soon, the molecules that miraculously made a bird will recombine as shark muscle that will hunt birds. So what *is* an individual? Who *are* we? *What* are we? At times the everyday incomprehensibility of it seems utterly dumbfounding. Embedded in mystery within miracle, how is it that daily life ever seems short of sheer magic?

The native Hawaiians certainly have felt close to sharks. I wonder if, in their veneration of sharks as guardians, they saw things in them we're missing—and vice versa; in our fascination with sharks as animals, we certainly see things that ancients overlooked. But how similar can humans and sharks be in our experience of the world? With no parental care, no bonding, their emotional lives must differ considerably. Do sharks feel love or compassion? Almost certainly not. But consider the range of loves people have. We use the same word, *love,* to say "I love my child"—an emotion sharks can't feel—and to say "I love food"—an emotion sharks almost certainly share in the sheer physical satisfaction of eating. A strange and confused concept we have of love, using one word to cover such a multitude of needs, wants, desires, indulgences, preferences, pleasures, passions, compassions, and ideals. You'd expect we'd have at least as many words for love as Eskimos supposedly have for snow. But we don't. So while there is a lot that sharks are missing about love, it seems that perhaps people have a long way to go yet, too.

Often when confronted with otherness, we assign a name and assume that's all we need to know; we make our summary judgment and apply this typecast to a whole race of beings. And in doing so we overlook almost everything there is. Perhaps if we instead look further and deeper, and be patient, the world will begin revealing itself, at a rate matching our openness and willingness to receive.

In this contemplative tone, we the people follow our thoughts, while letting the beeps from the unseen entity called "shark"—whatever that truly means—take us where they lead. Are sharks, as Chris says, "like people"? We are here because we are curious about these sharks. For Chris to be right, sharks would have to be curious about us.

Suddenly the signal cuts out. Then as unexpectedly, the signal comes in so strong that Chris can't determine the direction it's coming from. He says, "Wow, this shark must be *very* close."

I'm sitting on the cooler facing the rear of the boat when a huge dark shadow comes up almost to the engine, moving quickly and seeming agitated. It abruptly veers off, making a deep boil on the surface. Brad says, "*Whoooa!* I've never seen one do *that* before!" The sea's disguise conveys a perfect ability to startle; to ambush with delight or amazement or terror.

Suddenly there's a big square snout traveling just behind the engine's prop wash. And a big fin following us.

The trackers have become the tracked.

> ≻ ≻ ≻ ≻ ≻ ≻ ≻ ≻ ≻ ≻ ≻ ≻ ≻ ≻

HOME AMONG NOMADS

SOON AFTER SUNDOWN, when only the brightest stars have come onstage, the first Green Turtle appears in the surf wash. In Hawaiian she is called *Honu*. She moves in the solemn slowness of her own time. She has been doing this for 150 million years.

It seems fitting that someone so old should now claim her piece of the future. But she appears reluctant to leave home, even for a few hours. A female Green Turtle will swim the seas for twenty-five years before her first breeding. How alien and laborious it must feel, after all that duration and endurance, to emerge as never before onto dry land, and experience for the first time the weight of your own body, and struggle up the beach, where every movement is full of friction and heaviness and pressure, these things you've never felt before. Even an experienced turtle remains in the sea for several years between nesting attempts. Our *Honu* is hesitating to make that momentous transition from the fluid float of water to the stranding alienation of land. She turns away, and the waves cover her tracks in the sea.

Hours pass. Meanwhile, enveloping darkness reinforces the resolve of egg-bearing turtles. Now is the peak of a nesting season that starts in April and will run through September. For those readying to lay, the night blackness intensifies their mysterious motivation to enter the strange and difficult world of air, to undergo the ordeal of bringing forth new life.

Sometime near midnight, Julie Rocho is belly-down on the beach, her hand over the front of a flashlight, allowing just a little bit of brightness to escape through her fingers. The night sea wind is blowing her hair from the edges of her kerchief. I kneel.

The turtle Julie's watching has excavated a body-sized pit and dug a remarkable, almost perfectly cylindrical egg chamber about a foot wide and half again as deep. Her wind-dried shell looks dull. She has a small, grape-sized tumor at the base of her tail.

Every twenty seconds or so, her shell and tail dip down, her rear flippers flex inward just slightly, and she sighs with exertion. With each labored squeeze, two or three eggs fall from her. The gleaming eggs—a bit leathery, coated with mucus—look like large Ping-Pong balls. As minutes pass, her eggs pile up in the exquisite chamber.

What perception, what emotion, has made her do this? Does she have a suddenly irresistible yearning; is she somehow smitten with the urge to feel solid land beneath her stiff shell? What *feeling* draws her first to these faraway islands, then inexorably up and onto the beach, to exhaust herself digging and pressing her body into the sand, to lay eggs she will never even see, bearing young she will never know?

Only about half the Green Turtles that ascend a nesting beach will actually lay eggs that night. They'll keep emerging on other nights, and eventually each female will lay about four times in her season, about one hundred eggs at a time. Then she'll abstain from nesting for about three years.

When we've been lying with her half an hour, the turtle pauses for a couple of minutes. Now she moves very slowly forward, just a little. Using her rear flippers she begins gently mounding and patting loose sand over her eggs; a move Julie calls "patty-caking." Her rear flippers are surprisingly nimble and sensitive, working deftly, like hands in mittens.

She rests a few minutes, then continues the patty-caking. She seems a tired beast. Julie yawns. I notice a meteor. A frigatebird flies slowly by, in dark silhouette.

Twenty minutes later, our big turtle suddenly shifts gears, seemingly filled with a new energy. She's beginning the final phase of nest completion: filling in the entire body pit. Her first three long, powerful, flinging strokes lift so much sand that much of it lands far past the great depression she's trying to fill.

Everything about a turtle seems slow and measured except its efforts in digging. She is chopping into the ground as though swimming into the sands. Her front flippers, biting in vigorously like propellers, are snapping to the power stroke, slapping her shell startlingly. Each snap showers us with sand and small stones. When her flippers strike a large coral chunk, her nail and scales produce a sound that sends shivers, like a shovel scraping along a rock. After a few tries against this obstacle she stops chopping and rests. Resolute, but not foolish, she pivots for softer purchase. She is working with much exertion. She's making an energetic chop with her foreflippers every two to five seconds, then after a set of about three to five such chops she's spending half a minute to a minute resting.

Julie says, "Everything together usually takes around two hours; making the body pit, digging the egg chamber, laying, patty-caking, and backfilling. But we see turtles up longer than that, because—I don't know—they're picky. They do a lot of digging and moving before they finally decide on a spot to nest. Or sometimes afterward, they're so exhausted they fall asleep. I've seen them stay sleeping all night."

Seeking shelter from the wind and the path of flying sand, we move into an abandoned body pit. I raise my hood against the damp sea breeze. Julie's sitting with her legs pulled up and her arms around her shins, resting her head on her knees. I ask if she's warm enough. She says yes, but she seems chilly. Slowed to turtle time, we continue our sleepy vigil under a sky crowded with stars.

At one A.M., our turtle has moved slightly forward and is now pivoting a bit, seemingly trying to level out her job. Each phase in the complex, exacting nesting must satisfy some unknowable, motivating sensation to correctly perform different motions and tasks, in the right sequence. Something in her experience of reality makes her want to spend herself with such exertion, but it's all done by feel; she never visually inspects her work.

Half a moon emerges from the warm sea as though coming from a naked swim, and starts its pale ascent among light clouds. Moonlight floods the night enough to throw long shadows. It puts a silver outline to the contours of her shell and flippers and head. She continues chopping, thrusting, chopping, thrusting, filling her pit. And in between, she rests, and rests again. Out in the surrounding night, unseen shearwaters are moaning, unseen terns calling overhead. The rhythmic surf breaking. Our minds unwinding.

Taking much longer pauses now, she seems enfeebled with exhaustion. Some of her flipper thrusts are mere waves of her arms. Other thrusts, with gathered strength, still pelt us with pebbles, but now she follows each thrust or two with multiminute rests. I hadn't realized turtle nesting was this complicated, this arduous.

In this remote corner of night's run, one night-darkened albatross exercises in the moonlight. But most albatrosses are asleep. Julie, having pulled on some extra clothing from her pack, now lies in the fetal position, in the abandoned turtle pit, down out of the wind, likewise asleep. The turtle pauses longer, then also seems to doze off.

We are all adrift in a dream, in our souls all ancient nomads wandering a great sea, hoping to navigate to some safe harbor, some protected shoreline halfway between eternities; wishing to come at last to a good place, a haven from the troubled world, to rest our burden softly, to bring time to a halt and pass into a deep, secure repose; to feel, "You belong right here, you have done well, and for a while, you can rest."

Though the breeze may be blustery, it cannot sweep away the moonbeams. At two A.M., Julie rouses yawningly. We decide to move on. Let the sleeping turtle wake in her own moonlit solitude and drag herself to the water in her own ancient time.

WE MAY DREAM with the turtle, but the real effort here is trying to understand why sea turtles are suffering strange new tumors. When Hawaii's Green Turtles found their name entered under the Endangered Species Act, in 1978, the main listed threats to survival included egg collecting, hunting, hatchlings' disorientation by artificial lighting on beaches, and by-kill in fisheries. No one thought of tumors.

Someone had found a Green Turtle suffering external tumors in Florida in 1938. But the new disease—fibropapilloma—remained rare until the mid-1980s. Since then, this "Elephant Man–like disease," as it's been called, has become increasingly common. Now about 10 percent of these turtles suffer from tumors, and in certain places the percentage is much higher. In Kaneohe Bay near Honolulu, for instance, more than half the turtles carry tumors. Other hot spots exist in Hawaii, and in Florida, Indonesia, and Australia. The disease, first noticed in Greens, now affects several sea turtle species in every ocean.

The tumors can, over time, grow large enough to interfere with swimming or eating. Some turtles get hit by boats because their vision is impaired by tumors growing near their eyes. Fibropapilloma is now the most common cause of death in Hawaiian Green Turtles. It kills mostly immature animals. It rarely goes into remission. Its exact cause remains uncertain, but turtles in more polluted waters suffer more tumors.

Ninety percent of all Hawaii's Green Turtles migrate hundreds of miles here to French Frigate Shoals to breed, making it an excellent place for research. One nesting turtle tagged here in 1982 returned a couple of years later and was found here again in the mid-1990s. At that time, scientists fitted her with a transmitter before she went back to sea. For the next month the turtle voyaged mostly out of sight of land, over waters miles deep, and against prevailing winds and currents. During this trek, she averaged one mile an hour. Slow and steady. Eventually she arrived in Kahului Bay on the Maui coast, seven hundred miles from French Frigate Shoals.

The convergence of turtles at French Frigate Shoals from so far and wide makes this an extremely important breeding colony. Female sea turtles almost always lay their eggs on the same shore where they were born decades earlier. This fidelity to place of birth was originally a way of increasing the survival chances for their own young, gifting the eggs and nestlings with the advantage of starting life on a proven beach. Such faithfulness now makes turtles vulnerable to egg gatherers and meat hunters. Turtles have always had predators to contend with, but only humans are systematic and numerous enough to wipe out entire breeding colonies. On Laysan and Lisianski people have killed more turtles than nest there today. This may well account for the disproportional number at French Frigate Shoals. When hunters completely destroy a nesting population, reestablishment may take a thousand years; no one really knows how long because it's never happened. Hundreds of years is apparently not enough turtle time; turtles have never recolonized rookeries wiped out in the last two hundred years, including Bermuda in the Atlantic and the Caribbean's enormous Cayman Islands population.

The Cayman Green Turtle rookery was probably the largest that ever existed. Parts of the Caribbean at that time were so full of turtles we cannot really picture it today. Christopher Columbus's second voyage, in 1493, brought this impression of turtle numbers: "in those twenty leagues . . . the sea was thick with them . . . so numerous that it seemed that the ships would run aground on them and were as if bathing in them." During Columbus's fourth voyage Ferdinand Columbus described the Cayman Islands as "two very small and low islands, full of turtles, as was all the sea about, so that they looked like little rocks." He saw the islands full of turtles during the daytime, as we see today only in the Norwest Hawaiian Islands. Of a part of the Caribbean during the 1600s, one Edward Long wrote, "It is affirmed, that vessels, which have lost their latitude in hazy weather, have steered entirely by the noise which these creatures make in swimming." Recent calculations have estimated the original Cayman Green Turtle population at several million animals. Yet even the Cayman nation was exterminated, never to regroup.

Each existing breeding beach, each remaining population, therefore, is a distinct world treasure. The entire Hawaiian turtle population is geographically isolated and rather small; each year about five hundred female Greens go to nest at French Frigate Shoals, out of a population of about two thousand adult females living throughout all the islands. The good news is that the number of nesters has slowly risen, roughly doubling since the 1970s. Up till then, commercial hunting was depleting the population. Hawaiian restaurants served Green Turtle as recently as the 1970s, and the turtles' current upward trend reflects the hunting ban. The Hawaii turtle population enjoys the rare privilege of being effectively protected from most human predation *and* not subjected to drowning in shrimp nets; both things kill many turtles elsewhere. (There's no shrimp fishery in Hawaii, but Hawaiian turtles aren't entirely free of fishery problems—some die on longlines.) French Frigate Shoals enjoys the rare distinction of welcoming turtles nesting in *increasing* numbers, going from moribund to more abundant.

Responding to the news of increases, some people in Hawaii want to start killing turtles. Tumors or not, for certain people it's a matter of tradtional culture. One native Hawaiian fisherman, William Aila, was quoted in a Honolulu paper saying, "I can remember my uncles catching turtles and my aunties preparing them. But that has been lost over several generations."

Call me insensitive, but better we lose the recipes than the turtles. Let's realize that the world has changed and how we've crowded it, and how difficult it has become for animals like turtles. Let's make it our new cultural tradition to be able to afford to leave some things alone, to respect and protect some space for older beings, and to think that sea turtles are more deliciously savored by seeing them *alive* rather than in a bubbling, troubling stew. But even without hunting, the tumor disease is quite serious. The biggest question is: are these tumors now killing enough turtles, or depressing reproduction enough, to drive turtle populations down again?

DURING THE DAY the only sign of the "turtle people" is last night's footprints in the beach sand, astride the turtle tracks. They each take turns walking the beach every two hours from sunset till dawn, to locate nesting turtles coming ashore only during darkness. The rest of the team sits up in the barracks all night, waiting alongside the walkie-talkies for a call that says the beachwalker has found a new tumor-bearing turtle and needs help. This research entails long hours of boredom punctuated by irregular bouts of exhausting work. The boredom gets filled with videos and silliness—Julie and Aaron Dietrich have braided each other's hair—and talk. These all-night vigils are the only time to get to know the turtle crew, which, in addition to Julie, includes Aaron, Vanessa Pepi, and Nick Nickerson. If you're awake with them, you learn to avoid the kitchen in the dark unless you're fond of flying cockroaches just slightly smaller than skateboards. Either you will step on one while barefoot, or one will fly across the room and hit you—usually in the face.

Right now, Julie is preparing to circumambulate the island, gathering her radio and a snack, and stuffing her hair under her kerchief. She's just had the plaits taken out, leaving her with crimps. Julie jokes, "Yeah, every four days or so I'm going to try a new look." She closes her eyes and pulls on the ends of her hair in a gesture of mock glamour. Julie's another of the many army brats that have wandered their way to these islands. In her two dozen years, she's seen the landscapes of Korea, Italy, Alaska, Virginia, Kansas, Michigan, and Hawaii. "There're a few other places I've lived; but I can't remember." Her job experience is similarly wide-ranging. She's worked in Alaska rehabilitating hawks and eagles injured by everything from airplanes to leg-hold traps, tracked Hawaiian Hawksbill Turtles, and worked for a zoo that sent her into nursing homes. "It's amazing to see the therapeutic effects animals have on people. Many of the residents couldn't even feed themselves, and then they'd stroke a bunny and their face would transform." After earning her bachelor's degree in natural sciences, she thought she was done with volunteering, but she couldn't resist the opportunity to come to Tern Island for a four-month stint last fall. "I loved it—*loved* it." Now she's been hired to help study the turtles, and has arranged to get her master's degree simultaneously. She walks out the doorway and vanishes into the bird-loud night.

Our job now is just to wait, in case she finds a tumored turtle. And so the evening melts along. Vanessa plops onto the couch, and I notice her fondness for asymmetry: one painted fingernail (her left pinkie, painted deep red) and three gold rings in one ear, one in another. She has long, sandy-blond hair and blue eyes. She's also led a peregrine existence: born in Germany, she attended elementary school in Utah, junior high school in Washington State, and high school in Wisconsin. "For the past two years, I haven't really been *living* anywhere—mostly these remote islands." Now twenty-nine, she's also here as a graduate student and field assistant on the government-funded study comparing turtles with and without tumors to see if they differ in body condition and contaminant loads, and comparing their eggs' fat and protein composition and hatching success. One other aspect of the studies is to see whether turtles actually *gain* contaminants here at French Frigate Shoals, due to pollutants like PCBs leaching from old military matériel.

Also here is Nick Nickerson, an unusually senior (but new) member of the field crew, closing in on fifty and trying to engineer a new career. Another military brat, he grew up in Japan, Seattle, Florida, then Georgia. Nick wanted to be a marine biologist since the second grade, and he took that aspiration to college. But when his father was hospitalized, he quit school to help his mother. *That* cost him his draft deferment, and he was compelled to join the military; forced to abandon Mom to defend apple pie. Eventually he did become a marine biologist, surveying shrimp and crab abundance in Georgia waters, mapping seabeds, and managing a national marine sanctuary. "I really liked the work. But I just started getting itchy." He scratched that itch by moving to the Hawaiian island of Kauai, where, as an ordained minister with an honorary doctorate in divinity—all accomplished via mail with the Universal Life Church out of California—he began performing commercial weddings.

Aaron Dietrich is a youthfully sinewy, ponytailed and bearded blond twenty-seven-year-old whose body adornments include a ring through his left nipple and, on his shoulder, a large, tastefully drawn tattoo with the image of a sea turtle: "Turtle is my *'aumakua,* my spirit guardian. I feel a special connection." Aaron was raised in Utah and Colorado. After high school he went to the Big Island of Hawaii, where he worked with his father—an artist who sculpts molten lava—for half a dozen years. "Interesting work: we would scoop the lava into wooden molds while it was still two thousand degrees. By the time the lava cooled, the wood was gone, leaving a burned surface texture." Aaron entered the University of Hawaii but quit a year short of his degree. He worked two summers salmon fishing in Alaska. "At the beginning it was exciting, partly because dealing with anything in large volume can be exciting. But killing so many fish really got to me after a while. And there were other things I found disturbing—like captains and crew shooting at sea lions. I realized that I like biology more than anything; so now I'm back in school."

The sudden crackle of Julie's voice over the walkie-talkie startles us. She's found a turtle with tumors, on the south beach. Vanessa, Aaron, Nick, and I strike out. The beach looks like a thin light ribbon separating the black sea from the black land, under a cloud-blackened sky. My eyes begin adjusting to the dark as we walk the narrow wedge of beach at the water's edge. We walk past driftwood branches draped with roosting frigatebirds and boobies. And it's not always easy in the dark to tell the seals from drift logs. We give each the benefit of the doubt and a wide berth. An occasional phosphorescent jellyfish lights up in our footsteps in the wave-washed sand.

The tiny silent runners directly in our path on the beach are crabs abroad from daytime burrows. Vanessa says, "When the nests hatch out in a couple of months, the hatchling turtles will come up at night. That helps them avoid frigatebirds, but these ghost crabs will happily kill and devour them." About 80 percent of turtle eggs hatch. Hatchlings suffer horrifying mortality. Over the course of a life spanning fifty years, a female might nest in about eight seasons, laying thirty times, a lifetime total of three thousand eggs. Assuming there are as many males as females, a stable population requires that only two survive.

ONE BIG GREEN TURTLE—this one a male—is in our path, lying on the beach asleep. No animal looks more a geological feature, an outcrop of life. In fact, it's difficult to imagine anything *deader* looking than a sleeping sea turtle. The first time you see one you'll swear all life has left it. A wave catches the sleeping beast and the outwash begins sinking the creature's drooped head and splayed flippers into the sand. Sand begins burying its mouth—and still the eyelids droop. Finally, as if only to prove it lives—and thereby underscoring how unlifelike it seems—it lifts its eyes-closed head and inhales. You'll grow uncomfortable waiting for a sleeping turtle to take a breath. Don't hold yours. They breathe about once every ten minutes. When they do, it'll be a big gulp. The head will rise reflexively, because in a turtle's oceanic world air is always above you, breath always something you must reach for.

We walk around behind him, continuing for another quarter mile. When we meet Julie and the turtle she has found—also male—all talk is in whispers. We drop our equipment, then huddle, deciding a strategy of approach. Julie explains that this turtle has a small tumor on his neck. He also appears to have a couple of very small white growths in the corners of his eyes; these may become tumors. She whispers, "Most turtle tumors appear around the head and neck because that's where most of the soft tissue is."

Vanessa softly says, "A lot are in the eyes, on the shoulders, in the jaw—"

Aaron and Vanessa walk toward the turtle, which is about four and a half feet long. The animal is dry, not at all wet. His shell looks amazingly tough, thick, and rather rigid—almost mineralized. The skin-to-shell connection is very solid. Large scales on the flippers and head lessen the visual contrast between skin and shell. The skin itself is leathery, yet soft. What's really remarkable is how even the scaliest part of the flippers seem soft. Even his meaty, prehensile tail—a foot long, nearly five inches in diameter at the base and thirteen inches around—is soft; I can easily feel the bony vertebral structure through it. His eyes are wet with tears, adding to his lugubrious sense of melancholy, but the tears are just to keep sand from his eyes. The turtle's head is about the size of a softball. The tumor growing from his neck is olive-sized.

I ask whether the tumors are hard or soft. Aaron whispers, "They tend to be pretty soft and doughy." He touches it.

I do the same. It feels fleshy, about the consistency of a grape.

Julie whispers, "This tumor looks new, and very vascular. A lot of times they're just kind of bloody because they're so big they get scraped on things. They usually look pretty raw. But this one is dry."

Aaron suddenly volunteers to me, "There's no real danger in touching them, but they often involve a herpes virus—so don't touch your face. You'll want to go back to the barracks and scrub your hands with antibacterial soap later."

I'm no pathologist, but I know two things: one, herpes viruses are nasty and can be unpredictably contagious; and two, antibacterial soap has no effect against viruses. And now I feel very uncomfortable about my possibly contaminated hand. I wash it in an oncoming wave, then scour it with beach sand. Perhaps I'm being a bit of a hypochondriac. But if you can't be a hypochondriac about touching strange, not fully explained wild-animal tumors that you've just been told could possibly transmit an infection to you, what can you be a hypochondriac about? I suddenly have a Beatles lyric running circles in my mind: "Hold you in his armchair you can feel his disease. / Come together / Right now / Over me." I realize I've gained a more intimate sense of this creature's affliction, odd though that seems.

They place their net on the sand before the turtle, then tap him to prompt him to chug forward onto it. This done, they gather the wide edges of the net atop the turtle's shell, then lock the net into place with a carabiner. Encased in netting, the turtle is thus largely immobilized. But he is awake, and exceedingly powerful. He struggles but makes no attempt to bite. Aaron places a hood over the animal's eyes to calm him, and sits holding his big head. He whispers to me, "This is a special part of my job. There's a real specific technique of pressing your palms against their eyes very, very lightly—really gently—that makes them relax.

And to have them react to you by going almost totally limp and calm—that's a very neat feeling."

Julie opens an equipment kit and hands Vanessa a spray bottle filled with Betadine disinfectant. Vanessa washes away some sand with water and applies the disinfectant to the base of the turtle's neck, right where it meets the body. On the neck itself the skin is quite soft. She carefully palpates the skin, then inserts a needle fully, pulls it out partially, and inserts it a little farther, looking for the right spot. No blood comes. Without withdrawing it from the skin, she pulls the needle up and pushes it back in three times. Each attempt is a dry well.

I'm cringing at the sight of the needle going up and down, but the turtle is not acting as though it feels any pain. With Aaron holding him, he is staying quite calm.

A bit exasperated, Vanessa removes the syringe, goes to the other side of the neck, palpates, sticks, and draws. Now the blood begins coming slowly but evenly into the syringe.

The blood will be analyzed for the comparison of chemical contamination between turtles with and without tumors. In a couple of months, after the nests hatch, they'll dig out the remains of eggs laid by females with and without tumors, to compare how many hatched and how many didn't. The blood will also be analyzed to see if it contains vitellogenin, a protein indicating the presence of eggs. If it's found in *males*, it shows that chemical contaminants like PCBs, DDT, and less familiar sounding compounds have been functioning in the animal's body as mimics of female hormones. In offspring this can interfere with normal embryo development, sometimes causing individuals to be born "intersex"—half male, half female, a problem increasingly found in wildlife, and people, in various parts of the world.

There are many sounds in the night here: the waves and the birds, an occasional seal snort, the Bulwer's Petrels like little hooting owls. And though it's not quiet, all speaking—*all* speaking—remains whispered, making it almost impossible to hear unless you are close to a person who's talking directly to you.

About every two minutes, this turtle breathes. With each inspiration of breath, his entire shell rises. The deep occasional sighs with which he exhales sound labored. Weightless and winged as they are in water, sea turtles must feel unbearably heavy on land. He seems ineffably sad and tired, as though carrying the weight of the world. Hearing his breathing, it is easy to believe the mythology that a great turtle holds up the Earth.

With the blood drawn, Julie injects a tiny coded-wire tag in each of the animal's rear flippers. From now on, this animal's identity can be ascertained by merely waving the electronic wand.

Nick and Aaron have set up their large, heavy-duty, ten-foot tripod. Fully opened, it's big enough to frame a small tepee. They place it directly over the turtle. There is a type of lever-operated winch called a "come-along" rigged at the tripod's apex. It's stuck. It seems to be jammed with sand. Vanessa steps gingerly up on the turtle's shell, using the creature like a stepstool to get to the top of the tripod. Aaron says, "I like working with animals sturdy enough to put your weight on without hurting them." Vanessa has some trouble getting the tool to work, but finally gets it freed and lowers its strap to the turtle. She attaches a weighing scale and hooks the scale into the net. Nick starts pumping the come-along handle, and suddenly the turtle begins levitating over the sand.

The sky opens a little, liberating a few stars. The shrouded moon, waiting in the wings for its chance at another appearance, lights the outlines of some broken clouds.

This turtle weighs 230 pounds. Julie whispers in my ear, "We've seen some under two hundred, others over three." Julie's massive calipers tell us that the shell itself is 97 centimeters, a little over three feet long. The shell width is 76.7 centimeters, about two and a half feet wide. Aaron takes a portable handheld router and in a couple of strokes etches the number 11 on the shell, then sprays a little bit of paint over the number and wipes the shell.

While Julie is still transferring the blood samples into smaller vials, Nick, Vanessa, and Aaron lower the turtle, unclip the carabiner, and loosen the net. The turtle begins tractoring down the beach almost immediately. He stops near the water's edge as though trying to remember what his original motives were. The turtle walks into the sea until only his tracks remain on land. But in addition to tracks, he leaves us clues to his condition and the health of the overall population.

Another turtle, much smaller, begins crawling onto the beach fifty feet from us like a bright, shining amphibious unit, newly arrived upon the beachhead, still awash in the wavelets massaging the shore. Julie checks with her light. This turtle has a small number 48 near the rear of her shell. Julie waves her magic wand across her rear flippers, and the magnetic tag number comes up on her little screen. She says to me, "She's had everything done already. She's probably coming up to lay eggs."

We continue walking down the beach. Right now, we're looking only for tumored turtles that haven't already been tagged this season. If one has been tagged before, we just note who it is. If it has tumors and has not been worked on before, the team does its medical sampling.

The next turtle is another untagged male asleep on the beach, not quite beyond the reach of the highest breaking wave. This one has an unusually deformed, highly domed shell with a big concave dent running almost the whole length of one side. It has no tumor. We move on.

Fifty yards farther we come upon two more turtles, dry and dozy, separated by a few yards. They're completely quiet, heads down in the sand, utterly immobile. Neither has any tumors. Both are just resting.

The tracks of nesting turtles go past the beach, up beyond the berm, into the brush. They've done some quite impressive bulldozing up under the bushes where the birds are roosting. Julie follows one fresh track that goes over the berm, scanning with the flashlight for the turtle. There she is: she's dug a body pit but has not laid any eggs. She's calm and quiescent and still. We check to see if she needs to be sampled later when she's finished her mission. But she has no tumors. We leave her.

A few stars are shining in the south and overhead, and there's enough moisture to create little halos around them, like in Vincent van Gogh's *Starry Night*. In the north, clouds cloak the horizon and lightning flashes every few minutes. The overall sense is of being on a speck of sand in a vast sea on a mysterious planet suspended in a great galaxy.

Up ahead, another male, more heavily tumored, lies on the beach, sleeping. When Aaron and Nick attempt to stimulate him onto the net, he doesn't wake. They tap his shell and gently pull his tail. Yet he remains in resolute repose as though disembodied and departed. So they simply pull him up onto the net by his flippers. Still the turtle slumbers. Aaron and Julie work to clip the net in place.

This turtle has a tumor the size of a plum on his neck, plus a larger, knobby one on the right side of his head near the corner of his mouth and *another* knuckly one on the left side of his face.

When Julie inserts the blood-sampling needle, the turtle—now finally awake—tucks his head back. Julie waits a moment, then pulls back slowly on the plunger, and the syringe fills with dark blood.

The exact cause of this disease, and why turtles are now so affected by it, remains debated. Researchers have argued about whether the herpes virus that's involved is a primary infection or a secondary problem. Though the viruses might be the direct cause of tumors on turtles, certain algal and cyanobacterium "blooms"—bursts of rapid reproduction in which so many cells are created that they color the seawater—may set the stage. Some of the blooms produce toxins such as okadaic acid, which promotes tumors in laboratory mice, and lyngbyatoxin, another tumor promoter. Sea turtles seem most beset by tumors in certain semi-enclosed bays and harbors where those toxin-producing organisms now bloom in unusual densities because of pollution.

Aaron points and shows, "Even though tumors usually erupt from the soft fleshy parts, not the surfaces with large scales, this turtle has tumors coming directly out of his face, involving the big scales of his head, as well as the soft scales on his neck."

In slightly better light, I now realize that the tumor on the right side is bigger than I first thought—about the size of a peach. It bulges from his face in an overhanging shape from the mouth, growing over the hinge of the bottom jaw. Seeing so wonderful a creature so disfigured sickens me with sadness.

Julie palpates the tumors with her bare fingers. I'm thinking, Wear examination gloves. Using a U-shaped metal implement, Julie pries open the turtle's jaws. He does not approve of this maneuver. Apparently, turtles don't like dentists. Julie shines her headlamp into the balking animal's mouth and, with much effort, ascertains that the oral interior is clear of tumors.

Julie and Vanessa confer about how to score the tumors in the notebook. They have a classification system according to size: A tumor the diameter of your little finger rates a 1. Larger, up to the size of the circle your fingers form when you make the O.K. sign, is a 2. A 3 is smaller than your fist, and a 4 is larger than your fist.

The team wants biopsy samples of these tumors. Aaron covers and holds the animal's head. Julie switches her headlamp on. With a twisting motion she plunges the biopsy corer into the flesh between the fore-flipper and the neck, right into the small tumor there. The turtle cringes, pulling back and thrusting his net-confined flipper forward in a hunching motion. When Julie goes for a second flesh sample, he again seems to feel this acutely, giving another sharp shrug.

Julie is working with her face very close to the animal. She's precise with her actions. Considering that she's only twenty-four, her confidence is impressive.

This smaller turtle weighs 177 pounds. Nonetheless, he's extremely strong. Even through the netting, he somehow manages to get enough of his flipper dug into the sand to begin traveling down the beach, despite the fact that Aaron and Nick are trying to hold him back. An occasional wave washes up high enough to soak Nick, Aaron, and Julie, who are working at the front of the turtle, trying to measure his body dimensions.

As soon as they're done measuring, they unclip the net and the turtle shoves himself into the dark waves.

I mention to Julie that those tumors horrified me.

She says, "Yeah—and I've seen far, far worse."

Vanessa adds, "The *really* heavily tumored turtles don't come here; we think they don't have enough energy to make it this far."

As we continue on, I'm walking alongside Aaron. He volunteers, "This is a pretty fantastic job, I think. I don't like to be bossed around. I don't like corporate structure. I've seen people abuse authority—which has gotten me in trouble in the past. That's why volunteer work is very appealing. This job is probably the best thing that's ever happened to me. It's going to lead to bigger and better things, and the ability to do more of what I want to do."

When we come upon two more sleeping turtles, Aaron glances quickly at their shells. They've been marked; we don't need any more data from these. A little farther along, Aaron checks an unmarked turtle. He takes care to avoid shining the light in its eyes. Aaron checks carefully around the foreflippers, neck, and head, and under the shell around the rear flippers, working like a mechanic searching knowledgeably under a car. The verdict: clear and clean. We walk on.

About a hundred feet farther down the beach another turtle is lying on the sand. Aaron sweeps his dimmed flashlight to its shell, and I'm startled to see that a big piece of its left hind flipper is missing. The light goes up toward the turtle's head, revealing that the left front flipper is also mostly gone below the wrist, leaving a fleshy, meaty wound. This is a shark attack. Aaron whispers, "This turtle's been here the last few days." The appalling wound looks potentially fatal, because it seems like so much of the turtle's pulling power is gone. Aaron says, "There's been a lot worse that turtles have survived. When we first saw this turtle a few days ago the wounds were extremely fresh, still bleeding. Now the wound on the rear left flipper looks like it's closed up."

But the one on the front left flipper is still meaty and raw. All the flesh is clogged up with sand. It looks awful.

Aaron thinks that if they have the wrist joint they can survive. But he remembers a turtle with an entire foreflipper missing, its shell compressed with starvation. He found it dead a few days later in the same place.

Vanessa says that females with half a back flipper sometimes dig half a nest chamber, or one too shallow. "In that case, they end up scattering their eggs all over during the backfill, making a big omelette."

Julie guesses that about 10 percent of turtles coming ashore have shark bites.

A little farther along, several confused tracks lead up into the berm and back down. Aaron moves along the dark beach, checking into each tuck and cranny in the vegetation with the suppleness of a weasel on the prowl. He sweeps his light. No turtles.

But a minute later, amid lots of heavy tracks going up the beach, Aaron's flashlight catches some sand being thrown. He glances the light at the turtle and says, "That's number fifty digging a body pit. She's been in and out for a couple of weeks."

The moon, now broken clear of any clouds, is casting a wide silver path on the lagoon. In the beauty of that lagoon, turtles are fighting for their lives against everything from predatory monsters to unseen chemicals to tiny viral particles acquired in polluted waters hundreds of miles away.

We come to the end of the beach and step onto the runway. Those of us who have been carrying our flip-flops throw them onto the ground and slip our feet into them. We're back at the dark border of civilization.

⭢ ⭢ ⭢ ⭢ ⭢ ⭢ ⭢ ⭢ ⭢ ⭢ ⭢ ⭢ ⭢ ⭢

LEARNING AND LUCK

*D*URING THE FIRST WEEK of summer Amelia transnavigates the Bering Sea, looping and loping her way to the Pribilof Islands, squeezing between St. Peter and St. Paul, and bumping into the Aleutians' Umnak Island on July 4th, Independence Day in the United States. It is independence day for the chicks who are finally flying, too, and after this revolution comes the real challenge of seeing how well the fledgling nation will survive.

Amelia is also in a sense celebrating her own independence from the rigors of motherhood by wandering, with the single objective—when she has one—of feeding only herself. She has arrived in Albatopia, the promised land. It's a realm of hungry salmon and runaway herring and clouds of baby fishes pressed near the surface by both their fears and their appetites, and squids squeezed into narrow island passes, lusting and dying in the heated passions of the short summer. It's a fat, productive place, where sheer living abundance bursts the broad seam between ocean and land. Amelia lingers a week and a half, practically parking herself, making a slow counterclockwise circle a mere ninety miles in diameter. Just recently, crossing such a distance would have taken her less than a morning. Here she leisurely works the currents and fish schools and the krill swarms where whales are blowing, and she benefits from herring hurt by lunging humpbacks. She shares the view with flocks of sea ducks and skeins of puffins and dolphin pods, all here for the food, like crashers at a wedding feast. And though even here the water is warmer than it used to be and the pickings slimmer than necessary for some of the other kinds of animals, Amelia finds enough fish and squid day after day to fill the bill for an albatross.

. . .

THE TERN ISLAND BIRD team has just completed its final preflight count of albatross chicks. It's been the second bad year running. February's rains, plus El Niño's effects on weather, ocean temperatures, and food abundance, took a mounting toll on nestlings. Add to that: unknown additional mortality to chicks fed plastic debris; adults that simply skipped breeding because food was too sparse; plus other adults killed on long-lines who never returned to feed their chicks.

Fewer than half of the Black-footed chicks remain alive—far below the average 70 percent for both species. For the Laysans, the year's a catastrophe. The several days' difference between the two species' nesting peak made more Laysan chicks vulnerable to the rains. Consequently, the Laysans Albatrosses' experience of the year was quite a bit worse. The Laysans' dismal survival rate is only *eight* chicks per one hundred breeding pairs.

But day by day the survivors are losing that last fuzz of youth, looking more grown-up. We've watched them grow big. We've watched them go from wobbly to standing strongly to walking well. And we've seen them begin exercising their wings. With feet complete and wings waiting, the gift of flight is all that's needed for independence.

Almost daily, we've been visiting East Island. Its albatrosses have the highest survivorship among the atoll's islands, because its elevation was high enough to avoid flooding. Over fifteen thousand chicks are getting set to go. More than ever now, you see them lined up on the beach-top berm, flapping in the breeze like a little wind-energy farm. They're jumping straight up and down as if on trampolines, or running like colts, leaping and flapping, toes leaving the ground.

Urged by appetite, they want to go. Many of these chicks have seen their parents for the last time. Hunger, and everything about the way their bodies and brains are changing, is moving them toward the water. For days the activity has been intensifying, and more and more big young birds have moved to the beach.

Chicks normally remain on the beaches exercising vigorously for several days. When they've lost a third of their peak weight—the same formula that forces starving adults to desert nests—hunger and the wind propel them seaward. When the time comes, there are but two options: fly or die.

So finally this morning we're watching fledgers. Up on the breezy berm, one Black-foot spreads its exceptional new wings. It seems afraid to take that final plunge. It folds those wings, leans forward, spreads again. Closes. Leans forward. Then suddenly launches itself with con-

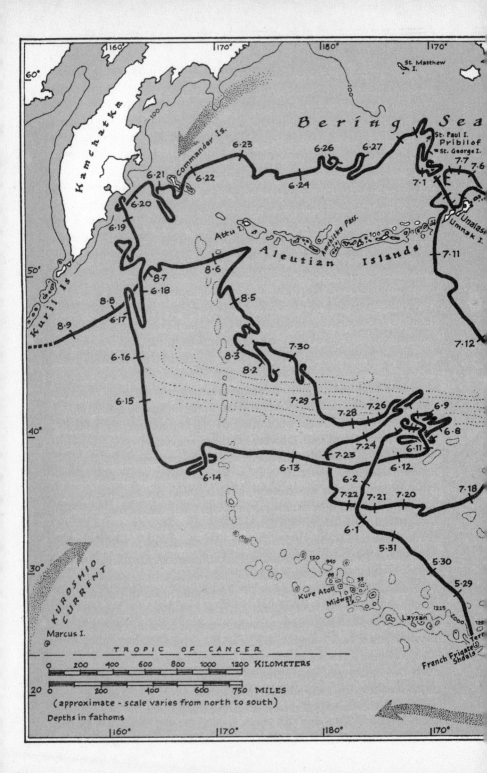

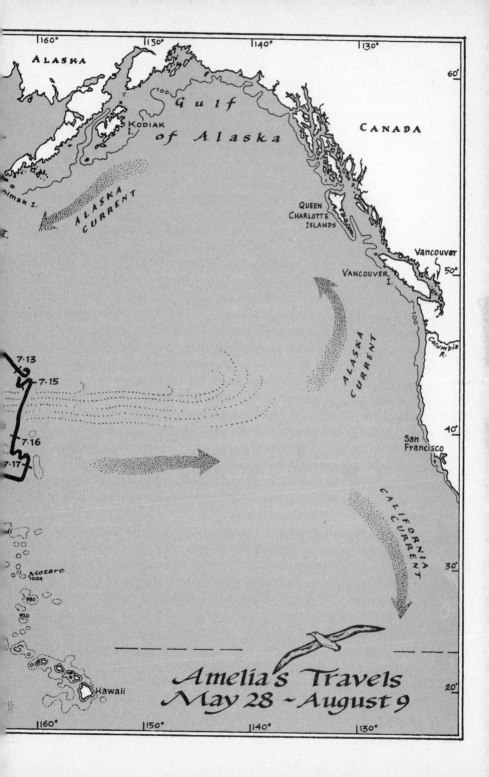

Amelia's Travels
May 28 ~ August 9

viction. Lofted by the breeze, it leaves the berm. Flapping for all it's got, and making a go of it, it flutters into the lagoon.

In addition to its first flight, this looks like its first swim. This feels different from the firm, fast land it has always and only known. It paddles awkwardly with its wings almost fully opened, as though trying to avoid getting wet. Ungainly and unsteady at first, it soon seems accustomed to the rhythm and the feel of the yielding water that will be its universe for the next few years.

Now begins the usual terror of adolescence: the race between learning and luck.

First flight is one of the great joys of creation. But trepidation suppresses our urge to cheer. We're not the only ones gathered for this much-anticipated event. Mitsuaki Iwago motions with his hand and swings his camera into the ready position. His gesture causes me to glance along the shore. There, an open-winged fledgling is paddling around, about fifty yards from the beach. Awkward movements are the norm among birds that have never before felt saltwater, but the surface around this fledger looks unusually disturbed. A sudden eruption of water shoves the bird aside. The young albatross shakes its body and wings and settles leisurely into the water. The Tiger Shark comes for a second attack, its dorsal and tail streaming through the surface. On this approach the chick, finally alarmed, pivots to actually bite the huge snout, which again misses due to the pillow of water it itself is generating. Like the thin and illusory protective cloth of a bullfighter's cape, only a thin diaphragm of water protects the bird from the charges of the shark. In their clumsy choreography, the shark's movements seem both unreal and absolute, abstract yet stark, oddly remote—yet imminent as death itself.

For animals capable of such exquisite grace of motion, the excruciating slowness is the most horrific aspect of it, like dreams in which you cannot run. But with each pass the shark grows more agitated and determined; the chick, more alarmed. Just ahead of the next oncoming bulge, the chick runs sloppily along the surface and manages to get airborne. In the last few minutes, its new ability of flight has gotten it into mortal danger—and out again.

The wind is up to a steady ten knots, invigorating the youngsters. Birds with entirely downy heads are fledging; I would have thought them too young. They fly on still-growing wing feathers that seem too short for an albatross. But they do get airborne, and fly forty or fifty yards into the lagoon. There they bob on the water, often with wings spread in the wind like little sailing ships. Other albatrosses go into the water by simply walking off the beach. They shouldn't do this. While walking into the water does not fit the strictest scientific definition of "fledging," it certainly fits the Tiger Sharks' looser definition.

One chick's entry has not gone unnoticed, and soon a long, dark shape approaches. The big, square snout followed by an awkwardly gaping mouth breaks the surface two feet from the fledgling. The bobbing bird, with wings half opened, peers at it quizzically. In the clumsy rush, the bow wave of this nine-foot Tiger Shark's wide head also shoves its intended target sideways. The shark turns, but fails twice more, giving up the attack after a third pass. Bad luck for the shark, good luck for the bird—different ways to value the same event even in the starkest moments of life and death.

Five minutes later, Iwago says in a simple hush, "Attack." A large Tiger is already closing on a nearby fledger. Its remarkable ability to approach so closely on this open flat without us seeing it is indeed an impressive display of the professional predator's craft. The big shark comes up from directly behind the blissfully bobbing Black-foot. And *this* time the big square head pushes the albatross forward, not sideways.

A big, square snout followed by an awkwardly gaping mouth breaks the surface. (*Norbert Wu/www.norbertwu.com*)

When that mouth closes, the aft half of the fledgling disappears, and in the next half instant the big dark bird is simply missing from the agitated water.

Several other chicks are paddling nearby. Nothing troubles them. But when the next fledger hits the water it attracts another big Tiger cruising near shore. In another clumsy bullfight, this chick does not read the message in time, and on the shark's third pass it gets its jaws around the bird's body, and the albatross—pecking furiously with its shiny, sharp, brand-new bill—vanishes. A slick of oil and some feathers appear at the surface.

Several sharks have converged in the lagoon like massive foxes in a watery henhouse. It's hard to say how many, but people have counted more than ten at a time here in past years. In the next attack, when the oncoming Tiger's mouth drops open like a castle drawbridge, the bird actually hops atop the great snout, toppling to safety over the shark's head.

Out of practice since last year, many of the sharks are clumsy. But already, some are refining their approach. An enormous Tiger vaults half airborne from a sudden explosion of foam. With energy and aim we haven't seen before, this shark hits a Laysan chick like a powered battering ram. This is the trick: don't just come up like you're still scavenging; aim high and come on fast. The sharks are getting the hang of this as though shaking off the fog of a memory. And while the sharks get better each fledger enters the water as naive as the last.

Over the next couple of weeks in this lagoon, one of every ten chicks that has survived all its severe infancy will nourish a Tiger Shark. This is the deal evolution has made with albatrosses: heavier mortality early in life will be compensated by extraordinarily high survival during a lifetime four to six decades long.

In all that lifetime—as for all these creatures—two surviving offspring are all that's needed to keep the population stable into the next generation. So it has been for aeons. Albatrosses as a whole can well cope with hard rain and howling wind, food scarcities, and the Tigers in the sea. But evolution leaves them unequipped to deal with high, or even moderate, adult mortality—the kind that usually comes at the hand of humans.

AT FRENCH FRIGATE SHOALS the surviving albatross chicks, rapidly mastering flight, will soon further press their luck upon the wide sea. When Amelia's chick makes his first over-water flight he travels about a hundred yards and lands in the lagoon. Scanning the wide world from the oddly unsteady platform of the wavy liquid, it never crosses his mind to return to land. Though he has never known it before, he suddenly seems to remember that he belongs on the sea. Opening his wings, he flaps and splatters along the surface for a few seconds. And though he has never before lifted off from water, he looks rather skilled at it—not polished, but not awkward either. As he clears the surface, the only thing about his flying that looks different from an older bird's is that he is beating his wings a little more and a little deeper, working a little harder. But so rapidly does he get the feel of this thing he was born to do that second by second you can see him growing steadier, smoother, the wing beats shallower and more effective, his motion more economical; until very soon he is at a surprising distance, sailing in long glides in a way that would be hard to distinguish from a more experienced bird. He lands in the lagoon again. And then again. And then is over the reef, outside the atoll. After so many months, his leave-taking was practically instantaneous.

A whole world ends and another begins when a young one you have loved leaves. And who is to say that these young, so strenuously and devotedly cared for, so luminous with beauty, have not been loved in their way?

Outside the reef, the atoll's slopes drop sharply away. Less than a mile from the shallow turquoise lagoon, the ocean runs purple with depth. A lone Black-footed Albatross is paddling in cobalt swells. So grown-up looking is it that only the sleek, uniform darkness of its feathers—no sun-bleached wear and tear—tells you it's this year's freshly minted chick. Amelia's chick lands nearby. This undulating ocean is a new world, beautiful in its austerity, like smooth skin. He scrutinizes it all intently, as you once studied with such wonder the smooth, curving surfaces of your first lover. Amelia's chick opens his perfect wings, the breeze lifts him, and he strides northward on the propelling wind, getting smaller, smaller, then is lost from view, somewhere beyond our ken. If a multitude of luck holds, in a few years he may again swing his feet down to touch dry land.

By MID-JULY, Amelia's chick is far from any shore, feeling the air pressing his wings up from below, rippling his feathers, holding his body aloft. Like most Laysan chicks, he heads northwest, wandering toward the coasts of Japan and Russia. He is exploring the sea for the first time, and everything seems new as the first day of school, greatly interesting. In his years traveling at sea, he will learn the limits of the ocean and of life.

Gone to extremes—Amelia

Amelia is wandering now, too. When she leaves the Aleutians, Amelia is fat and as close to happy as an albatross ever gets. She heads straight south until she crosses the transitional waters of her favorite hangout, the subarctic front, then follows the current boundary west. Amazingly, she hooks back almost *exactly* to the same area where, during the first week of June, she spent a week loitering within a sixty-mile radius. Here she now lingers a few days before traveling northwest and foraging heavily again. Her travels are taking her toward Russia's Kuril Islands, north of Japan—twenty-six hundred miles from Tern Island. Here, on the western rim of the North Pacific Ocean, at the limits of the world's greatest water, in a few weeks Amelia and her chick may cross paths.

➤ ➤ ➤

*B*RIAN ANNOUNCES THAT the plane will be here in half an hour. In a few minutes, everyone on the island will help clear the runway, walking and biking along, shooing birds.

In the past four years the plane has killed only one albatross. But this year it's hit four, killing two. Even this is a consequence of the hot, calm weather with reduced wind—making albatrosses much slower at getting airborne.

Brian brings out the tractor—the only motorized land vehicle for hundreds of miles—in case a crash necessitates moving bodies in a hurry. Fire extinguishers are readied. All in accord with official protocol.

We hear the distant plane—very faintly.

One Laysan Albatross walks straight from the vegetation toward Melissa, as though it knows she's a veterinarian and it has a health question. She raises her arms and encourages it to go back into the brush. So intent on coming out is it, Melissa has to chase the bird twice.

A few birds—mostly noddies, some boobies, an albatross or two—are constantly in the air nearby. Up high swirl a few hundred Sooty Terns. Another much larger flock of terns and frigatebirds is wheeling out over the breakers on the reef edge, out of harm's path.

Melissa has to chase that one Laysan back yet again, talking to it, lifting her arms, trying to shoo it back. It seems to have bonded with her; perhaps it thinks they're dancing.

Exactly on time, the plane appears in the sky. A Black-footed Albatross is flying low over the runway and another one is just walking out. Anthony runs to scare the walker back, but it goes straight in the direction the plane is coming from.

Frightened birds—mostly noddies—rise and crowd the air chaotically as the plane approaches. No albatrosses are in its path, but some noddies and boobies are still streaming across the airstrip. The plane hits the ground and runs the entire length of the strip—and in some fierce combination of skill and luck, it does not strike a single bird of any kind.

Now the albatrosses' clapping bills seem like applause. The tension relaxes, and everybody walks slowly toward the plane. Almost immediately, Melissa's one persistent albatross walks onto the runway yet again.

The plane as usual brings letters, supplies, goodies, film, food.

Brendan and I are leaving. Everyone exchanges addresses, telephone numbers, and e-mail information, hoping these precious and intense new friendships can be made to outlast the unforeseeable miles and years.

Reluctantly I lift my feet from the island and into the plane. Waving, waving, waving, we take off.

We swing out over the reef edge, gaining altitude and a splendid view of the atoll: the sandy islands, that emerald lagoon, the stark pinnacle, the dark ocean. Outside the gleaming, creamy breakers, a whale blows three times as it swims along. Brendan points and leans back so I can see it. I nod.

We climb to seventy-five hundred feet and level off, wrapped in a blue flannel sky. The flying is smooth.

As we speed east along the chain, each occasional island looks perfectly inlaid into the blue enamel of the sea below, like a piece in a sacred mosaic. Yet each seems to float. It's hard to fully comprehend that these are just the tips of an enormous mountain range, grown from a seafloor thousands of feet below. Anne Morrow Lindbergh responded to the idea that no one is an island by saying, "I feel we are all islands—in a common sea." That is an appealing refinement of the idea, but there is something else deeper. Perhaps we only seem like islands because all our shared underpinnings, which have brought us up and hold us into the sunlight, lie unseen below the surface. Now and then we think we might detect submerged connections by a whiff of something familiar, by an upwelling of memory or empathy or the urge to show kindness to another creature, like a visible pattern of ripples at the surface caused by something lying far below. The rock-hard ties to all these other islands—human and nonhuman, current and past—lie out of sight, deep in time, massively holding together all our fragile little islands, yet barely recognized and seldom acknowledged. What a different view of life we would have if we mapped our islands not by their perimeter as seen from the surface but by their profile and foundation, showing always the roots and connections within the shared mountain chain. Could we not recognize ourselves as part of the same chain of Life, originated from the same hot spot? Are we not little kindred isles adrift a sea of time, on a conveyor of space? We are born. We have our adventures. And we are sucked back in, to be reintegrated, recast in the continuing saga of our singular island home afloat the oceanic universe.

A broken rim of clouds rings the horizon, as though the entire planetary ocean is an atoll lagoon fringed with a reefy white surf. The clouds seem to cushion the ocean from the weight of so large a sky. Again we can see fronts of darker blue water bordering lighter blue masses of ocean that run for miles. Brendan is asleep. I'd like to sleep too, but I can't. In the midst of all this beauty, my one thought is of a loved one, many clouds away.

The airplane is loud. My legs feel cramped. An island slides by below. Clouds slip by beneath us. I get relaxed. Too relaxed to sleep. The clouds themselves begin to seem like islands, like mountains, like the surf, like white lava heads and puffy coral pinnacles. Like there is nothing to see up here, and everything to imagine. Time slows. Minutes pass between thoughts. Finally this waking dream dozes me, and my eyes flicker shut.

SELECTED REFERENCES

AUSTIN, O. L. 1949. The status of Steller's Albatross. *Pacific Science* 3:283–95.

BJORNDAL, K. A., ed. 1995. *Biology and Conservation of Sea Turtles.* Rev. ed. Washington, D.C.: Smithsonian Institution.

BROTHERS, N. P., J. COOPER, and S. LOKKEBORG. 1999. *The Incidental Catch of Seabirds by Longline Fisheries: Worldwide Review and Technical Guidelines for Mitigation.* FAO Fisheries Circular 937. Rome: Food and Agriculture Organization of the United Nations.

BURGER, J., and M. GOCHFELD. 2000. Metals in albatross feathers from Midway Atoll: Influence of species, age, and nest location. *Environmental Research* 82:207–21.

CAMPBELL, D. G. 1992. *The Crystal Desert: Summers in Antarctica.* New York: Houghton Mifflin.

COE, J. M., and D. B. ROGERS, eds. 1997. *Marine Debris: Sources, Impacts, and Solutions.* New York: Springer-Verlag.

COLBORN, T., F. VON SAAL, and A. M. SOTO. 1993. Developmental effects of endocrine-disrupting chemicals in wildlife and humans. *Environmental Health Perspectives* 101:378–81.

ELY, C. A., and R. B. CLAPP. 1973. *The Natural History of Laysan Island, Northwestern Hawaiian Islands.* Atoll Research Bulletin 171. Washington, D.C.: Smithsonian Institution.

FEFER, S. I., C. S. HARRISON, M. B. NAUGHTON, and R. J. SHALLENBERGER. 1984. Synopsis of results of recent seabird research conducted in the Northwestern Hawaiian Islands. *Proc. Res. Inv. NWHI.* UNIHI Seagrant-MR-84-01.

FERNANDEZ ERAZO, A. P. 1999. Foraging biology and reproductive rate of albatrosses. Master's thesis, Wake Forest University.

FISHER, H. I. 1949. Populations of birds on Midway and the man-made factors affecting them. *Pacific Science* 3:103–10.

———. 1967. Body weights in Laysan Albatrosses. *Ibis* 109:373–82.

———. 1969. Eggs and egg-laying in the Laysan Albatross. *Condor* 71:102–12.

———. 1971. The Laysan Albatross: Its incubation, hatching, and associated behaviors. *The Living Bird* 10:19–78.

———. 1975. Mortality and survival in the Laysan Albatross. *Pacific Science* 29:279–300.

FISHER, H. I., and M. L. FISHER. 1969. The visits of Laysan Albatrosses to the breeding colony. *Micronesica* 5:173–221.

FISHER, W. K. 1904. On the habits of the Laysan Albatross. *Auk* 21:8–20.

FLINT, E. 1999. Status of seabird populations and conservation in the tropical island Pacific. In: *Population, Development, and Conservation Priorities.* Vol. 2 of *Marine and Coastal Biodiversity in the Tropical Island Pacific Region,* edited by L. Eldredge, J. Maragos, P. Holthus, and H. Takeuchi. Honolulu: Pacific Science Association.

FURNESS, R. W. 1990. Easy gliders. *Natural History.* August, pp. 63–68.

GALES, R. 1993. Cooperative Mechanisms for the Conservation of Albatross. Hobart: Australian Nature Conservation Agency.

GOULD, P. J. 1992. Population dynamics of the Laysan Albatross and other marine birds in the north Pacific. Manuscript.

HARRISON, C. S. 1990. *Seabirds of Hawaii: Natural History and Conservation.* Ithaca, N.Y.: Comstock.

HARRISON, C. S., T. S. HIDA, and M. P. SEKI. 1983. Hawaiian seabird feeding ecology. *Wildlife Monographs* 85:1–71.

HARVELL, C. D., et al. 1999. Emerging marine diseases—climate links and anthropogenic factors. *Science* 285:1505–10.

HOLBROOK, S. J., R. J. SHMITT, and J. S. STEPHENS JR. 1997. Changes in an assemblage of temperate reef fishes associated with a climate shift. *Ecological Applications* 7:1299–1310.

HOOVER, J. P. 1993. *Hawaii's Fishes: A Guide for Snorkelers, Divers and Aquarists.* Honolulu: Mutual.

JACKSON, J. B. C. 1997. Reefs since Columbus. *Coral Reefs* 16:S23–32.

JOBLING, JAMES A. 1991. *A Dictionary of Scientific Bird Names.* New York: Oxford University Press.

KANE, H. K. 1997. *Ancient Hawaii.* Captain Cook, Hawaii: Kawainui Press.

KEPLER, C. 1967. Polynesian rat predation on nesting Laysan Albatrosses and other Pacific seabirds. *Auk* 84:426–430.

KIRCH, P. V. 1985. *Feathered Gods and Fishhooks.* Honolulu: University of Hawaii Press.

LEFEBURE, M. 1975. *Samuel Taylor Coleridge: A Bondage of Opium.* Briarcliff Manor, N.Y.: Stein and Day.

LOOSER, R., O. FROESCHEIS, G. M. CAILLIET, W. M. JARMAN, and K. BALL-SCHMITER. 2000. The deep-sea as a final global sink of semivolatile persistent organic pollutants? Part II: Organochlorine pesticides in surface and deep-sea dwelling fish of the north and south Atlantic and the Monterey Bay Canyon (California). *Chemosphere* 40:661–70.

LUDWIG, J. P., C. L. SUMMER, H. J. AUMAN, V. GAUGER, D. BROMLEY, J. P. GIESY, R. ROLLAND, and T. COLBORN. 1998. The roles of organochlorine contaminants and fisheries bycatch in recent population changes of Blackfooted and Laysan Albatrosses in the North Pacific Ocean. Chap. 19 in *Albatross Biology and Conservation,* edited by G. Robertson and R. Gales. Chipping Norton, N.S.W., Australia: Surrey Beatty and Sons Pty. Limited.

MACINTYRE, I. G. 1996. *Laysan Island and Other Northwestern Hawaiian Islands: Early Scientific Reports with a Laysan Bibliography.* Atoll Research Bulletin Nos. 432–34. Washington, D.C.: National Museum of Natural History, Smithsonian Institution.

MATHEWS-AMOS, A., and E. A. BERNTSON. 1999. *Turning Up the Heat: How Global Warming Threatens Life in the Sea.* Washington, D.C.: World Wildlife Fund and Marine Conservation Biology Institute.

MELVIN, E. F., and J. K. PARRISH, eds. 2001. *Seabird Bycatch: Trends, Roadblocks, and Solutions.* Fairbanks: University of Alaska Sea Grant.

MOLONEY, C. L., J. COOPER, P. G. RYAN, and W. ROY SIEGFRIED. 1994. Use of a population model to assess the impact of longline fishing on Wandering Albatross populations. *Biological Conservation* 70:195–203.

MURPHY, R. C. 1947. *Logbook for Grace.* New York: Macmillan.

NAKUINA, E. M. 1994. *Nanaue the Shark Man and Other Hawaiian Shark Stories.* Honolulu: Kalamaku Press.

NEVITT, G. 1999. Foraging by seabirds on an olfactory landscape. *American Scientist* 87:46–53.

NORRIS, K. S., B. WÜRSIG, R. S. WELLS, and M. WÜRSIG, et al. 1994. *The Hawaiian Spinner Dolphin.* Berkeley: University of California Press.

PAULY, D., and V. CHRISTENSEN. 1995. Primary production required to sustain global fisheries. *Nature* 374:255–57.

POMERANCE, R. 1999. *Coral Bleaching, Coral Mortality, and Global Climate Change.* Washington, D.C.: Bureau of Oceans and International Environmental and Scientific Affairs, U.S. Department of State.

RANDALL, J. E. 1996. *Shore Fishes of Hawaii.* Vida, Ore.: Natural World Press.

ROBERTSON, G., and R. GALES, eds. 1998. *Albatross Biology and Conservation.* Chipping Norton, N.S.W., Australia: Surrey Beatty and Sons Pty Limited.

ROPER, C. F. E., M. SWEENEY, and C. E. NAUEN. 1984. *Cephalopods of the World.* Vol. 3 of *FAO Species Catalog.* FAO Fish. Synop.

RYAN, P. G., and C. L. MOLONEY. 1993. Marine litter keeps increasing. *Nature* 361:23.

RYLANDER, L., U. STROMBERG, and L. HAGMAR. 2000. Lowered birth weight among infants born to women with a high intake of fish contaminated with persistent organochlorine compounds. *Chemosphere* 40:1255–62.

STEINER, R. 1998. Resurrection in the wind. *International Wildlife.* Sept.-Oct. 13–21.

STEVENS, W. K. 1999. *The Change in the Weather.* New York: Delacorte Press.

TENBRUGGENCATE, J. 1999. Albatrosses abandoning nests in record numbers. *Honolulu Advertiser.* March 7, p. 1.

TICKELL, W.L.N. 2000. *Albatrosses.* New Haven: Yale University Press.

VAN RYZIN, M. T., and H. I. FISHER. 1976. The age of Laysan Albatrosses at first breeding. *Condor* 78:1–9.

WEIMERSKIRCH, H., N. BROTHERS, and P. JOUVENTIN. 1997. Population dynamics of Wandering Albatross and Amsterdam Albatross in the Indian Ocean and their relationships with long-line fisheries: conservation implications. *Biological Conservation* 79:257–70.

WETHERBEE, B. M., C. G. LOWE, and G. L. CROW. 1994. A review of shark control in Hawaii with recommendations for future research. *Pacific Science* 48:95–115.

WILKENING, K. E., L. A. BARRIE, and M. ENGLE. 2000. Trans-Pacific air pollution. *Science* 290:65–67.

INDEX

Page entries in *italics* refer to maps and photographs.

ABOUT THE AUTHOR

CARL SAFINA grew up loving the ocean. He is a recipient of a MacArthur "genius" Fellowship and a Pew Scholar's Award in Conservation and the Environment. His first book, *Song for the Blue Ocean,* won him a Lannan Literary Award. Safina earned his Ph.D. studying seabirds and later founded the National Audubon Society's Living Oceans Program. He is a Visiting Fellow at Yale University.